Crossing the Line of Departure

Battle Command on the Move
A Historical Perspective

by John J. McGrath

Published by Books Express Publishing
Copyright © Books Express, 2012
ISBN 978-1-78039-680-4

Books Express publications are available from all good retail and online booksellers. For
publishing proposals and direct ordering please contact us at: info@books-express.com

Foreword

John McGrath's *Crossing the Line of Departure* is a wide-ranging historical overview of that most difficult aspect of military leadership, the art of battle command. McGrath leads the reader through case studies beginning with Alexander the Great leading up to the recent war in Iraq. Among others, he analyzes Napoleon's technique, French and British practices in World War I, the German experience with "Blitzkreig" in World War II, and the Soviet approach to battle command. McGrath also extends his historical analysis to the present day by presenting a description of battle command theory in the "Modular Army" and the Infor• mation Age. Through it all, he finds that the key to successful command in battle, particularly in mobile operations, is found in the successful interplay between technology and personal technique.

Unlike some pundits today, McGrath does not conclude that information age technology is likely to shift the balance between these poles in favor of technology dependence. The commander's personal sense of where to be on the battlefield, where to locate and how to use his headquarters staffs, and how to communicate with his subordinates have been—and re• main today—crucial elements of successful battle command. A 21st century commander has use of technology beyond the comprehension of an Alexander, a Napoleon, or a Guderian; but he will continue to grapple with the same issues of personal presence and technique that they mastered so well.

Crossing the Line of Departure brings to the fore insights, trends, and leadership qualities needed for successful battle command. While possessing knowledge of these traits does not guarantee success on the battlefield, their absence will almost assuredly bring defeat. We at the Combat Studies Institute believe that McGrath's monograph, by casting light on the art and science of battle command through the ages, will be a useful tool for commanders and staffs as they prepare for future operations. *CSI—The Past is Prologue*.

Timothy R. Reese
Colonel, Armor
Director, Combat Studies Institute

ACKNOWLEDGEMENTS

I wish to thank the Combat Studies Institute and the United States Army for providing the opportunity to do important historical research in support of victory in the Global War on Terror.

This is my second collaboration with CSI editor Michael Brooks, without whom this work would not have seen publication. I also wish to thank Research and Publications Team Chief LTC Steve Clay for his support in the completion of this project as well as past CSI colleagues LTC Brian DeToy and Robin Kern, who all had key roles in this project at earlier stages.

Finally I'd like to acknowledge friends and family whose constant support have greatly assisted in completing this project. Debi Bush is the person in Kansas I've known the longest. My son William has two prairie visits under his belt away from our home area of Massachusetts. Son Andrew and daughter Barbara have been unable to visit but provided long distance support. Dr. Robert Wright, enjoying his retirement in sunny, shark-infested Florida, has always provided guidance and support.

Hopefully this work, in some small way, will help support the soldiers and officers of the United States Army worldwide in their vigorous pursuit of victory in the Global War on Terrorism. This work is dedicated to these soldiers and to those who will not be coming home.

John J. McGrath
Fort Leavenworth, Kansas
3 February 2006

CONTENTS

TABLE OF FIGURES

Key to Military Symbols

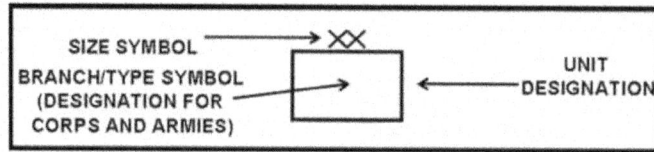

SIZE SYMBOL ⟶ XX

BRANCH/TYPE SYMBOL (DESIGNATION FOR CORPS AND ARMIES) ⟶

UNIT DESIGNATION ⟵

HEADQUARTERS UNIT

ENEMY UNIT

UNIT OF UNSPECIFIED SIZE

FIRST ARMY — BRIDGING EQUIPMENT

IV CORPS

ARMORED DIVISION — 1

INFANTRY DIVISION — 2

MOTORIZED DIVISION — 3

TANK BATTALION — 1-33

AIRMOBILE INFANTRY BATTALION — 1-7

CAVALRY UNIT

MECHANIZED INFANTRY UNIT

AIRBORNE UNIT

MARINE UNIT

ARMORED CAVALRY UNIT

TANK DESTROYER TASK FORCE — TF

RANGER UNIT

SP ARTILLERY

MODULAR COMBINED ARMS MANEUVER BATTALION

BRIDGING EQUIPMENT

SIZE SYMBOLS

XXXX	XXX	XX	X	III	II
ARMY	CORPS	DIVISION	BRIGADE	REGIMENT	BATTALION

ENTRENCHMENTS   INFANTRY ON LINE   AIRFIELD

TROOP MOVEMENTS

AIRMOBILE TROOP MOVEMENTS

FRONTLINE POSIITONS

NOTE: On maps with gridlines the distance between any two lines is 0.6 mile or 1 kilome•ter. All other maps have scales of miles.

INTRODUCTION

"Audaces fortuna iuvat- Fortune favors the brave."
—Virgil, The Aeneid

This work discusses the historical development of technology and techniques to command and control large military forces actively engaged in combat operations against an armed enemy in fast-paced, mobile-style actions. The 'mobile' nature of such operations can be defined as the movement of a military force swift enough to either surprise its enemy by its speed of advance or retreat, or which forces the enemy to respond in a manner that he is either unprepared for or less likely to be successful. In modern terms this usually, but not always, equates to the operations of armored, mechanized, and motorized forces. However, it can also refer to forces moved operationally or strategically by helicopter or air transport. In the pre-mechanized age, mobile operations are characterized not by the predominant use of one arm of the service, such as cavalry, but by the ability of army commanders to quickly move their forces both operationally and tactically, while retaining control, against deployed enemy forces. The focus will be on the operations of United States Army forces, though telling examples from foreign armies will also be used as necessary. This work will also discuss the development of particular operational tools and techniques designed to the facilitate command and control of forces on the modern battlefield, as well as organizational and equipment related issues.

Command and control has always, through the ages, been the bedrock of battlefield suc•cess. The commander whose army both followed his intent for battle, and was able to adjust to changes of this intent based on the actions of the enemy was invariably the successful one. Command and control has traditionally, been an arduous process in mobile campaigns, particularly since the growth and dispersion of armies beyond the direct vision of the com•mander. The complexity is magnified by shortened time spans to make decisions, much more widely dispersed forces, and forces in motion at distances which limits the effective•ness of communications. Additionally, the actions of the enemy in such campaigns may be less predictable or more fluid as well.

Historically, two key intertwined elements have enabled a commander to succeed on the battlefield or in a campaign: technology and technique. Technology is the hardware of battle command, the means available for a leader to control his forces. At times this has included the horse, voice commands, signal flags, battle flags, the telegraph, field telephones, radios and satellite computer uplinks, as well as armored command vehicles and helicopters. Tech•nique is the software of the command and control process: how the commander or army or•ganizes itself to lead its forces based on the available technology. Technique applications to battle command include the use of standardized units and operating procedures, battle drills, systems of couriers or household cavalry units, command post organizations, standardized decision-making and operations order formats and even the use of map overlays and graph•ics. This work will analyze the use of technology and technique in the effectiveness of com•

mand, starting with a background discussion of mobile command through the ages, and then focusing on the modern era of armored and other mobile forces.

Battle Command on the Move and Army Doctrine

How does battle command on the move fit into US Army doctrinal concepts about battle command? Army doctrine on this subject is outlined in two field manuals, *FM 3-0 Operations* (formerly 100-5), published in June 2001, and *FM 6-0, Mission Command: Command and Control of Army Forces*, published in August 2003. FM 6-0 supplanted portions of the former staff operations manual FM 101-5. These two documents define and elaborate the Army's concept of battle command and battle command on the move.

Battle command is defined as "the exercise of command in operations against a hostile, thinking enemy."[1] It is distinct from command in general, which is in Army terms lawful authority exercised by an individual in the Army over his designated subordinates because of his rank and position. In contrast, battle command is essentially the exercise of command in the face of the enemy.

To exercise battle command doctrine spells out a framework: the commander is expected to visualize the nature and design of the operation, describe his intent to his staff and subordinates in terms of time, space, resources, purpose and action, and direct the actions of subordinates. Battle command on the move comes into play in particular in several areas of this process.

While visualizing how he will execute an operation, the commander is expected to use the various elements of operational design outlined in FM 3-0 as tools. These elements concern themselves primarily with the determination of objectives, lines of advance, and operational pauses. While these are all elements found in mobile campaigns, two elements operational reach and tempo are particularly related to battle command on the move.

FM 3-0 defines operational reach as the distance over which military power can be employed decisively. Tempo is defined as the rate of military action.[2] Operational reach requires the ability to effectively exercise battle command over an extended distance in order to be employed decisively. The ability of a commander to command his force while it is moving directly affects his ability to project operational reach. Tempo, the speed at which a military force executes its operations, equally is dependent upon mobile systems of battle command. Battle command needs to be seamlessly continuous if the force is to keep a fast paced tempo based on maneuver and movement.

After visualizing and developing a concept for an operation, the battle commander needs to describe this to his staff and subordinates through his planning guidance and commander's intent. Subordinate understanding of this intent is vital to the success of battle command on the move. As will be discussed throughout this work, effective command of mobile operations requires the commander juggling the available communications technology with organizational techniques designed to facilitate the command of forces in motion. In the latter category, one of the key points is that the commander cannot be everywhere all the time himself. Accordingly, when he is not there, and previously issued orders do not spell out direction for his subordinates on the spot, the subordinates need to have a clear understanding of the commander's intentions for the operation as a whole and their piece of it. They can then act in the best interests of what their commander expects them to do, even when he cannot tell them himself.

Battle commanders are expected to direct the actions of their subordinates in executing the operation. This is done primarily through the publishing of operations and fragmentary orders, and the continuous synchronization of the various battlefield operating systems.[3] Battle command on the move is concerned primarily with the synchronization of one of these systems, command and control.

FM 3-0 defines command and control as the exercise of authority and direction by a properly designated commander over assigned and attached forces in the accomplishment of the mission.[4] In essence, battle command on the move is a way of providing the commander with an effective means of retaining command and control over a moving force.

While FM 3-0 discusses combat operations, FM 6-0 is devoted specifically to providing a doctrinal framework for the exercise of command and control. FM 6-0 discusses command and control in relation to two major components: the commander, and his command and control system. A command and control system is defined as the arrangement of personnel, information management, procedures, and equipment and facilities essential for the commander to conduct operations.[5] The ability to operate an effective command and control system while a force is moving, or otherwise conducting mobile operations, is the main theme of this book, *Crossing the Line of Departure*. The bulk of this work discusses the evolution of command and control systems for mobile operations through examples from armies of the past, both distant and recent. This work divides battle command on the move command and control systems into two basic components- technology, and technique. Technology provides a means of effecting command and control through the use of equipment, devices or technological advances. Technique provides a means through the use or organization, training, command style, etc. In other words, technology is the hardware and technique is the software of battle command on the move.

FM 6-0 discusses the environment of command and control, whose basic elements are the human dimension, uncertainty, time, and land combat operations.[6] The importance of these elements is even more so in mobile operations and more difficult to effectively harness. In the human dimension, for example, the chaotic nature of battle can be exaggerated when large swatches of territory separate the force's various components and the unit commander cannot readily turn to his superior for immediate direction. Uncertainty is increased and time compressed when the operation is a mobile one. The nature of mobile land operations—primarily conducted in two dimensions, across varied terrain and in a continuous fashion—are intensified in mobile operations. This intensity increases the complication of the operation making command and control even more difficult, but usually rewards the successful practitioner with decisive results.

FM 6-0 also emphasizes mission command, defined as the conduct of military operations through decentralized execution based on mission orders for effective mission accomplish•ment. The manual also states "successful mission command results from subordinate leaders at all echelons exercising disciplined initiative within the commander's intent to accomplish the mission."[7] Mission command is contrasted with detailed command—detailed centralized command controlled from above. Given the general fluidity of combat operations and the relative frailty of communications and information equipment, doctrinally the Army prefers mission command in almost all cases.[8]

The contrast between mission command and detailed command techniques parallels the difference between battle command on the move and battle command in a stationary environ•ment. Mobile operations are marked by great fluidity and test the fragility of communica•tions systems. While a permanently static force could be controlled in a detailed, centralized manner, such control in a dispersed force on the move would prove to be virtually a recipe for disaster, particularly when faced with an enemy operating in a decentralized manner.[9]

Despite the inherent difficulties in exercising battle command on the move, such operations by their nature inflict the same difficulties on the enemy force commander. An army commit•ted to retaining the initiative through offensive operations can best be successful through the use of mobile operations. For the potential is great that the side with the initiative can over•come these difficulties before the enemy can do so and the subsequent sequence of events bring success that can often prove decisive.

Summary

This monograph takes a historical look at how commanders effectively and ineffectively controlled mobile campaigns in the past and will draw conclusions about the nature of battle command on the move, particularly concerning its two major components, technology and technique. In addition to highlighting general historical trends, this work uses the methodol•ogy of the historical case study to illuminate it's points. As such, it is concerned with the op•erational (campaigns and series of battles) and tactical (battles) levels of battle command on the move. Historical examples include the employment of whole armies in the case of Geng•his Khan, Napoleon, Washington at Yorktown, Scott at Mexico City, and Grant at Petersburg and on the road to Appomattox. As technology enhanced command and control and caused the dispersion of units at the tactical level, most modern examples include the operations of portions of, rather than whole armies. These include the German right wing in France in August 1914, the US VIII Corps in Brittany in August 1944, the 1st Cavalry Division at Khe Sanh in 1968, a corps-sized Israeli Defense Force element in two battles in the Sinai in 1973, and the operations of American corps-sized forces in Iraq in 1991 and 2003.

Notes

1. US Department of the Army, *FM 3-0, Operations* (Washington, DC: Department of the Army, 14 June 2001), 5-1.

2. Ibid., 5-10, 5-12.

3. Per *FM 3-0*, 5-15, these battlefield operating systems are intelligence, maneuver, fire support, air defense, mobility/countermobility/survivability, combat service support, and command and control.

4. *FM 3-0*, 5-17.

5. US Department of the Army, *FM 6-0, Mission Command: Command and Control of Army Forces* (Washington, DC: Department of the Army, 11 August 2003), 1-6, 1-7.

6. Ibid., 1-8,1-9.

7. Ibid., 1-17.

8. Ibid., 1-16.

9. The obvious difficulties inherent in centralized control of mobile forces did not stop the Soviet Union and states patterned after it from employing just such a doctrine, though with predictable results. See Chapter 8 for a detailed discussion of the Soviet approach.

BATTLE COMMAND IN THE AGE
OF THE HORSE (ANTIQUITY TO NAPOLEON)

"The strength of an army, like the power in mechanics, is estimated by multiplying the mass by the rapidity; a rapid march augments the morale of an army, and increases its means of victory. Press on!"

—Napoleon (Maxim IX)[1]

Ancient Times

Organized armies first appeared with the rise of kingdoms in the Near East and Asia. The introduction of bronze and the bronze sword as a battlefield weapon occurred sometime before 2000 BC in Assyria. In the 'heroic' or Bronze Age, armies were relatively small and composed of two basic elements—a large mass of unarmored infantry carrying pikes and shields and an elite contingent of horse-drawn chariots from which the nobility or royal family fought. This age of chariots was often called the heroic age because the nobles in the chariots frequently faced off one-on-one with similar personages from the opposing army in dismounted combat.[2] Such combat is depicted in Homer's *Iliad*. Later, in the Bronze Age, the chariots carried elite bowmen. Battles increasingly became contests between the op•posing chariotries, with the victor then shattering and pursuing the massed infantry of the enemy army.[3] At the end of the Bronze Age, from about 1200 BC, massed infantry again replaced the chariot as the centerpiece of warfare. Throughout this era army commanders controlled their forces by planning the battle and then usually leading its most important part personally, or, if an elderly king, observing from a nearby vantage point. In such battles where the commander was a participant, once battle was joined, he became an individual fighter whose command and control was merely represented by personal example. Since combat took place at such close proximity, commanders who observed from a distance were confined primarily to being capable of committing reserve or otherwise uncommitted forces to the battle.

Later, during the Classical Age beginning about 600 BC, massed infantry units evolved into the highly successful Greek phalanx and Roman legion. Alexander the Great conquered the Persian Empire and beyond using a phalanx army which he personally led and fought with on the battlefield, positioning himself on the key wing of the army. Most of Alexan•der's Hellenistic successors led the same way, but instead of actually participating in the fighting directly, led the key wing forward or switched between wings, but did not control the army as a whole once the battle started. Communications included the use of bugles or trumpets and messengers. Messengers and commanders could move around the battlefield via horse, though this became impractical as a method of command once the battle became a close fight. Alexander's forces always fought united under his command and never as separate columns or maneuver forces. In the only instance in which he did divide his force, it was out of logistic concerns, not operational. And in that case, little enemy opposition was expected.[4]

The rise of the Romans showed the use of technique to overcome the relative limitations of technology in the command and control of armies. While the Greek phalanx system of control was designed to minimize the number of separate units the army commander had to worry about controlling, the Romans organized their armies into many quasi-independent subunits, centuries, maniples and cohorts—each with its own experienced commander, the centurion. Bugle and standard flag use went down to this level. Such units were organized and trained to be capable of fighting with minimum overall direction. The legions these units belonged to practiced various battle drills and the centurions, being able to see the battlefield situation around them, were frequently able to make decisions for themselves. This was particularly important because Roman custom usually gave key military commands at the legion and above level to inexperienced nonprofessional aristocrats. While early Roman commanders had fought hand-to-hand in the traditional style, later commanders like Caesar, though not averse to combat, preferred to assess the battlefield situation and influence it as necessary. Such commanders let their subordinates do their jobs using initiative and battle drills to execute the overall battle plan. Through these methods, Roman armies proved to be remark•ably flexible on the battlefield. Additionally, a figure like Caesar could inspire his soldiers by his mere appearance among them without having to actually limit himself to personal combat with the opposing army.[5] Roman armies, while primarily composed of infantry, were capable of mobile operations when properly motivated and led. A good example of this is Caesar's seizure of Italy at the beginning of the civil war in 49 B.C.

Genghis Khan and Mobile Leadership

"The greatest pleasure is to vanquish your enemies and chase them before you, to rob them of their wealth and see those dear to them bathed in tears, to ride their horses and clasp to your bosom their wives and daughters."

—attributed to Genghis Khan[6]

While weapons technology ebbed and flowed from the time of Caesar to the Nineteenth Century, there were no real technological advances in communications to facilitate command and control. Throughout this long period commanders depended on various organizational techniques, such as signal flags, the use of messengers, and the horse to control their forces. Generally, campaigns were not highly mobile and armies were not dispersed far beyond the commander's ability to see and direct them. An exception to this was the medieval Mongol army of light cavalry led by Genghis Khan and his successors.

Between 1204 and 1227, through conquest, Genghis Khan created an empire consisting of most of central Asia and northern China. Using his highly mobile cavalry army and his battle command techniques, his successors would expand this empire into Europe, the Middle East, and the rest of China as well. As with the Romans, a lot of Genghis' mobile command success can be attributed to his organizing his army into effective subordinate units led by very com•petent commanders. Unlike the Romans, however, these units were composed exclusively of cavalry and were much larger. On campaign, Genghis usually organized his forces into several different armies each consisting of two or more *tumans*. The 10,000-rider *tuman* was the basic Mongol military unit and was in turn divided into smaller units by tens culminat•ing in a squad of ten riders.[7] When not at war, each unit, as with the Romans, was thoroughly drilled and trained for specific battlefield maneuvers, which were controlled through a system of flags, whistling arrows, fire arrows, and horns. Battle drills controlled by these signals al•lowed troops to be moved into preplanned positions or execute various battlefield maneuvers (attack, retreat, charge, move to the flank). Additionally, as similar to the Romans, subordi•nate commanders were empowered to make battlefield decisions.[8]

The Mongol cavalry was primarily lightly armored, consisting of archers and riders equipped with swords. Warriors fought for the most part mounted and, following their no•madic heritage, carried virtually all their necessary supplies with them. Accordingly, during mobile operations Mongol columns were not tied to conventional lines of supply and com•munications, either bringing along what they needed or, if necessary, foraging in the invaded territory.

The innovative and highly mobile Mongol army generally faced much less experienced armies composed of either peasant infantry or heavy, armored cavalry (as were the knights of contemporary European armies), both of which were tied to cities or roads or rivers for supply and support. Particularly when fighting on open steppe or prairie-style terrain, Mongol armies were nearly irresistible. Through force of arms an empire was soon forged consisting of most of the Central Asian steppe lands and adjoining areas.

Genghis Khan's method of battle control for his mobile forces was based primarily on orga•nization and technique. His well-trained columns, under good, experienced leaders down to the squad level, were fully capable of operating independently and completing a preplanned general campaign plan. However, once the operation was placed in motion, even Genghis had to depend on his immediate subordinates for its execution—most of them being his ownd sons. Once the army had taken to the field, he could only control the actions of the column he was with until his forces rejoined each other. Accordingly, the great khan usually placed himself with the one column he considered to have the most important or most decisive mis•sion and personally directed its activities. The 1220 campaign against the Turkish-Iranian Khwarizm Empire provides a good example of a typical Mongol mobile campaign.

The Khwarizm Empire was a Moslem kingdom in Central Asia centered on the valley of the Oxus River, with its capital at Samarkand. The original Khwarizmians were Iranians, but several hundred years before Turkish nomads from East Asia had conquered the region and continued to rule it as an Islamic kingdom. The populace was in the process of becom•ing Turkic in language and custom.[9] The ruler of the empire at the coming of the Mongols was Shah Mohammed II Ali ad-Din, who had spent the previous two decades expanding his domain into Persia to the south and across the Oxus into the eastern regions of Transoxiana and Khurusan. This gave the empire control of fertile valleys and cities along the Oxus and Jaxartes Rivers, and the Ferghana Valley on the lower reaches of the Jaxartes River point•ing east to the neighboring kingdom of Kara-Kitai. Beyond Kara-Kitai lay the empire of the

Mongols, united only since 1206, but expanding beyond Mongolia to the south and southwest in the intervening years under its gifted martial leader, Genghis Khan.

After ten years of arduous campaigning in East and Central Asia, and in Mongolia, Genghis had, in 1217, demobilized his army except for a two *tuman* force under his best general Chepe, which he sent west against the Buddhist kingdom of Kara-Kitai. The throne of Kara-Kitai had recently been seized by a renegade Mongol chieftain named Kushlak. This kingdom was located just east of the Khwarizmian lands and after its swift conquest, placed the Mongols on Shah Mohammed's own doorstep. After a breakdown in diplomacy when the arrogant shah executed the emissaries of the 'infidel' khan, both sides mobilized large armies for a now inevitable conflict.[10]

The Mongols mobilized roughly 200,000 riders, practically their whole male population, while the Khwarizmians already possessed an army of roughly a half million, which the shah had planned to use against the Caliph of Baghdad. Instead he would fight the Mongols. This army consisted of a small force of elite Turkish heavy cavalry, and larger masses of Turkish and Persian infantry—mostly inexperienced and low in morale. Mohammed placed his forces along a 500 miles stretch of the Jaxartes, the first defensible terrain inside his empire facing the east.[11]

Meanwhile, Genghis Khan began operations in 1219 with the movement of two armies commanded by Chepe and Genghis' son Juji (Jochi) with a total of three *tumans* against the Ferghana Valley. This force clashed with a much larger army under Shah Mohammed's son Jalal at Jand and the Mongols retreated. The Khwarizmians believed they had beaten an attempt to outflank their forces along the Jaxartes River farther to the north. In reality, however, the whole maneuver had been a feint designed to prevent interference while the Mongols assembled their forces for the main campaign that would take place the next year.[12]

The Mongol plan for the conquest of the Khwarizm Empire was based on mobility, surprise, and offensive action. Drawn up by Genghis' strategic advisor, Subotai Bahadur, the plan involved dividing the army into five main elements. The first two elements advanced late in 1219 directly against the city of Otrar, on the Jaxtares, and consisted of large detachments under the khan's sons Ogatai and Jagatai (Chogatai). They promptly besieged the city, a siege that would last seven months. Simultaneously Juji led a force out of the Ferghana Valley against the southern portion of Mohammed's line along the Jaxartes, quickly capturing Kojend and besieging its army, under the able Timur Malik, on an island in the river. These forces were designed to divert attention from the other two forces: 20,000 men under Chepe—the only major Mongol subordinate commander who was not Genghis' son, but actually an old adversary of the khan, and the recent conqueror of Kara-Kitai—advancing around the southern flank through mountains against Mohammed's main forces from the south. The second force was a 50,000 rider force under Genghis himself, moving far to the north and east around and behind Mohammed's army from the northwest crossing the unguarded Kyzil Kum desert using a dragooned local guide. In March 1220, while gearing his forces to fight Chepe, and losing 50,000 men in the process, Mohammed was shocked when Genghis ap

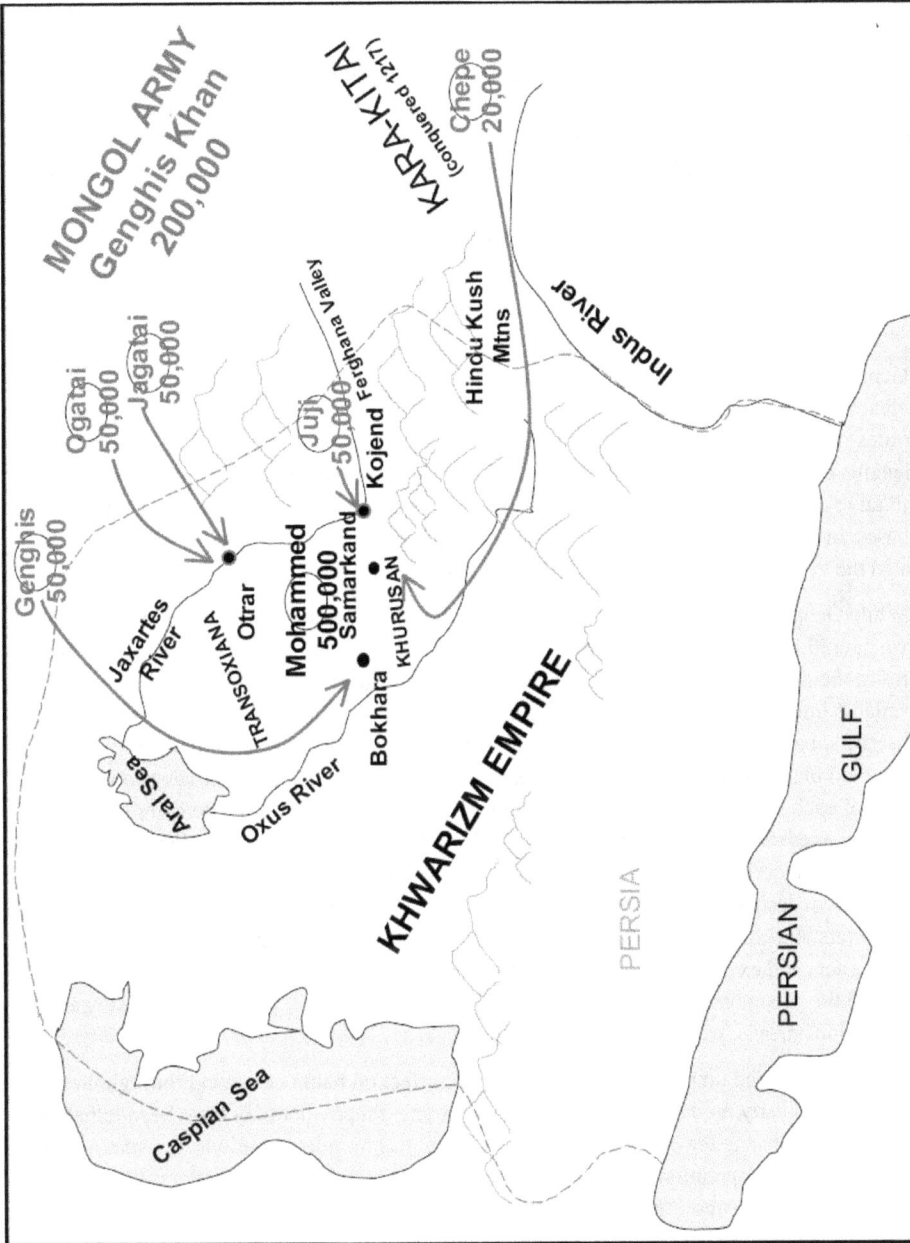

Figure 1. Mongols conquer Khwarizm Empire, 1220.

peared before the fortified city of Bokhara, 400 miles behind his main lines on the Jaxartes. In a panic, the shah threw the bulk of his forces into the fortresses of Bokhara, Samerkand and other cities.[13]

Bokhara soon fell, as did Otrar and Kojend. All the Mongol forces were now advancing to converge on Mohammed's capital, Samarkand, in the center of the Transoxiana region. The shah fled in great haste with his family to the south. Samarkand surrendered in five days, with its citadel holding out only a few additional days. The Mongols spent almost a year consolidating their hold over Mohammed's former domains. An army of 30,000 pursued Mohammed through the remaining portion of his kingdom before he finally died on the shore of the Caspian Sea. The shah's son and successor, Jalal, fought on in the area of present-day Afghanistan, but was defeated in 1221 by Genghis himself at the Battle of the Indus before fleeing to India and obscurity.[14]

Genghis and his strategist Subotai had planned a perfect mobile campaign, allowing them to defeat a much larger, very dangerous enemy force. The movements of the different Mongol armies were synchronized based on those of the others. However, once the operation started, Genghis only directly controlled his own column. He had to depend on the experience and initiative of his other commanders for the success of the campaign. Of course in the later phases, indirect word from reports, rumors, and indirect communications would have indicated the general situation of the other components of the Mongol army.

While Genghis Khan retained a personal bodyguard, he was for all practical purposes, his own operations officer. In later campaigns he used the talents of key subordinates who had proven themselves to be adept at military operations. Prior to a campaign, he analyzed all available intelligence information on the enemy using the Mongol's keen system of spies and observers, based primarily on merchants and traders. With this intelligence, the khan drew up a detailed plan of operations. The plan determined axes of advance objectives and the composition of each subordinate force. Once operations commenced, subordinate commanders—on different axes than Genghis himself—were allowed great latitude to reach their objectives. Such commanders were only required to comply with the general overall plan, leaving details to their own design. Communications with Genghis were facilitated by a sophisticated system of couriers and courier way-stations. This system not only enabled the Mongol leader to relay orders and exchange information with subordinates at a speed fast for its day, but it also allowed the Mongols to adapt to the combat situation before their enemies, using slower communications means, were able to.[15]

Technological and martial innovations had little effect on battle command throughout the medieval and early modern periods. The longbow and gunpowder may have been lethal but they did not enhance the commander's ability to control mobile operations. For maximum control of mobile operations a commander still needed to either have a large, well drilled army consisting of subordinate elements led by experienced leaders of great initiative, or a relatively small army led by the commander himself.

6

The period following the Mongol age of conquest saw in Europe the former ascendancy of heavily armored mounted knights eventually give way to massed infantry forces armed with crossbows, pikes, and later muskets and rifles. The advent of gunpowder did not really change tactics and warfare until Swedish king Gustavus Adolphus arrived on the scene in the first half of the Seventeenth Century. Gustavus Adolphus changed the massed formations of musketeers and pikemen who fought battles much like those of the Greek phalanx, depending on brute force and attrition, into one more akin to the style of the Roman legions. He reduced his number of pikemen and increased his musketeers, while placing them into smaller units which could be maneuvered to greater effect on battlefields and during campaigns. Gustavus Adolphus organized combined pike-musket units of about 400 men, half armed with each weapon. The pikemen were in the center of the formation with half the musketeers on each side. These units, called squadrons, advanced with the lines of musketeers firing while the pikemen protected musketeers in the rear reloading. Muskets were fired in volleys to add to their shock effect. Once a squadron closed with the enemy, the 11 foot long pikes were used to finish him off much like bayonets would be employed later. Combining this system with cavalry and more mobile artillery, Gustavus had increased the offensive battlefield power of the infantry on the battlefield. In the period from 1630 to 1632, the Swedish army, under its innovative king, and fighting for the Protestant cause in the Thirty Years War, dominated the battlefields of central Europe. Gustavus Adolphus was killed at the Battle of Lutzen in 1632, but his innovations were soon copied and ultimately became the basis for infantry linear tac•tics up until World War I.[16]

Despite these innovations, however, mobile campaigns as seen in the Mongol era, did not exist. This void was more than just the difference between light cavalry and heavy infantry. Campaigns characterized by the rapid movement of forces as a method of operations did not exist. Gustavus Adolphus tied his cavalry in closely with his infantry forces and the maneu•verability of his army on the battlefield did not translate into a general quicker pacing of campaigns. These forces were still tied to the marching pace of heavily equipped infantry, the need to besiege fortresses, and the maintenance of clear lines of communications for logisti•cal purposes.

Napoleon and Battle Command on the Move

Large mobile operations did not return to the battlefield until the French revolutionary army reorganized itself into self-contained, well-led subunits called army corps, late in the Eighteenth Century. Unlike the Mongol armies, however, Napoleon's forces were composed primarily of infantry, with cavalry typically playing a supporting role. The new French head of state and general, Napoleon Bonaparte, then refined the organization of these corps.[17] The rise of Napoleon, whose genius in mobile operations matched that of Genghis Khan, accord•ingly saw the return of such operations to the battlefield. Napoleon campaigned for almost twenty years. Most of his successful operations depended on outmaneuvering his opponents by moving faster than them and consolidating his forces to face a portion of their army on ground of his own choosing. Two campaigns stick out as examples of this mobility and his methods of commanding such an operation: the 1805 Ulm Campaign, which was a movement to contact operation, and the 1806 pursuit after the twin victories over the Prussians at Jena and Auerstädt.

Napoleon's ability to conduct successful mobile operations with an army largely composed of masses of infantry was based almost entirely on technique rather than technology. He organized the first modern staff to facilitate his battle command. As the last major historical field commander to also be a head of state, his army headquarters was also the forward headquarters for the government of France. Nevertheless, through organization and management, i.e. technique, Napoleon was able to command his forces in the field as thoroughly as possible given the technology of the pre-Industrial Age, and conduct complicated mobile operations using armies composed of masses of conscripted citizens or allied soldiers.

These forces were thoroughly organized in a manner reminiscent of the Roman legions. However, Napoleon's equivalent to the legion was a much larger force, the army corps. The Imperial Army's standard tactical unit, the army corps was a combined arms force consisting of two to four infantry divisions, each consisting of two or more infantry brigades and its own battery or two of artillery, a brigade or division of light cavalry, one or two batteries of artillery at the corps level, one or two companies of engineers and support and service elements. Corps organization was not totally standardized, both as a security measure, and because corps size was, to some extent, based on the perceived capabilities of the commanders.[18] Napoleon selected these commanders carefully, awarding most the elite rank of marshal, which soon became the usual rank for the men who commanded corps. By design their commands were to be able to fight on their own for short periods of time. Once he had his self-styled *Grande Armée* reorganized this way, Napoleon employed it in his classic style of using corps as separate entities, each advancing and moving under general instructions. Each able to hold its own, if necessary, until the rest of the army could come to their aid, but remaining in mutual supporting distance of each other. The corps would then concentrate by forced marches for a climactic battle.[19]

Napoleon controlled his martial orchestration through a field headquarters, called the general headquarters, which operated under the emperor's personal headquarters (the *Maison*), which was essentially the government of France operating from the field. The general headquarters sent out mounted messengers and aides with written dispatches out daily to each corps and received messages from the corps and the cavalry forces. Napoleon also retained a small staff of aides-de-camp of general officer rank who he employed on any special missions that came up.

The general headquarters, headed by its chief of staff Marshal Louis-Alexander Berthier, executed all the detail work required for a campaign, including the reproduction of orders, preparing and receiving reports, and movement control. Army logistics were handled by a rear headquarters, which usually established a line of communications following the path of the corps in the center of the army's deployment of advance. Corps and divisions had smaller versions of Napoleon's general headquarters.[20]

As the army advanced, Napoleon moved his headquarters forward, always trying to place it where he could both control the army the easiest, and to be near where he felt the decisive action would take place. As his army concentrated, he placed himself where he could best control it via messenger, retaining the reserve with him, or otherwise collocating with the corps with the key projected role.

The Ulm Campaign of 1805, while planned out, was an operation of expediency for Napoleon. He had originally assembled his army for an invasion of England, but the formation of a new continental alliance against him consisting of Austria and Russia, proved a more immediate danger. The French emperor had to defeat the Austrians before they combined with the Russians or delay or damage that meeting as much as possible.

In the October 1805 Ulm operation, Napoleon crossed the Rhine from French-controlled Alsace into Germany (French ally Württemberg) with an army of 200,000 organized into seven army corps and a cavalry corps, with corps varying in strength from 16,000 to 37,000 soldiers. The corps initially advanced on a broad 150 mile front but not too broad that they could not concentrate in a matter of three or four days. The Austrian forces facing Napoleon, commanded by the Habsburg Archduke Ferdinand and his deputy, the professional soldier General Karl Mack, pushed forces forward into neutral Bavaria as a prelude to a coordinated invasion of France once the Russians arrived. Mack expected the French to advance on him through the traditional invasion route through the Black Forest. The Prussian enclave of Ansbach, farther to the east, blocked the most direct north-south road network and Mack expected the French to have scruples about violating Prussian neutrality. Accordingly, he covered the Black Forest with light cavalry and prepared to advance westward from the Danube near Ulm to defeat the French forces as they advanced out of the forest.

Napoleon, however, after sending his cavalry under Marshal Joachim Murat as a feint into the Black Forest, actually sent his corps advancing diagonally across the Austrian front from the Main and Rhine rivers southeast to the Danube and the Austrian forces. Both sides were deceived as to the dispositions and intentions of the other. Napoleon planned to advance to the left (east) of the enemy forces near Ulm, cross the Danube and advance down the Lech River to Augsburg, threatening the forward Austrian forces with being cut off from Vienna. He fully expected the Austrians to retreat to the Lech or beyond. He anticipated concentrating in the general vicinity of Augsburg and defeating the Austrians in a decisive battle.[21]

Napoleon remained at Strasburg initially, controlling the campaign through his orders, which generally covered periods of from three to five days and daily horse-mounted messengers to and from the corps commanders. After some delays because of a shortage of bridges, his corps got across the Rhine and advanced toward the Danube, commencing on 25 September 1805. The only initial command and control difficulties were an inability to gain a clear knowledge of enemy dispositions and intentions. Despite Austrian expectations, Napoleon had no compunctions about passing his corps through the enclave of Ansbach. The Prussian governor protested but otherwise the only effect was that the Prussians now allowed the Russians to cross their territory farther to the east in their movement to join the Austrians.

By 6 October, the first corps elements were crossing the Danube. Skirmishes and full-scale battles with Austrian defenders along the line of the river slowed the crossing. The French emperor moved his field headquarters forward to Donauworth on the north bank of the Danube on the 7th and was immediately dissatisfied by the speed of the advance. Napoleon wanted to get his entire army across the river and concentrated near Munich and Augsburg as quickly as possible. He expected to fight a major battle near one of those cities within days, as the Austrians fell back to keep from being cut off from their capital, Vienna. Accordingly he dispatched a senior staff officer to relay orders for three corps to speed up their move-ments. However, in an eagerness to comply, the corps ended up entangling their columns into each other. The resulting traffic snarl causing unnecessary delays. Nevertheless, by the 12th, all major French forces were across the Danube, leaving a small force of cavalry, the main body of the army's trains and a single division of infantry on the north bank.[22]

The Austrians, however, were not in flight. Until the first French elements reached the Danube, they still were watching the exits from the Black Forest to the west. The Austrian cavalry had failed at its mission to provide early warning for the command. Once the French

26 September-12 October 1805

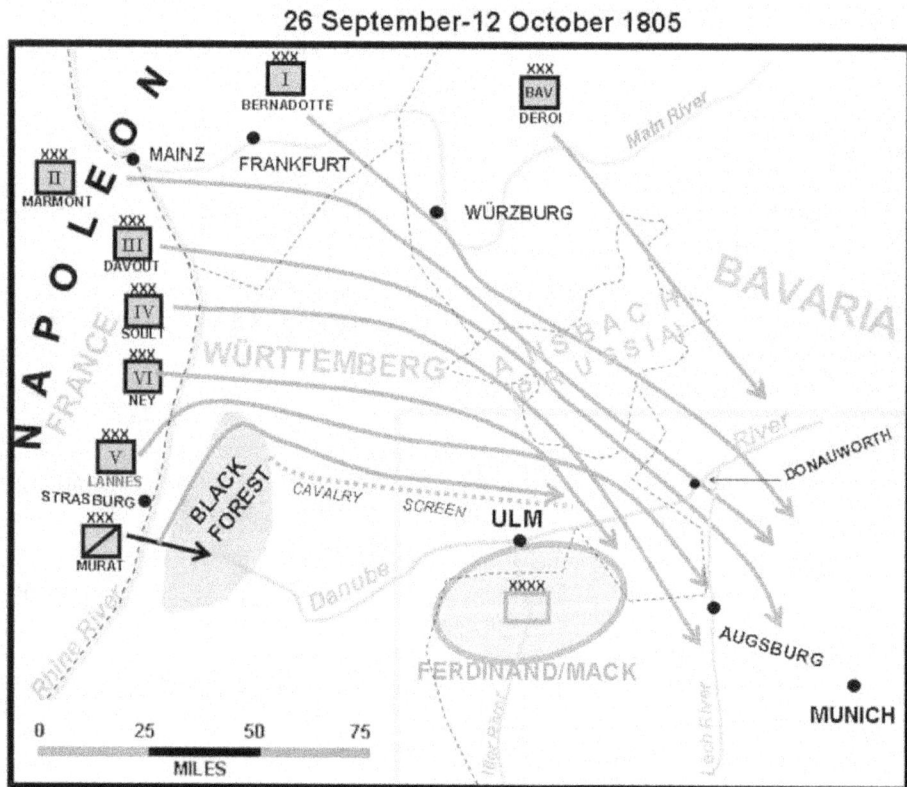

Figure 2. The 1805 Ulm Campaign, Inital Phase.

10

were discovered on and crossing the Danube, the Austrian command was at mixed opin•
ions on what to do. The timid royal Archduke Ferdinand wanted to retreat immediately. The
professional, Mack, saw instantly that Napoleon was repeating his maneuver from the 1800
Marengo campaign where he cut the line of retreat of the Austrian forces and baited them into
retreating into a battle of his time and choosing. Mack also soon realized that while Napoleon
stood on his army's lines of communication, so he did on Napoleon's. An advance along the
north bank of the Danube would not only capture the French trains, but also serve to possibly
cut off the corps on the wrong side of the river and defeat them in detail. Even if unsuccessful
at this, the Austrians would still have escaped the trap at Ulm and been able to join up with
the advance elements of the Russian army. Several times Mack tried to issue the orders to
advance out of Ulm, but his aristocratic commander refused to allow it. And then it was too
late. Napoleon had realized his misjudgment and scrambled to correct it.

The ability of Napoleon to command his forces while on the move and in battle was now
tested. Finally, with a true understanding of Austrian dispositions, on 12 October he recog•
nized the dangerous situation he had placed his forces in by advancing them so far forward
and across an unfordable river. Behind him and astride that river was the bulk of the enemy
army in position to attack his lines of communication and poised to destroy the supply trains,
ammunition trains, heavy artillery and, possibly, isolate the army. Since 9 October his head•
quarters had been at Augsburg near most of his corps. Accordingly he rapidly responded to
this crisis with a hail of new orders. Sending two corps (I, III) to advance on Munich to the
southeast to cover the army's eastern flank and prevent the Russians from coming to the
Austrian's rescue, he turned the rest west to face the Austrian concentration at Ulm. Accom•
panied by his division-sized force of Guards, he traveled with the two corps (II, V) moving up
to surround the Austrians in the Ulm defenses. He sent the IV Corps on an envelopment to the
south and west then back eastward to surround Ulm from the west, and sent another, the VI,
to cover both banks of the Danube towards Ulm. The cavalry, under Murat, was first sent to
screen this advance and hold the Austrians in place, and then sent across the Danube to cover
the trains and pursue various enemy elements that had escaped the encirclement. Forces be•
yond Napoleon's immediate control acted on their own. For example, it took couriers a whole
day to find the VI Corps division that had been initially left as the only infantry north of the
Danube. This division had retreated after fighting off a corps-sized Austrian element escaping
from the Ulm trap.[23]

Archduke Ferdinand left General Mack in the lurch. The archduke refused to allow his chief
subordinate to act aggressively against the French before Napoleon discovered his mistake.
Once Napoleon turned towards Ulm, Mack, based on a false rumor of unrest back in Paris,
misinterpreted the French actions as the beginning of a retreat back to France. The true na•
ture of French intentions, however, was quickly apparent when the advancing French corps
mauled part of the Austrian force. By the 16th, the Austrians were trapped in Ulm. Before the
trap was sealed, however, Archduke Ferdinand handed command over to Mack and, not want•
ing to become a geopolitical prize, Ferdinand took a force of cavalry and infantry and fled to
the north bank of the Danube, ultimately escaping across the French lines of communication

after 12 October 1805

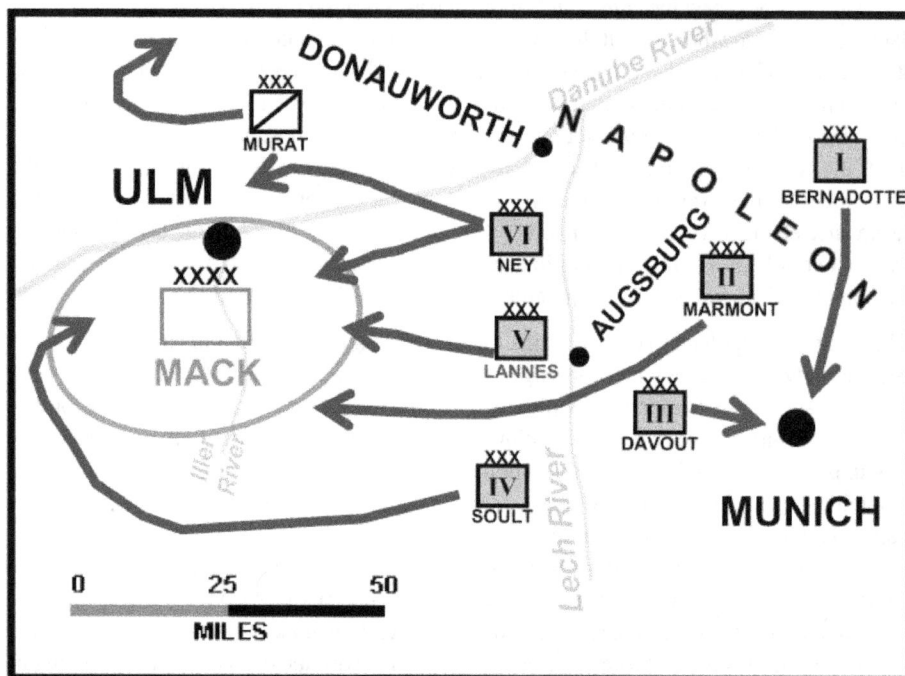

Figure 3. 1805 Ulm Campaign, Final Phase.

to Bohemia, partially pursued by French cavalry. Mack stayed at Ulm, hoping to buy time for the other Austrian armies and the Russians. Mack's forces were poor and some of his subordinates unfit. Accordingly he was unable to stand a long siege. Driven out of their fortifications into the city proper by the 15th, the Austrians surrendered on the 20th.

The Ulm campaign was over. Despite minor glitches, Napoleon's ability to command and control his army given the technological limitations of the day was excellent. Using its superb corps organization and following general plans and frequent messages which gave more of Napoleon's intent rather than specific instructions, he was able to control the army dispersed over an area of up to 150 miles. Once concentrated, he was able to control the various components with frequent exchanges of messages, orders, reports and personal contact.

The overall campaign did not end at Ulm. Napoleon pursued the remaining Austrian armies into the heart of Austria, occupying Vienna and then fighting and thrashing a combined Austrian-Russian army at Austerlitz in early December, forcing the Austrians to sue for peace. Despite the great victory, there was one major command and control failure along the way. While advancing along the Danube after the Russians into the Austrian heartland in early

November 1805, the French forces moved in corps columns spread out as in the approach to Ulm, though on a shorter front. Five corps were south of the river, one ad hoc corps under Marshal Edouard Mortier, was north. The Russians turned away from Vienna, retreating north of the Danube into Moravia to the northeast. Napoleon intended his forces to follow the enemy, not capture undefended Vienna. But somehow instructions got misunderstood and instead cavalry leader Murat and the V Corps headed to the Austrian capital. Left unmolested, the retreating Russians turned on Mortier's unsupported corps north of the river and badly mauled it. Napoleon's belief that a corps could fight unsupported for up to two days was here proven, as Mortier's corps drove off Russian forces almost three times its size attacking from three directions before retreating across the Danube.[24]

After Austerlitz, the Russians, while still at war with France, did not immediately field new armies in central Europe. Instead Prussia, smarting from various slights and basking in the past glories of Frederick the Great, joined the Russians in alliance against the French. In the fall of 1806, however, Napoleon moved to forestall the Prussians, who had decided to fight alone, before the Russians were ready. He had assembled his army in central Germany when the Prussians invaded the buffer state of Saxony and forcibly made it an ally.

ADVANCE ON VIENNA NOVEMBER 1805

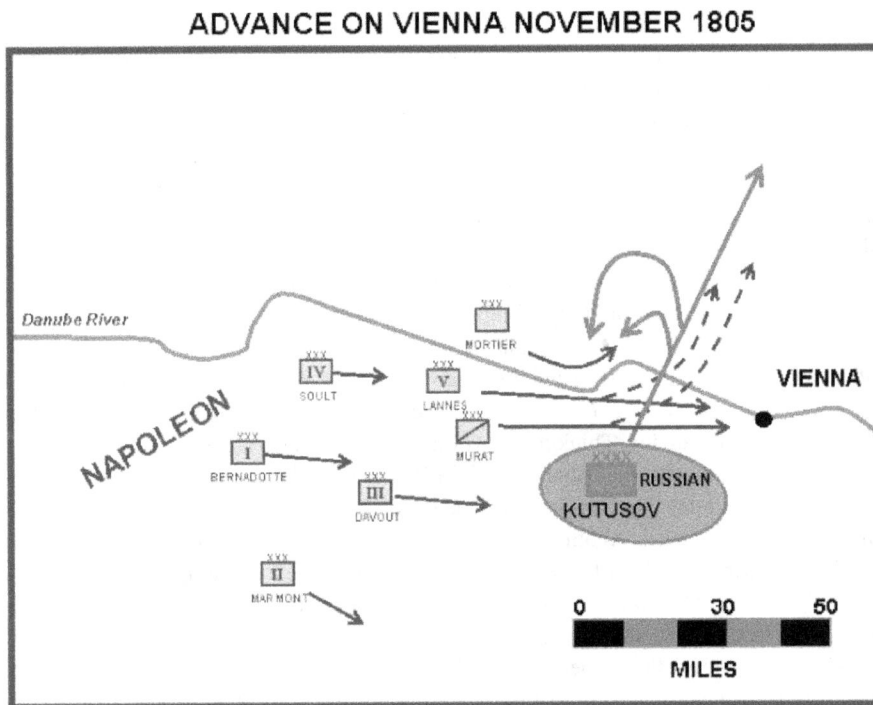

Figure 4. The Advance on Vienna, November 1805.

The subsequent campaign against Prussia showed all application of Napoleon's superior technique to the successful pursuit of a defeated army and swift occupation of a hostile nation. Once again Napoleon used his superior organization and the initiative of his subordinate leaders to execute a complicated, multi-faceted operation when contemporary technology precluded instant and continuous contact and communications with his subordinates.

Napoleon advanced on the Prussians in multiple corps columns, hoping to concentrate and beat them piecemeal before they themselves could concentrate. He was partially successful in that he met only a portion of the Prussian army at Jena with almost his entire army. However, a detached corps, the III under Marshal Louis Davout, was faced with the bulk of the Prussian forces at Auerstädt about ten miles north of Napoleon's force. Davout and Marshal Jean Baptiste Bernadotte's I Corps were designated to outflank the left of the Prussian forces facing Napoleon at Jena. Instead, Bernadotte stayed out of the battle completely and Davout fought off the bulk of the Prussian army with his single corps while Napoleon defeated the rest with the bulk of the French army. Jena-Auerstädt saw several command and control failures on Napoleon's part. Firstly, before the battle Davout, Napoleon's most reliable subordinate, failed to report to the Emperor's chief of staff, Marshal Louis-Alexandre Berthier, in his daily dispatches that he faced a large Prussian force, merely commenting that he had secured himself against attack.[25]

Then, on 14 October 1806, as Napoleon himself fought (with four corps and 96,000 soldiers) and defeated 51,000 Prussians under General Fredrick-Ludwig Prince Hohenlohe and Lieutenant General Ernst-Friedrich-Wilhelm-Philipp von Rüchel, he had no idea of the location and actions of two of his corps, Davout's III, and Bernadotte's I. The previous night Napoleon had ordered these corps to advance deep into the rear of the Prussians facing him. However, once the action at Jena started, the Emperor himself had no idea of the activities or situation of the two corps. Bernadotte chose to interpret his orders as a call for inaction, ignoring the sounds of battle and maintaining a position between the two battlefields. Meanwhile Davout's single corps of 26,000 fought off 63,000 Prussians under the Field Marshal Karl, Duke of Brunswick, with the Prussian king, Frederick William III, present. Davout's position was perilous, but his skill and the timely battlefield death of the Duke of Brunswick led to a rout of the much larger Prussian force when a local French counterattack ended up outflanking the Prussian line. Thinking he was facing the whole Prussian army, Napoleon, after a back-and-forth morning battle, routed the Prussians in the afternoon. Napoleon did not realize until the next day that Davout had faced the bulk of the enemy army and defeated it until he received dispatches. Another corps (Bernadotte's) was out of command and control and did not contribute to either battle. Luckily for Napoleon, he had the right subordinate (Davout) at the right place and time, as, essentially the key battle of the campaign was fought and won for Napoleon by one of his corps commanders acting on his own initiative beyond all timely direction from the Emperor.[26] Napoleon had to decide how best to control and command his force as a whole and chose, through a combination of bad intelligence and luck, to be in direct command of the bulk of his forces facing a secondary enemy force.[27]

The pursuit of the Prussians after Jena-Auerstädt is considered the classic mobile pursuit of the pre-mechanized era. After routing the Prussians on the battlefield, the French had to en‑ sure the victory by not allowing their enemy to regroup and make a stand elsewhere or to es‑ cape and join the Russian forces moving into play far to the east. Lasting from 15 October to 7 November 1806, this mobile operation effectively knocked Prussia out of the war, with only minor detachments left to join the Russians in the subsequent Eylau-Friedland campaigns.[28]

Napoleon initially only ordered the troops with him to begin the pursuit. Once he regained contact with Davout and Bernadotte, they were urged on as well. The first goal of the pursuit was to get across the Elbe River quickly and catch the retreating enemy forces. After crossing the Elbe, Berlin was a key objective as well.[29]

Napoleon spread out his forces for this mission. Murat with the bulk of the cavalry, support‑ ed by Marshal Michel Ney's VI Corps, swung wide to the west through the Harz Mountains to hopefully beat the retreating Prussians to the fortress city of Magdeburg on the Elbe. Mar‑ shal Nicolas Soult and his IV Corps would nip directly at the heels of the retreating survivors

PURSUIT AFTER JENA/ AUERSTÄDT 1806

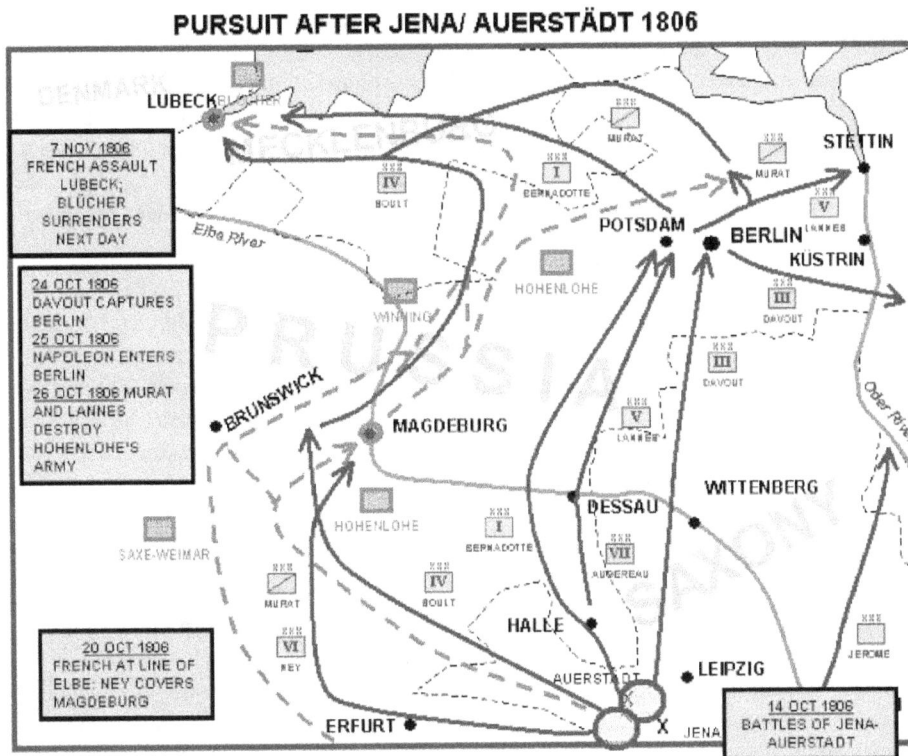

Figure 5. The pursuit after Jena-Auerstädt, 1805.

of Jena-Auerstädt. Bernadotte was to advance to the middle Elbe after blocking a previously uncommitted Prussian force under Eugen, the Prince of Württemberg, from joining the other retreating Prussian forces, pushing any stragglers to the west where Soult could deal with them. Davout would clear the eastern Elbe, preparatory to a march directly on Berlin. Cavalry commander Murat quickly captured the important city of Erfurt and Napoleon made this his new base of operations.

Within five days the various French forces had chased the Austrians across the Elbe, destroying Württemberg's force at Halle and placed Magdeburg under siege. With the Elbe breached, the Prussians, after leaving small forces behind at Magdeburg, retreated to the northeast, hoping to get across the Oder River beyond Berlin and then regroup in the eastern provinces of the Prussian Kingdom. Davout entered Berlin on 24 October, 9 days after the pursuit began, then moved to the east, blocking Prussian escape routes over the Oder River. Farther to the west, the two main remaining Prussian forces, Hohenlohe's force at Magdeburg and the Duke of Saxe-Weimar's army near Brunswick, attempted to escape to the northeast pursued by the French cavalry, and Soult and Ney's infantry. After being roughed up by Soult on the 23d, Saxe-Weimar crossed the river north of Magdeburg. Napoleon left Ney's corps behind to cover Magdeburg while the rest of his army chased the Prussians across a broad front. The main force under Hohelohe was finally caught and destroyed northeast of Berlin by Murat and part of Marshal Jean Lannes' V Corps on the 26th. Two French corps and Murat's cavalry pursued the other major force, Saxe-Weimar's former command and part of Hohenlohe's command—both under Lieutenant General Gebhard von Blücher—northwest to the free city of Lubeck on the Baltic coast. On 7 November the French assaulted and took the city with Blücher surrendering the next day, effectively ending Prussian organized resistance 28 days after the battles of Jena-Auerstädt.[30]

Napoleon controlled this mobile operation very indirectly. He made Erfurt his base on 16 October, then moved up to Wittenberg on the Elbe on the 22d, and entered Berlin on the 25th. He controlled his corps with general instructions such as those given to Murat and Ney after the fall of Erfurt to act as a "sword point to [the enemy's] kidneys."[31] Daily dispatches and reports allowed him to adjust operations as necessary, but the corps commanders on the ground formulated most of the details. Good organization and leaders with initiative enabled him to execute an operation he could not really control directly.[32]

Summary

From antiquity to the beginning of the industrial age, mobile battle command was hindered by a lack of technological advances, which made communications over great distances difficult. To make up for this problem, successful mobile commanders depended on technique—systems of organization and the initiative of distant subordinate commanders—to synchronize and coordinate operations. Some commanders, such as Alexander the Great, preferred to retain the bulk of their forces under their own immediate control, using the mobility and coordination of various subordinate units only on the battlefield itself rather than in the overall campaign.

16

The Romans developed an organizational system based on the legion and its subunit—the cohort. By giving the Roman field commander a series of reliable cohorts of similar capabil•ity, it allowed him to deal primarily with the operational employment of these units, rather than having to fight with them as well. Commanders of such stature as Julius Caesar were able to use this flexibility to maneuver large units both on the battlefield and in campaigns. Caesar's swift advance into Italy in 49 B.C. at the beginning of the Civil War with Pompey (Gnaeus Pompeius Magnus) is a good example of the mobility of such a force.

While European military developments in the Middle Ages shifted to armies composed of massed infantry and heavy cavalry, the central Asian Mongols, led by their first overall ruler, Genghis Khan, applied an organizational flexibility similar to that of the Romans to a large force of light cavalry. Using the mobility of his cavalry, Genghis typically split his forces into several subordinate elements which all advanced on different axes aiming to reach predeter•mined objectives or to accomplish predetermined general missions. With an overall general plan and a system of speedy couriers, the Mongol leader managed to synchronize his forces over large geographical expanses in the first real mobile campaigns in history. Genghis, how•ever, had to depend on the abilities of his subordinate commanders, as his battle command over any of his forces he was not with was indirect at best.

While in the early modern period, Swedish king Gustavus Adolphus devised the organiza•tional structure of infantry, cavalry and artillery which evolved into linear tactics, it was Na•poleon who took these organizations and applied them at the operational level to effectively control fast moving forces. The army corps system gave the French emperor large, self-con•tained units with which he could conduct campaigns, spreading the forces out to overwhelm his enemies, then massing them for decisive battles.

Methods of technique—such as reliance on mission orders or the organizing of one's army into self-contained units which could operate independently, then deploying them to acting mutual support of one another—were the hallmarks of battle command on the move in the long epoch before the industrial revolution. During this expanse of time, battle command saw no technological developments. By the time of Napoleon, however, this was about to change, with the development of the telegraph and the railroad.[33] Before moving to these technologi•cal advances, the beginning of the American experience, which had predated Napoleon by two decades, requires attention.

Notes

1. Napoleon, *Napoleon's Art of War*. General Burnod, ed., Lieutenant General Sir G.C. D'Aguilar, CB, trans. (New York: Barnes and Noble, 1995), 19.

2. R. Ernest Dupuy, and Trevor N. Dupuy, *The Encyclopedia of Military History: From 3500 B.C. to the Present*, Revised Edition (New York: Harper and Row, 1977), 2-3.

3. Robert Drews, *The End of the Bronze Age: Changes in Warfare and the Catastrophe CA. 1200 B.C.* (Princeton: Princeton University Press, 1993), 105-7.

4. Martin Van Creveld, *Command in War* (Cambridge, MA: Harvard University Press, 1985), 25, 44.

5. Ibid., 45-47. Roman army commanders, including Caesar, traditionally wore a scarlet cloak called a *paludamentum* into battle, which not only identified them to their own troops but to the enemy as well,. This was a key psychological point for Caesar once his battlefield reputation was established. See Julius Caesar, *The Gallic War*, Loeb Classical Library, trans. H.J. Edwards, 1994 ed. (Cambridge, MA: Harvard University Press, 1917), 506-7. This cloak is mentioned in the New Testament as the one placed on Christ by the soldiers when they were mocking Him. See Matthew 27.28.

6. This famous quote is often cited in various translations and was paraphrased in the Arnold Schwarzenegger movie *Conan the Barbarian* (1982). The quote originated in the 14th century Persian language *Jami'at-tawarikh (Collected Chronicles)*, compiled by Rashid ad-Din. See Paul Ratchnevsky, *Genghis Khan: His Life and Legacy*, Thomas Haining, ed/trans. (Cambridge, MA: Blackwell, 1992), 152, 264 note 29.

7. The other units were called *arban* (tens-squad), *jaghun* (hundreds-troop), *mingghan* (thousands• regiment). See Stephen Turnbull, *Genghis Khan and the Mongol Conquests 1190-1400* (London: Osprey, 2003), 17.

8. James Chambers, *The Devil's Horsemen: The Mongol Invasion of Europe* (New York: Atheneum, 1979), 54, 59-61.

9. The modern day inhabitants of the region speak Turkish languages-Uzbek, Kazakh, Kyrgyz, although a type of Iranian is spoken to the south in Tajikistan and Afghanistan (Pashtun).

10. Dupuy, 336-7: Chambers, 6.

11. Chambers, 3, 6-7.

12. Ibid., 7-9.

13. Ibid., 10-12.

14. Ibid., 16-18; Dupuy, 337-8.

15. Dupuy, 343; James Dunnigan and Daniel Masterson, *The Way of the Warrior: Business Tactics and Techniques from History's Twelve Greatest Generals* (New York: St. Martin's Griffin, 1997), 55-6.

16. Dupuy, 526, 529-30, 537-40; Dunnigan 83-5.

17. Robert M. Epstein, "Patterns of Change and Continuity in Nineteenth-Century Warfare", *Journal of Military History*, 56, (July 1992), 376; David G. Chandler, *The Campaigns of Napoleon* (New York: Scribner, 1966), 136, 159. 266.

18. Chandler, 146-7, 266; BG Vincent J. Esposito and COL John R. Elting, *A Military History and Atlas of the Napoleonic Wars* (New York: Praeger, 1968. Arms and Armour press Reprint 1978), v.

19. Esposito, ix, Chandler, 154, 185; Corps were expected to be able to fight on their own unsup• ported for up to two days. Napoleon expected a well-led corps to be capable of being sent anywhere. See Epstein, 377 and Chandler, 154, 185.

20. Chandler, 266, 367-73; Esposito, vii.

21. Chandler, 394-5; Esposito, text accompanying Map 48; Connelly, 80.

22. Chandler, 396-9; Esposito, text accompanying Map 48.

23. Chandler, 399-400; Esposito, text accompanying Map 50.

24. Chandler, 405-6; Esposito, text accompanying Map 52; Connelly, 85-6.

25. Chandler, 462-4, 467-8, 477-8, 488; Esposito, text accompanying Map 62.

26. Davout's excellence as a corps commander was greatly enhanced by his divisional commanders, *Générals de Division* Louis Friant, Charles Morand and Charles Gudin, collectively referred to as "the three immortals."

27. Chandler, 488, 503; Esposito, text accompanying Maps 65, 66 and 67; Connelly, 101-3.

28. Chandler, 497.

29. Chandler, 498.

30. Ibid.,498-502.

31. Esposito, text accompanying Map 67; Chandler, 497-8.

32. Chandler, 503-5.

33. The British and French had developed sophisticated systems of visual signaling by the 1790s, the most prominent being the French Chappé telegraph. See Note 7, page 122 for more information. Such systems were primarily of use at the strategic and sometimes operational levels, but were far less useful in mobile operations.

THE AMERICAN EXPERIENCE TO 1861

"There is nothing so likely to produce peace as to be well prepared to meet an enemy."
—George Washington[1]

The Yorktown Maneuver, 1781

American experience with mobile operations was fairly limited prior to the American Civil War. Before that war, campaigns were typically between small forces of infantry moving along clearly defined lines of communication at a steady pace. The lack of road networks, the predominance of forests and the large logistical tails inherent in the armies employed in America in the Revolutionary War, and War of 1812 resulted in more deliberate operations.

However, in the Revolutionary War, the campaigns in the Southern colonies during the period 1778-1781 resulted in the one major operational maneuver of a mobile nature ex- hibited in that war—the shifting and concentration of American and French forces against British forces at Yorktown. The preceding campaign in the South had seen frequent marches and countermarches across South and North Carolina, particularly after the capitulation of Charleston in May 1780. Most of these movements ended in pitched battles, but, aside from a rout at Camden in August 1780, the British were unable to destroy the American forces in the Carolinas, even suffering defeat themselves at Kings Mountain in October 1780, and at Cowpens in January 1781. Except for some troops at the port of Charleston, the British forces, under Lieutenant-General Lord Charles Cornwallis, moved on to Virginia to combine with other British forces there. For various reasons the British command decided to shift Cornwallis' force out of Virginia and, accordingly, he moved to the port of Yorktown on the York River estuary and occupied defensive positions awaiting evacuation by sea.

In response to Cornwallis' movement into static positions at Yorktown, the American Commander-in-Chief General George Washington managed to slip the bulk of his army out of its cordon around British-occupied New York in 1781 and move it unmolested to York- town to bring about the surrender of Cornwallis' force. At the time, Washington was being reinforced with a French force under Lieutenant-General Jean-Baptiste Donatien de Vimeur, Count de Rochambeau, which had landed at Newport, Rhode Island, and was marching to New York. The plan in early 1781 was to use this force to eject the now outnumbered main British force in America—the 17,000 soldier garrison occupying New York city under British American theater commander, Lieutenant-General Sir Henry Clinton. Several things changed the plan. First, Clinton realized forces were being massed against him and conse- quently ordered Cornwallis to send part of his army to New York to reinforce the garrison. Cornwallis, accordingly, moved to the port of Yorktown to await the arrival of ships. Mean- while, the French appeared ready to challenge the British control of the sea off the American coast, providing a large fleet (29 ships) and 3,000 troops under Admiral [*Lieutenant-Général des Armées Navales*] François Joseph Paul, Count de Grasse, to be on station off Virginia and Maryland in September and October 1781. Upon getting word that de Grasse was en route in August 1781, Washington and Rochambeau changed gears, deciding to shift the bulk of their forces to Virginia to destroy Cornwallis.

As with Napoleon later and with earlier commanders, Washington relied on technique as the technology of his day did not facilitate battle command via swift communications. In fact, as an operational technique, he relied on the time lag in communications to allow him to sneak his army away from New York before the British realized it and to finish off Cornwallis before they could then do anything about it. While he personally led the bulk of the army in its grand maneuver until it was well away from New York, he also relied on the proven abilities of Lafayette to keep Cornwallis at bay while the maneuver was executed, and on the French fleet to do its part of providing Lafayette with reinforcements while keeping the British fleet away from Cornwallis or Chesapeake Bay. Washington's plan depended on a lot of smaller pieces coming together, which they did because he had organizationally set the stage for them to come together.[2]

Moving the bulk of his army south was risky for Washington. Were Clinton to realize what was going on, he could sortie out and attack the Americans. Or he could move to reinforce Cornwallis, or withdraw his force before the trap could be set. The latter option was temporarily nullified when the British Royal Navy committed one of its few lapses in professionalism during the war. De Grasse, who had arrived off the coast of Virginia at the end of August, encountered a slightly smaller British fleet out of New York, under Rear-Admiral Thomas Graves, at the mouth of Chesapeake Bay and fought the tactically indecisive Battle of the Capes on 5 September. After the battle, both fleets drifted south off the North Carolina coast, facing each other until the 10th when they lost mutual visibility of each other's force. De Grasse returned to Chesapeake Bay. The British turned to do so as well, but on the 13th, Graves received news that French had beat him back to the bay and were now being reinforced with their squadron from Newport. Fearing renewed battle with a larger French force with his weakened fleet, Graves chose to return to New York to refit his damaged ships, leaving de Grasse with control of the Chesapeake.[3]

Washington began his movement on 19 August, crossing the Hudson River miles upstream at Stony Point the next day, followed by the French contingent. A force of 12,000 was left behind under Major-General William Heath to cover the withdrawal and then protect the strategic Hudson Highlands. While the fleets were maneuvering, Washington and Rochambeau continued to march. To deceive Clinton as to his intentions, Washington had his forces cross the Hudson and move in a big loop through northern New Jersey, simulating a possible massing for an attack on British controlled Staten Island. He also refused to allow the French to do standard route reconnaissance and logistical preparations for the move and did not tell his ultimate intentions to any of his subordinate commanders.

On 25 August Washington finally let his subordinate commanders in on the actual objective of the army's maneuvers.[4] The army then concentrated and camped for one day at the end of August near Chatham, New Jersey, to fool the British as to its intentions before beginning a straight march to Philadelphia and beyond to transports assembling at the head of Chesapeake Bay.

22

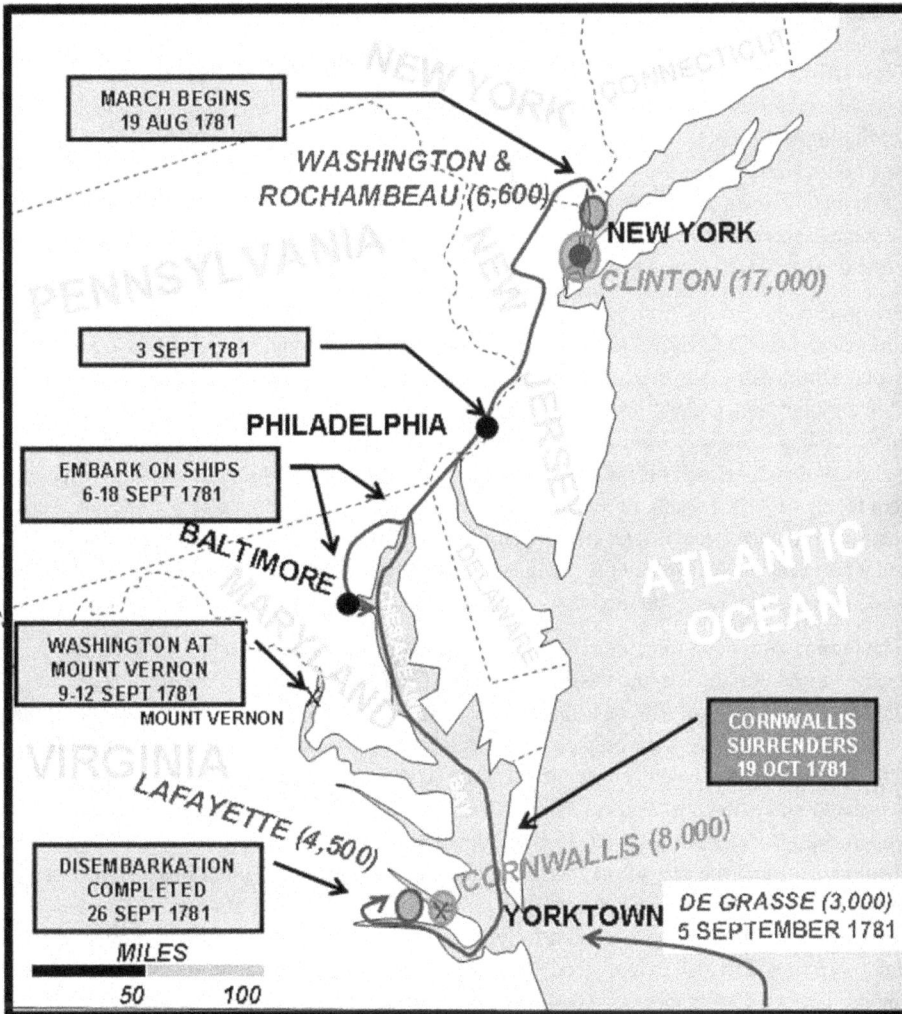

Figure 6. Redeploying to Yorktown, 1847.

The ruse worked. As late as 1 September, Clinton still expected an attack on New York. What finally convinced him of Washington's true intentions was a combination of word of the French fleet movements on the Chesapeake, and reports of the obvious movement of Wash•ington and Rochambeau's armies to the south away from New York. But with Washington far to the south and Heath's force watching New York, Clinton was, for all practical purposes, in no position now to prevent the movement. He had sent his fleet out to look for the French fleet, and without its support dared not move against the Americans.[5]

Washington had finally abandoned the deception at the end of August, as reports were received that the British had sent out their fleet from New York. Previously, with a portion of the British West Indies fleet, Rear Admiral Sir Samuel Hood had pursued de Grasse from the Indies to the Chesapeake, but somehow made a faster passage and beat the French there. Not finding any French at the mouth of the bay, Hood sailed to New York where his squadron joined with Graves' squadron. This combined fleet, under Graves' command, then sailed out to find de Grasse on 29 August. When Washington received word of this, he cancelled all deceptive measures. Either Clinton was already onto the move, or he now had no fleet to react to it and most of the army was out of his overland striking distance.[6]

Previous to the Battle of the Capes, de Grasse had landed 3,000 French infantrymen to reinforce a small American force opposing Cornwallis led by Major-General Marie Joseph du Motier, Marquis de Lafayette. Additionally, while the fleets drifted southward opposite each other, another French naval force under the admiral who now commanded the naval squadron which had brought Rochambeau to Newport, Louis Jacques- Melchior, Count de Barras de Saint-Laurent, arrived off the Chesapeake. On 10 September, while the two larger fleets were facing off to the south, de Barras landed the remaining French troops from Rhode Island along with Rochambeau's siege artillery and supplies, which had accumulated in New England. De Barras' arrival scared off the British commander Graves, when the former's force linked up with de Grasse the next day.

The Franco-American force marched south to Trenton, crossed the Delaware River and marched through Philadelphia, passing in review, from 2-6 September. The army began concentrating at Head of Elk, near the northern end of Chesapeake Bay, on the 6th. But it was soon apparent that there were only enough available boats there for about a third of the force, so the bulk proceeded to Baltimore, where more boats were available. The army embarked on boats to move down Chesapeake Bay to the James River where it would disembark near Williamsburg between the 6th and 18th of September, with the loading delayed for two days when it was feared the British may have defeated the French fleet. The troops disembarked upon arrival with the amphibious operation completed on the 26th. Lafayette had been containing Cornwallis since the 8th and now, with the arrival of reinforcements, a proper siege of the surrounded British commenced. The siege ended with Cornwallis' surrender less than a month later on 19 October. As an after-note, upon the return of Graves' fleet to New York, Clinton realized the dire straits Cornwallis was in and planned a relief expedition. Fearing the now enlarged French fleet, though, he allowed delays for ship repairs until the fleet of 25 ships of the line and three admirals finally sailed on the day Cornwallis surrendered. En route the British force encountered a small merchant vessel, which related the news of Cornwallis' surrender. The British returned to New York.[7]

Washington controlled his Yorktown movement carefully as he faced large enemy armies on both ends. He crossed the Hudson with the vanguard and stayed with the main body during the deception. To ease movement, the army moved in three columns—French and American infantry in separate columns with the artillery baggage train in the middle.[8] Once removed far enough from New York to not worry about immediate enemy action, Washington and

Rochambeau moved with their staffs ahead of the Army, to plan the rest of the movement and subsequent operation. Once agreeing upon a movement to the northern end of Chesapeake Bay (Head of Elk), where boats and supplies awaited, Rochambeau returned to his forces and Washington went ahead to Philadelphia to confer with the Continental Congress and remained in the city for a week as first the American forces passed through, then the leading elements of the French.[9] From there he issued orders for the march to Head of Elk. Depart‐ing on 5 September, he received de Grasse's dispatch en route at Chester and stopped there to await Rochambeau's arrival by boat to confer with him about the new development.

After this, Washington moved to Head of Elk the next day and set about coordinating the moving of the army by sea. After two days there, he left the troops to be embarked under command of Major-General Benjamin Lincoln and moved south with Rochambeau ahead of the rest of the following troops to Baltimore.[10] On 9 September, with everything in motion, Washington rode ahead to his estate at Mount Vernon, 60 miles south of Baltimore, where he remained for three days—his first and only visit during the course of over seven years of the war. While there he continued to receive and send dispatches. Rochambeau arrived the next day and the two generals and their staffs rode out for Williamsburg on the 13th, arriving the next day and moving to the lines of Yorktown shortly thereafter as the campaign moved to its siege phase.

When not directly with his command, or portions of it, Washington depended on horse-borne couriers, or ships and boats to pass messages. He used a special detachment of dra‐goons to communicate directly with the commander of the army's rearguard during the move‐ment. This rearguard also carried the boats to be used later.[11] Word of de Grasse's arrival in Virginia took five days to reach Washington. From New York on 17 August he had sent as a courier French Colonel Louis Duportail to tell de Grasse about the army's movement. Dupor‐tail did not reach de Grasse at Hampton until 2 September. The French admiral promptly sent back dispatches to Washington via ship to Baltimore. From there a dispatch rider was ordered to find Washington wherever he was and deliver his parcel of accumulated dispatches. He found Washington at Chester, Pennsylvania, just below Philadelphia, on 5 September.[12] En‐route from Mount Vernon to Williamsburg on 13 September, he received dispatches that the French fleet had left the Chesapeake on the 5th and hadn't been seen since. Ironically, by the time Washington had found this out, the fleet had already returned, but the time lag of com‐munications was at play. Washington immediately sent back messages halting the movement of the army down the bay until further news of the naval situation was received.[13] The good news of the French success he received upon arrival at Williamsburg the next day.

Washington managed to successfully control his force and that of his French allies during its over 300 mile march and sea movement between two large enemy forces by a balanced and judicious use of personal command, able subordinates, and dispatch couriers. The French allies cooperated fully with the operation, subordinating themselves to American command, and Washington's subordinates ensured he was kept informed. The campaign was swift for its day, Cornwallis surrendering less than two months after the first troop movements and only 23 days after the disembarkation of the last troops. This celerity paralyzed British commander

Clinton and his naval subordinate Graves from playing a key role in the operation. By the time they realized what was happening, it was over.

Advance On Mexico City, 1847.

Sixty-six years after Yorktown, Major-General Winfield Scott, the Commanding General of the US Army, took to the field and personally commanded the American expedition against Mexico City in the War with Mexico. In many ways this operation was a precursor of the Baghdad campaign of 2003. Scott's force was small, smaller than he had expected, and out-numbered. He was forced to operate on a single line of communications and advance to the enemy capital quickly, fighting battles on the way and halting for an operational pause two-thirds of the way there. After several pitched battles, the capital was taken without a block-by-block fight and subsequent operations included those against guerillas operating against the American supply lines. A contemporary military observer, Britain's Arthur Wellesley, the Duke of Wellington, even pessimistically proclaimed "Scott is Lost!" when told of Scott's maneuvers which violated conventional wisdom about supply lines and lines of communi-cation.[14] But Scott was not lost, executing one of the classic mobile operations in US Army history, which proved to be the decisive campaign of the war.

Though employing primarily infantry forces, Scott's campaign was a mobile one, advancing from the port of Veracruz to the Mexican capital 260 miles to the west in two swift advances separated by an extended operational pause caused primarily by the expiration of the enlist-ments of many of the Army's volunteer troops. After assembling 13,000 troops, partially taken from Major-General Zachary Taylor's now idle force in northern Mexico, Scott made an unopposed landing south of Veracruz on the Gulf of Mexico on 9 March 1847.[15]

Following a twenty-day siege, Veracruz surrendered and a week later Scott commenced his advance on Mexico City. This movement proceeded in three phases. In the first phase, the army moved by taking the northern of two possible routes, the Mexican National Road from Veracruz, defeating a larger Mexican force under off-and-on-again Mexican President General Antonio López de Santa Anna at Cerro Gordo, then advancing to Jalapa, 12 miles ahead. Scott sent his lead division, followed a few weeks later by the rest of the army over the Sierra Madre mountains onto the Plateau of Anahuac to the town of Puebla, 70 miles short of Mexico City. There on 15 May, the army paused for reinforcements as the short-term enlist-ments of the volunteer troops had expired and they had returned home. This left his army at less than half the size of the opposing Mexican forces—too dangerously small to proceed. Accordingly Scott paused until August when newly raised regiments finally arrived, before renewing the advance on Mexico City.

In the second phase of the advance, from Puebla to the outskirts of Mexico City, Scott, reinforced up to 11,000 soldiers (from 5,000) boldly renewed his movement on 7 August 1847. He left a small supply base at Puebla, but otherwise abandoned his long line of commu-nications. The American forces faced about 30,000 Mexican defenders under the command of Santa Anna. Scott chose to advance initially along the northernmost of several available

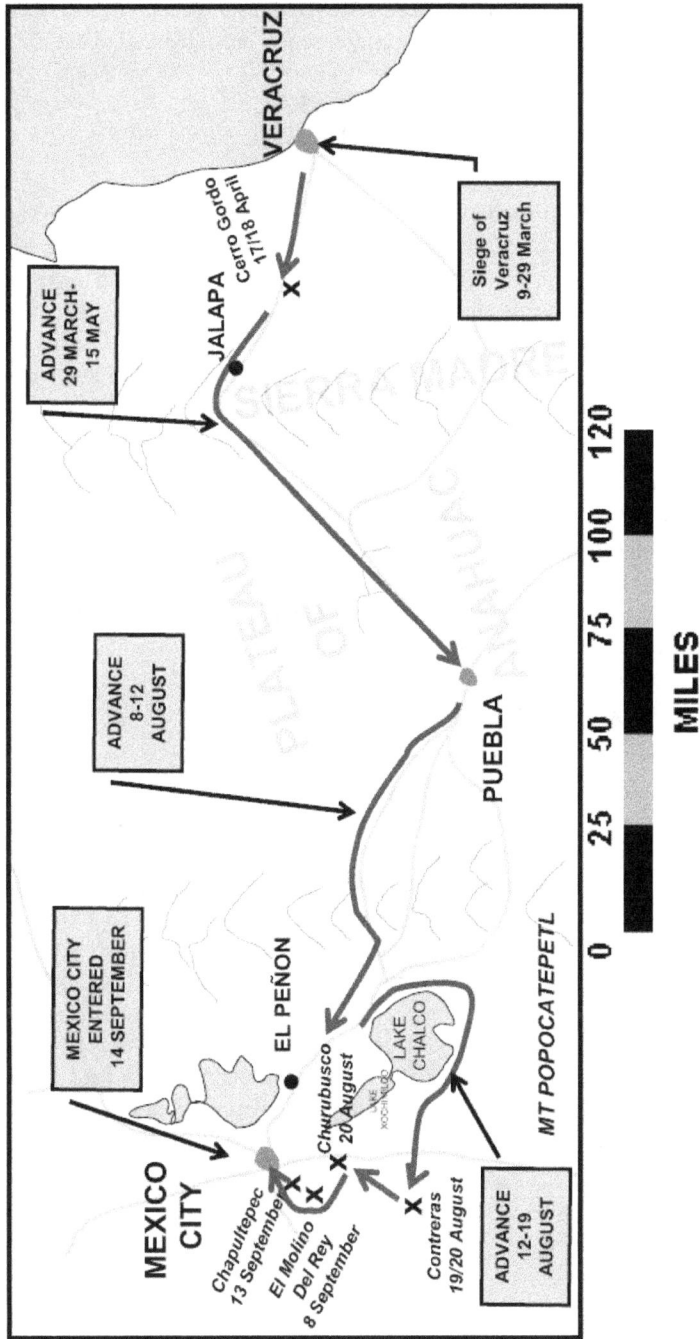

VERACRUZ

JALAPA
Cerro Gordo
17/18 April
X

ADVANCE
29 MARCH-
15 MAY

Siege of
Veracruz
9-29 March

SERRA MADRE

PLATEAU OF ANAHUAC

PUEBLA

ADVANCE
8-12
AUGUST

MEXICO CITY
ENTERED
14 SEPTEMBER

EL PEÑON

MEXICO
CITY

Chapultepec
13 September
X

El Molino
Del Rey
8 September
X

Churubusco
20 August
X

LAKE
XOCHIMILCO

LAKE
CHALCO

Contreras
19/20 August
X

ADVANCE
12-19
AUGUST

MT POPOCATEPETL

MILES

0   25   50   75   100   120

Figure 7. Scott's advance on Mexico City, 1847.

27

routes. But when on 12 August his forces discovered the direct approach to the Mexican capi•tal well defended at El Peñon, he turned onto a poorly defended trail to the south of two large lakes, Lake Chalco and Lake Xochimilco. By going this way, the vanguard of the American force managed to get as far as San Augustin by 13 August, only 9 miles south of Mexico City, an advance of over 60 miles in six days. The bulk of the army arrived over the next three days.[16]

Santa Anna, though surprised by the new direction of the American approach, managed to redeploy his forces to block the American advance. On 19 and 20 August the two armies fought battles at Contreras and Churubusco. By a combination of good maneuvering and aggressive assaults, US forces defeated the Mexicans, inflicting heavy casualties and forced them to fall back into the defenses of Mexico City. Still outnumbered, Scott hoped to broker a peace and a two-week truce followed, resulting, ultimately, in failed negotiations as Santa Anna used the time primarily to reorganize his forces. Hostilities were renewed on 7 Septem•ber after Scott felt that the Mexicans were violating the truce.[17]

The final phase of the advance commenced the next day when Brevet Major-General Wil•liam Worth's 1st Division assaulted Mexican forces defending a series of fortified foundries at El Molino del Rey. After a fierce fight, the Mexicans were defeated. Between the victori•ous Americans and the city stood the fortified heights of the Mexican military academy, Chapultepec. Scott's forces stormed that citadel on the 13th and, after skirmishes at the gates of the city, Mexico City fell the next day. The conventional phase of the war ended with the capture of Mexico City. An unconventional phase lasted until the signing of the Treaty of Guadalupe Hidalgo in February 1848.

Scott had his share of command and control difficulties in this campaign. During the ad•vance Scott preferred to send forward a lead division or two, while he followed farther back, ensuring the trains and supply wagons were in good shape. He counted on his staff contingent of couriers and aides-de-camp to provide him with information rather than going to each location himself. And he prepared detailed and clear orders. At Cerro Gordo, a mountain pass 60 miles northwest of Veracruz, the advance elements encountered Santa Anna's army en•trenched astride a mountain pass. Scott rushed up from Veracruz and drew up a plan, utilizing paths improved by his engineers, designed to cut the Mexicans off from their route of retreat and then push them into the trap with a secondary attack.[18] Unfortunately, his subordinates failed to follow the plan with one—Brigadier-General David E. Twiggs (who led the van•guard)—attacking the Mexican position frontally instead of going around it and blocking its escape. A brigade commanded by political appointee Brigadier-General Gideon Pillow, was supposed to advance along a covered route towards the Mexican position, but instead took a route closer to the enemy position, which exposed it to enemy fire while it advanced. Despite these failings, the Mexican forces were routed, though the American command difficulties precluded their planned destruction as Santa Anna escaped with a disorganized portion of his army.

Scott depended on superior organization, and a corps of superb regular Army officers to command the mobile phases of his campaign, despite the lack of constant, immediate communications as reflected in the technology of the day. Commanding through his division commanders, Scott was able to easily overcome even their mistakes because of the overall high quality of his forces.

Summary

The American experience with mobile battle command begins with the Yorktown campaign where General and Commander-in-Chief George Washington executed an operational-level maneuver, moving the bulk of his Continental Army, and a French allied army, from positions covering New York city to the vicinity of Yorktown, almost 500 miles to the south to overwhelm a smaller British force under Lord Cornwallis. Washington did this under the nose of the British commander in New York, who was unable to react fast enough to change the outcome once he realized the actual situation. For his battle command technique for this operation, Washington worked in close concert with the French commander Rochambeau and accompanied the advance element of the force, stopping at various times to review progress as the force passed by and then moving forward again to make sure everything was working according to his design.

In the 1847 campaign against Mexico City, Major-General Winfield Scott conducted a swift advance similar to Washington's, though in two distinct phases. However, Scott had at his disposal a smaller, though well-trained, force and had to advance along a single axis against Mexican opposition. After an initial swift advance, a combination of logistical and personnel difficulties resulted in an extended operational pause. When Scott resumed his advance, it was equally as swift as the previous advance and he moved against the Mexican capital from an unexpected direction. Scott controlled his forces through key subordinates, dividing his force generally into a forward, central and rear element. He generally stayed with the central element or coordinated logistical matters with the rear element. He controlled elements he was not with by a combination of couriers and pre-arranged plans.

The American Civil War saw the first mass armies in the experience of the United States. Industrial age technology would finally see military applications, making battle command on the move no longer solely dependent upon superior organization (technique), but on the combination of superior organization and superior use of available technology.

Notes

1. Robert Heinl, *Dictionary of Military and Naval Quotations* (US Naval Institute: Annapolis, 1966), 312.

2. Washington had organized the Continental Army under a flexible system of brigades commanded by hand-picked brigadier generals. Additionally, he had set up a defensive scheme around New York which made the British wary to test it. See, John J. McGrath, *The Brigade: A History* (Fort Leaven•worth: Combat Studies Institute Press, 2004), 4-9. The latter point allowed him to slip away before the British could respond and pursue, as Clinton, the British commander, was fearful of even facing the portion of the American forces Washington left behind. Having a proven commodity such as Lafayette on the other end ensured the forces there were doing exactly what he wanted them to do without him having to personally direct them.

3. Lee Kennett, *The French Forces in America, 1780-1783* (Westport, CT: Greenwood, 1977), 136; Burke Davis, *The Campaign that Won America: The Story of Yorktown* (Washington, DC: Acorn Press, 1979), 162-5; George Washington, *The Diaries of George Washington 1748-1799: Volume II 1771•1785*, John C. Fitzpatrick, ed. (Houghton Mifflin, Co., 1925), 254, 260. Since Graves, had left New York before it was known that the American and French forces were moving to Virginia, he did not re•alize the immediate consequences of his action in relation to Cornwallis, expecting to be able to return after refitting.

4. Kennett, 129; Davis, 26-7, 29.

5. Clinton had received a bloody nose at Springfield, NJ, when his army forayed against American defensive positions out of the range of the fleet the previous June (1780).

6. Davis, 31-2, 51.

7. John A. Tilley, *The British Navy and the American Revolution* (Columbia, SC: University of South Carolina Press, 1987), 266-8.

8. Ibid., 28; Washington, 257-8.

9. Tilley, 71; Kennett, 133; Washington, 258.

10. Davis, 83; Washington, 259.

11. Davis, 27; Washington, 259-60. Placing the boats at the rear was part of the deception—if the British pursued, seeing the boats would make them think the movement was, perhaps, an assault cross•ing of the Hudson.

12. Davis, 67, 79; Kennett, 131; Washington, 258.

13. Kennett, 136; Davis, 84-5.

14. The full quote is "Scott is lost! He has been carried away by success! He can't take the city [Mex•ico City], and he can't fall back on his base." See Lieutenant-General Winfield Scott, *The Memoirs of Lieut-Gen. Scott, LLD* (New York: Sheldon & Co, Publishers, 1864), Volume 2, 466N.

15. Taylor, of course, with his small force fought off Mexican General Santa Anna's attack at Buena Vista in February 1847 during the interval of time before the beginning of Scott's operation.

16. Richard Bruce Winders, "Mexico City Campaign: The March to Mexico City" in *The United States and Mexico at War: Nineteenth Century Expansionism and Conflict*, Donald S. Frazier, ed. (New York: MacMillan Reference USA, 1998), 254-5.

17. Thomas W. Cutrer, "Scott, Winfield," in Frazier, 381.

18. Ulysses S Grant, *Personal Memoirs of U.S. Grant*. E.B. Long, ed. (New York: Da Capo Press, 1982), 62-4.

MOBILE BATTLE COMMAND IN THE
AMERICAN CIVIL WAR AND AFTER

"...[W]e did not want to follow [Lee], we wanted to get ahead of him and cut him off."
—Ulysses S. Grant.[1]

After thousands of years, technological advances finally reached the realm of the command and control of armies with the development of the telegraph and railroad in the mid-Nineteenth Century. In the later Napoleonic wars, campaigns of opposing armies composed of army corps had been supplanted by campaigns of opposing groups of several field armies composed of army corps.[2] Such large-scale campaigns were hard to control. For example, Napoleon lost the decisive battle of the 1813 campaign when a subordinate prematurely blew up a bridge over the River Elster at Leipzig. The development of faster means of communication (the telegraph) and transportation (railroads) did not have an immediate effect on command and control in the American Civil War as many of the early troop movements and campaigns were conducted by marching infantry. In the later stages of the war, however, railroads allowed higher commanders to redeploy their forces to distant theaters and the telegraph allowed such commanders to control the actions of forces spread out over great distances almost instantly, as well as receive and process information in a far more timely fashion than in the past. At the amateurish First Battle of Bull Run in 1861, the use of railroads and semaphore flag communications even proved to be decisive.

These technological developments, coupled with the vastness of the theater of war and the large size of the armies that fought it, made Civil War battle command at the corps and above level challenging and unique. Major-General George Meade, the commander of the Union Army of the Potomac at the end of the war, even lamented about the "the difficulty of getting two bodies to advance simultaneously... if [the operation] is dependent on a simultaneous movement past experience bids me despair."[3] In an era before the use of codified military correspondence, graphics and control measures, confusion often reigned over poorly named geographical features, unknown missed dispatches and coordination between two adjacent units not belonging to the same higher command.[4] Additionally, as will be discussed below, methods of command could also increase this difficulty.

The technological advances in communications and transportation first made an impact on American military operations in this war. The railroad allowed commanders at the higher levels to move bodies of troops over great distances relatively quickly. The railroads had less impact upon tactical operations and battle command, although the capture or destruction of rail lines often became military objectives in their own right at these lower levels.[5] However, the telegraph, providing almost instantaneous communications between commanders and subordinates down to corps level and sometimes division-level, allowed army and theater commanders to control forces not within their direct sight or easily reached by couriers.

The electric telegraph was invented in 1844. The new device was adopted much more quick•ly in the geographically expansive United States, than in the much more compact Europe.[6] Soon the telegraph was applied to military operations, the first major technological advance in military communications since the domestication of the horse.[7] While the telegraph easily replaced the courier system over long distances, its use tactically over shorter distance was limited by the technology of the early models. As with later field telephones, the telegraph was tied to wire lines either placed on the ground or strung on poles. Both laying this wire and the sending of messages by the apparatus required specialized training or civilian con•tractors.[8] By the end of the war, telegraph lines were routinely laid from army headquarters to corps headquarters and sometimes even to divisions. Normally chiefs of staff, a new position found in the small headquarters of all units above division in size, controlled and monitored message traffic, both telegraphic and courier.[9] While used almost universally at higher levels, at the tactical level the telegraph could not hope to keep up with mobile operations and was used to augment the traditional means of couriers or commander's face-to-face contact. In this respect the new technology did not yet have a great impact on battle command.

Similar to the Napoleonic era, the American Civil War was primarily characterized by relatively slow moving operations executed at the pace of marching infantry. Equally similar to some of Napoleon's operations, several operations late in the war stand out as examples of the capabilities and failings of command and control of a rapidly moving army, and will be examined in detail in this chapter.

Grant's Move on Petersburg, June 1864

The first of these, an operational level movement of the main elements of two field armies occurred at the end of US Army commander Lieutenant-General Ulysses Grant's overland campaign across Virginia. This maneuver culminated in a loss of command and control that saw the negation of a great tactical advantage gained from a highly successful preliminary surprise maneuver. Grant and his key subordinate, George Meade, failed to impress a sense of urgency upon their subordinate commanders who displayed a lack of aggression while acting on their own initiative.

By mid-June 1864 the Union armies operating in central Virginia had failed in three at•tempts to envelop the defending Confederate forces under General Robert Lee at the Wilder•ness, Spotsylvania and Cold Harbor.[10] This relentless offensive maneuver had culminated on 2 and 3 June with the bloody repulse at Cold Harbor a few miles east of Richmond. After the Union failure, the armies faced each other from entrenchments only feet apart. Grant wanted to outflank Lee again and possibly cut his supply lines by moving south, crossing the James River, at this point a broad tidal estuary, and capturing the key rail hub of Petersburg.

Such an operation was risky. It required Grant to withdraw his troops from under Lee's nose, crossing two major rivers, the Chickahominy and the James, without interference from the Confederates, and then swiftly advancing and capturing Petersburg before Lee could rein•force it's small garrison.

Grant's method of command at this stage of the war included a small headquarters staff linked into telegraph lines back to Washington and forward to his army commanders. He commanded from this headquarters and, by choice, rarely moved forward, preferring to com• mand by telegraph.[11] For most of this campaign, Grant directly controlled a single army, the Army of the Potomac, commanded by Major-General Meade. Meade's command consisted of the 2d, 5th, 6th, 9th and Cavalry Corps, though all but one cavalry division had been recently detached on a separate mission. Also in the theater under Grant was Major-General Benjamin Butler's Army of the James, located at Bermuda Hundred between Petersburg and Richmond. Butler's command consisted of the 10th and 18th Corps. The 18th Corps, commanded by Major-General William F. Smith, had been detached to fight at Cold Harbor with the Army of the Potomac. The forces for this operation would primarily be those of Meade.

Like his superior, Meade was not an up front commander. Similar in method to Grant, he preferred to sit at a headquarters and manage the battle by telegraph and couriers.[12] Granted their commands were large and usually spread out. However, as frequently shown by com• manders such as Caesar, Napoleon and Alexander the Great, there were always critical places and times, and usually action was drawn out enough that a commander could visit all im• portant places during an action. Instead of doing so, however, Grant and, especially, Meade usually preferred to either order various corps to "cooperate" or appoint a corps commander to command a large portion of the army. The two depended on talented corps commanders to execute their orders. A Congressional committee would later criticize Meade for this method of command.[13] Despite their detachment from on-the-spot battlefield involvement, Meade and Grant still presumed that their knowledge of the bigger picture trumped their subordinates' knowledge of the local situation facing their own troops and accordingly gave extremely detailed orders, which they expected to be obeyed, even if the actual situation did not match. Grant in particular used detailed orders with subordinates he did not totally trust, while giving only vague general instructions to those he did.[14]

Subordinate commanders would have difficulty following rapidly changing orders given from distant command posts via poor transmission means without clear cut overall opera• tional objectives. In modern armies, commanders like to give their subordinates their intent directly for what they want an operation to accomplish. In this way subordinates do not need revised, detailed instructions to deal with changes in the situation. They can use initiative to respond in a way that still reflects the commander's general plan.[15] Control measures such as the axis of advance (general area along which forces are to move), and phase lines (lines perpendicular to a movement or attack) are drawn on maps to simplify execution. In the Civil War, the concept of the commander's intent and use of such control measures were unknown. In many cases, while Grant had a general intent, his desire to control infantry corps and divi• sions by fiat negated initiative on the part of the commanders of such units.

The distant approach allowed Grant and Meade to detach themselves from the casualties re• sulting from their orders. It also resulted in detachment from changing battlefield conditions. Unlike their superiors, the corps commanders typically did lead from the front. This made the carnage and defensive strength of well-fortified enemy positions not just abstract concepts to them.[16]

In addition to command and control methods in place before battles started and those depending on revised instructions sent via courier or telegraph dispatch, in the fog of war Civil War battlefield commanders at all levels often used the sounds of weapons fire to make battlefield decisions.[17]

Meade's forces were to commence their movements at dusk on 12 June 1864, after having endured over a month of grueling attrition warfare and working under the above-described system of command and control. Prior to the beginning of the operation, Meade had ordered the preparation of a second entrenched line at Cold Harbor. At dusk on 12 June the 2d Corps, commanded by Major-General Winfield Scott Hancock, and the 6th Corps, commanded by Major-General Horatio Wright, fell back to the secondary line to cover the movement of the rest of the army. Smith's 18th Corps marched down to boats on the Pamunkey River to the east, traveling by water down the York River and around to the James River and back up to the Bermuda Hundred positions held by Butler's army. Once Smith had rejoined Butler, how•ever, Grant, through Butler, instructed him to cross the Appomattox River to the south and advance to seize Petersburg. Meanwhile the rest of the Army of the Potomac, led by Han•cock's corps, would cross the Chickahominy, advance southward and cross the broad James via a bridge to be built by regular Army engineers on 14 June, and by ferries. After crossing Hancock and the following corps were to move rapidly on Petersburg as well. Brigadier-General James Wilson's cavalry division and Major-General Gouverneur Warren's 5th Corps would move to the south of the Cold Harbor position and take up new positions screening the movement of the rest of the army. Then Warren and Wilson would follow as well. The large army wagon train was also part of the movement as Grant intended to shift his logistics base to the south side of the James.

As a prelude to the operation, Grant initiated two minor moves designed to distract or mis•lead Confederate commander Lee and draw forces away from the main action or otherwise facilitate it. One was a diversion in the vital but somewhat distant Shenandoah Valley, while the second and third involved troops facing Lee or the Confederate forces just to the south at Petersburg. In the first diversion Grant had by telegraph instructed Major-General David Hunter to advance boldly down the Shenandoah Valley roughly 100 miles to the west and northwest of Richmond. in this operation Hunter managed to defeat one small Confederate force on 6 June at Piedmont, which compelled Lee the next day to transfer 2,000 infantry troops to the Valley. Hunter then joined up with two other Federal forces under Major-Gen•eral George Crook and Major-General William Averill. Upon learning this, Lee, on 12 June, hours before the commencement of Grant's maneuver, dispatched 8,000 men of the 2d Corps, under command of Lieutenant-General Jubal Early, to reinforce the troops he had previously sent to the Valley.[18]

A more deliberate diversion was Grant's 7 June dispatch of part of the Army of the Po•tomac's Cavalry Corps, under Major-General Philip Sheridan, on a raid designed to destroy

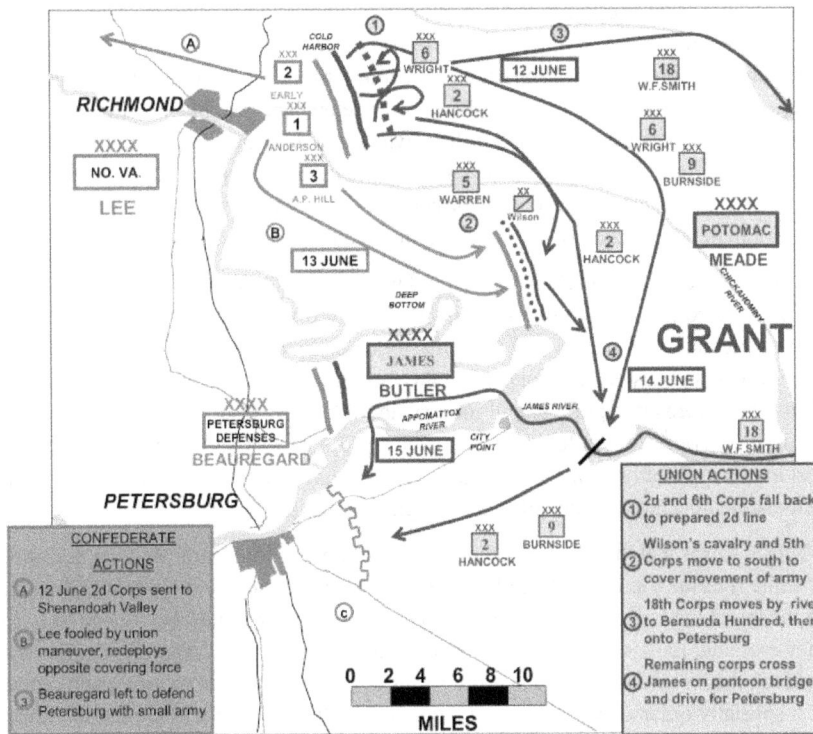

Figure 8. Grant moves on Petersburg

rail lines leading out of the Valley to Richmond. Sheridan was to ultimately link up with Hunter if possible. For the raid he took cavalry divisions commanded by Brigadier-Gener•als David Gregg and Alfred Torbert, leaving behind a single cavalry division with Meade's army.[19] Lee immediately sent almost all his cavalry after Sheridan, retaining only minimal sorely needed reconnaissance assets during the Union move to the James.[20]

Meanwhile, Butler executed a third move: a direct attack on Petersburg itself. He did so on his own initiative, completely independent of Grant's overall scheme and without the senior commander's knowledge. Grant in fact feared that the Confederates, upon discovering the abandonment of the Cold Harbor positions, would concentrate against Butler's position at Bermuda Hundred across the Appomattox River to the northeast of Petersburg. Additionally, any premature move in the direction of Petersburg could alert the confederates to the possible weakness of their position south of the James River. In any event, when he did discover the abandoned Cold Harbor positions, Lee merely saw it as another attempt to tactically outflank his own positions from the south and acted accordingly rather than concentrating against Butler.

On 9 June Butler therefore attempted to capture Petersburg on his own. He sent a small part of the 10th Corps, under its commander Major-General Quincy Gillmore, and a cavalry force under Brigadier-General August Kautz to try to capture the city in a coordinated attack from two directions. Kautz swung around the defenses of Petersburg and attacked the city from the south, driving off the poorly trained militia, who were then the city's main defenders. Artillery and the timely arrival of a cavalry force repulsed Kautz. Meanwhile, Gillmore, who was supposed to attack the city from the northeast in coordination with Kautz' attack, did not move and ultimately retired across the Appomattox River to Butler's main position.[21]

The main movement of Meade's forces to the James went off like clockwork on 12 June. After dark all the corps were in motion. Wilson's cavalry division moved to the south and crossed the Chickahominy at dawn on the 13th, followed by the 5th Corps. Wilson immedi•ately moved west aggressively, encountering the Confederate cavalry and making it seem like the Union forces were attempting one of their standard left flanking maneuvers. Since the sector Wilson was operating in led right into Richmond, Lee was immediately convinced that this was Grant's main effort. This belief and his conviction that any move south of the James could not escape detection would color his thoughts for days.[22]

Smith's 18th Corps marched to the Pumunkey river to board transports arriving at dawn. The 125-mile riverine trip to Bermuda Hundred would take almost two days, but would still outpace the marching columns. Between 12 and 14 June the corps marched relentlessly for the James crossing. Early on the evening of the 13th, Hancock's 2d Corps was the first ele•ment to reach the river. The rest of the army would take up to the 17th to arrive and cross. On 14 June a specially organized task force of engineers built a 2100-foot long pontoon bridge across the James. Ultimately the 9th Corps, the army wagon trains and the rearguard 6th Corps would cross the bridge. The 2d Corps began crossing via ferry before the bridge was completed and was followed by the 5th Corps.

Lee's troops woke up on the morning of the 13th to find the trenches opposite them empty. A 115,000-man army had slipped away during the night undetected. With news of Wilson's cavalry activity to the south, Lee immediately ordered his two remaining corps, the 3d under Lieutenant-General A.P. Hill, and the 1st under Lieutenant-General Richard Anderson, to move south and form a new line opposite Wilson. By the time the Confederates were in posi•tion, only Wilson's troopers were facing them. The 5th Corps had already begun its move to rejoin the rest of the army moving to the James. Lee received no reports about the mass movement of troops across the James.[23] Long after troops from the Army of the Potomac were fighting at Petersburg, Lee still clung to his belief that the majority of that army was still north of the James.

While the officers and soldiers executed the movement with great urgency, care and drive, completely fooling the Confederate defenders, their commanders displayed less aggressive•ness. Smith and his corps led the operation. Butler, through whom Grant controlled the initial attack, gave Smith Kautz's cavalry division and additional infantry. The river movement of Smith's force had not gone without glitches. Upon being told he was expected to cross the

Appomattox at a pontoon bridge four miles downstream from where his troops were slated to land, Smith changed the landing point of his boat-bound troops. However the changed destination did not reach the first several boats. Additionally, several other vessels sat too deep in the water to travel inland on the shallow Appomattox as far as the bridge site and had to disembark at the other site as well. These troops had to march the four miles to the bridge site.[24] Unaware of the urgency Grant placed on his speedy advance on Petersburg on the 15th, Smith ended up wasting most of the day in deploying his command on line. Conducting a detailed personal reconnaissance, and advancing the meager eight miles to Petersburg Smith finally ordered the attack on the Petersburg defensive line—called the Dimmock Line—to start at 6 pm.

Alerted by Butler's abortive attack on the 9th, militia alone no longer defended Petersburg. However, the city's defenders on 15 June were not much more numerous. General Pierre G.T. Beauregard, commander of the Confederate Department of North Carolina and Southern Vir‑ ginia, was responsible for both garrisoning Petersburg and containing Butler's army at Ber‑ muda Hundred between Petersburg and Richmond. In Petersburg, Beauregard had defending against Smith's 14,000 Union soldiers a mere 2,200 infantry and artillerymen under the direct command of Brigadier-General Henry Wise, the former governor of Virginia. The defenders were too slim in numbers to adequately defend the whole five miles of fortifications, so they only defended the left portion, using a small group of cavalry to cover that flank.[25]

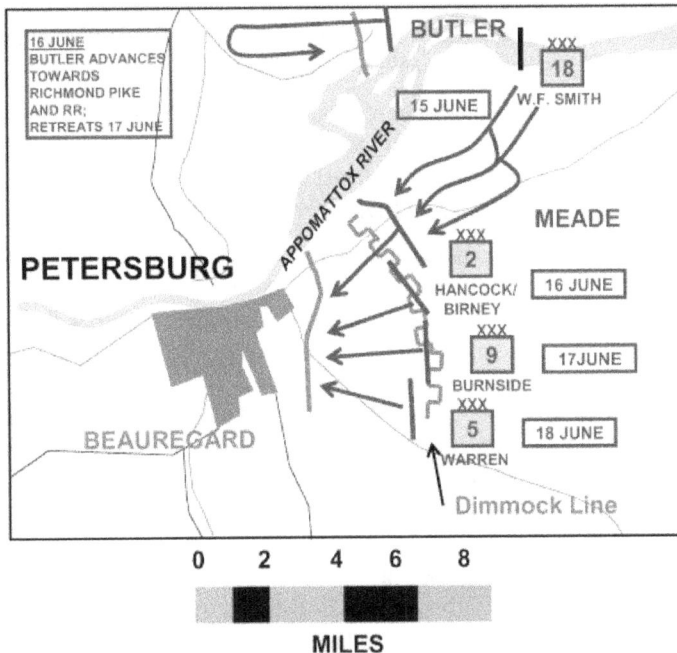

Figure 9. Union attacks on Petersburg, 15-18 June 1864.

Smith's attack was further delayed an hour while the artillery recovered from a positioning error. What Grant had envisioned as a sunrise attack had now become a sunset one. Between 7 and 9 pm, the 18th Corps attacked with each of its three divisions on line and the cavalry covering the left flank. In rapid succession, key positions on the Dimmock line fell. The small number of defenders simply made the Federal push irresistible, with only a few scattered positions of the Dimmock Line remaining in Southern hands.

In Grant's scheme, Hancock's 2 Corps was to follow up and support Smith's attack on 15 June. As the vanguard of the marching component of the movement, that corps had been fer•ried across the James on the 14th and was ready to move on Petersburg at dawn on the 15th. However, Grant had not told either Meade or Hancock about the planned attack on Petersburg that day. Accordingly, neither pressed forward to advance on the city. On the morning of the 15th both generals allowed long delays while the troops awaited the issuance of rations. In any event, the rations were never issued and Hancock began his march on Petersburg at 10:30 am. This march itself was not marked by urgency, being delayed by faulty maps, and a lost division. Finally, once on the correct route, the two advance divisions of the corps made 14 miles in four and a half hours.[26]

Hancock finally realized Petersburg was to be attacked that day about 5:30 pm when he re•ceived dispatches from both Grant and Smith indicating his role in supporting Smith's attack. At dusk his two lead divisions began to link up with the 18th Corps. At about 9 pm Hancock had a face-to-face meeting with Smith and, despite his seniority, subordinated his command to Smith and had his troops begin relieving Smith's leftmost division in its captured Dim-mock line positions. This relief was completed by 11:30 pm.[27]

Despite his success, the clear visibility of a moonlit night, and the arrival of reinforcements, Smith stopped his advance. He feared Confederate reinforcements and a counterattack and was content to rest on the laurels of having almost completely captured the enemy defensive works. As darkness fell, the initial Union advance halted.

The Confederates were being reinforced, but not from the Army of Robert Lee. Beauregard did request such reinforcements, but Lee, still fearing the large Union force he thought was north of the James, refused him. The ever-resourceful Beauregard then took the troops out of the Bermuda Hundred line opposing Butler and through the night of 15-16 June, they arrived and reinforced his weak Petersburg position. Beauregard knew the Bermuda Hundred posi•tion was important because it was between Petersburg and Lee's army, but he also realized that Lee would have to reinforce Bermuda Hundred. Early on the 16th Butler noticed that the Confederates had abandoned the positions opposite him and he sent forces forward to occupy the positions and cut the rail and road link between Petersburg and Richmond with pickets. Lee quickly discovered his cut communications with Beauregard and sent two divisions im•mediately to push Butler back. Even though Grant was sending Butler reinforcements in the form of two veteran divisions of the rearguard 6 Corps, the timid Army of the James com•mander pulled his forces back to their original lines.[28]

After the initial attacks on 15 June, Union forces renewed their attacks with the addition of newly arrived forces on the 16th, 17th and 18th. During the night of the 15th/16th Beauregard had reinforced his position with the troops that formerly opposed Butler at Bermuda Hun•dred. The Union forces observed this reinforcement but did nothing to hinder it. When news reached him at the river crossing site on the James of Smith's success, Meade stopped the crossing of the army wagon train and immediately ordered the crossing of 9th Corps. He also gave instructions for the 5th Corps to begin ferrying across.[29]

On the 16th Hancock now commanded the combined forces of the 18th and 2d Corps and the arriving 9th Corps. As on the previous day, the Union commander spent most of the day reconnoitering the enemy position and conducting other attack preparations. The Confeder•ates easily repulsed several Union brigade-sized probes in the morning. The attack delay allowed Beauregard to fill out his new defensive line with freshly arrived troops.[30] Grant visited Smith in the morning and toured the captured Dimmock Line positions. Later on the road back to City Point he conferred with Meade, who he had requested to come forward. Apparently unperturbed by the inaction of the Union forces, Grant now gave direct command of the Petersburg operation to Meade and ordered another dusk attack, employing the arriving 9th Corps, in addition to the 18th and 2d Corps.[31] Despite the massing of Union forces, only part of the 2d Corps actually attacked, while the 18th Corps merely conducted a demonstra•tion and the 9th Corps, though in support of the 2d Corps attack, actually saw little combat. The frontal attacks attained only limited success. Though outnumbering the Confederates on the field of battle almost four to one (roughly 50,000 against 14,000), the Federals could not bring their strength against the defenders enough to crack the defense.[32]

On the 17th, with information indicating Lee had yet to reinforce the Petersburg defenses with his own troops, Meade was determined to attack early and take Petersburg before Lee's reinforcements could arrive, using Major-General Ambrose Burnside's 9th Corps. Burnside's 2d Division, ably led by Brigadier-General Robert Potter, attacked at dawn in a surprise as•sault on the Confederate right flank position. The attack was highly successful, breaking open a mile wide hole in the Confederate defenses, while suffering only light casualties. Immediate exploitation of this opportunity was essential. But this did not happen. A division of the 2d Corps was supposed to support Potter on the right and a division of the 9th Corps on the left. Neither did, the 2d Corps division because its men were exhausted from the previous days of marching and combat, and the 9th Corps division because it was poorly led and had to march through rough terrain.[33] The attack was not renewed until 2 pm when Brigadier-Gen•eral Orlando Willcox's 3d Division of the 9th Corps, supported by a brigade of the 2d Corps attacked. Preparations were poor and the attack failed with heavy casualties, as the Confeder•ates had recovered from the disaster of the early morning and had reinforced their new line. Burnside made one more attempt on the 17th, with an attack by his one fresh division, the 1st under command of Brigadier-General James Ledlie, at 6 pm. Ledlie's attack went over the same ground as Willcox's earlier in the day, but was more successful, led on the field by one of the brigade commanders, Colonel Jacob Gould, normally the commander of the 59th Massachusetts. Gould's attack broke the center of the Confederate position, creating a horse•

shoe-shaped salient in the line. After dark, the Confederates began continuous counterattacks against the salient, culminating in a full-scale counterattack by two brigades at 10 pm which threw Ledlie's men back almost to their original positions of the afternoon.[34]

18 June was the day the Union forces were to execute a combined attack by four corps against the enemy positions in front of Petersburg. The 5th Corps had arrived on the 17th and formed up on the 9th Corps left. Meade planned another dawn attack with all available forces.

After the success of his night attack, Beauregard and his subordinates did not rest. Fearing the proximity of Federal troops to his line and its irregular shape, he had prepared a new, shorter line 500 to 800 yards to the rear and now fell back to it. Beauregard was also relieved to hear that Lee had finally discovered Grant's location and was immediately dispatching the vanguard of A.P. Hill's corps to reinforce Petersburg.[35]

Beauregard's withdrawal disrupted the projected Union dawn attack. Meade did not want to blindly assault the new line. However, fearing that delay would allow Lee to link up with Beauregard, Meade ordered the advance to continue. Moving forward through rough terrain in battle line formations disrupted the advance and affected coordination between adjacent corps. Delays persisted even after the Federals closed up on the new enemy line. The new attack start time was noon. Meade desired to wield a hammer of massed attacks conducted by all his corps simultaneously. But only part of the 2d Corps was ready and attacked at noon, being repulsed. Meade had trouble coordinating the attacks of his various corps. In some cases his orders to attack were blatantly ignored. In others, terrain hindered their timely execution. He was forced to send orders for an immediate attack by all corps, rather than coordinate a time.[36] Ultimately the attack took place between 4 and 6 pm. However, instead of the projected coordinated attack, the action resulted in a series of unsupported brigade-sized attacks which had only limited success.

Beauregard had been reinforced with one of A.P. Hill's divisions early on the 18th. By the end of the day, Hill's entire corps had arrived. With the failure of the 18 June attacks, Grant and Meade both realized Petersburg was not going to fall. Grant called off offensive operations for the present.[37] One of the most successful operational-level maneuvers in United States Army history had ultimately ended in failure. While many factors such as troop exhaustion and excessive loss of leaders contributed to the repulse at Petersburg, the root cause was a loss of effective command and control where such control most counted.

Command and control in the Petersburg maneuver was a mixed bag. Up to a point, the movement itself was superbly executed and well controlled. However, once across the James, the final movement and attack on Petersburg—-the whole objective of the operation—was hardly controlled or commanded at all. This was in spite of the establishment of effective methods to control the force.

At the highest level, Grant failed to impart a sense of urgency as to his intent throughout the operation. He commanded indirectly, primarily through Meade. Throughout the operation, however, Grant failed to provide his personal presence at any critical time and place where he could have instantly made a difference. The lieutenant-general preferred to command from a centralized location at his new logistics hub at City Point, with occasional visits to his forward commanders, never during a key action. On 14 June while the movement was well underway, he had taken a naval craft up to Butler's location and talked to him face-to-face about the actions he expected of Smith's corps and the support required of Butler.[38] On the 16th Grant went up to the lines in front of Petersburg and conferred with Hancock, ordering him to attack at 6 pm, then meeting Meade on the way back to City Point and placing him in command.

From City Point, telegraph lines were quickly strung connecting Grant with Butler and Meade. After giving general direction to Meade, the commanding general remained some·what detached for the rest of the operation, preferring to receive telegraphic reports rather than impress upon his subordinates the operational urgency of moving on the enemy quick·ly.[39] In the last three days of the Petersburg attacks, the lieutenant-general only visited Meade once, for a half hour on the 17th.[40] Even when dawn attacks became dusk attacks and army attacks became brigade attacks, Grant, were he even aware of the situation, did not act.

Smith did not realize, as the operation commenced, that his command was the spearhead of the army, nor did he realize the urgency required of him to get his corps into Petersburg.[41] Meade and Hancock were similarly in the dark. Grant's explanation for this in his memoirs written twenty years later was murky at best, making it seem that Hancock's corps was not supposed to participate in the attack in one sentence, then in another a few lines later, excus·ing Hancock for not understanding that he was expected to participate that day at Peters·burg.[42]

In a comment in a dispatch sent to Major-General Henry Halleck, the Army Chief of Staff, on 17 June, Grant commented: "Day and night has been all the same, no delays being allowed on any account."[43] Had he personally been up front at Petersburg, he would have readily real·ized this was not the case at all.

Grant knew his soldiers were physically exhausted and their leaders were both physically and mentally exhausted, but assumed they were still driving with his own sense of urgency to beat Lee to Petersburg.[44] They were not. Wasted opportunities, such as Smith's breakthrough on the 15th, Butler's breakthrough on the 16th and Potter's penetration on the 17th were not followed up.[45]

Meade, Grant's primary subordinate commander, initially spent most of the movement at the James River crossing sites, which he apparently viewed as the critical point. While his subordinates were commanding at Petersburg and failing to understand the urgency of taking the city, Meade remained miles away.

Even once he was in command at Petersburg, Meade's presence was felt from courier's mail pouches and telegraph keys rather than physical presence. On 18 June when four corps were arrayed against the Confederates, Meade was not on the field himself. Despite having excellent telegraphic communication down to division-level, he could not get his four corps and eleven divisions to act in concert.[46] The technological advantage of fast communica•tions brought about by the telegraph did not negate the moral advantages of a commander on the scene directly impressing his will on subordinate commanders who were physically exhausted and mentally worn thin by the previous 40 days of relentless attrition. Additionally, Meade (and Grant as well) only had an abstract understanding of the situation on the ground. The corps commanders on the ground were hesitant to attack formidable defenses unless the whole army participated. The situation on the ground, particularly for those who remembered Cold Harbor, often looked different than that at the headquarters.

Though he did not personally confront his corps commanders, Meade did try various methods to control his subordinates. He located himself on a high rise to the rear of the lines behind some artillery pieces from which he could see parts of the various battles.[47] He also sent couriers to Grant, and on the 18th dispatched aides-de-camp to corps headquarters to fre•quently send him telegraphic updates. Ironically, while Meade remained aloof from the battle, his corps commanders often met face-to-face to discuss their plans and battlefield realities.[48] As 18 June dragged on with delays, some brought on by Beauregard's surprise retreat and some by the corps commanders' hesitancy to respond to orders received in dispatches, or by telegraph, which seemed to them to show a lack of understanding of the battlefield, Meade got angrier and angrier. However, he did not confront his subordinates directly. Instead he threatened them through dispatches and telegrams.[49] In desperation, Meade even sent out a courier to bypass the chain of command and direct a forward brigade of the 5th Corps to im•mediately attack. The commander of the brigade, like his superiors, believed the order was made without knowledge of the tactical situation, where the enemy defenses were formidable, and the attack of a single brigade would be suicidal. So he requested clarification that the army commander was directing his brigade to attack. The courier returned shortly with both clarification and an indication that the brigade was attacking in concert with the whole army. The brigade then attacked with only one other brigade and was repulsed easily, with the bri•gade commander being grievously wounded in the process.[50]

The technological advance of the telegraph provided a commander the ability to communi•cate with, and control spread out forces almost instantly. However, it did not replace the need for a commander to be physically present at critical times, and places where he could imme•diately impress his will and intent upon subordinates, or equally change plans to make them more representative of battlefield realities.

The Appomattox Campaign, 1865

After the repulse of 18 June, the Union and Confederate forces settled into siege warfare for the next nine months, marked by occasional battles when the Federal forces tried to envelop the Southern lines, or penetrate through perceived weak points. It wasn't until late March 1865 that the situation developed into a mobile operation again.

Aside from the Petersburg maneuver, one of the few other major mobile campaigns of the Civil War involving large masses of combined arms (infantry, cavalry, field artillery) units was the Appomattox Campaign of late March-early April 1865. In this campaign, Grant, com•mitted large forces to the western flank of the Petersburg fortifications and, upon the ultimate success of these operations, set his combined force of several armies and cavalry in pursuit of Confederate General Robert E. Lee's retreating troops, ultimately surrounding Lee and forc•ing him to surrender eight days later after a chase 50 miles to the west.[51] Grant had to employ multiple columns, traveling different routes during this march, in order to get around and trap Lee. Grant and his immediate subordinate commanders controlled these fast paced operations very successfully. In many ways this campaign was the culmination of command and control developments made during the war.

The prelude to the Appomattox pursuit was a series of battles and maneuvers beginning on 29 March and concluding in the 1 April 1865 Union victory at Five Forks. This short cam•paign was one of mobility as well. Grant reshuffled his forces to mass two infantry corps and a cavalry corps on the far western (left flank to the Federals, right flank to the Confederates) end of the twenty mile entrenched Southern line in front of Petersburg. His intent was to outflank Lee's fortifications or otherwise overextend it, making it vulnerable to a penetration attack elsewhere. The forces involved contained two distinct components: an infantry com•ponent consisting of the 2d and 5th Corps, under Meade's direction, and a cavalry element consisting of three cavalry divisions (formerly subordinate to Meade) under the command of Major-General Philip Sheridan. Sheridan had been an army commander in the recently con•cluded Shenandoah Valley campaign and was treated by Grant as a separate army commander even when his troops were not more than corps-sized in strength.[52]

Grant and Meade both moved forward, to separate headquarters behind the infantry corps, tied into telegraph lines, which were soon also laid to the headquarters of the infantry corps.[53] The cavalry under Sheridan basically disappeared over the horizon and then fought and lost a separate battle with a larger combined arms force of infantry and cavalry sent by Lee under Major-General George Pickett at Dinwiddie Courthouse on 31 March. Sheridan was effectively not under Grant's command and control once away from the Union lines. Grant lamented the long delay in communications with Sheridan and the need to base decisions and coordination on old information as to his activities or expectations of his actions based on such information.[54] In this void, dependence was often made on the hearing of sounds of battle or couriers cut off from reaching Sheridan.[55]

Meanwhile, to the east of Sheridan, but not in contact with him, the 5th and 2d Corps ad•vanced against the extreme western end of the Confederate line. After a series of marches and battles, hindered by muddy roads from continuous rain storms, these corps pinned the Con•federates into their fortifications on 31 March and were then poised to envelop that defensive line and then cut the right-of-way of the Southside Railroad, Lee's last key supply line from the south.

On the 31st Sheridan communicated with Grant through a series of dispatches that resulted in Grant ordering the 5th Corps to abandon its current line of advance and move to aid Sheri•dan. Despite a series of confusing orders by telegram, Warren managed to disengage his corps and move it to join Sheridan early on 1 April. With this combined force of infantry and cavalry, Sheridan decisively defeated and mostly destroyed Pickett's force at Five Forks. On the next day, the 2d, Federal troops captured Sutherland Station north of Five Forks, cutting Lee's direct supply lines, while the 6th Corps and Major-General Edward Ord's corps-sized force, the Army of the James/ 24th Corps, attacked the weakened Confederate fortified line and advanced on Petersburg from the west. Lee had little choice but to abandon his Petersburg lines and began his retreat from Petersburg and Richmond on the night of 2/3 April.

Command and control issues marred the Five Forks campaign. The command structure itself was unusual with three army commanders, Meade, Sheridan and Major-General Ord controlling the equivalent of three infantry corps and a cavalry corps, with their forces adjacent or even intermingled. Ord, Butler's replacement as the Army of the James commander, commanded an ad hoc corps-sized force (the 24th Corps), which was also under the direct command of its own corps commander, Major-General John Gibbon. Ord's other corps, the 25th, remained far to the north near Richmond. He also commanded a small cavalry division led by Brigadier-General Ranald MacKenzie which came south with Gibbon's force, which was moved into the Union line just to the right of the advancing 2d and 5th Corps. Therefore, this separate command was in the middle of Meade's Army of the Potomac forces. While two corps moved out on the left, Meade still controlled the 6th and 9th Corps in the Petersburg entrenchments. Sheridan essentially controlled a corps worth of cavalry, but two of his divisions worked under a corps headquarters commanded by Brevet Major-General Wesley Merritt, while the third division, led by Major-General George Crook, reported directly to Sheridan. This unusual arrangement was set up because Crook, a former departmental and corps commander, was senior to Merritt.[56]

Command by telegraph still caused control difficulties. Twice a whole division of the 5th Corps had to turn around and retrace its steps because higher commanders, above corps, either changed instructions or sent guides out too late.[57] Grant and, particularly, Meade peppered 5th Corps commander, Major-General Gouvernor Warren, and 2d Corps commander, Major-General Andrew Humphreys, with telegrams containing instructions, requests, refinements of plans, and requests for reports. Warren felt so inundated by these messages that he located his corps headquarters away from most of his corps where the telegraph line ended and delayed moving forward to his corps on 31 March waiting for an expected dispatch from Meade.[58]

With the commencement of Lee's retreat from Petersburg and Richmond, the Union forces found themselves in a mobile operation only matched by the march north that resulted in the Battle of Gettysburg in June 1863 or the previously described June 1864 advance on Petersburg. At Gettysburg the initiative of several key commanders in the army vanguard allowed the army to concentrate where the enemy was attacking part of it. At Petersburg the lack of initiative and loss of control in the army vanguard allowed the enemy to concentrate and the whole objective of the operation to be defeated. In the pursuit of Lee in April 1865, all things would come together in the execution of the most successful US Army mobile operation before the age of modern communications technology.

While not formally reshuffling his forces, Grant reconfigured them for the pursuit. He controlled three army headquarters (Sheridan commanding the Army of the Shenandoah[59]; Meade heading the Army of the Potomac, and Ord with the Army of the James), and six corps of infantry, one corps of cavalry and two independent cavalry divisions. Command for this campaign was more simplified in practice than it had that been in the preceding Five Forks campaign. Basically, Sheridan commanded the advance guard, consisting of Merritt's cavalry corps (and Crook's cavalry division), and initially the 5th Corps, but later briefly the 6th Corps. The main body was led by Meade and consisted of the 2d and 6th (later also the 5th) Corps. Ord commanded the left wing flank guard consisting of most of his own Army of the James (parts of the 24th and 25th Corps), while Meade's 9th Corps followed Ord but was used to provide security along the line of communications.

The aim of the pursuit operation was to get in front of and block Lee's route of retreat. Unlike the initial operations at Petersburg, a sense of urgency permeated the Union forces. The troops marched and rode at top speed until the goal was achieved.

Lee managed to escape being trapped in the Petersburg area, consolidating his army at Amelia Courthouse roughly 40 miles west of Petersburg. There he could be resupplied and retreat along the line of the Richmond and Danville Railroad to Danville and a possible union with the army under General Joseph Johnston in North Carolina. Unfortunately, logistics mistakes followed by swift Federal troop movements made resupply impossible and forced Lee to shift his starving troops farther to the west.[60]

Grant, once he discovered Lee's move to Amelia Courthouse, almost immediately understood Lee's operational choices and made moves to counter them.[61] The Confederate commander's best choice was to try to move south in the direction of Danville in order to link up with Johnston. If unable to do this, he'd then try to move farther west towards Lynchburg where he could again try to turn south. Key geographic points would therefore be Burkeville (Burke's Station), where the east-west Southside Railroad met the north-south Richmond and Danville Railroad, and Farmville where the Southside Railroad crossed to the south of the Appomattox River for the last time. Grant organized his forces to prevent these options. Ord moved out along the line of the Southside Railroad to provide a distant block against enemy moves from the south and to get to Burkeville and Farmville as soon as possible. Closer in, Sheridan, leading the vanguard of three cavalry divisions and an infantry corps, was to put continual pressure on Lee and, if possible, get in front of him with part of his force. Meade's follow-on infantry corps would then close the trap from the rear.

From Sutherland Station, Sheridan led the pursuit with the cavalry corps and the 5th Corps. Lee had paused on the 4th at Amelia Courthouse to resupply, but the supplies never came and his efforts at forage in the countryside produced meager results. Thus he had lost a day and in the interval the Union forces closed on him and now had a general idea of his intentions.[62] Sheridan had pursued aggressively and, once realizing Lee was headed towards Amelia, he swung part of his force to the south and blocked the railroad line out of Amelia at Jetersville on his own initiative.[63] Meanwhile his wide-ranging cavalry managed to capture part of Lee's

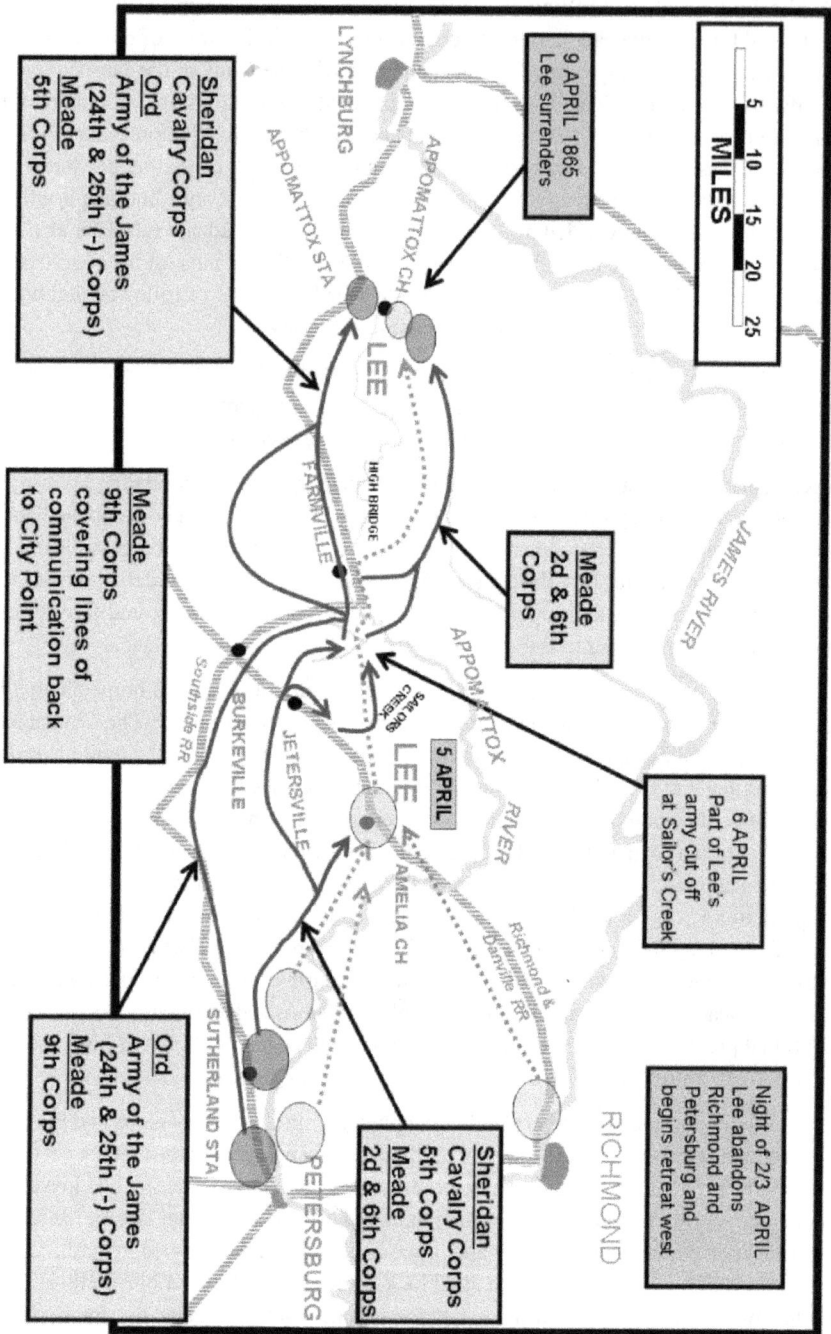

Figure 10. Pursuit to Appomattox.

48

supply trains, before it could join the rest of the army. Farther to the south, Ord reached Burkesville on the 5th.[64]

Lee's pause allowed Meade's infantry to catch up with Sheridan at the Jetersville roadblock on the 5th. A planned Federal attack scheduled for the morning of the 6th was changed into renewed pursuit when Lee began moving himself on the afternoon of the 5th and through the night. Not wanting to test the roadblock, Lee had turned his forces to the west towards Farmville using country roads. Humphreys' 2d Corps detected the movement early on the morning of the 6th and Meade and Sheridan's combined force was soon in motion after the Confederates. Despite the head start, the Confederate movement was slowed by the size of the army and the poor quality of the roads, allowing the Federal pursuers to notice the movement and quickly shift from attack to pursuit mode.

While Lee's vanguard under Lieutenant-General James Longstreet, got away from the pursuers, the following corps, led by Lieutenant-General Richard Ewell, and Lieutenant-General Richard Anderson and the rearguard, commanded by Major-General John Gordon were not so lucky. Humphreys caught up with Gordon at dusk, while the latter's force was delayed crossing a bridge at the confluence of Big and Little Sailor's Creeks. Ewell had shifted Gordon with the army wagon train to a more northerly route to escape the rapidly approaching Union infantry. In the resulting action, Gordon lost almost a third of his force while Humphreys captured over 300 wagons. Farther to the east following the main Confederate column, Merritt, Sheridan's subordinate cavalry commander, managed to get cavalry between Longstreet and Anderson, cutting Anderson and Ewell's forces off from the rest of Lee's army, while Major-General Horatio Wright's 6th Corps pressed Ewell from behind. Ewell formed a hasty defensive position behind Little Sailor's Creek, but Wright's assault proved irresistible and the Confederates were soon overrun, their force being virtually destroyed and Ewell himself a prisoner of war. At the front of that column, Anderson discovered his route blocked by Merritt with 10,000 cavalrymen to oppose his 6,300 tired Confederate infantrymen, most of them being the survivors of the defeat at Five Forks six days earlier. Merritt's attacks were coordinated with that of Wright as both forces were in visual contact. After an initially staunch defense, Anderson's command crumbled, with roughly half its numbers captured and the remnants escaping as a disorganized mass to the west.[65]

Even as the Battle of Sailor's Creek progressed, the part of Lee's army not pressed there, Longstreet's ad hoc corps, was being pressured to the southwest at Rice's Station on the Southside Railroad line, as Ord's Army of the James was advancing up that line from the east. By two consecutive night marches and despite the debacle at Sailor's Creek, the Confederates had beaten the Federals to Farmville where rations awaited them. However, the Union cavalry and infantry refused to let up their relentless pressure and Lee moved his forces across to the north side of the Appomattox to Cumberland Church where he entrenched.[66]

Confederate attempts to destroy the bridges across the Appomattox at Farmville, including an elaborate railroad trestle called High Bridge, were only partially successful and part of Humphreys' corps streamed across and was soon closed up to Lee's new position. Humphreys

promptly attacked with his vanguard, attempting to outflank Lee's position on the left. How•
ever, the 2d Corps commander was unaware that destroyed bridges at Farmville had delayed
the advance of the 6th Corps, which had been advancing directly behind the Confederates
while his corps advanced to the north. Hearing the sounds of firing to the south and believ•
ing it to be the expected 6th Corps attack, Humphreys ordered his lead elements to move
into position to attack. In fact the sound Humphreys heard was a skirmish between Crook's
cavalry division and the Confederate rearguard. The small 2d Corps attack was repulsed and
Humphreys fortified his position as the rest of his corps arrived and then awaited the arrival
of the rest of the army.[67]

From Cumberland Lee hoped to move due west about 30 miles to Appomattox Station
on the Southside Line, from whence he could move to Lynchburg and escape to the south.
However, Lee had erred in crossing the Appomattox at Farmville. The route to Appomattox
Station south of the River was shorter. If the Union forces reacted swiftly, they could beat Lee
there.[68] With the Federal forces already closing fast on his position, Lee ordered another night
march and the Southern forces began abandoning their Cumberland church position after dark
on the 7th, less than a day after arriving.

Lee hoped to steal a march on Grant. However, talkative prisoners captured by Humphreys
indicated the Confederate goal was Lynchburg.[69] Even before getting this information, Grant
had dispatched Sheridan's cavalry to the south of Farmville on a broad sweeping maneuver
designed to cut off the Confederate route to Danville. The troops then turned west and biv•
ouacked on the evening of the 7th south of the Southside Railroad, already almost halfway to
Appomattox Station. Behind Sheridan's horse soldiers followed the foot soldiers of Gibbon's
24th Corps from Ord's command, and Brevet Major-General Charles Griffin's 5th Corps from
Meade's. On his own initiative, Sheridan sent his cavalry to Appomattox Station early on the
8th to capture reported supply trains Lee had moved from Farmville because Federal pressure
had not given him time to distribute the supplies.[70] With Meade's main force of the 2d and
6th Corps following behind Lee from the east, Sheridan's move put his cavalry in a blocking
position in front of the Confederates. Lee's plan was thwarted almost from the start.[71]

During the evening of 7/8 April and throughout the following day, Lee marched his troops
westward and southwestward along the axis of the Richmond-Lynchburg Stage Road towards
Appomattox Station. At dusk, Lee's army halted around a small village centered on the Ap•
pomattox county courthouse, three miles north of the station. At the same time at the station,
Sheridan's lead element, Brevet Major-General George Custer's 3d Cavalry Division, were
capturing the supply trains and the station. Custer then pushed up the stage road encountering
Lee's cavalry.[72] On the other side of the Confederate force, Meade's 2d and 6th Corps fol•
lowed the retreating Rebels, though only their skirmishers and scouts maintained contact. At
the end of the day, the two corps were roughly a mile east of the Confederate positions and
prepared to attack on the 9th.[73]

Lee realized he was trapped, but, after resting his troops through the night of 8/9 April,
expected he could push through the Union cavalry blocking the road to the south in the

morning of the 9th. The Confederate commander undoubtedly thought it unlikely that Federal infantry could have marched up fast enough to join Sheridan's cavalry before he could break through the horse soldiers' roadblock.[74] However, the Union infantry was on the way. As Sheridan pushed for Appomattox Station on the 8th, the 24th and 5th Corps followed right behind him.[75] Urged by Ord and Griffin, the infantry marched relentlessly, advancing over 30 miles on the 8th while continuing into the night. After a short break only a few miles from the station, the advance resumed early on the 9th, reaching Appomattox Station in time to help repulse Lee's last attack.[76]

On the 9th Lee attempted to break through the cavalry blocking his movement to the southwest, while the Union 2d and 6th Corps were advancing against him from the east.[77] After some success against Sheridan's cavalry, the Southern infantry bumped heads with Ord's lead elements and pulled back. Lee and Grant had been corresponding for two days about a Confederate surrender. With his escape route blocked, Lee now asked for a meeting with Grant, along with a ceasefire. At the afternoon meeting in a private residence at Appomattox Courthouse village, Lee formally surrendered, effectively ending the greatest pursuit operation of the war and giving Grant his third captured enemy army of the war.[78]

Throughout the pursuit, command and control was problematic as always. Sheridan led from the saddle and always had his own command under complete control. Meade was ill for most of the operation and rode forward in an ambulance wagon. Nevertheless, unlike in previous campaigns when he was not sick, he was forward with his advance troops, even ahead of them at one point (with Sheridan). In a show of mutual cooperation, Meade, when he first linked up with Sheridan at Jetersville, allowed him to position Meade's troops as they came up, while he tried to recover from his illness.[79] During Sheridan's final advance on Appomattox Station, the following infantry advanced behind him even before receiving notification through their own respective commanders and even affirmed their movement in an enclosure to a dispatch from Sheridan to Grant asking that those corps be moved up as soon as possible.[80]

Grant, in overall command, moved with the advance, usually staying with one of his subordinate commanders. He had moved his headquarters up behind the left wing of the army in late March during the Five Forks campaign. After returning to Petersburg to confer directly with President Abraham Lincoln, who was at City Point, Grant returned forward, initially advancing with Ord's Army of the James along the line of the Southside Railroad.[81] While Grant was able to communicate with his rear headquarters at City Point via telegraph, his primary means of communication with his army commanders (except, of course, when he was traveling with their headquarters) was via couriers, who also provided direct observation of troops movements.[82] And while he sometimes went hours without hearing from Sheridan and Meade, they were very clear of his intent and were doing exactly what he expected them to do.[83] Grant made extra efforts to insure that his generals coordinated their actions and did not fall back into the inaction that lost opportunities in June 1864. On the evening of 5 April, Grant, though thoroughly exhausted from riding all day, with a small staff and escort left Ord's command at Burkesville and moved cross country 16 miles to join Sheridan and

Meade at Jeterville. Meade and Sheridan were at odds on what to do the next morning. With Lee entrenched at Amelia Courthouse, Meade wanted to wait until all his troops were up and then advance on Lee's left. Sheridan, fearing that this would facilitate what he presumed to be Lee's desired withdrawal to the west, wanted to attack first thing in the morning and keep the pressure on Lee, while trying to cut across his line of retreat. Grant sided with Sheridan, but did so in such a persuasive manner that Meade promptly issued orders for the movement.[84] The result was the smashing victory at Sailor's Creek the next day. Grant returned to Burkeville in the evening of the 6th and remained with Ord's command until both main columns closed up at Farmville the next day.[85] For the remainder of the campaign Grant collocated with Meade's headquarters behind the pincer of the 2d and 6th Corps.[86] On 9 April when Lee asked for a meeting, Grant moved cross country from Meade's headquarters to Sheridan's position, as he felt it would be easier to pass through the lines there.[87] Grant had clearly learned the lessons of the previous June and applied them with vigor in this operation.

Despite being ill, Meade displayed uncharacteristic drive during the pursuit operation. As already mentioned, in this operation his headquarters was always located up front with his advance troops. He spent the first night (3 April) at Sutherland Station where his headquarters was located next to Grant's. He personally helped resolve traffic jams caused by the supply trains of Sheridan's forces in front of him.[88] Meade spent the second night about a day's march behind Sheridan, while poor roads, cavalry and wagon trains from the vanguard slowed up the advance of his own infantry. On the 5th Meade collocated with Sheridan's headquarters, even moving ahead of his own troops, as the infantry caught up to the cavalry while Lee was paused at Amelia.[89] This proximity greatly enhanced the employment of their forces in concert and when Grant joined them on the evening of 5th, the conditions were in place to execute the destruction of a Confederate corps the next day at Sailor's Creek. Meade and Grant traveled together for the rest of the campaign, Meade remaining with his troops while Grant went to obtain Lee's surrender.[90] Meade controlled his forces through continual communications and personal observation and presence. He was able, accordingly, to adjust to changing circumstances, such as destroyed bridges at Farmville, instantly.[91]

The biggest difference between the Petersburg Maneuver and the Appomattox Campaign was the presence of Phil Sheridan commanding the vanguard. He commanded from the front with his troopers, and had a single-minded emphasis on the objective of cutting off Lee's army. Sheridan had learned from his mistakes in previous campaigns and never let up.[92] His attitude proved to be contagious.

Though played out with many of the same troops and some of the same commanders as the June 1864 maneuver, the Appomattox campaign was executed far differently. A sense of urgency permeated the command.[93] Grant and his subordinates had command and control of their troops at all times.[94] In this operation, instead of delaying movement to wait for rations or to rest the troops, commanders kept the pressure on the Confederates, foregoing rest and meals.[95]

Generals cooperated to resolve potential misunderstanding. For example, at the very beginning of the pursuit there was some confusion over whether Sheridan or Meade controlled
Humphreys' 2d Corps. Instead of leaving the corps in limbo, the two generals cooperated
without missing a step and coordinated with Grant. The corps continued in the pursuit.[96]

While Meade and Grant occasionally located their headquarters along telegraph lines, the
nature of the campaign precluded management by telegraph.[97] Instead, commanders depended
on a combination of couriers and locating themselves close to the action. Grant usually collocated with either Ord or Meade to facilitate command and Meade and Sheridan were located
together or near each other for all but the final phase of the campaign as well. While dispatches could take an hour or more, and contact was occasionally lost with far-flung commands,
Grant's clear intent allowed such lapses to have virtually no effect on the operation.[98] This
clear intent and Grant's complete trust in Sheridan's judgment allowed the employment of the
multiple columns that placed direct pressure on Lee, while ultimately enveloping him. The
employment of such columns also gave the Union commander a certain flexibility to cover
contingencies until Lee's exact intentions could be discerned.

Mobile Command in the Indian Wars 1865-1890 and Beyond

The period from 1865 to 1890 saw United States Army units committed to multiple campaigns against American Indians in the western portions of the nation. These operations were
almost entirely mobile in nature and many, because of the Indian's preferred style of hit and
run warfare, resembled the pursuit of Lee's army, except that cavalry was usually the main
strike force rather than infantry.[99] The great geographical distances involved in many of these
campaigns precluded the use of telegraph lines, which could not be expected to follow the
troops into the field and, in any event, after the Civil War, the army restricted the use of the
telegraph to time sensitive matters.[100]

Battle command in these movements almost always found the force commander with the
column he commanded. The use of multiple columns converging on the presumed location
of the hostile Indians was the preferred technique. Converging columns allowed multiple
opportunities to find the hostiles and trap them.[101] However, when multiple columns were employed, the limitations of technology and technique were clearly evident. Commanders were
usually, but not always, appointed for expeditions using multiple columns. But realistically
these commanders lost control of any columns with which they were not personally traveling
and had to depend on general instructions, link up locations, and the initiative and abilities
of their subordinate commanders. Naturally this made coordinated operations, as seen in the
Appomattox Campaign, very difficult, if virtually impossible.

Part of the problem with Army operations in the west was the mindset that military operations in this environment were, by their nature, of a level less than full wartime operations.
There were disputes in Congress over whether Indian fighting was to be considered war as
such.[102] The restrictions on the use of the telegraph are but one example of this mindset. The
Army fought these actions organized into its peacetime structure of geographical commands

called military divisions with subordinate commands called departments. Although task forces, usually called columns, composed of companies from various regiments were often formed on a temporary basis, no permanent or even temporary units above the size of regiments existed or were created. When not participating in offensive actions, the Army often had its units scattered to provide local defense from fixed posts. Forces were cobbled together from available troops for particular mobile operations. Further, there was at times a certain contempt of the fighting abilities of the Indians that was sometimes reflected in the preparation for campaigns. Higher commanders considered coordination between columns, even if possible, unnecessary because each column, it was thought, could easily defeat the enemy by itself.[103]

Therefore columns, in most cases, became virtually independent in operations once they left their fixed posts. Logistics—even small columns required a large supply wagon train to subsist in the inhospitable prairie land—frequently slowed down columns and even halted operations, hindering them as much as command and control difficulties did.[104]

A good example of battle command in a mobile campaign during this era is the 1876 campaign against the Sioux. Overall commander of operations was Lieutenant-General Philip Sheridan, who commanded the Military Division of the Missouri, a large area command whose responsibilities included all of the Great Plains east of the Continental Divide. Subordinate to Sheridan were four departments, each responsible for all the Army forces and operations within their own specified areas. This campaign involved two of the departmental commanders. In the north, Brigadier-General Alfred Terry commanded the Department of Dakota, with headquarters at Saint Paul, Minnesota. Terry was slated to provide 41 infantry and cavalry companies from five different infantry regiments and two cavalry regiments for operations. In the south Brigadier-General George Crook commanded the Department of the Platte, with his headquarters at Omaha, Nebraska, and deployed 35 companies from three cavalry and three infantry regiments for the campaign.[105] While Sheridan was overall commander, in the sense that he was in charge of all Army operations on the Plains in 1876, he did not appoint a separate field commander for the Sioux expedition. With his two departmental commanders, Crook and Terry, in the field, Sheridan left these peers in charge of determining how they would coordinate their operations.

The objective of the campaign was to find and subdue bands of hostile Sioux warriors operating in the general area of eastern Montana and Wyoming territories between the Bighorn River in the west and the Powder River in the east. Unofficial Army doctrine called for winter campaigns against hostile Indians. Sheridan, in his campaign directive of 8 February 1876 to his subordinates Crook and Terry, clearly indicated he expected a campaign as soon as possible.

However, while Crook was ready—because a visit east had tipped him off to the projected operations—Terry's command would not be able to mount up until the spring, a delay of several months.[106]

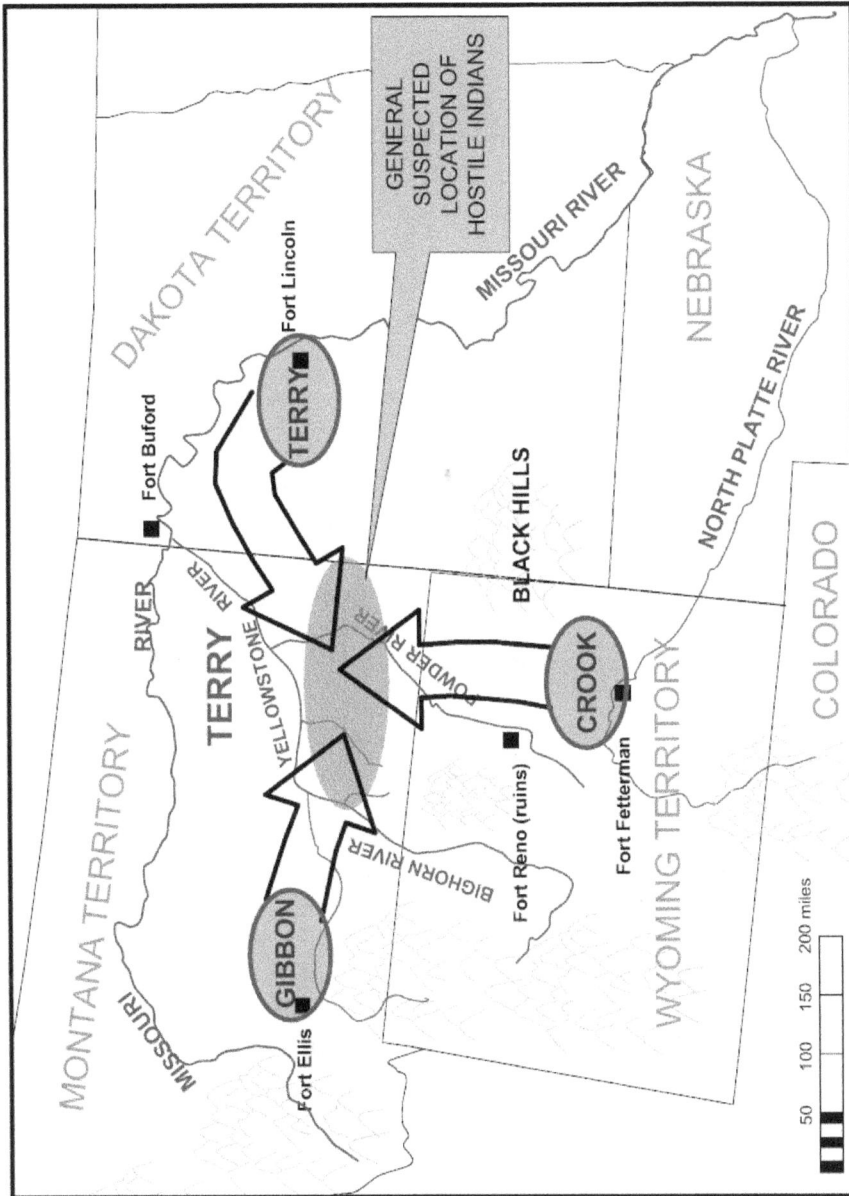

Figure 11. Campaign plan against the Sioux.

Sheridan also indicated that, although Terry planned to use two columns and Crook intended to advance towards Terry from the south, the columns were not expected to necessarily act in concert, as the Indians were mobile themselves.[107] These rather broad instructions included no provision for an overall operational commander, forcing Crook and Terry to coordinate their operations informally, if at all.

Crook assembled his force at Fort Fetterman on the North Platte River in the Wyoming Territory. From there he planned to march northward 150 miles into the hunting grounds of the hostile Sioux with ten companies of cavalry and two of infantry, scouts and support personnel.

Terry massed the forces for his portion of the expedition in two places: in the east at Fort Lincoln in the Dakota Territory, and in the west at Fort Ellis in the Montana Territory. At Fort Lincoln he assembled a primarily cavalry force, most of which came from Lieutenant-Colonel George Custer's 7th Cavalry Regiment.[108]

This column Terry would command himself, though he planned to give Custer an independent command if the situation warranted it. Terry planned to supply his column by using the Missouri and Yellowstone Rivers as lines of supply. And he also intended to use the rivers to maintain communications with the force advancing eastward from Fort Ellis, Montana.[109] Both columns would also depend on couriers bringing messages forward from telegraph stations located at permanent posts.

While Sheridan may have had little concern about coordinating these columns, Terry felt otherwise, feeling that his columns should support Crook from the north by initially preventing the escape of the Indians, then turning south and helping Crook defeat them.[110] Of course this was easier said than done.

At Fort Ellis in the Montana Territory, Colonel John Gibbon assembled Terry's other column, a force of five infantry companies and four cavalry companies. Gibbon's force formed up to the west of the projected area of operations in early April. Gibbon was to march down the Yellowstone River eastward. Cavalry forces from Fort Ellis had already marched out in February to bring back some traders being harassed by Indian raiders on the Yellowstone at the mouth of the Bighorn River.[111] Terry felt that if Gibbon could get his force moving as soon as possible, he'd at least minimally fulfill Sheridan's intent for a winter campaign.[112] But Gibbon would not be ready to go for weeks.

Accordingly, when Crook's force set out on 1 March 1876, a cold Plains winter day, it did so as the sole column and the only one to actually do so in what was considered the optimal operational weather. From the start small groups of Indians harassed the march but Crook shook them off by leaving his trains and infantry behind at the ruins of Fort Reno abandoned almost a decade before as the terms of peace in a previous Sioux war. With the cavalry and scouts, Crook moved north in search of the Indians. After fruitless ridings along the Tongue River, scouts finally found a Cheyenne Indian village near the Powder River. Crook detached six companies under Colonel Joseph Reynolds to attack the village. Advancing through an icy blizzard, Reynolds' surprise attack was initially successful. But, hypersensitive to his force's security, he withdrew without adequately destroying the Indian resources, making the engage‑ ment effectively indecisive. Reynolds rejoined Crook and the whole force returned to Fort Fetterman twenty-six days after it had set out.[113] Crook refitted and reinforced his command, planning to return to the field in May.

With Crook in the field, Terry prepared to advance his columns. While bad weather delayed his own departure, Gibbon left Fort Ellis at the start of April, and advanced down the Yel‑ lowstone, pausing briefly to resupply. By the 21st he was near the western edge of the area of operations near the junction of the Yellowstone and its tributary, the Bighorn River. Here, 200 miles east of Fort Ellis, near an abandoned civilian post called Fort Pease, which had been evacuated in February, Gibbon received instructions to halt from Terry. The orders came via courier forwarding telegraphic dispatches from Fort Ellis, dated the 15th.[114] Terry, now aware of Crook's return to Fort Fetterman, and well aware of his own eastern column's delays in getting started, feared an Indian concentration against Gibbon. In an effort to coordinate movements, Terry had Gibbon pause for almost three weeks.[115]

While Gibbon remained static, the Sioux began harassing his camp, leading him to send out scouts who soon discovered a large Indian village on the Tongue River on 16 May, 35 miles away. By its size, this village had to be the ultimate objective of the whole campaign.[116] Gibbon ordered a night march in order to attack the village at dawn. However, after delays

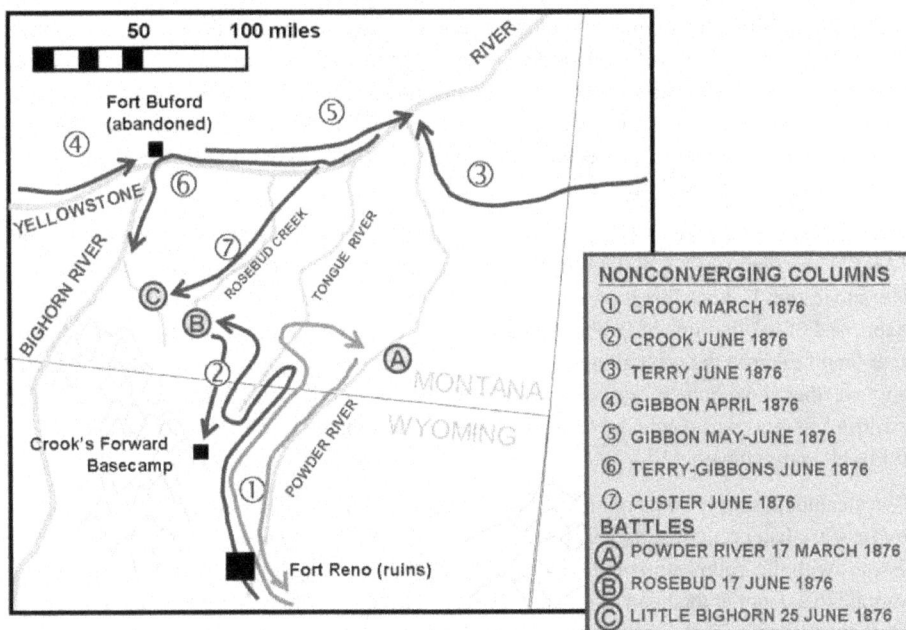

Figure 12. Nonconverging columns in the Little Bighorn Campaign.

caused by the lack of sufficient boats to get the cavalry quickly across the Yellowstone, Gibbon cancelled the movement when Sioux scouts were noticed observing it. He realized he could not get to the camp fast enough to still have surprise, an essential ingredient to the attack's success.[117]

On the 18th Gibbon received a situational update from Terry dated the 8th that reiterated the need to cover the north bank of the Yellowstone to prevent Indians from escaping in that direction, and providing an update on the eastern column. Meanwhile Gibbon had failed to report the sighting of the large village or his failed attempt to move against it and the prob•ability that the Sioux were aware of his presence.[118]

Despite bouts of bad weather, Gibbon's scouts remained active, as did the Indians. Gibbon established a new camp location nine miles farther east opposite the mouth of Rosebud Creek and moved to it on 21 May, where he would remain immobile per Terry's instructions for two more weeks, as supply difficulties and Sioux harassment began to mount. Mysteriously, however, all Indian presence stopped on 23 May. But on the 27th the scouts discovered the large village had moved to a point on the Rosebud only 18 miles from the Army camp. The Indians apparently felt little threat from Gibbon's column, having moved closer to him rather than away.[119] Gibbon reacted to this news with an apparent lack of concern. In a dispatch sent to Terry by small boat down the Yellowstone on 27 May, Gibbon mentioned the village's discovery merely in passing, citing that its discovery might slow his renewed march down the Yellowstone. This renewal of the advance was in response to a telegram Terry had sent Gibbon on the 14th telling Gibbon to advance eastward to join up with Terry's own column as Terry expected to find the hostile Indians farther to the east. Even though he received these instructions on the 28th, Gibbon did not renew his movement to the east until 4 June, after his supply trains and other detachments had been concentrated for the advance. Even if Gibbon himself did not realize it, his scouts were fully aware that they were moving away from the very Indians they were seeking out.[120]

Bad weather delayed the assembly of Terry's eastern column. But it finally got underway on 17 May. The cavalry-heavy column initially moved cross-country towards the Little Missouri River in western Dakota Territory, roughly 150 miles west of the Fort Lincoln start point. Unapprised of the findings of Gibbon's scouts, Terry believed the Indians to be massed there rather than farther to the west along the Tongue River where Gibbon's scouts had found them. Rainy weather slowed the movement down, and it was not until the 27th that the vicinity of the Little Missouri was reached. Naturally, signs of the Indians were sparse, forcing Terry to modify his campaign plan.[121]

Two steamboat supply ships on the Missouri supported the column. One of the steamers, the *Far West*, had brought supplies up the Missouri to Fort Buford near the junction of the Missouri with the Yellowstone in late May and was then ferrying infantry south on the Yel•lowstone to a depot at the head of Glendive Creek. The steamer met up with Gibbon's boat-mounted couriers, adding a new, tenuous communications link between the two columns.[122]

Command and control difficulties now had Terry finding no Indians where he expected them to be, one of his subordinates rushing to help close the prey-less trap, and another subordinate who, in reality, knew the location of the prey. Trying to be as flexible as his limited control al• lowed, on 3 June Terry revised his plans. Now in courier communications with the new depot at Glendive Creek, he sent orders to Gibbon to stop his eastward march and for the *Far West* to move to the mouth of the Powder River, to which his command would also shift. This river was reached on the 7th.[123]

Unfortunately, on the 8th Terry found out that his written orders to Gibbon instructing him to halt had been not dispatched, the couriers having turned back when their path was blocked by a large Indian war party. Terry, fearful of uncoordinated actions and wanting to obtain intelligence from Gibbon's scouts as soon as possible, left with a small party to join the *Far West* on the Yellowstone, in anticipation of taking it south to Gibbon's position. Terry left Custer and the bulk of the 7th Cavalry on the Powder River. Aboard the *Far West*, he dis• covered a small advance party of Gibbon's force already there, having taken boats down the river. From them Terry first heard of the large Indian village. He sent a boat downriver to order Gibbon to halt his command immediately, and to then come himself to the *Far West* for a meeting.

Not wanting to waste any more time, Terry took a boat southwesterly along the Yellowstone on the morning of the 9th and met Gibbon along the way. On the small craft they conferred while the boat continued on to Gibbon's camp. The result was a new plan—Gibbon would return to his old Rosebud camp and watch to the south to insure the large Indian village did not try to cross the Yellowstone. Meanwhile, Terry would move part of his column southwest along the river to Gibbon's location, arriving in about a week, while half of the cavalry would do a sweep to the south to gather intelligence and drive off any warriors not with the main vil• lage.[124]

This six company strong cavalry detachment, led by Major Marcus Reno of the 7th Cavalry, was to scout the valleys of the Powder River, and the Mizpah Creek and Tongue Rivers to the west, rejoining Custer and the rest of the 7th Cavalry at the junction of the Tongue with the Yellowstone. After the reconnaissance, Terry intended to then move his combined force against the Rosebud village through the use of two parallel columns, a cavalry-heavy one under Custer moving southwest along the Tongue River, which would then swing around to the west and north to attack along the Rosebud from the south and a slower moving infantry heavy column under Gibbon moving directly south along the Rosebud. While Reno conduct• ed his reconnaissance, Custer and the rest of the eastern column would move the 25 miles to the mouth of the Tongue where a new supply base would be established.[125]

The new depot was quickly set up and some infantry, cavalry recruits and heavy baggage were left behind there as Custer's portion of the 7th Cavalry marched out on the 15th while Terry and his staff were transported down the river on the *Far West*. Before departing the de• pot, Terry rerouted communications with his rear headquarters through Fort Buford and down the river. Custer moved west along the Yellowstone to meet Reno at the prearranged rendez•vous and was joined there by Terry the next day. Reno did not appear for three days.[126]

Reno began his scouting mission on 10 June. After finding little in the east, he decided, on his own initiative, to move to the abandoned Tongue River village site so his scouts could de•termine the size of the massed Indian group. After doing so on the morning of the 16th, Reno decided to further stretch his orders by trying to determine where the village had gone and ad•vanced towards the Rosebud, where his scouts examined the now abandoned Rosebud village site as well. The size of the Indian group was estimated at about 400 lodges and 800 warriors. Reno moved south along the Rosebud, with his scouts finding several fresher abandoned vil•lage sites. They estimated the cavalry was only a day's march behind the large Indian village, though at that very time the Indians were fighting Crook's command some miles farther to the south. Reno then moved to make his rendezvous, arriving opposite Gibbon's camp at the mouth of the Rosebud on the 18th.[127]

Bad weather had delayed Gibbon's countermarch but he finally reached his designated campsite on the 14th and then sent out a cavalry patrol 60 miles to the west to determine if the Indians had crossed to the north side of the Yellowstone. The patrol returned with no signs of such a crossing. The large Indian village was still south of the river.[128]

Reno communicated with Gibbon across the unfordable Yellowstone via swimming couri•ers and signal flags. Reno then moved a day's march northeasterly along the river towards the rendezvous site. Rather than continue, he then sent couriers forward to Terry and Custer. Reno's patrol had discovered where the Indians were not and roughly where they were headed. Size estimates of the Indian encampment at about 800 warriors, which became the expedition's planning figure, did not, however, account for additional warriors joining the vil•lage since it moved.[129]

Reno's behavior had given Terry a personal lesson in how little control he actually had over his forces when he was not in constant communication with them. He was upset that Reno had not followed orders and questioned his motives and worried that the patrol could have compromised surprise. But Terry did use the intelligence that Reno gathered to revise his plans. Under the new plan, Custer, with the entire 7th Cavalry, would ride to the southwest along the Rosebud to its headwaters, then swing to the west to the Little Big Horn River and follow it north to the Bighorn. He had the flexibility to follow the Indian trail if he found it, but if the trail went west from the Rosebud, he was to sweep south before turning west to make sure the Indians could not escape to the south. Gibbon's primarily infantry force would travel south along the Bighorn to the mouth of the Little Bighorn. Ideally Custer's force would drive the Indians north into Gibbon's force.[130]

On the 20th, Terry's forces began moving to their respective start points, Gibbon to the mouth of the Big Horn, Custer to Reno's camp, then to the mouth of the Rosebud. Custer be•gan on his movement on the 22d. Meanwhile the supply steamer ferried Gibbon's command across the Yellowstone to the east bank of the Bighorn. Gibbon then started his southerly march to the mouth of the Little Bighorn. The *Far West*, loaded with supplies and with Terry aboard, followed in the river.[131]

By the end of May, after several delays, Crook had assembled his Big Horn and Yellowstone Expedition at Fort Fetterman. His force was composed of 15 cavalry and five infantry companies and a mule train. Leaving on the 29th, the force suffered through terrible weather to move northward and reach the abandoned Fort Reno site on 2 June. A shortage of experienced guides resulted in the column being misdirected on the prairie over the next week before scouts finally brought it into a preplanned supply camp at Goose Creek, which was then made into the expedition's forward base.[132]

After a pause from the 11th to the 16th to await the arrival of Crow Indian scouts, Crook moved north heading for the headwaters of the Rosebud, to the west of where Reynolds had fought in March. The next day, after a short morning march, and while Crook rested his command, his Indian scouts skirmished with a large body of Sioux and Cheyenne warriors to the north, falling back to the main body's position. Crook advanced his force to gain control of some commanding high ground.[133]

In the ensuing three-hour battle, the Sioux and their Cheyenne allies fought so fiercely that Crook suspected their village had to be nearby. He detached a cavalry force to the east to look for the village. Meanwhile on the other side of the action a cavalry force had become separated from Crook's main force and was saved from annihilation by several timely counterattacks, eventually rejoining the main force after suffering relatively heavy casualties. To ease the pressure against the separated force, Crook ordered the column to the east to swing back around and attack the Indian flank. While this force did so, it did not do it fast enough to ease the pressure on the separated unit that ended up having to push through heavy Indian fire to reach Crook's main force. However the attack of the eastern force surprised the Indians facing Crook. They then retreated. Without a village discovered, Crook decided to return to his Goose Creek camp to refit.[134] The Battle of the Rosebud was over. Crook's column would remain inactive during the decisive operations of Terry's columns.

While the Indians fought fiercely, they did not stand and fight, falling back when pressured and pressuring where they found weakness. When Crook divided his force to seek out the phantom village, he extended the action right when the Indians were beginning to weaken under the strain of his manpower advantage, which was roughly 1000 to 700.[135] Even though his force was split into as many as four separate elements during this action, several of which were in motion at the same time, the Army commander managed to maintain positive command and control with these elements by deploying them in mutually supporting positions and using couriers and aides to send revised instructions.

Back with Terry's forces, Custer advanced his column south along the Rosebud and discovered the large Indian trail. Terry's orders to Custer implied he should continue south before moving towards the Little Big Horn where the trail led. Custer chose to follow the trail on 25

June instead. His scouts discovered the village and he chose to immediately attack it from the march in the late afternoon while he still had surprise.

For the attack Custer divided his command into three battalions, the largest, 221 soldiers strong, he personally commanded, with Major Reno leading a force of 175 and Captain Frederick Benteen commanding 120 troopers. He also maintained a force of 136 to guard the regimental pack train. Operationally, Custer sent Benteen to the south to make sure the Indians were not retreating that way. Benteen was to then rejoin the command and act as the reserve. Reno was to attack the Indian village from the south while Custer's own force would support him with an attack on the flank of the Indians facing Reno, hopefully reinforced with Benteen's command.

Reno's charge across the Little Big Horn into the Indian village opened a hornet's nest. The Indians were in much larger numbers than ever before encountered, and they were stand•ing and fighting. After fierce combat, Reno was forced to retreat across the river to a hilltop defensive position where he faced annihilation. Custer, already farther to the north and having now seen the immense size of the Indian village, had sent a courier to find Benteen and bring him forward with the pack train and its ammunition supply. But when scouts reported Reno's defeat, Custer went forward to attack and relieve the pressure on Reno before Benteen and the packs could arrive.

To the south, Indian pressure decreased against Reno as the Indians massed to annihilate Custer's force. Benteen and the packs soon joined Reno. Meanwhile the Indian forces con•centrated four miles to the north against Custer and annihilated his force to the last man. Reno and Benteen, unsure of what was going on, moved a force under Captain Thomas Weir to the north to look for Custer. But, upon the destruction of Custer's force, the Indians shifted back to the south, forcing Weir back to the hilltop position in which the combined Reno-Benteen force was besieged throughout the night of the 25th and into the morning of the 26th. In the afternoon of the 26th, the Indians withdrew and Reno's men observed the whole village mov•ing off to the southwest.

Terry and Gibbon's column had advanced sluggishly down the Big Horn, checking a false lead of a village location on the way. The *Far West* followed along the river, anchoring at the wrong place. The force finally reached its blocking position at the mouth of the Little Big Horn on the morning of the 26th. Rumors of Custer's disaster reached Terry through Indian scouts who had fled the battle and smoke plainly visible to the south. Terry, therefore, after consolidating his command, the infantry having lagged behind, moved south along the Little Big Horn. He sent two scouts forward to find Custer and pass on the message that he was coming. These dispatches ultimately reached Reno.[136] Terry halted for the night only eight miles north of Reno's besieged position on the opposite side of the Little Big Horn. On the following morning Terry's force discovered the scene of Custer's destruction and relieved Reno.

The Indians scattered after Custer's defeat, while Terry moved back to the camp at the head of the Big Horn and awaited reinforcements. Crook, now himself reinforced, moved north again in mid-August and joined forces with Terry, advancing north along the Tongue River then resupplying at the depot at the mouth of the Powder River. Terry then moved north to the Missouri, ultimately ending up at Fort Buford. Crook moved east into the Dakota Territory and south towards the Black Hills. On 8-10 September, he fought a three day drawn battle with a much smaller Sioux force under Crazy Horse at Slim Buttes. Supply difficulties precluded pursuit as Crook moved into the Black Hills for resupply. Campaigning after this included operations by Colonel Nelson Miles south of the Missouri in eastern Montana where his 5th Infantry continued to pursue and harass small bands of Indians throughout the winter, culminating in a defeat of Crazy Horse's band at Wolf Mountain in January 1877. Crook had meanwhile launched his third expedition from Fort Fetterman in November 1876 with a large force of soldiers and Indian scouts, attacking and destroying a Cheyenne village near old Fort Reno on 25 November. Sheridan's winter campaign came a winter too late.

Command and control in the 1876 campaign displayed many of the same techniques and limitations exhibited during the Civil War. Telegraphic messages lost their immediacy when relayed by couriers. Couriers employed were often either aides or civilian scouts who were motivated by personal reputation to get the message through.[137] Coordination between several different forces spread out geographically was lumbering at best. A commander in the field, while losing a bit of communications time by not sitting in a headquarters with its own telegraph line, did manage to at least have immediate and complete control over the force he was with at all times. Once in the field a commander ran a great risk of losing control if he divided his force. However if he did not do so, the objective of the operation—the destruction of the hostile Indian forces—may not have been obtained given the hit and run nature of Indian warfare. Unfortunately in this campaign the Indians fought pitched battles and massed large forces. An operational division of forces proved dangerous, while a tactical division proved disastrous.[138]

While at the operational level forces were hard to coordinate, even at the tactical level communications between forces depended more on the individual initiative of subordinate commanders and their understanding of the commander's operational intent. At Little Big Horn, Custer broke up his unified command into three smaller ones. Once the action commenced, he only controlled the column he was with. His subordinate commanders, acting under their own impression of the situation, failed to adequately comply with the dispatches Custer sent out from his column. They did not understand his intent. Accordingly, the Indians, acting as one large group in concert, were able to defeat Custer's small forces in detail, first attacking Reno's battalion, then switching to Custer's force before renewing attacks against Reno's command now consolidated with Benteen's battalion.

Things were different at the Rosebud. Much more experienced at both fighting Indians and leading large forces divided into several separate subforces, Crook, though surprised by the Indians tenacity, managed to place his forces in positions where they could support each other and masterfully used couriers and aides to control his forces, even correcting an error when he sent a force on a wild goose chase just when he needed it the most.

It is at the operational level that the difficulties of command and control of moving forces is most evident. Crook's command had fought a pitched battle only 30 miles southwest of the site of Custer's battle a week later. His command was resting at its Goose Creek camp to the south. Neither knew of the actions of the other. Additionally, Terry's column was less than a day's march north of Custer the day of the battle. Coordination between each of these ele•ments, despite their relative proximity to each other, was extremely limited. Communications technology limited the precision required to execute successful mobile operations consisting of more than one moving force. Even though the Indians were standing and fighting with their largest concentration of warriors ever, the combined Army forces still outnumbered them and, if they were operating in better concert, could have accomplished the mission they had been sent into the field to do.[139]

While the Indian Wars were marked highly mobile campaigning on both sides, the Little Bighorn campaign best illustrates the difficulties and capabilities of such campaigns, particu•larly when multiple columns were employed. When single columns were employed, typically the Indian forces managed to elude battle and drift away, moving across the border to Canada or back to their reservations in small groups.

US forces participated in no real mobile campaigns after the Indian Wars until World War II. Mobility in the War with Spain and the subsequent campaign in the Phillippines was primar•ily of the strategic nature, with naval transports bringing the ground forces to the critical places and times. The campaign in Cuba was not a mobile one, as the army massed against the main Spanish force after landing from ships, then attacked and defeated it, then besieged it in the city of Santiago for two weeks until it surrendered. In operations in both Puerto Rico and Manila in the Philippines, Spanish forces surrendered after little resistance. The follow•ing extended operations against insurgents in the Philippines resembled the operations against the Indians, except the geography was far different, favoring the use of infantry rather than cavalry as the main strike element.

Summary

The Civil War saw the first effective application of the railroad and electric telegraph to large military operations. While providing timely long distance communications, the tele•graph was, however, less of use for mobile operations, which could be hindered by being tethered to lines of wire. Coordination between different units on campaign, even when under the same commander, proved difficult and was only facilitated by traditional methods of good planning, good follow-up by the commander and good selection of subordinates.

A comparison of the initial Union advance on Petersburg in June 1864 and the April 1865 pursuit to Appomattox is a tale of two completely different campaigns even though most of the troops and commanders were the same. In the advance on Petersburg, Union commander U.S. Grant planned and executed a masterful operational maneuver which placed most of the Union forces near Petersburg before the Confederate commander, R.E. Lee, realized what had happened. However, Grant and his primary subordinate, George Meade, lost effective battle command over their forces in the final, decisive stages of the operation. Instead of pressing on resolutely against smaller, second rate Confederate forces defending Petersburg, Grant and Meade allowed their subordinate commanders to halt after minor setbacks, to move out without expediency and to execute their attacks with inadequate coordination and synchronization. Accordingly, Lee's Confederates we able to overcome their initial confusion and build up a solid defensive line before Grant and Meade could execute a coordinated mass attack. The Union commanders were rarely on the spot to see that their forces were being led with a lack of sense of urgency, and allowed misunderstandings or misinterpretation of orders to fester until it was too late.

In contrast, Grant's next major mobile operation, the pursuit from Petersburg to Appomattox against Lee's retreating Confederates, was handled with far greater skill. Though Grant's forces were organized into a complex combination of field commands, the reality of the pursuit and the clearcut imparting of Grant's intent to his subordinates combined for excellent battle command on the move in this campaign. The aggressive Sheridan led the relentless spearhead. The highly competent, but somewhat less aggressive Meade led the main body and Ord led the left wing force designed to cut off Lee's escape routes from a distance. Unlike in previous campaigns, both Grant and Meade were far forward moving with the troops. After a preliminary envelopment at Sailor's Creek, Sheridan and Ord successfully cut off Lee's route of retreat while Meade's forces faced him from the other direction.

Campaigns against the American Indians after the Civil War proved to be typically highly mobile and involve multiple columns over vast swatches of territory. In the Little Big Horn campaign, US Army forces organized into three columns under two co-equal commanders, hoped to converge on the Sioux and Cheyenne forces before they could disperse to avoid the blow. With communications depending on couriers and arrangements made before the forces took to the field or separated, coordinating the operations of the various columns was virtually impossible. One column failed to pass on intelligence information in a timely manner, while parts of the other two fought separate battles against the Indians. The Sioux/ Cheyenne forces were allowed to fight two columns separately, fighting the first to a standstill then moving against and annihilating a large portion of the second. Although the American commanders had three columns within striking distance of the Indians and supporting distance of each other, lack of an overall commander and lack of effective communications turned each column into an independent entity. Communications technology had not yet advanced to the level where a commander could maneuver multiple forces, which were not close together geographically.

The invention of the telephone in 1876 and a practical field version in 1892 did not affect operations in the War with Spain, but would have marked effect on operations in the next century.[140]

Notes

1. Grant, 540.

2. Epstein, 380-2.

3. US War Department, *The War of the Rebellion: A Compilation of the Official Records of the Union and Confederate Armies* (Washington, DC: Government Printing Office 1880-1901) (cited here•after as *OR),* Series I, Volume 46, Part III, 349-50.

4. *OR*, 46, Pt III, 228-9.

5. Exceptions to this where the railroad proved to be tactically decisive were 1st Bull Run and, to a lesser extent, the September 1863 Battle of Chickamauga.

6. Van Crevald, 103

7. Advanced uses of signal fires and signal flags or visual telegrpahic had been developed over the course of time, with the French developed Chappe system used by Napoleon. See Randy Katz, *Na•poleon's Secret Weapon: The Optical Telegraph,* April 2, 1997, http://http.cs.berkeley.edu/%7Erandy/Courses/CS39C.S97/optical/optical.html, (accessed February 23, 2005).

8. The field use of the telegraph was initially developed by the Army's Chief Signal Officer, Colonel Albert Myer. See Rebecca Raines, *Getting the Message Through: A Branch History of the U.S. Army Signal Corps.* (Washington, DC: US Army Center of Military History, 1996), 18, 31.

9. At divisions and brigades messages were handled by officers designated as assistant adjutant generals.

10. The US Army uses the doctrinal term envelopment to indicate "an offensive maneuver in which the main attacking force passes around or over the enemy's principal defensive positions to secure objectives to the enemy's rear." See US Department of the Army, *Field Manual 101-5-1 Operational Terms and Graphics* (Washington, DC: Department of the Army, 1997), 1-61. In this work the terms envelop and outflank will be used interchangeably.

11. Grant admitted this at the Warren Court of Inquiry. See *Proceedings, Findings and Opinions of the Court of Inquiry Convened by Order of the President of the United States in the Case of Lieutenant Colonel G. K. Warren.*(hereafter *Proceedings)* 3 vols (U.S. Government Printing Office, Washington, D.C., 1883), 1035. Grant usually wrote out dispatches that were then carried to his telegraph center and sent out.

12. Ibid., Grant wrote that Meade and Sherman "are the fittest officers for large commands I have come in contact with." See Ulysses S. Grant. *Personal Memoirs of U.S. Grant.* E.B. Long, ed. New York: Da Capo Press, 1982, 424 and Wainwright, Charles S. Wainwright, *A Diary of Battle: The Per•sonal Journals of Colonel Charles S. Wainwright, 1861-1865*, Allan Nevins, ed. (New York: Harcourt, Brace & World, 1962. Reprinted Gettysburg: Stan Clark Military Books, 1987), 372n. Grant's high opinion of Meade might have been because they both managed battle similarly.

13.   Michael A. Cavanaugh and William Marvel, *The Battle of the Crater "The Horrid Pit." June 25- August 6, 1864*, The Petersburg Campaign, Virginia Civil War Battles and Leaders Series, 2d ed. (Lynchburg, VA: H.E. Howard, Inc., 1989), 111.

14.   Major-General George Thomas lamented Grant's telegrams trying to give tactical advice from 500 miles away. See Shelby Foote, *The Civil War: A Narrative: Red River to Appomattox* (New York: Vintage Books, 1988), 683-5.

15.   Department of the Army, *Field Manual 100-5,Operations* (Washington, D.C., US Government Printing Office, 1993), 6-6.

16.   The previous several paragraphs paraphrase pages 149-151 of the author's "Humiliation in Vic‧ tory: The Relief of General Warren at Five Forks." MA Thesis, University of Massachusetts at Boston, 1997.

17.   One observer with a scientific background has even postulated a theory that strange effects of sound waves had decisive effects on the results of several key battles. In these cases, battlefield sounds were either muted or magnified at the commander's location, causing him to make poor decisions. See Charles D. Ross, *Civil War Acoustic Shadows*, (Shippensburg, PA: White Mane, 2001).

18.   Thomas J. Howe, *The Petersburg Campaign: Wasted Valor June 15-18, 1864*. Virginia Civil War Battles and Leaders Series, 2d ed.(Lynchburg, VA: H.E. Howard, Inc., 1988), 11.

19.   Eric J. Wittenberg, *Little Phil: A Reassessment of the Civil War Leadership of Gen. Philip H. Sheridan.* (Washington, DC: Brassey's, 2002), 36-7. Sheridan never linked up with Hunter. He was defeated by Confederate cavalry at the Battle of Trevilian Station on 11-12 June, and ultimately forced to rejoin the Army of the Potomac.

20.   Howe, 11.

21.   Ibid., 12.

22.   Ibid., 13.

23.   Ibid., 18-9, 38.

24.   Ibid., 21-2.

25.   Ibid., 27.

26.   Ibid., 30.

27.   Ibid., 35.

28.   Ibid., 38, 43, 51-2.

29.   Ibid., 40, 48.

30.   Ibid., 44-6: Grant 456.

31.   Howe, 48-9; Grant, 456. Hancock was temporarily relieved from command for medical reasons, both as field commander and as commander of the 2d Corps, with Major-General David Birney assum‧ ing acting command of the corps.

32. Howe, 57.

33. Ibid., 67-8.

34. Ibid., 94, 97-99.

35. Ibid., 102, 107.

36. Ibid., 122-3.

37. Grant, 457.

38. Ibid., 454.

39. Ibid., 105, 140.

40. George Meade, The *Life and Letters of George Gordon Meade, Major-General, United States Army*, Vol. II. (New York: Charles Scribner's Sons, 1913), 206.

41. Ibid., 13,15.

42. Grant, 455, 457.

43. *OR*, 40, Pt II, 116.

44. *OR* 40, Pt. II, 117.

45. Howe, 69.

46. *OR* 40, Pt. II, 167, 179. Telegraphic lines were advanced as the troops advanced. See *OR* 40, Pt. II, 167, 172.

47. Lyman, 165.

48. Ibid., 168. Burnside, commander of the 9th Corps, was at Warren's 5th Corps headquarters on the morning of 18 June.

49. *OR* 40, Pt. II, 167, 172, 174-7, 179. Meade only heard of the repulse of the 2d corps attack on the 18th via telegraph. See *OR*, 40, Pt. II, 168.

50. Joshua Chamberlain, *Bayonet Forward: My Civil War Reminiscences* (Gettysburg,: Stan Clark Military Books, 1994) 47-8; Howe, 128, 134.

51. While Appomattox is roughly 80 miles west of Petersburg, the circuitous routes marched by both armies made the course of the pursuit almost twice a distance than that.

52. Sheridan usually signed his dispatches with "Cavalry Headquarters" as the designation for his de facto army headquarters.

53. *OR*, 46, Pt.III, 242, 256, 362-3.

54. *OR*, 46, Pt.III,336.

55. *OR*, 46, Pt III, 336, 338.

56. Crook had commanded the Department of Western Virginia. He was out of favor with Secretary of War Edwin Stanton because he had been kidnapped by Confederate partisans from his quarters in Cumberland, Maryland, on 21 February 1865, and was only exchanged on 20 March. See Ezra J. Warner, *Generals in Blue: Lives of the Union Commanders* (Baton Rouge: Louisiana State University Press, 1964, reprint 1981), 103. A detailed discussion of the complex command relationships in the Five Forks campaign may be found in McGrath, "Humiliation in Victory," 47-50.

57. *OR*, 46, Pt III, 254-5;Joshua Chamberlain, *The Passing of the Armies: An Account of the Final Campaign of the Army of the Potomac Based Upon Personal Reminiscences of the Fifth Army Corps* (New York: G.P. Putnam's Sons, 1915; reprint New York: Bantam, 1993), 32-3; *Proceedings*, 250; Ed Bearss and Chris Calkins, *The Battle of Five Forks*, Virginia Civil War Battles and Leaders Series, 2d ed. (Lynchburg, VA: H.E. Howard, Inc., 1985), 83N. On the first day of the operation, 29 March 1865, the Five Corps was ordered to turn around, backtrack and follow a new route after it was discovered that the 2d Corps was unable to maintain contact with its sister corps if it took the original route, as rough terrain restricted the length of the 2d Corps frontage. The other occasion took place early in them morning of 1 April 1865 when a division of the 5th Corps moving to reinforce Sheridan was marched past a turn because of a combination of a lack of route instructions and late posting of guides, who did not anticipate the speed of the infantry's march.

58. *Proceedings*, 1197-8.

59. Sheridan usually referred to his command in dispatches simply as "Cavalry Headquarters."

60. Lee had preplanned for a supply train including 350,000 rations from Richmond to meet him at Amelia Courthouse. See Chris M. Calkins, *The Appomattox Campaign: March 29- April 9, 1865.* Great Campaigns (New York: Da Capo Press, 2001), 75. Lee then ordered up rations from Danville to Farmville on rail line farther to the west. On the 4th Ord's force captured a railroad employee who told Federals about the supplies being sent to Farmville. See *OR*, 46, Part III, 557. Adding to Lee's problems, on 4 April elements of Sheridan's cavalry caught up with and destroyed a large part of Lee's supply train north of Amelia Courthouse. See *OR*, 46, Part III, 582.

61. Grant, 540-1.

62. Calkins, *Appomattox Campaign*, 85.

63. *OR*, 46, Pt III, 556, 560.

64. *OR*, 46, Pt III, 572.

65. Frances Kennedy, ed, *Civil War Battlefield Guide,* 2d ed, The Conservation Fund (Boston: Houghton Mifflin, 1998), 426; Calkins, *Appomattox Campaign*, 11-12; *OR* 46, Pt. III, 596-7,605.

66. The relentless nature of the Union pursuit is exemplified by union cavalry under Brevet Briga• dier-General Irvin Gregg almost captured Lee himself when the Confederates were moving into posi• tion at Cumberland Church. A timely Southern counterattack prevented general's capture. See Calkins, *Appomattox Campaign*, 143-4.

67. *OR*, 46, Pt. III, 623-4; Calkins, *Appomattox Campaign*, 131-4.

68. Calkins, *Appomattox Campaign*,129-30.

69. *OR,* 46, Pt III, 624.

70. Ibid., 653.

71. In his memoirs, Grant claimed that the 6th Corps was assigned to Sheridan's command for the rest of the campaign after Sailor's Creek (see Grant, 548). While it is clear that corps was under Sheridan's control at Sailor's Creek, after that battle Meade clearly controlled its movements. See *OR* 46, Pt. I, 55-6, 605, 907-8, Pt. III, 647-8.

72. *OR,* 46, Pt III, 653.

73. Ibid., 642, 644-5.

74. Calkins, *Appomattox Campaign*, 155-6.

75. *OR* 46, Pt. III, 654.

76. *OR,* 46, Pt. I, 841; Calkins, *Appomattox Campaign*,151-2, 155,162.

77. *OR,* 46, Pt III, 667, 669-70.

78. Ibid., 663. Grant had captured armies at Fort Donelson in 1862 and Vicksburg in 1863.

79. *OR,* 46, Pt III, 576; Grant, 544-5.

80. *OR,* 46, Pt. III, 654.

81. *OR,* 46, Pt. III, 528, 576; Grant, 545.

82. *OR,* 46, Pt. III, 572-3.

83. Ibid., 572.

84. Grant, 545-6; *OR,* 46, Pt. III, 573, 577-8

85. *OR,* 46, Pt. III, 596.

86. Chris M.Calkins, *Lee's Retreat A History and Field Guide (*Richmond: Page One History Publica•tion, 2000), 66, 76.

87. Calkins, *Appomattox Campaign,* 171-2.

88. *OR,* 46, Pt. III, 512-3.

89. Ibid., 576.

90. Calkins, *Appomattox Campaign,* 172.

91. *OR,* 46, Pt. III, 620-1, 623-5.

92. For a critical analysis of Sheridan's failings as a cavalry corps and army commander see Chapters 2 and 3 (pages 24-90) of Wittenberg's *Little Phil.*

93.   An example of the sense of urgency: On 6 April as his corps was preparing to move towards what became the Battle of Sailor's Creek, Humphreys, the 2d Corps commander, discovered his 2d Divi•sion, commanded by Brigadier-General William Hays, to not be in motion per orders. When he went to Hays' headquarters, Humphreys discovered the whole headquarters to still be asleep. Humphreys sacked Hays on the spot and his replacement got the corps moving out promptly. See *OR*, 46. Part III, 597-8. The new division commander, Brigadier-General Thomas Smyth, was mortally wounded the next day at Farmville, the last Union general officer to fall in the war.

94.   The only troops Grant, Meade or Sheridan lost direct control of for any length of time were the troops providing security on the lines of communication. And these simply obeyed their previous orders which were, in fact, unchanged. See *OR*, 46, Pt. III, 605.

95.   *OR*, 46, Pt. III, 576.

96.   Ibid., 512-3.

97.   Ibid., 620.

98.   Ibid., 644-5.

99.   William G. Robertson, Jerold Brown, William M. Campsey and Scott R. McMeen, compilers, *Atlas of the Sioux Wars* (Fort Leavenworth: Combat Studies Institute, 1993), text accompanying Map 8; Robert M. Utley, *Frontier Regulars: The United States Army and the Indian 1866-1891* (Lincoln: University of Nebraska Press, 1984), 50.

100.   Clayton K.S. Chun, *US Army in the Plains 1865-91*, Battle Orders series, (London: Osprey, 2004), 76.

101.   Chun, 15-6.

102.   Utley, 21

103.   Robertson, et al., text accompanying Map 8.

104.   Utley, 48.

105.   Chun, 34-37.

106.   Lieutenant-General Philip H. Sheridan, *Annual Report, Military Division of the Missouri*, No•vember 25, 1876, enclosure to the 1876 *Annual Report of the General of the Army*, 440. John S. Gray, *Centennial Campaign: The Sioux War of 1876* (Norman, OK: University of Oklahoma Press, 1988), 36-7.

107.   Sheridan, 441: Robertson, et al., text accompanying Map 8.

108.   Custer was originally supposed to command this column, but Terry replaced him after Custer's indirect Involvement in the Belknap scandal made his commanding an expedition politically infeasible, The Belknap scandal was a graft case involving the Secretary of War and President Grant's brother and Army post sutlers. Gray, 67-8.

109.   Ibid., text accompanying Map 11;

110. Gray, 42.

111. see note 108 below.

112. Gray, 41-2.

113. Robertson, et al., text accompanying Map 9.

114. Fort Pease had had a brief existence. Established in 1875 as a trading post, Indian war parties harassed the small group of civilians who spent the winter of 1875-6 there. Under orders from Terry, Gibbon had sent a relief party there which brought the civilians back to Fort Ellis in March. Gray, 19, 40-41.

115. Brigadier-General Alfred Terry, *Annual Report Department of Dakota*, 1876; Gray, 75-6.

116. Gray, 80, 85.

117. Ibid., 80.

118. Ibid., 81.

119. Ibid., 82-3.

120. Ibid., 85, 89, 106-7.

121. Ibid., 98-9.

122. Ibid., 87, 102-3.

123. Ibid, 103.

124. Ibid., 108-9.

125. Ibid., 125-8.

126. Ibid., 129-30.

127. Ibid., 132-4.

128. Ibid., 130-1.

129. Ibid., 135-8.

130. Ibid., 137, 139-41; Robertson, et al., text accompanying Map 17.

131. Gray, 139-40, 147.

132. Robertson, et al., text accompanying Map 12.

133. Ibid., text accompanying Maps 13 and 14.

134. Ibid., text accompanying Maps 15 and 16. In actuality the village was already moving into the valley of the Little Big Horn about 30 miles to the northwest and the Sioux, far more aware of the sol•diers' location, had assembled a force of warriors to attack Crook before he got closer to their village. See Gray, 120.

135. Gray, 122.

136. Ibid., 190.

137. Ibid., 143-4,190

138. Ibid., 141.

139. Modern estimates are that the Indian village on the Little Bighorn had 1780 warriors. Custer's command, before it was divided, had 566 enlisted men. Gibbon's strength was roughly 400. Crook's force initially was about 662. Together or working in concert, these forces were, numerically, a match, for the Indians. But separately there were greatly outnumbered. See Gray, 47, 141, 357.

140. Chun, 76.

BATTLE COMMAND IN THE INDUSTRIAL AGE

"One seldom sees much on the modern battlefield."
—Major Glover Johns, World War II Infantry Battalion Commander[1]

World War I Battle Command

With the dawning of the Twentieth Century, armies were still organized and led not much differently from the days of the Civil War. Telegraph lines could assist in controlling slow moving operations or defensive lines, but were far less useful in fast moving campaigns. Technology was beginning to creep forward to facilitate the command and control of large forces over large areas in mobile operations. The first step in this was the development of the telephone, which, once an adequate portable version was fielded, would simplify com• munications by not requiring specially trained operators who had to translate Morse code into text. However, though handy the field telephone would operate under many of the same restrictions found with the telegraph. It too required the laying of delicate wire lines and the maintenance of such lines. Additionally, the telegraph was retained for many years because the early versions of the telephone had far shorter ranges and required more power than did the telegraph.

The biggest technological advance in relation to command and control was the develop• ment of wireless telegraphy or radio. The development of radio was slow at first and early versions were merely wireless versions of the Morse code telegraphs. Early radio was better suited for naval operations. Radio's impact for ground operations would not be felt until the refinement of the technology after World War I.[2]

The development of the airplane in the early Twentieth Century was another technology that would later on have a great impact on battle command, but during World War I its im• pact on battle command was minimal. In practical terms, its contribution to battle command was limited to allowing commanders at higher levels gain situational awareness through the use of aerial reconnaissance to discover the location of enemy forces.[3]

In addition to the airplane, the motorized vehicle also had applications to military battle command. By the eve of World War I, most armies had already established motor dispatch service. Those that did not have such means available at the start of the war soon adopted them. Motor dispatch services provided courier and message services through the use of automobiles, small trucks, or, more commonly, motorcycles, replacing, for the most part, the horse-bound couriers of earlier wars.[4]

But while communications technology was about to make command and control simpler, weapons technology was about to make it even more difficult by forcing armies to imple• ment new, harder to control techniques of tactical organization. Soon commanders would have increasing complications controlling even troops sharing the same battlefield space as themselves.

At the beginning of the war, advancements in weapons development, particularly artillery, had not been paralleled with a similar advancement in tactical and operational technique. Antiquated tactics were being used against industrial age weaponry. Until new organizational techniques were adopted and tested, the war sunk into the morass of trench warfare.

In trench warfare, the two sides faced each other with massed infantry armies dug into extensive systems of entrenchments. They were supported by machine guns, and indirect fire from concentrated artillery located safely in the rear. In its refined state, the commanders of trench warfare armies controlled their forces through the extensive use of field telephone systems. The field telephone had a range of between 15 and 25 miles. For longer ranges, up to hundreds of miles, armies used the telegraph.[5]

For example, in a typical American division in 1918, the signal battalion at the division headquarters strung wire down to each frontline battalion and between them, as well as to the intermediate brigade and regimental headquarters. Divisions had a large switchboard and bri•gades employed a slightly smaller version. Battalions ran wire out to their companies in the frontlines. A special wireless telephone technique, called earth telegraphy, was developed dur•ing the war. Earth telegraphy required a telegraph line to be set up along the ground parallel to the front line as an antenna. Once set up, any unit within two or three kilometers (roughly one to two miles) could patch into the telephone line simply by setting up their own wire 'antenna.' In attacks, advances or in rough terrain this precluded the requirement to string wire out all the way to the front. Unfortunately the enemy could also easily tap into the line and relatively easily disrupt the signal. Radio technology between the wars would ultimately make earth telegraphy obsolete.[6]

The primary importance of technological advances in communications in World War I was seen in the employment of field artillery. Before the development of the field telephone, artil•lery fire was difficult to control. It often had to be wheeled to where the force commander could control it and direct which targets for it to fire on via signals, couriers or personal contact. This usually brought the artillery up into range of both the enemy's small arms and artillery, making it very vulnerable and less effective. While technology had greatly improved artillery effectiveness, range and technique since the Civil War, it was not until the develop•ment of the field telephone that field artillery was able to dominate the battlefield. Use of the telephone enhanced the employment of artillery guns as indirect fire weapons, firing from positions behind the front lines with firing data computed based on the instructions of ob•servers linked to the batteries via telephone. This new communications means also allowed commanders to mass artillery fires and rapidly change fires. Since most artillery was not very mobile and required extensive ammunition stockpiles, these technological advances had the greatest effect on static defensive operations or attacks with limited objectives. Attempts at mobile operations were, therefore, often stopped for a lack of effective artillery support, or only employed artillery in their initial phases. Attacks forced to be paced by the movement of artillery barrages and subsequent movement of batteries, such as the 1916 British attack at the Somme, could hardly be considered mobile at all. And the same problems with the use of wire lines in any mobile operation also impacted on communications with the artillery, the support of which was essential to the success of such an operation. In addition to deploying and fighting his troops, battle commanders would now also have to contend with planning and executing indirect fire support.[7]

France 1914: Lack of Command and Control Defeats a German Mobile Operation

"An order which can be misunderstood, will be misunderstood."
—Old German General Staff Proverb.[8]

The most significant mobile campaign of World War I took place at the beginning of hostili‑ ties in August and September 1914, long before the American entry into the war. This cam‑ paign saw the large conscript armies of Germany and France, supported by a small contingent of British regulars and formerly neutral Belgians, face off in a war of movement that ended with a hasty retreat of the German right wing and a subsequent stalemated front in eastern France. A loss of battle command and control directly contributed to the German failure in this campaign.

By 1914 detailed staff planning had enhanced strategic mobility to a far greater level than was seen in the American Civil War. The railroad allowed commanders to move their forces rapidly to a theater of war or to mass forces in one place. However, once there the deployed forces operated again at the speed of the marching infantryman. However, those who marched faster, on an exposed flank and in concert with other similar units, were capable of executing mobile operations at this pace.

The German plan called for a massive wheeling of their right flank through Belgium against the French left flank, hopefully pushing it against the German left flank on the Franco-Ger‑ man frontier, thus defeating the French quickly so the Germans could then turn to face their other major enemy, the Russians.

For the World War I era, the German advance through Belgium into France was positively mobile and fast. The infantry advanced at an average pace of twelve miles a day. As the war began in August 1914, the German high command, the OHL (*die Oberste Heeresleitung)* directly controlled the German field forces, which consisted of seven armies in the west and one army in the east. Though the Kaiser (Wilhelm II) was present, the OHL was in actuality led by the German Army's chief of staff, *Generaloberst* Helmuth Count von Moltke.[9] Von Moltke personally directed the actions of the eight armies from his headquarters initially at Koblenz, then later at the city of Luxembourg, primarily through the use of the telephone. With this headquarters ultimately located 150 miles from its farthest deployed army in the west, effective command and control of such a large force would be problematic at best and depended on communications technology rather than command technique.[10]

While the field forces remained within the boundaries of Germany, they were able to use the excellent German civil telephone system. However, once deployed outside of Germany in

Belgium and France, the advancing armies depended on new lines strung up from the forward units back to their bases in Germany and into the OHL line. While most armies employed the telephone for short-range communications (15-25 miles), and the telegraph for longer ranges; the Germans abandoned the telegraph altogether in 1910, preferring to depend on a combina‑ tion of radio and telephones.[11]

Radio and telephone technology was still in relative infancy in World War I. To expect to use it as the primary means of command and control over a mass army conducting what was anticipated to be the nation's decisive military campaign in the war was wishful thinking at best. Nevertheless, this is exactly what the Germans did. The telephone, when using lines just strung, as those of an advancing army in a foreign country, had a much more limited range than when used on a permanent line. Radio sets were large and limited in frequencies so that often different models could not even communicate with each other.[12]

In August 1914 the Germans had deployed one large Telefunken 2-kilowatt model radio to OHL and one to each army headquarters. The Telefunken, under optimal conditions, had a range of between 150 and 180 miles. Additionally, each army headquarters also had a Poulsen large radio set, which was used for armies to talk to each other. Two smaller model Telefunk‑ en sets, with ranges of about 40 miles, were provided to each cavalry division in the Army. These divisions were also provided with one or two of the larger Telefunken sets. Except for the cavalry divisions, below army level there were no radio sets. Corps and subordinate units were expected to rely on the telephone. There was also no redundancy as the headquarters usually only had one set. If it broke, there was no back up.[13]

This was the communications background to the mobile campaign the Germans intended to conduct in August 1914. The Germans massed the preponderance of their forces (44 infan‑ try divisions in the four armies of their right flank) on the Allied left to envelop the French by marching through formerly neutral Belgium, opposed initially only by the Belgians' six divisions. The Germans hoped to use a combination of their soldiers' swift marching and the coordinated action of their armies to get around and behind the Allied forces and pin them against the German left flank in a large wheeling envelopment operation.

To coordinate this operation, the German high command controlled the army headquarters directly, using telephone lines of semi-permanent standard construction built by signal troops from the armies, and radios. The armies themselves controlled large forces as well, between three and seven army corps, each of two infantry divisions. Army commanders controlled these corps via personal contact and temporary field telephone lines laid down by signal troops assigned to the corps. Corps controlled their divisions principally through personal contact, though sometimes the corps laid telephone lines to the divisions.[14] In 1914, corps were expected to usually fight as single units on narrow fronts allowing the corps commander to control his force without the need for telephones.

For their mobile campaign, the Germans planned on using a standardized command and control procedure developed in prewar maneuvers. Every evening commanders at each level held staff conferences to plan the next day's operations. Liaison officers from the subordinate

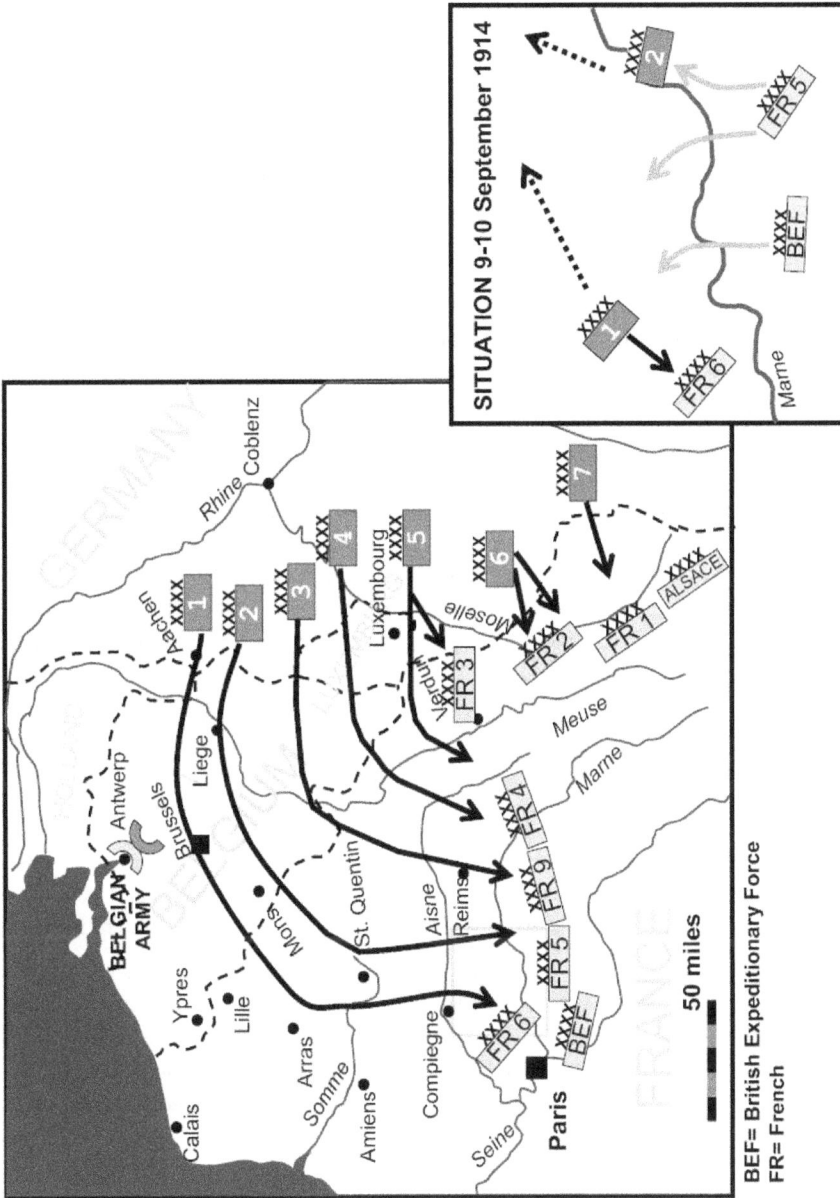

Figure 13. German advance to the Marne, August-September 1914.

SITUATION 9-10 September 1914

BEF= British Expeditionary Force
FR= French

50 miles

79

units received the commander's intent or concept for the next day then returned to their own commands where, at their own conferences, warning orders for the next day could be issued to subordinate units. Formal orders were typically prepared after these conferences and sent to the units via mounted messenger or, preferably, dictated over the telephone. But as the campaign progressed, the system of regular daily staff conferences soon broke down. The radio, down to army level, and the telephone was forced to fill the void.[15]

As the German forces advanced, the infantry averaged a pace of about twelve miles a day. But the signal troops stringing the telephone lines could not keep up, averaging between five and six and a half miles a day. Whenever an army got two days march ahead of the end of its semi-permanent wire lines and had to depend on temporary wire lines, there was great difficulty communicating via telephone. By 23 August, just six days after the commencement of the German advance, the radio had become the primary means of rapid communication between the OHL and the armies, and between neighboring armies. But even by the 23d the great wheel the Germans had set in motion had placed their far right army, the First, at the edge of radio range limitations, forcing time-consuming message relays. Additionally, the small number of sets and the need to encrypt transmissions also slowed radio transmissions.[16]

The sheer bulk of radio transmissions allowed the French to intercept the messages and over time break the code. This led to German intentions being known to their enemies ahead of time. On 31 August as the German First and Second Armies advanced towards the Marne, the Germans planned to exploit a large gap in the Allied line between the French and British. The OHL, via radio, ordered a cavalry corps to attack and raid through the gap. But, tipped off by the radio transmission, the Allies were ready and completely defeated the raid, which had had great promise of disrupting the French retreat.[17]

As the telephone before it, the radio system was failing the Germans. Routine situation reports took up to 26 hours to reach OHL. Time delays allowed situation reports to pass in transmission orders which timely receipt of the reports would have made obsolete. And this would directly affect German operations.[18]

Reporting difficulties had already made von Moltke think the Germans were more success-ful in the late August Battle of the Frontiers than they had been, so that he had felt free to reduce the troops on the right flank by two corps, dispatching the corps to the eastern front where the Russians were advancing.[19]

A series of time-delayed reports and orders from von Moltke resulted in confusion on the German left wing at the end of August and on into September 1914. In response to these diffi-culties, von Moltke had temporarily placed the First Army under control of the Second Army and later sent out one of his staff officers to act as his on-site representative with the various army commanders.[20]

As the Germans stumbled for command and control, the French and British regrouped and reorganized. General Joseph Joffre, the French commander, shifted forces to his left wing to cover Paris, support the small British Expeditionary Force, and to stop the seemingly relentless German advance.[21] On 28 August Joffre counterattacked with his Fifth Army against the German Second Army near Saint Quentin. Although this unexpected maneuver was repulsed, Joffre's action changed the whole situation on the German right, causing decisions and actions to swiftly outpace the delivery of reports and orders and, essentially, forced each German army to act on its own rather than as cogs in a machine executing a larger mission. And these piecemeal actions then gave the French and British the opportunity to act in unison themselves and stop the German advance.[22]

While the German Second Army had repulsed the French at Saint Quentin, the army commander, *Generaloberst* Karl von Bülow had been forced to stop and take up a temporary defensive posture. Meanwhile to von Bülow's right (west) the First Army, under *Generaloberst* Alexander von Kluck was under orders to drive west of Paris. Von Bülow, however, wanted von Kluck to move away from Paris to the east and support his attack on the French Fifth Army, both to provide security in that direction and to overwhelm what the German generals felt was the French left flank. Von Kluck, unable to get timely instructions from von Moltke, and having earlier been placed temporarily under von Bülow's command, decided to cooperate with von Bülow. Therefore on his own initiative he turned the First Army away from Paris, moving to the southeast instead of to the south on 31 August. Unfortunately, von Bülow remained in position for a day after his fight with the French, allowing von Kluck to get a day's march in front of him. Von Kluck's First Army was now exposed on both flanks, in the west by the reinforced garrison of Paris (the redeployed French Sixth Army) and in the east by a 15-20 mile gap developing between his advancing forces and von Bülow's a day behind. Into this mix, finally, orders were received from von Moltke on the evening of 2 September. Over 150 miles removed from his right flank forces with his headquarters freshly relocated from Koblenz to Luxembourg city, von Moltke interpreted von Bülow's battle as the indicator that the Allies had been defeated and the Germans should now go into pursuit mode before their enemies could slip away. Accordingly, new orders indicated the First and Second Armies should advance to the south. Von Kluck himself was to fall back a little behind the Second Army to provide it a flank guard against the French forces forming near Paris.[23]

Ironically, the Germans championed 'mission-type' orders (*Auftragstaktik*), in which orders were given as general guidelines and the commanders in the field were expected to use their own judgment based on the general intent of their superiors. However, when lacking even minimal guidelines, or timely updates of the commander's intent, the *Auftragstaktik* system broke down.[24] The German army commanders tended to sub-optimize their own missions, each fighting their own separate battles without any overriding authority looking at the picture as a whole. Accordingly, the armies in the center all attacked the French forces in front of them, fighting unnecessary bloody battles when, if the right flank armies did their job according to the plan, the French opposite the center would have been caught in the encirclement anyway.[25]

Von Kluck evaluated the situation against his new orders, which he received late on 2 September. He was advancing to the south east supporting and a day's march farther south than his neighboring army, the Second. His new orders were to fall back and hold a flank guard, while changing direction to due south. Uninformed by von Moltke of the French build-up around Paris, the First Army commander chose to continue southeast towards the Marne River with three corps, leaving two corps and his cavalry to cover his flank facing Paris. Von Kluck figured only his forces were in the right place and at the right time to envelop the French left flank.[26]

Von Moltke had lost control of his forces. Von Kluck's report on his movements took over a day to reach OHL. Von Moltke's two right armies were separated by a 20-mile gap between them and the rightmost (von Kluck's) was exposing its flank to a large body of French forces in Paris. Von Moltke radioed instructions for both armies to immediately stop moving to the south and to face west towards Paris while the armies of the center tried to execute a smaller encirclement. This order took about eleven hours to reach the field. With his communications too slow, von Moltke was forced to find another expedient: dispatching a senior general staff officer to personally issue the order and gain an estimate of the situation at the front. The officer he sent, Lieutenant Colonel Richard Hentsch, his intelligence section chief, made two tours of various army headquarters, the first on 5 September, the second on 8/9 September.[27]

During the first of his visits, Hentsch explained the overall situation to von Kluck. Von Moltke had given Hentsch instructions to get the First Army to fall back to the north across the Marne. Von Kluck agreed to withdraw his command to the northwest over the course of the next several days to cover the flank from the German forces in Paris. While conferring with Hentsch, one of the corps (IV Reserve Corps) that von Kluck had placed on his flank ended up in a fight with the French Paris forces. The aggressive German corps commander, *General der Artillerie* Hans von Gronau, attacked and soon discovered he was facing far larger forces. Von Kluck sent the second corps not committed to the south in that direction, while leaving the bulk of his army still facing southeast across the Marne. Eventually he had to dispatch a third corps as well. Therefore, on 6 September the German First Army was fac• ing both west on the River Ourcq against the French Sixth Army out of Paris and south on the Marne facing the British Expeditionary Force.[28]

The French had planned their counteroffensive for 6 September. The Germans soon learned this through a captured order. Remarkably enough, von Kluck, now aware of the size of the French forces to his west, chose to redeploy his army along the Ourcq to defeat them, leaving only security forces to his southern front. He believed he could take this risk because he mis• takenly felt that the British commander seemed unwilling to fight. But Joffre had met with the British and planned a coordinated attack against the German right wing. The Allied attack de• veloped slowly, allowing von Kluck to have virtually his whole army facing the French Sixth Army on the 8th when the force of the Allied attack became apparent. While von Kluck's small cavalry-infantry security force held off the British initially, his movements along with those of von Bülow had created a huge 30-mile gap between their armies.[29]

By the 8th the French counteroffensive had tied down von Bülow's command. Meanwhile, with his army massed, von Kluck was beating the French and was fully capable of pushing them out of Paris. Neither army commander, however, was in a position to do anything about the gap. And on the 8th and 9th, the French and British found the gap and started moving through it.[30]

At this point, Hentsch was making his second tour of the headquarters of the armies. He was tasked with determining the situation at each army and had been given the authority to coordinate the actions of the armies for the OHL.[31]

The French Fifth Army, now under a new, more daring commander, attacked into the evening of the 8th against von Bülow's right flank through the gap. Though the Germans were hardly defeated, the ever cautious Second Army commander decided his flank was unsecured and he ordered a short retreat which effectively widened the gap with the First Army an additional ten miles.[32]

Nevertheless, von Kluck felt he had the French beaten in front of Paris and presumed their defeat would result in a German envelopment of the Allied northern wing, thereby making developments along the Marne moot. His security force under *Generalmajor* Georg von der Martwitz, though now opposed by both French and British troops, was holding its own. Accordingly, von Kluck planned to continue his attack on the 9th. To him "victory on the decisive wing seemed certain."[33]

But to von Kluck's east, von Bülow had ordered on the 9th that his Second Army retreat northeast to the line of the Aisne River. Unless he was successful quickly, this maneuver would place von Kluck out on a limb. And there was no way for the two-army commanders to communicate to effectively coordinate their activities. When the OHL representative, Hentsch, arrived at von Kluck's headquarters, this relatively junior staff officer took up this role himself, effectively coordinating the actions of all the German right wing armies by ordering a retreat to a line generally along the Aisne. Hentsch never talked to von Kluck, who was not at his headquarters at the time, issuing the new orders to his chief of staff, *Generalmajor* Hermann von Kuhl, instead. While, under the precepts of *Auftragstaktik,* von Kluck did not feel bound to necessarily follow the instructions of the high command's representative if he felt the situation boded well for a great success. With the other armies, particularly the Second, falling back he realized that even with success his army would be isolated. Accordingly, he ordered an immediate northerly retreat to the Aisne on the afternoon of the 9th. On 10 September, von Moltke again placed von Kluck under the orders of Second Army's von Bülow.[34]

After the fact, von Moltke approved all decisions made both by his army commanders and by his representative Hentsch during periods in which he did not have direct control over his forces. The decisive decisions of the campaign had been made not by the force commander, but either by his subordinates or by his emissary, a relatively junior officer. Von Moltke was soon replaced and the Western Front sank into a stalemated war of competing systems of entrenchments.[35]

After the failure of this campaign, the Germans revamped their communications systems, reintroduced the telegraph, established a motor dispatch service, and added a new echelon of command, the army group.[36] In a smaller campaign concurrent with the actions in France, a single German army showed what command and control could accomplish against a larger force. At Tannenberg, the German Eighth Army held off one Russian army and adroitly redeployed to envelop and destroy another. Here the Germans were greatly helped by poor Russian command and control, which included the sending of radio messages in the clear.[37]

Von Moltke failed to properly execute his battle command in a campaign he expected to be mobile because he himself remained immobile and depended on weak communications tech•nology without any realistic redundancy. While the technical aspects failed him, so too did organizational technique, which in past mobile campaigns had often managed to make up for a lack of technology. Von Moltke's span of control was too great, directly controlling seven field armies in the west and an additional one in the east. It was unrealistic to expect to be able to control so many subordinates, most of whom were in battle daily and pulling farther away from the immobile higher headquarters, even if the communications were better. He was forced to fall back on the individual initiative of his subordinate commanders. Without an overall commander available to coordinate and settle disputes, conflicts in intent like those between the impetuous von Kluck and the cautious von Bülow would end up in each going their own way and the overall operation becoming a *fait accompli* rather than the will of the commander.

Development of New Style Infantry Tactics

In the midst of trench warfare, the Germans reflected on the causes and effects of the stalemate and then developed an organizational technique to overcome the lethality of entrenched defenders employing industrial age weapons. Essentially what they ultimately called infiltration tactics were open order infantry tactics long employed by the skirmishers placed out if front of units by all armies to provide security and forces to cover large fronts with few troops. Instead of fighting in closely compacted lines, these skirmishers fought in small groups, spread out, and used the terrain for cover and concealment and shifted around the battlefield as necessary, ultimately withdrawing back into the main body. The German solution to the failure of the attack was to apply such tactics to offensive actions, and, because even successful defensive actions were casualty-intensive, to defensive operations as well.

The modern lethality of the defender should have come as no surprise to the Germans, or the later success of infiltration tactics. The prowess of the defense was clearly illustrated as early as the 1864-65 Overland, Petersburg and Atlanta campaigns in the American Civil War. The Germans themselves had similar experiences in the 1870 Franco-Prussian War, where French firepower had decimated dense Prussian formations.[38]

In these previous wars, the firepower of infantry small arms halted offensive action. In 1914 this happened again, even though both sides initially only deployed a relatively small number of machine guns, forcing defenders to entrench. Entrenched defenders, now supported by bar•riers, obstacles, increased machine guns and indirect firing artillery, made even the simplest of attacks like assaulting a medieval fortress.[39]

Ironically, while the Germans had emphasized mission-type orders and initiative at their higher levels, and expected an amount of independence in its officer corps, there was a certain amount of ambivalence about applying open tactics to infantry attacks, as fears of commanders losing command and control over units up to battalion size (which would be extended over almost 3000 meters) overrode fear of excessive casualties. Accordingly German drill regulations in the 1880s reversed post-Franco-Prussian War innovations with a return to close formations, where a company commander could still verbally and visually control a company of over 250 men. However, after the 1899-1902 Boer War and the 1904-5 Russo-Japanese War, in both of which closed up formations suffered from modern weapons, the German drill regulations accommodated the possibility that units might have to spread out and smaller units might have to fight without being under the direct personal control of their commanders.[40]

This flexibility in drill meant that in 1914 some German infantry fought closed up, while others fought in more open formations. Those that fought closed suffered heavy casualties, while those who fought open, far fewer, even within the same unit fighting the same defender.[41] The Germans responded to their early war experiences. Accordingly, official bulletins issued in October 1914 adopted the open tactics as German doctrine. With the adoption of these new tactics, small squad-sized units led by noncommissioned officers (NCOs), with soldiers spread 2-3 meters apart and firing at will rather than as a whole platoon or company became the norm. The feared loss of control did not happen as the NCOs proved to be up to the task and the increased survivability of the soldiers decreased panic. The smaller German units were also better able to support each other, with one unit providing covering fire as another moved forward to advanced positions. This smaller unit flexibility also allowed the Germans to develop the tactic of enveloping or outflanking their enemy, an operational favorite German move now adopted at the tactical level.[42]

As the war progressed, the Germans continued to innovate in ways that increased the complexity of command and control at lower levels, while also increasing the flexibility and survivability of their forces. As with the offensive, the Germans were soon dissatisfied with their way of doing things. While there were great advantages to being on the defensive, massive artillery barrages, upon which all infantry attacks of the period 1915-16 were based, could equally decimate the defender, particularly if he inflexibly chose to defend every inch of front tenaciously. Here too, dense formations proved to be a flaw and by 1917 the Germans had reorganized their entire defensive posture. The new defense, much like the open order offensive, was flexible and relied on depth and firepower to defeat attackers rather than mere masses of soldiers. Relatively few troops held the front-most positions which would be most exposed to the fury of the enemy artillery, and the attackers would have to face several successive defensive positions rather than one main line. Forward lines would shift to escape artillery fire and create strongpoints built around machine guns that would then hinder the attacker's advance. Once the attack was spent, the Germans would counterattack using their open order tactics.[43]

As in the attack, the infantry squad became a key level of tactics. As the war progressed, the squad was rebuilt around the light machine gun, with one team being the machine gun crew, the other essentially providing security for it.[44] Fire and maneuver, formerly conducted at levels as high as battalion, was now executed at the lowest possible level—infantry platoon and sometimes squad.[45]

Towards the later years of World War I, the Germans synthesized their new doctrine for attack and defense with the specialized use of artillery and created an operational level version of their new offensive tactics that became referred to generally as infiltration, or stormtroop tactics. Starting late in 1917, the Germans conducted a series of successful offensives using these new assault tactics. The essence of the new tactics were the employment of specially trained assault troops (stormtroopers) equipped lavishly with light machine guns and supported by flamethrowers and their own pocket artillery to spearhead the assault, followed by conventional infantry. The attack was conducted in depth with advance elements probing the enemy defenses, followed by the specialized assault troops who would sweep between nests of resistance and either bypass them or attack them from the side or rear. Bypassed positions would be later attacked by the follow-on troops, as the assault troops were to try to get as deep into the defender's position as possible. Massed aircraft would strafe the defenders while the artillery would fire a much shorter preparatory fire synchronized with the infantry advance, which would also shift forward ahead of the advancing troops.[46]

Such tactics were fraught with possible command and control problems. In the past, commanders had directly controlled their units. But now success depended on the initiative and aggressiveness of leaders down to the lowest level, and sometimes on that of the individual soldier. Commanders would not normally be nearby to bark orders or to provide continual guidance. The soldiers, particularly the junior leaders, had to understand what was expected of them and act almost automatically in accordance with this overall intent. In the past, such dependence on orders stressing mission over details and the initiative of subordinates was usually the hallmark of a campaign of multiple columns, such as most of those of Napoleon, but this decentralization did not normally go below the operational (corps and, by 1914, division) level. However, with the new lethality of industrial age weaponry, battlefield survival necessitated just such decentralization down to the lowest levels. So, as a twist of historical irony, just when communications technology in the form of the portable radio was presenting military commanders with the ability to talk with their subordinates over distances, weapons technology was making it more difficult to control units that in the past had been relatively easy to control.[47]

While successful at the tactical and sometimes briefly at the operational level, the German use of infiltration tactics was ultimately unsuccessful. The defenders were always capable of building up new defensive lines either by redeploying troops via railroads or motor vehicle while the German attackers became exhausted. Once exhausted and facing fresh defenders, the German attack halted. By 1918 the Germans did not have enough fresh troops to commit to overcome the ability of the Allies to place reinforcements in front of their exhausted attackers.[48]

86

Despite the ultimate failure of German innovation in World War I, the importance of their experience and that of the other participants is that modern infantry techniques and organiza- tion spring from it, including the complexities of commanding and controlling so many small, independently operating cogs. Initially commanders controlled such formations through a combination of messengers (often now called runners) and field telephones. Variations of the small unit fire and maneuver tactics first used by the Germans in 1914 were eventually ad- opted by all major nations including the United States, mostly via the process of reorganizing small infantry units with automatic weapons.

For the US Army, the World War I experience led to a major organizational restructuring that affected command and control. This was the gradual replacement of the battalion with the company as the basic element of maneuver and the battalion becoming the lowest echelon capable of providing all but the most light fire support. Such a shift necessitated the battalion commander to coordinate the support rather than personally lead the advance.[49] While most armies provided their infantry squads or sections with light machine guns, the United States provided its squads with an automatic rifle, the Browning Automatic Rifle (BAR) instead. However, the US infantryman was equipped upon its entrance into battle in World War II with a semi-automatic rifle, the M1 Garand, which gave each individual a superior level of fire- power to both Allied and Axis troops.[50]

World War II and Korean War Infantry Battle Command

After World War I the development of motorized and mechanized vehicles and, to some extent, aircraft, dominated mobile operations. However, to a lesser extent, forces dependent primarily on foot soldiers were still able to conduct battle command on the move at a pace su- perior to that of previous armies because of the development of the radio and field telephone.

Even with the addition of reliable portable radios, World War II and Korean War infantry battle command still greatly resembled that of the last stages of World War I. Of course infan- try commanders in these later wars could expect much better tank, artillery, and air support. But, essentially, the field telephone or, if necessary, the portable radio provided communica- tions between elements, particularly from company level on up. The field phone was even used in the offensive, at least until enemy action or the pace of the advance cut the lines.[51]

In World War II, US infantry commanders used a combination of wire, radio, runners, and personal contact to control their units. While wire was the primary means and each echelon of command down to battalion-level had assigned signal personnel to lay wire, artillery fire and other enemy action often cut the wire lines. A shortage of wiremen and signalmen in general at regimental and battalion levels also hindered the laying and maintenance of wire lines.[52] Units usually ran two telephone networks controlled by a small switchboard and operator. The command line, which included all subordinate units and the switchboard of the higher headquarters, and a separate line for the artillery, which connected the artillery forward observers with the battalion field artillery liaison officer and with the fire direction center of the supporting artillery unit.[53] Technology had even improved the field telephone. The Army developed and deployed a field telephone that was powered by sound rather than batteries. Such a piece of equipment, though of relatively short range, was reliable and ideal for use in the conditions of frontline service.[54]

The drawbacks of wire, particularly in offensive operations, added to the importance of newly developed portable radios to the infantry. The US Army pioneered the use of FM frequencies in addition to the AM frequencies used exclusively by all the other major com•batants. FM, invented by an American in 1936, provided a virtually static-free radio medium capable of providing numerous frequencies and minimal skipping of those frequencies. Although FM sets could theoretically range up to 25 miles, since they required line of sight to be effective, the actual range in the field was closer to three miles or less. This made their use ideal for small units only having to communicate relatively short distances. For use in World War II, the Signal Corps developed a series of tactical radios. The SCR 300, the famous "walkie-talkie" was a 32-pound backpack radio used primarily for companies to com•municate with battalions and battalions with regiments. To make the radio portable, it was equipped with a newly developed dry cell battery. In the field it had a practical range of about five miles. At the company level, AM was still used as the company commander communi•cated with his platoon leaders via a small handheld AM radio, the SCR 536 "handie-talkie" with its one mile range. Portable FM radios also became the primary means of communica•tion between the field artillery and the units they supported.[55]

Even with good communications, in rough terrain like the Normandy hedgerows, parts of units could get lost in the new style dispersed tactical movements. In one documented in•stance, for example, a battalion lost contact with several squads in one of its lead companies, contact only being reestablished when the company commander personally found the miss•ing units.[56] In another, a division lost contact with a whole regiment that was located across a patch of rough terrain from the rest of the division. The division commander had to pass through a contested sector to personally regain control of the regiment. He sacked the regi•mental commander.[57] Such instances of loss of control of small units would have been virtu•ally impossible when using the linear tactics common as late as 1918.

A good example of US Army World War II and Korean War era infantry battle command at the battalion level can be found in the memoirs of (then) Major Glover S. Johns, Jr. Johns commanded the 1st Battalion, 115th Infantry, 29th Infantry Division, in the June-July 1944 Normandy campaign, fighting offensive and defensive actions against elite German para•troopers north of the city of St. Lo. Johns organized his command with a rear command post under his executive officer (XO) or second-in-command, or headquarters company com•mander, which stayed behind the lines with the battalion supply sergeants and cooks, and other support personnel. Johns himself was up front with a relatively small forward command post (CP) consisting of himself; the battalion operations officer (S3); battalion intelligence officer (S2); the heavy weapons company commander; his field artillery liaison officer; an or•derly; several runners supplied by the companies; two radio operators (one for battalion radio net, other for the regimental net); and the battalion's wire section, which was responsible for laying and maintaining telephone lines from where the regiment line ended down to any ad•

vanced CP locations and to the companies.[58] The battalion reserve company, if there was one, stayed near the forward CP to provide security for it and to allow it to be ordered into action immediately, which Johns in fact did several times.[59]

The battalion command post, though allocated a small tent, was more typically located in a dugout position with overhead cover, several chairs, a small table and the sleeping rolls of the command group. Johns informally organized his CP into a first and second team. The first team consisted of himself, the battalion S3 and the artillery liaison officer. The backup team consisted of the battalion executive officer, the battalion S2 and the artillery liaison noncom‐missioned officer (NCO). The two teams would sleep apart and be prepared to take over operations immediately, providing needed continuity. When Johns had to issue combat orders or instructions to the battalion as a whole, he assembled an orders group, either at the forward CP or on a prominent piece of terrain overlooking the area of the projected operation. The orders group consisted of the battalion commander, S3, the company commanders and the artillery liaison officer.[60]

While Johns commanded through a combination of personal contact, runners, wire and radio, his higher headquarters, the regiment, generally controlled operations through wire and radio communications and an intense demand for immediate situation reports and map overlays showing the most current positions of Johns' subordinate companies. The regiment posted the overlay onto a situation map maintained by the regimental S3. During mobile operations, the S3 kept this map wrapped in a blanket in his jeep. After receiving overlays from all the subordinate battalions, the regimental S3 made a consolidated copy that was then forwarded to the division operations section (G3).[61]

Despite his efforts at positive command and control, during at least one German night coun‐terattack, Johns lost communications and effective control of his subordinate units. German scouts had apparently cut his wire communications and radio communications was limited as the Germans timed their attack to maximize the time between routine American radio checks with the artillery. Even with communications weak but intact, Johns had a difficult time controlling his battalion as his CP group came under direct attack from Germans who had overrun one of his companies. The battalion recovered sufficiently to immediately execute a previously planned attack the next morning.[62]

To augment the division's wire and radio communications, in Normandy the 29th Infantry Division commander had set up a pool of officers to act as personal liaison assistants. These he sent out to be his eyes and ears and to send messages directly to the regimental or battalion commanders, much like aides de camp had been employed in a less technological era.[63]

Until the advent of the helicopter in the late 1950s, infantry mobility and battle command was almost exclusively left at the pace of the foot soldier on the ground, much as it had been since antiquity. Such a pace minimized battle command difficulties, especially in the age of the portable radio receiver-transmitter and field telephone.

Summary

Modern battle command on the move begins with the 1914 Marne campaign in France. The Germans were ultimately unsuccessful in that campaign because the German field command‧ er, Von Moltke, lost command and control of his forces at key moments, primarily due to Ger‧ man failure to understand the weaknesses of contemporary communications technology. In a twist of historic irony, while technology was devising new means of communications which could, theoretically, greatly facilitate battle command of moving forces, the same technology also created more lethal weaponry which, in turn, resulted in the adoption of more open tacti‧ cal formations which were inherently harder to control. Offensive and defensive formations and systems adopted by the Germans were soon universalized, with infantry tactics in both World War II and the Korean War resembling tactics used by the Germans in the latter years of World War I. The addition and improvement of field telephone systems and portable radios enhanced command and control, particularly of stationary units or those operating on narrow frontages. Command and control, even of units as small as a battalion, still remained at times problematic in World War II, where commanders had to rely on a combination of personal contact, runners, field telephones and radios to keep in contact with subordinates, adjacent units and higher headquarters. Nevertheless, as long as infantry mobile operations moved at the pace of a marching soldier, battle command difficulties, even when the unit was in mo‧ tion, were relatively minimal.

Notes

1. Glover S. Johns, Jr., *The Clay Pigeons of St. Lo* (New York: Bantam, 1985), 2.

2. Raines, 172.

3. At the Battle of the Marne in 1914, Allied airplanes were instrumental in discovering a gap between the German armies. See Daniel David, *The 1914 Campaign: August-October, 1914*, The Great Campaigns of History (New York: Military Press, 1987), 149.

4. Paul W. Evans, "Strategic Signal Communication—A Study of Signal Communication as applied to Large Field Forces, Based on the Operations of the German Signal Corps During the March on Paris in 1914," *Signal Bulletin* 82 (January-February 1935), 27, 32, 54.

5. Ibid., 180.

6. Ibid., 185; A.E. Kennelly, "Advances in Signalling Contributed During the War" in *The New World of Science: Its Development During the War*, Robert M. Yerkes, ed (New York: Century Co, 1920), 243.

7. Jonathan B.A. Bailey, *Field Artillery and Firepower* (Annapolis, Naval Institute Press, 2004), 227, 243, 268-9.

8. Bradley John Meyer, "Operational Art and the German Command System in World War I" (PhD diss., Ohio State University, 1988), 146.

9. Timothy T. Lupfer, *The Dynamics of Doctrine: The Changes in German Tactical Doctrine During the First World War*, Leavenworth Paper No. 4 (Fort Leavenworth: Combat Studies Institute, 1981), vii, 2.

10. Van Creveld, 154; for various reasons concerned with the existing communications networks and the presence of the Kaiser, von Moltke chose not to move the OHL headquarters during the campaign. For legalistic reasons (technically he only gave orders through the emperor), von Moltke did not feel he could leave his sovereign at OHL and travel to the army headquarters himself. See Meyer, 138.

11. Evans, 33-4, 41.

12. Ibid., 33-4; Meyer, 135-6.

13. Evans, 34-5.

14. Ibid., 38.

15. Ibid., 46-7.

16. Ibid., 47-50; Meyer,135-7. The German troops on the outer edge of the advance, i.e. the First Army, marched up to 30 miles a day. See William R. Griffiths, *The Great War*, West Point Military History Series (Wayne, NJ: Avery, 1986), 31.

17. Evans, 52.

18. Ibid.

19. Griffiths, 33.

20. Ibid., 25, 31, 35-7.

21. Ibid, 33-4.

22. Van Creveld, 154-5.

23. Meyer, 141; Griffiths, 34-5; Van Creveld, 154.

24. Meyer, 144-5.

25. Van Creveld, 154-5; Griffiths, 35; Bruce I. Gudmundsson, *Stormtroop Tactics: Innovation in the German Army 1914-1918 (*New York: Praeger, 1989), 32, 40.

26. Meyer, 144-5; Griffiths, 34-5.

27. Meyer, 145, 150-1, 156; Griffiths, 35.

28. Meyer, 156-62; Griffiths, 35-6.

29. Meyer, 162-3.

30. Meyer, 169, 186, 189, 196-7; Griffiths, 36-7.

31. Meyer, 171, 173, 185.

32. Alexander von Kluck, *The March on Paris and the Battle of the Marne, 1914* (New York: Longmans, Green and Co., 1920), 137; Meyer, 197.

33. Von Kluck, 131-2, 134, 137. The French before Paris were, in fact, planning to retreat. See Von Kluck, 139.

34. Ibid., 137-8, 140-1; Evans, 53-4; Meyer, 199-200, 214-5, 217-8.

35. Meyer, 252-3, 255-6. Meyer contends that the German command system unwittingly worked because Hentsch's decision mirrored the exact decision von Moltke desired at the same time.

36. Evans, 54; Lupfer, 9.

37. Van Creveld, 155.

38. Gudmundsson, 7-8. The initially highly successful attack of Hancock's corps against the Confed•erates on 12 May 1864 at Spotsylvania, using a variation of skirmisher tactics developed by Colonel Emory Upton, showed a way to defeat a dug in defender, although after the penetration, command and control was utterly lost.

39. Bailey, 243.

40. Gudmundsson, 8, 19, 21-2.

41. Ibid., 23-4.

42. Ibid., 24-5.

43. Lupfer, 4, 7, 11-15.

44. Ibid, 20, 27.

45. Virgil Ney, *Evolution of the US Army Infantry Battalion 1939-1968*, CORG Memorandum CORG-M-343 (Fort Belvoir, VA: Combat Operations Research Group, 1968), 8; Gudmundsson, 100-2.

46. Lupfer, 40-2; Gudmundsson, 80, 113.

47. Gudmundsson, 18, 40, 101-2, 173.

48. Ibid., 177-8.

49. Ney, 8.

50. Ibid., 9, 13. The light machine gun was found in the company's weapons platoon.

51. Robert S. Rush, *Hell in the Hürtgen Forest: The Ordeal of an American Infantry Regiment* (Lawrence, KS: University Press of Kansas, 2001), 253-5; Glover S. Johns Jr., *The Clay Pigeons of St. Lo,* (New York: Bantam, 1985), 13.

52. The General Board, United States Forces, European Theater. *Organization, Equipment and Tactical Employment of the Infantry Division,* Study Number 15, 1945, 4-5, 7 (hereafter referred to as General Board, Infantry Division).

53. Johns, 46, 116.

54. George R. Thompson and Dixie R. Harrison, *The Signal Corps: The Outcome (Mid 1943 through 1945)*, The United States Army in World War II: The Technical Services, (Washington, DC: Office of the Chief of Military History, 1966), 634.

55. Karl G. Larew, "Signaling the American Blitzkrieg." Unpublished manuscript. Copy at Office of the Command Historian, U.S. Army Signal Center, Fort Gordon, GA., 9-11; Rush, 157; Johns, 29; Thompson and Harrison, 222-3, 638; Joseph Balkoski, *Beyond the Bridgehead: The 29th Infantry Division in Normandy* (Harrisburg, PA: Stackpole, 1989), 106-8.

56. Johns, 32-33; Ney, 49.

57. Ibid., 53, 62; Balkoski, 186-7; 195-6.

58. The weapons company consisted of six 81mm mortars, eight .30 caliber heavy machine guns, one M3 .50 caliber heavy machine gun and six 'Bazooka' antitank rock launchers. See Ney, 14, 73.

59. Johns, 3, 8, 12. On one occasion when he employed his reserve company to outflank German paratroopers holding up the advance of another company, Johns forgot to tell the other company, causing him to fear that the companies would shoot at each other or that the stationary company, thinking itself being enveloped, would stop its advance. Johns had to use runners and personal contact to regain control.

60. Johns, 44, 46-7, 74. Johns used soldiers from the Ammunition and Pioneer Platoon found in his battalion Headquarters Company to prepare his command post position.

61. Johns, 37-8.

62. Ibid., 116-7, 125-7.

63. Ibid., 53-4.

ARMORED AND AIRBORNE MOBILE OPERATIONS
BATTLE COMMAND 1939-45

"...I don't want to have anything to do with you people. You move too fast for me."
—*Generaloberst* Ludwig Beck, German Chief of Staff, 1935-8.[1]

Blitzkrieg Command and Control—German Theory and Practice for Command of Mobile Units Conducting Mobile Operations

In 1918 the Germans had been unable to maintain the momentum of their infiltration tactics attacks once their assault troops became exhausted and the Allies had managed to move forward fresh troops to plug the holes created by the attack. What was needed was a means of attacking faster than the pace of the infantry, comparable to the speed at which the defender could reinforce by railroad or truck. The solution was the addition of the tank (and supporting armored vehicles), and the radio to the infiltration tactics technique. The result was the mobile blitzkrieg style of warfare seen in World War II and further developed later into modern combined arms mechanized operations.

The Allies had developed the tank as their technological solution to the trench warfare deadlock in World War I. However, when used in a purely infantry support role, the tank, as demonstrated at the November 1917 battle of Cambrai, could be overcome by counterat-tacking infantry employing infiltration tactics.[2]

Though the ultimate technique the Germans adopted, sometimes called *Blitzkrieg*, but more accurately described as panzer, or armored operations, has many claimants for its authorship, *Generaloberst* Heinz Guderian was the foremost practitioner of the art in the 1939, 1940, and 1941 campaigns. In essence German panzer operations were a merging of the techniques of infiltration tactics, with its emphasis on combined arms synchronization, targeting enemy weak points, and speedy advances into their rear areas with the technology and employment of massed tanks, each equipped with a radio set, and supported by mecha-nized infantry, supporting branches, and close air support. The Germans organized panzer divisions based on this concept, a force later expanded into panzer corps and panzer armies. The higher units were organized to command and control mobile operations, with motorized headquarters and long-range radio equipment.[3] Later in the war, the operational distinc-tion between panzer and non-panzer corps and armies was virtually lost as the Germans dispatched subordinate divisions to these higher commands with virtually no distinction between panzer and non-panzer.

An analysis and comparison between the organizational structures of the panzer and non-panzer headquarters at the division, corps, and army echelons in the German army shows that by the end of the war, panzer headquarters at all levels were larger and contained more motor vehicles, more radios, and the signal unit at each echelon had two armored command vehicles. German mobile force commanders clearly planned to depend on radio and com-mand motor vehicles to control their forces in the field.[4]

The development of radios in headquarters signal teams and in individual tanks was the key ingredient to controlling the mobile operations of massed armored forces. Guderian, a former signal officer himself, along with the German chief signal officer, in the 1930s pioneered the development of tactical radios for use in armored units up to corps size. The mass employment of radios made the mass employment of tanks possible and successful.[5] The development of doctrine and techniques for mobile armored operations followed from the technological advances in terms of radio communications and the tank.

Many of the techniques of command and control pioneered by the early panzer commanders virtually became standards for battle command of armored operations in most other armies as well. Commands used specialized command tanks with dummy guns, or command vehicles with extra and larger radios. Orders were given essentially in the form of map overlays with coded sectors, axes of advance, objectives and roads assigned to each subordinate unit.[6] A system of complex military map symbols was adopted as well. As many of the techniques of mobile command utilized by the Germans were similar to those later adopted for use in the US Army, they will be discussed later in this work in greater detail.

In France in 1940, Guderian found himself but a cog in the German panzer machinery, but a key cog nevertheless. As a *General der Panzertruppen*, he commanded the XIX Motorized Corps, consisting of the 1st, 2d and 10th Panzer Divisions and *Großdeutschland* Motorized Infantry Regiment, a separate unit not assigned to any division. In this campaign, the Germans massed seven of their ten panzer divisions along with three motorized infantry divisions into a strike force of four corps. These corps moved along parallel axes through the Ardennes forest of Belgium seeking to escape the forest and breach the line of the Meuse River on its far side before the Allies could respond. Once across the Meuse, the panzers were to thrust deep into the Allied flank, presumably to cut the Allied armies in half by reaching the English Channel coast, then rolling up the forces in northern France and Belgium from behind in a grand envelopment.

Despite this ambitious plan, Guderian's superiors were not yet believers in panzer operations, preferring to delay actions such as the crossing of the Meuse until slower moving infantry forces could catch up to the panzers. Therefore they placed the cautious *General der Kavallerie* Ewald von Kleist over Guderian and two other corps in a provisional panzer group.[7]

In the ensuing campaign, Guderian ignored caution, which was usually reflected in excessive concerns about flanks and pauses to wait for the foot-mobile infantry divisions to catch up to the panzer forces. He moved at great speed, brushing aside weak Belgian defenses in the Ardennes and crossing the Meuse near Sedan as soon as he reached it on 13 May 1940, only four days after the start of the campaign. Once across he had his forces strike west to break free of the French defenses. A captured French order had revealed to him the confusion the French were facing against this unexpected armored thrust and he intended to allow no hesitancy to give the French an opportunity to recover, as they had during the German offensives of 1918. Guderian pushed his three divisions forward on a broad front.[8]

96

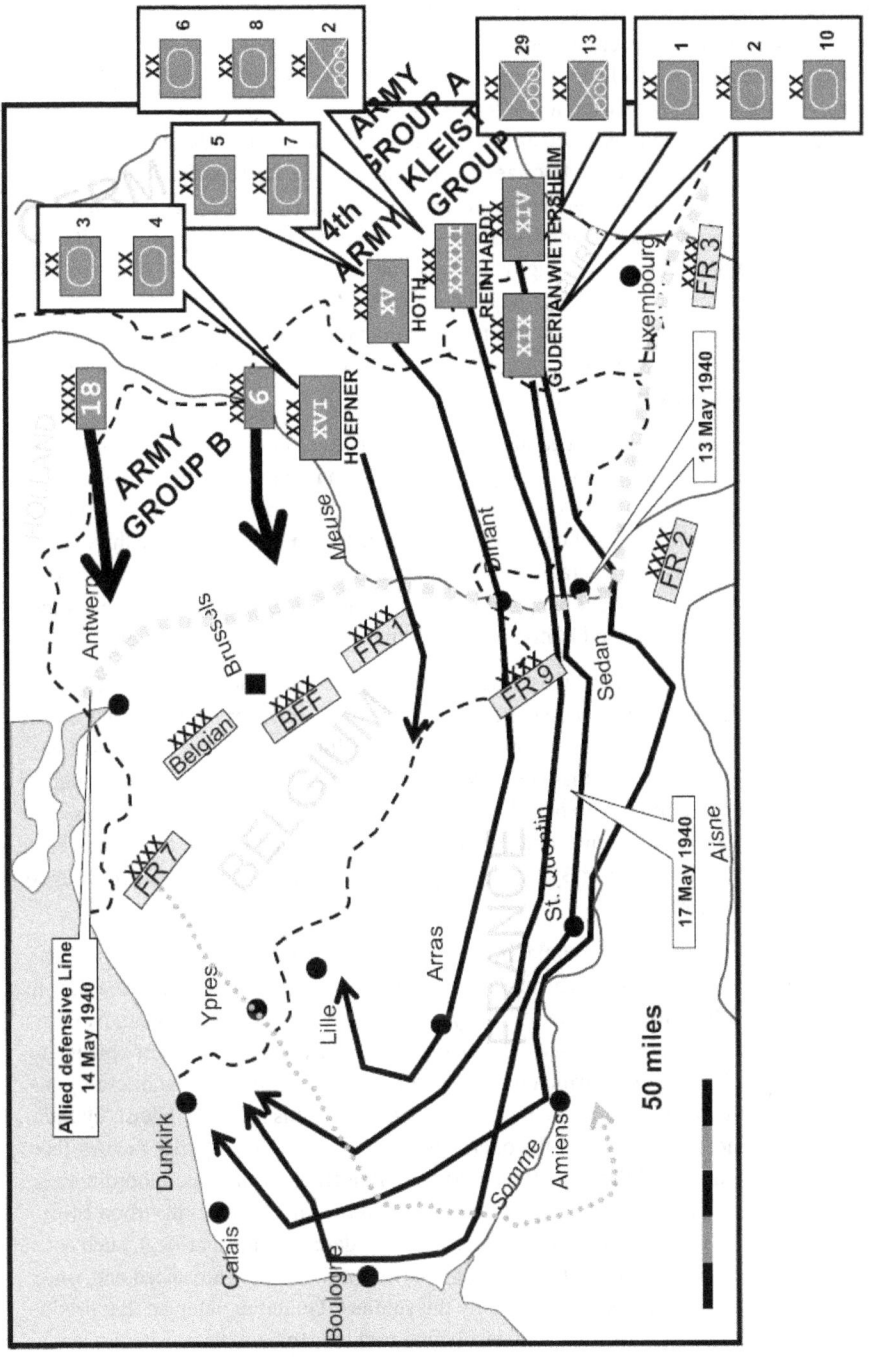

Figure 14. German advance to the Channel, May 1940.

Throughout the operation, Guderian continually fought with his superior, former cavalry commander von Kleist, over fear concerning flanks, diversions of panzer forces and desired halts. Several times Von Kleist had Guderian flown back to his command post for planning sessions, or Von Kleist flew forward to Guderian. These sessions were often highly argumen•tative.[9] The biggest flare-up took place on 17 May, immediately after Guderian's corps and its neighbor to the north, the XXXXI Motorized Corps, had pressed forward from the Meuse. On that day Kleist ordered an immediate halt to the advance, even going so far as to berate Gude•rian for exceeding his previous orders. Kleist wanted to wait for the infantry of the following 12th Army to catch up before continuing with the advance. Guderian naturally disagreed. Von Kleist immediately accepted Guderian's request to be replaced. However, the replacement order was countermanded by the higher chain of command. Guderian was pacified when told that the halt order was from the high command itself and that he would be allowed to conduct a reconnaissance-in-force while his corps was halted.[10]

Characteristically, Guderian advanced his corps forward under the guise of the reconnais•sance-in-force. In fact, the corps never really halted. Guderian laid wire between his rear and forward headquarters so he could talk to his rear staffers without using the radio that could be overheard by his superiors. The halt order was formally lifted on the 20th. In the three days of the so-called reconnaissance operation, Guderian had advanced his corps almost 70 miles. His advance troops reached Abbeville on the English Channel coast on 21 May, effectively cutting off the French, Belgian and British troops north of the panzer breakthrough.

On 24 May, after shifting the advance to the north along the coast and investing the cities of Boulogne and Calais, the panzers were halted again, this time on Hitler's own orders. By the time the Germans resumed the advance on Dunkirk on the 26th, the trapped British had be•gun a full-blown evacuation from that port city. The advance German units were less than 15 miles from the port when ordered to halt.[11] While the Belgian army surrendered en masse on 28 May, Dunkirk itself fell only on 4 June, after 337,000 British and French troops had been successfully evacuated to Britain.[12] By that time, Guderian had already been shifted away to form his own panzer group.

Guderian's preferred method of command was via a modified armored half-track vehicle equipped with banks of radios. He typically established his command post in an area near the front of the advance and moved frequently, daily, while his command was moving. At one point the command post was so far forward that a counterattack by French armor reached to within a mile of the headquarters, which was defended only by some small antiaircraft guns. The motorized corps commander normally communicated with his superior, Kleist, by radio. In fact, during the most hectic days of the operation, he did not see his superior face-to-face for nine days in the middle of the campaign. Guderian himself controlled his subordinate units through a combination of radio communications and by daily visits to his troop com•mands, where he paid particular interest in places he considered the most critical, such as the capture of Calais. He rode around between the various units as they advanced and, once victory was assured, was universally cheered by the soldiers. Guderian believed that tired forward troops and commanders often saw insolvable problems where there were not any as excuses to stop advancing. The true situation he could only discover this through personal observation. For example, one of his division commanders wanted to halt because of a perceived lack of fuel. Guderian discovered the fuel was readily available due to good staffwork and he set the wheels in motion to ensure the fuel was pushed forward.[13]

There were teething pains involved in the deployment of the panzer forces in France. Guderian had created a system of personal coordination with the supporting air force commander, which was almost ruined when higher headquarters tried to change the support arrangements at the last minute. Not expecting an advance of such a pace, the German higher commands sometimes didn't provide specific guidance to coordinate the movements of their various sub-

This image unavailable digitally due to copyright restrictions.

Deutsche Campaign Series*

Figure 15. Guderian in his command vehicle.

ordinate units, forcing Guderian and his neighboring corps commander to coordinate corps sectors and routes of march between themselves.[14]

After the Dunkirk operation, the German high command and army as a whole embraced panzer operations fully. Guderian was given his own independent panzer group for the second phase of the Battle of France. After that campaign the panzer force was greatly expanded by halving the number of tanks in each division and, although only a fraction of the German army was panzer or even motorized, both offensive and defensive operations for the rest of the war were built around the use of panzer forces.[15] Where earlier panzer corps and groups were placed under infantry armies, after the Battle for France, panzer groups were roughly equated a similar status as infantry armies and were formally renamed as panzer armies in late 1941 and early 1942.

The panzer and motorized (later partially mechanized and retitled panzer grenadier) divisions were so important to the Germans in the later stages of the war because most of their

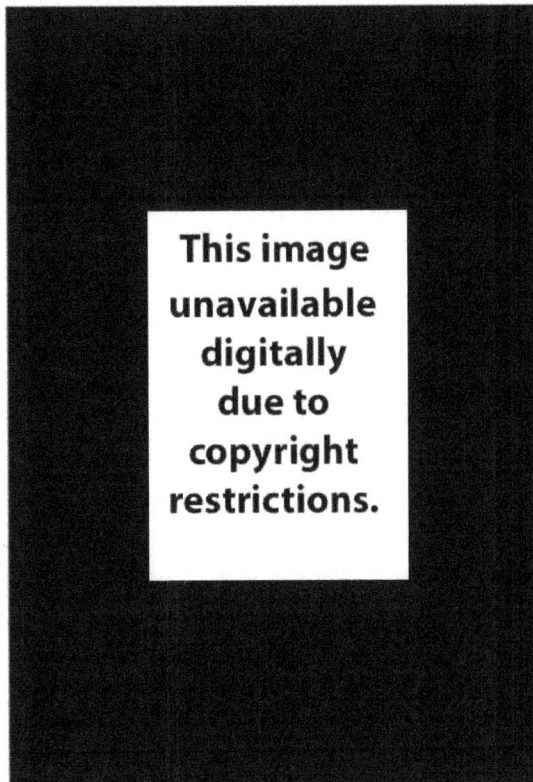

army was only foot-mobile, supported by horse-drawn wagons and artillery. A microcosm of this was found in the German infantry division, which, once placed permanently on the de‑ fensive, had its former reconnaissance battalion converted into a motorized infantry battalion, called a fusilier battalion. In this role, along with the motorized divisional engineer battalion, these two units typically became the division commander's reserve, as they were the only units in the division capable of moving around the battlefield at a pace faster than foot march‑ es. In Italy the Germans managed to motorize their whole defending force by commandeering the motor vehicles of the Italian armed forces after they surrendered in 1943.[16]

In the later years of the war, the Germans conducted mobile and panzer operations primarily to either counterattack on the defensive or to close gaps created by Soviet or Allied attacks. As the war progressed and the overall situation in relation to mobile forces became more fluid, particularly on the Russian front, the Germans issued combat orders almost exclusively orally, based on simple map overlays or other sketches. Subsequent written orders were dis‑ tributed usually only as reminders or for formal inclusion in unit operational records. Orders were only transmitted by radio when units were in a road march or fluid combat, where a rapidly changing situation diminished the possible effects of enemy interception of the orders. The placing of vehicles with radios strategically within columns allowed commanders to control the columns as they moved and minimize traffic jams.[17]

Guderian's fortunes went up and down for the rest of the war. He commanded a panzer group/ army in the 1941 Russian campaign and advanced faster and farther than he had in France. After the failure to take Moscow, however, Hitler removed him from command.[18] In early 1943, when the southern portion of the Russian front seemed about to collapse, Hit‑ ler brought Guderian back as an armed forces-wide troubleshooter for the German armored forces. Subsequently he served almost to the end of the war as the Chief of the General Staff, a formerly prestigious post which by then had become nothing more that the senior opera‑ tions officer for the Eastern Front.

A literal bridge between the World War I infiltration tactics and the panzer tactics of World War II was Field Marshal Erwin Rommel. As a junior infantry officer, Rommel had partici‑ pated in an attack in late June 1915, which demonstrated many of the characteristics of later infiltration tactics.[19] Later in the war he led a specialized mountain battalion in the vanguard of the Caporetto offensive in Italy in late 1917, the first major infiltration tactics style offen‑ sive executed by the Germans. In World War II, though without armored experience, Rom‑ mel commanded, in turn, a panzer division in France, and a panzer corps, group, and army in North Africa. Rommel's method of battle command combined a synthesis of the mobile command style espoused by the German panzer forces, his own infantry 'up-front' style of leadership and a dependence on the fine staff officers provided to him by the German general staff officer corps system. He used a specially designed command vehicle rigged with long range radios and, when separated from his headquarters while at the front, expected his opera‑ tions officer or chief of staff to make appropriate decisions, or even countermand his orders based on a temporary superior overall grasp of the situation.[20]

Rommel commanded the 7th Panzer Division in the 1940 French campaign. His division advanced and fought north of Guderian's force as part of *Generalleutnant* Hermann Hoth's XV Motorized Corps. Rommel's force reached the Meuse near Dinant and crossed even before Guderian, rapidly expanding the division's bridgehead.[21] The 7th Panzer commander pushed his command forward as hard as Guderian did his, earning the unit the nickname "Ghost Division" because its quick movements made it seem like a phantom. Rommel was in the frontline bringing his motorized infantry forces forward on 21 May when the British executed their one major counterattack of the campaign. During this counterattack near the city of Arras, Rommel personally directed artillery fire against the British.[22]

In North Africa, initially with the *Afrika Korps*, then *Panzergruppe Afrika* and its descendent organization *Panzerarmee Afrika*, Rommel continued his up front style of battle command. For almost two years he fought a seesaw mobile war with the British forces based in Egypt, culminating in a long retreat across Egypt and Libya in late 1942-early 1943 to Tunisia. He later commanded Army Groups in Italy and Normandy, being wounded in July 1944 and dying later in that year as a complication to his very minor involvement in the 20 July 1944 assassination plot against Hitler.

In North Africa, Rommel commanded from one of a fleet of three available specialized armored command vehicles, a *Sonderkraftwagen* (Sd Kfw) 250 lightly armored half-track equipped with several high-powered radio sets. His operations section also had a similar vehicle. The latter vehicle usually remained with the command post whenever Rommel went forward to the front. During advances Rommel preferred to move about between his units in a Storch light aircraft, during which he had the habit of dropping messages to stationary troops ordering them to get going. He typically spent most days up front with his subordinate units, against normal German practice, usually accompanied by his chief of staff. During critical actions, he'd always be up front, even for days at a time. There was one notable example of this: in November 1942 the Axis forces were fighting a highly mobile battle with the British (their Operation Crusader) between the key port of Tobruk (held by Australian troops and besieged by Rommel) and the Egyptian border to the east from where the rest of the British forces were trying to relieve the Australians. Rommel and his chief of staff, *Generalmajor* Alfred Gause, stayed up front away from their command post for five days. The relatively junior operations officer (Ia in German parlance), Colonel Siegfried Westphal, with a better understanding of the overall situation than Rommel, was effectively left in command of the panzer group as a whole, even countermanding some of Rommel's orders given in the field, moves later ratified by Rommel upon his return. One of the panzer group's staff officers considered occasional lapses like this to be more than made up for by Rommel's keen ability to be at critical places at the right time in the fluid North African battles.[23]

On a typical day Rommel would return to his battle headquarters in the evening and receive situation updates. From these he would issue orders for the next day to subordinate units. The orders were radioed separately to each unit. During the night, unit situation reports would be received and maps and charts updated by the headquarters night shift. A concise summary of the reports would be radioed to higher headquarters back in Germany and Italy by long-range radio. Rommel continued to coordinate operations with his staff as necessary in the evening. In the morning he would depart early with his chief of staff to visit corps and division head-quarters. During the day the units would keep the battle headquarters updated with situation and intelligence reports via radio, and the staff would monitor the command net to hear if Rommel was giving subordinate units orders via radio. If the battle headquarters was slated to move during the day, the administrative staff (IIa in German usage) and signal personnel would select a specific location and the headquarters would move to the location in two ech-elons with the operations officer and his mobile command vehicle moving first, the second echelon moving once the new location was operational. Rommel would return to receive a situation briefing, coordinate with higher headquarters by radio and to issue orders for the next day.[24]

While Rommel may be an extreme example, his battle command technique does generally illustrate the German panzer commanders' method of commanding mobile operations. While controlling mobile forces, German commanders and their command posts were usually far forward.[25] Aside from urging placing them as far forward as possible to control operations, German doctrine did not address the echelonment of command posts.[26] In practice, German command posts and staffs, particularly at the lower levels, in general were austere by design. Additionally, the Germans organized the theater of war in such a manner that the rear areas and key installations and geographical features (like towns or bridge sites) at each command echelon had separate area commands responsible for not just logistical functions within its area of responsibility, but also for combat operations there. In a pinch these other headquar-ters could fill in for the more forward headquarters of combat units.[27]

US Army World War II Mobile Operations Battle Command Theory and Practice

After World War I the US Army promulgated for the first time a separate regulatory manual for field service. In the 1923 edition of this manual, command and control was covered in great detail. The exercise of command was cited as being dependent on the transmission of information, reports, and orders. Communications was to be effected through technical means or messengers. The higher unit was responsible for establishing and maintaining communica-tions with its subordinate units via field telephone wire and later radio. Adjacent units had similar obligations. Signal officers at each command post down to battalion level were to establish message centers to execute the dispatch, recording, coding and decoding of messag-es. The message center was responsible for the prompt delivery and receipt of messages and, accordingly, normally determined the best means of transmission and prioritized messages based on the commander's guidance. By their nature, these message centers were hubs of the field telephone wire networks and best suited for static operations or slow moving advances.[28]

In the 1923 doctrine, command and control of fast paced situations was not ignored. In more mobile operations, command posts, while in motion, would depend on messengers mounted on motorcycles and bicycles for maintaining communications. Meanwhile the signal section would immediately establish a forward message center tied into the higher telephone network and connected initially with lower units via messenger until wire could be laid. Forward command posts, once established, would be located near advance message centers. The laying of wire forward would depend upon the rate of the advance and new forward message centers would be set up as necessary based on the tactical situation.[29]

The 1941 field service regulations formalized the division of command posts for units of division-size or larger into a forward and a rear element. While the 1923 regulation specified that command posts could move in echelon, the 1941 edition codified this, specifying that units of division or larger size would echelon its headquarters into a rear and a forward element. The forward element, called the command post, was responsible for combat operations and supporting the commander in commanding and controlling his subordinate units.[30] Reports, particularly current situation reports, were the primary means of doing this. The then current staff procedural manual emphasized the maintenance of situation maps, updated at least on a daily basis. Even in highly mobile operations, command posts were expected to keep situation maps updated while on the move. The operations section (G/S-3) was responsible for updating the friendly situation, while the intelligence section (G/S-2) kept what was known about the enemy situation current.[31] During the war itself, as previously mentioned, the immediate press to provide current map overlays showing unit dispositions was very strong, so strong that on at least one occasion a battalion commander personally delivered the overlay to his regimental command post at the end of a day's operations in Normandy.[32]

As the United States Army organized an armored force in 1940, long before actual combat, its creators reflected on battle command in mobile operations, using a combination of study of concurrent German panzer operations and the results of field exercises. Among the concepts espoused included an emphasis on mission-type orders and orders based on map overlays; the use of short and clear oral fragmentary orders once an operation had commenced; and the development and extensive practice on a series of drills to be used by vehicle commanders in specific situations or upon code-worded orders.[33] Advances would be controlled by the use of radios, which armored units received an extensive supply of, and the use of geographical graphic control measures, primarily phase lines and march objectives. There would be specifically designed command vehicles that would monitor the radio network of both their own command and the next higher echelon.[34] Command post organization for mobile operations was first divided into the three portions familiar to US Army personnel for the rest of the century and beyond: a rear command post, a forward command post, and a third element called the command group. The rear command post handles supply and personnel activities. The forward command post consists of the operations and intelligence sections of the headquarters, as well as any necessary communications, and transportation assets which would immediately be needed by the commander to help him oversee tactical operations. The command group, consists of those portions of the forward command post which accompanied the commander when he left the command post and moved forward to combat, or to visit the higher headquarters.[35] The table of organization and equipment (TO&E) of Army units, while organizing headquarters elements into headquarters and headquarters companies, did not organize them into these various command post elements, making their organization an *ad hoc* or standing operations procedure (SOP) item for the units, the details of which could vary even between units organized with exactly the same TO&E.

The United States raised 16 armored divisions in World War II, all of which fought in the European Theater. Additionally, by German standards, every American infantry division was already motorized. Unlike the Germans, no armored corps or armies were fielded. However, most US Army corps and army headquarters were already equipped similarly to German panzer headquarters, and, as mentioned above, by 1944 even the Germans were using panzer corps and armies interchangeably with similar non-panzer command elements.[36]

In World War II, the US Army first employed large airborne (a combination of parachute and gliderborne troops) units. These units, though able to get to the battlefield fast and in a unique manner (by parachute or glider), were basically as mobile as the rest of the infantry once on the ground. As originally designed, one infantry regiment was to be paratroopers, and the remaining two gliderborne. However, as the war progressed, the ratio was ultimately reversed.[37] In the European theater, additional parachute units were attached to divisions, resulting in a division often consisting of up to four parachute regiments and one glider regi‑ ment. Airborne units, once on the ground and properly assembled, operated similarly to other infantry units. However, particularly in mass drops in World War II, command and control of the divisions was lost during the initial assault when units and personnel were often scattered over great distances or intermingled with other units. Often key communications equipment was lost in the initial drops as well. Command and control via radio communications was of‑ ten hindered by the need for equipment to be portable even at the division level.[38] In addition to the delays caused by the nature of the initial assault, in the September 1944 MARKET‑ GARDEN operation, bad weather delayed for days the arrival of the glider portion of the divisions as well.

The World War II airborne division operated as a mobile unit essentially only during its initial entry into combat. Unfortunately a combination of air-ground techniques, combat ac‑ tion and weather often made this mobile entrance into combat to be the precise instance that commanders often lost command and control of their units until they could be assembled and communications reestablished. In these circumstances, commanders had to depend upon the initiative and motivation of junior leaders and their understanding of the overall missions of the unit. In most cases in World War II they were not disappointed. As with German panzer corps, the single US airborne corps (XVIII) was by the end of the war used interchangeably with all the other corps headquarters.

The First Modern US Army Mobile Campaign- Brittany, August 1944

The US Army's first major large scale operation using armored forces advancing quickly over great distances was the August 1944 Brittany campaign. In this operation one armored division was sent 150 miles to the west while another was sent 50-75 miles to the south while a third infantry division was fighting Germans in a besieged port in a third location between the distant armored division and the corps command post. Command and control of this operation at levels above the division left a lot to be desired. For long periods of time, orga·nizations as large as division were out of contact with corps and had to operate based on their own initiative and understanding of the corps and army commanders' intents and their own understanding of the enemy situation.

Before Brittany, command and control at the corps and army levels was geared to the pace of an infantry advance. As in World War I, field telephones, physically wired together by signal corps soldiers on the ground, were the primary means of communications between units.[39] In such a fast paced operation, however, alternate means—primarily high-powered radio and teletype, but also couriers, both ground and air—were less reliable or speedy. Battle command of such an operation, therefore, was bound to have its difficulties. Command and control was even more complicated than in Guderian's similarly scaled 1940 operation, since in 1944 the US VIII Corps was moving large units in several different directions at the same time.

After the Operation COBRA breakthrough on the western side of the Normandy front, the German left wing collapsed during the last few days of July 1944. Exploiting this, the US VIII Corps, Major General Troy Middleton commanding, which was on the extreme western (right) portion of the Allied line, advanced using its two assigned armored divisions, the 4th Armored Division (4th AD) and 6th Armored Division (6th AD), to secure the key crossroads city of Avranches and the key bridge across the Selune River four miles south of Avranches at Pontaubault. These successes opened the door for a rapid advance into the peninsula of Brit·tany.

Brittany was important for the Allied effort because of its collection of ports and its prox·imity to the Atlantic and the United States beyond. Army planners had originally envisioned clearing the peninsula using between two and four corps. But the sudden collapse of the German front changed this.[40] The VIII Corps had always been earmarked for the Brittany mission, but now was given the mission alone of seizing the major ports of Brest, St. Malo, Lorient, St. Nazaire and Nantes with two armored divisions and two (later one) infantry divi·sions. While the advance from Avranches was to spread westward almost 200 miles to Brest and southward to St. Nazaire and Lorient, over 100 miles distant, no special provisions were made to assist the corps headquarters in controlling its dispersed formations during their rapid advance. Normal procedures and equipment were expected to be adequate. The seasoned corps commander, Middleton, expected to execute a phased, orderly advance which would facilitate his command and control over subordinate units, much as the corps had operated in Normandy when it was primarily composed of infantry divisions.[41] A long serving in·fantryman who had commanded infantry units up to regiment level in World War I and had commanded an infantry division in Sicily and Italy the previous year, Middleton had never commanded armored forces before being given the 4th AD to support his infantry advance in Normandy several weeks previously. He anticipated the advance into Brittany to be more of the same sequenced, methodical style of operation as he had conducted in Normandy, with an advance on two axes, each with an armored division followed by an infantry division.

However, Middleton's new army commander, Lieutenant General George Patton, was to have different ideas.

Unlike Middleton, Patton, the commander of the newly activated Third Army, under which the corps would be assigned on 1 August, was an experienced armor commander with clear ideas about rapid advances. By direction of the army group commander, Lieutenant General Omar Bradley, in preparation for assuming operational command, Patton had been unofficially overseeing the operations of the VIII Corps in its rapid advance on Avranches.[42] Patton expected bold, rapid advances that would challenge command and control. While accepting this as a risk of mobile operations, given the technology of the day, he also took concrete steps to ease the problem. One of the first acts as army commander was to convert the army-level reconnaissance force, the 6th Cavalry Group, into something he designated the "Army Information Service," sometimes also referred to as the household cavalry. As such, this force, employing jeeps and armored cars, provided reports on unit activities down to battalion level which were then consolidated at the group headquarters and sent as teletype messages directly to Patton's advance command post, with the messages monitored by the echelons of command in between.[43]

The VIII Corps headquarters was not specially equipped to command an operation consisting of far-flung armored advances moving in completely different directions at the same time. The primary means of communications for the corps, both with higher and lower units, was the field telephone. This naturally was difficult in mobile operations with units advancing in different directions and over great distances. To augment the wire, the high-powered radio set SCR-399 was used. As a high frequency radio set, the SCR-399 was designed specifically for long-range transmissions, having a 100-mile range for voice transmissions while in motion and much farther using continuous wave transmissions in Morse code. The set was mobile, being rigged in a shelter, and mounted on the standard 2 1/2 ton cargo truck.[44] Corps also augmented the 6th AD with a radio-teletype team equipped with VHF radios and beam antennas designed to be beamed back to a receiving station. But this equipment was unreliable beyond 50 miles. Accordingly, more time consuming and less sophisticated means of communication would have to be employed, including the use of couriers, both traveling by ground vehicles and by air. Before units got too far away, both Patton and Middleton were to conduct personal visits to the advance units as well. But once the armored units were advancing, regular communications were not maintained until the advance stopped.[45]

At division level, the armored divisions usually organized into three compact elements, two advancing columns and a rear echelon. The division command post was located with one of the columns and controlled division operations by radio or personal contact or couriers. With the distances between elements ordinarily being much shorter than that of the divisions themselves with corps and army, command and control difficulties were minimal.

Middleton added to his command control difficulties by keeping his headquarters far to the rear, only a few miles south of Avranches, in order to retain telephone communications with the Third Army headquarters, located about 15 miles farther to the north. Except for what the

VIII CORPS IN BRITTANY AUGUST 1944

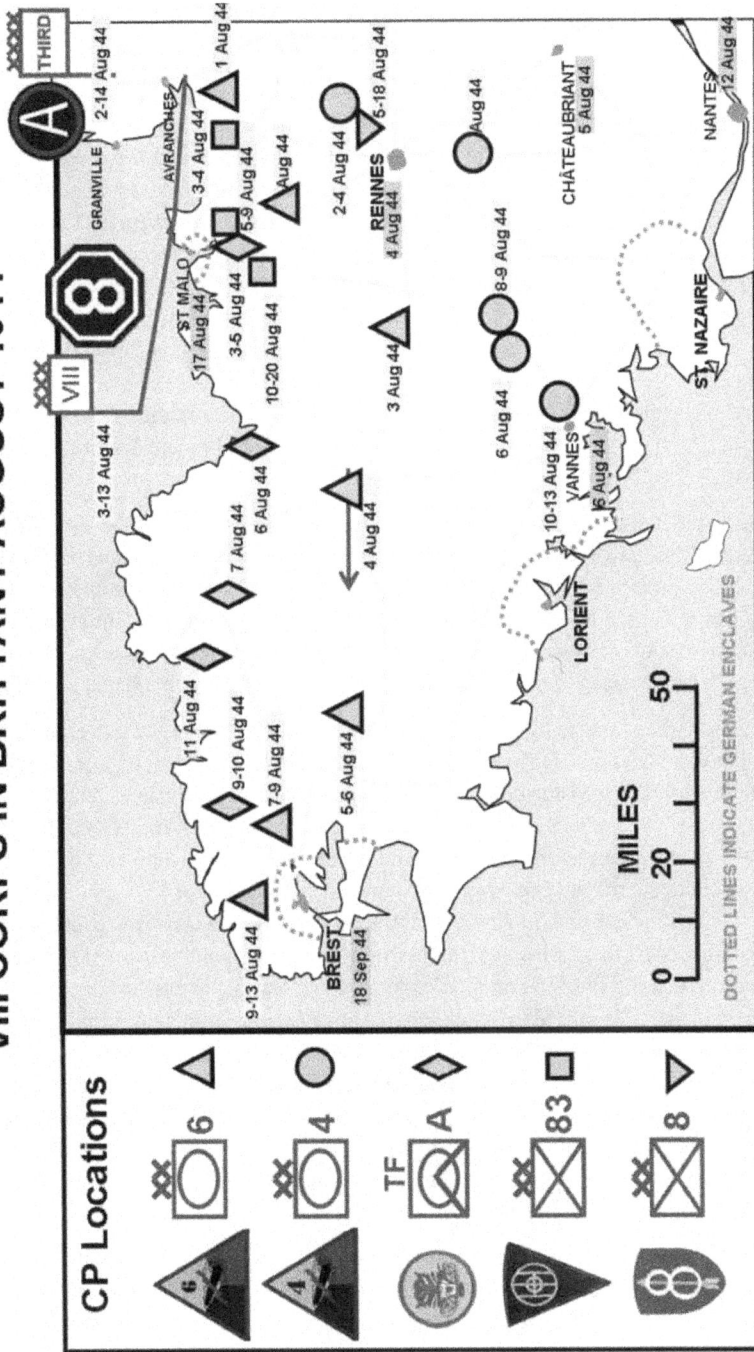

Figure 16. Command Post locations in the Brittany Campaign, August 1944.

divisions carried with them and a Third Army POL dump established about halfway to Brest, logistics elements also remained near Avranches during the mobile operation.[46]

Once the two armored divisions under the VIII Corps cleared the bottleneck around Avranches on 1 August, they advanced against weak German opposition. The 4th AD, under Major General John Wood, drove 50 miles to the south to the key crossroads town of Rennes, and had a projected advance from there another 50 miles to the south near the mouth of the Loire River and the ports of Lorient and St. Nazaire, a move which would cut off the German forces in Brittany. The 6th AD, under Major General Robert Grow, advanced 50 miles westward first to the area south of St. Malo, and was then slated to move on to Brest another 150 miles to the west. Each of these divisions was to be followed by an infantry division, the 83d Infantry Division (83rd ID) after the 6th AD, and the 8th Infantry Division (8th ID) after the 4th AD. A special force composed of tank destroyer, mechanized cavalry and engineer units under Brigadier General Herbert Earnest, called Task Force A, followed the 6th AD on the northern axis with a mission to clear the north shore of Brittany and secure a series of vital railroad bridges.

Almost immediately the corps commander lost control of the operations of the two armored divisions as radio communications broke down—primarily due to the geographical distances. The speed of the advance precluded the use of wire and the various types of radio communications equipment with each division proved to be unreliable. Given that the initial corps operational instructions gave only a very general direction of advance for the divisions, current situation reports were necessary for the corps to maintain adequate command and control.[47]

To add to the difficulties caused by communications technology, human factors entered the picture as further complications. Different levels of command had different expectations of the campaign. The armored division commanders expected sweeping advances that entailed even the bypassing of large enemy strongholds such as Rennes and St. Malo. Wood, in fact, preferred to turn his division east towards Paris and the Seine, rather than proceeding from Rennes to the south to cut off the Germans in Brittany. In this the new army commander, Patton, who felt a swift advance would secure all the ports before the Germans could react to protect them, supported them. However, at the corps level, Middleton expected a more tempered advance, securing lines of communication and not leaving bypassed Germans behind until the infantry was poised to attack them. Above Patton, at the new 12th Army Group headquarters, General Omar Bradley, though refusing to interfere directly in Patton's command, clearly favored Middleton's approach, an approach they had worked out together before Patton assumed command. With the campaign shaping based on day-to-day events, and a deteriorating enemy situation, Middleton and his subordinate commanders suffered under conflicting leadership styles and even unclear commanders' intent at the army (Patton) and army group (Bradley) levels.[48]

Efforts to maintain command and control were initiated on both sides of the communications void. Both armored divisions employed couriers. But, as the distances got farther, it would take from 12 to 48 hours for couriers to complete their roundtrips, often resulting in orders and information long being overcome by intervening events.[49] Before the advance got too far afield, both Patton and Middleton drove over fifty miles out to the advance units, Patton to Grow's 6th AD near St. Malo, and Middleton to Wood near Rennes. These personal visits both reaffirmed the operational situation and gave the field commanders immediate directive guidance. But distance precluded this from happening once the advance moved on and Patton depended on his household cavalry to provide updates, while both the corps and army commanders utilized spotter planes to get indications as to how far the lead units had advanced.[50]

With the armored divisions effectively out of communications with their highers and different interpretations of the intent of the operation being bandied about, the advance suffered two major control breakdowns, one with the 6th Armored Division near St. Malo, the other with the 4th AD at Rennes. In one case an armored division's advance was delayed because the corps headquarters was unclear about the division's location, while in the second situation, an armored division commander interpreted his orders in a way they were not intended to be interpreted.

In the first instance, the 6th AD was delayed 24 hours on its advance to Brest because of confusion in the chain of command caused by inadequate communications. As the division advanced south of St. Malo to the German strongpoint of Dinan, Grow, the division commander, interpreted his mission as one of bypassing Dinan and continuing on to Brest. Middleton, the corps commander, misunderstood a cryptic message from the division which implied it had taken Dinan and ordered follow-on troops of Task Force A and lead elements of the 83d ID to follow through the town. When these elements met resistance at Dinan and outside St. Malo, on the 3d, Middleton, believing the 6th AD to be nearby, ordered it by radio and courier to support the attack on Dinan and St. Malo. The division's forward elements were in fact between 15 and 30 miles to the west when Grow halted them to comply with the corps order. While Grow concentrated his division for the attack on St. Malo, he sent radio messages and a courier to protest the order. In the meantime, Middleton had gotten a better appreciation of the tactical situation and rescinded the order, giving the St. Malo mission exclusively to the 83d ID. Before Grow got this word, however, he had already put his division back in motion westward as Patton had arrived at his headquarters by jeep and verbally countermanded the corps orders. The 6th AD had lost 24 hours on the road to Brest. Similarly, Task Force A would lose 48 hours on its advance by lingering near St. Malo under confused orders.[51]

In the second case, Wood, the 4th AD commander, advanced on Rennes. He then decided to interpret his orders as allowing him to bypass the city to effectively cut off all the roads leading out of it. After this Wood intended to advance to the southeast to isolate the Germans in Brittany while posting his division eastward in anticipation of participation in the advance across the rest of France to the German border. Immediately upon arriving north of Rennes on 3 August and meeting resistance, he set his bypass plan into motion sending his Combat Commands A and B on arcs to the west of the city. While Wood dispatched a messenger to tell corps what he was doing, orders arrived telling him to take Rennes. However, with two combat commands already in motion, Middleton, after driving out with a small armored half-track escort to see Wood personally, partially approved Wood's plan. Middleton dispatched part of the 8th ID to take the city, but urged Wood to cover Brittany by placing reconnais• sance units along the length of the north-south Vilaine River from Rennes to the coast. A regiment from the 8th ID, the 13th Infantry, attacked Rennes soon after it arrived north of the city in trucks late on the 3d. This prompt attack encouraged the Germans to evacuate Rennes, which they did on the evening of 3/4 August.[52]

Middleton's concessions to Wood, however, did not take into account Third Army directives to take the port cities of Lorient and St. Nazaire. When Third Army G-3 Major General Hugh Gaffey found out about Wood's maneuvers, he dispatched the household cavalry directly to Wood's command post to reiterate the army's intent that the 4th AD was expected to move to Lorient. A copy of this order was also sent to the VIII Corps, which simply acknowledged the mission without further comment.[53]

The division promptly complied, advancing on the 5th 70 miles to the southwest to the key crossroads town of Vannes near the coast between Lorient and St. Nazaire. After repulsing a German counterattack the next day, the 4th AD reached the outskirts of Lorient finding the city well defended and fortified. Given the uncertain situation in western Brittany, both Patton and Middleton were fearful of needing to use the 4th AD to respond near Brest. Accordingly, the 4th AD was kept in place containing Lorient and St. Nazaire for the time being.[54] Wood was still looking east and was able to shift the bulk of his division that way when Middle• ton had Wood send a combat command 80 miles to the east to relieve a force from the 5th Infantry Division of the neighboring XV Corps at Nantes on the Loire River on 10 August. Two days later, after the division had secured Nantes, Wood received his wish: the 4th AD was relieved from the VIII Corps and sent to join the bulk of the Third Army push east across central France.[55]

Corps and army maintained relatively good communications with most of its units once the 4th AD had completed its advance to the southern coast and remained relatively stationary covering the large German troop concentrations at St. Nazaire and Lorient. Between the corps headquarters near Avranches and the 4th AD was posted the bulk of the 8th ID near Rennes as the corps reserve. And the 83d ID was investing St. Malo 50 miles west of Avranches.

However, the revival of good communications and command and control were not dupli• cated to the west beyond St. Malo as the 6th AD and Task Force A had disappeared over the horizon advancing rapidly on Brest and along the north coast, by-passing most opposition as they went. The 83d ID, originally earmarked to follow the 6th AD to Brest, was now fully committed to taking St. Malo, a systematic operation against determined German defenders fighting behind fortifications, which would take until 17 August.[56] To the west, periodic situa• tion reports from the 6th AD were taking almost 36 hours to get to the corps, making Middle• ton and Patton very anxious as early as 6 August about the division's status and in wonder concerning the situation at Brest. Patton dispatched his household cavalry and Middleton attempted to use unreliable radio communications to request the division's location. That day a fighter-bomber pilot relayed a message from Grow giving his location as 15 miles from Brest and a request for infantry support in the imminent attack on Brest. In response to Grow's request, an infantry regiment of the 8th ID was dispatched on the 8th, although it would not arrive until the 10th. In addition, more long-range signal equipment was also sent to the division, but its use upon arrival was hindered by small parties of Germans operating in the division area. Attempts to land small artillery liaison aircraft to provide courier service were also similarly hindered. Adding to this vague situation, Grow implemented radio silence on his command prior to his projected attack on Brest, but had been forced to cancel the pro• jected 9 August attack when the bulk of the German 266th Infantry Division was discovered to be in the 6th AD's rear area. Breaking his radio silence, Grow sent a cryptic message via high-powered radio that made it seem his division was in peril, a message that caused Patton and Middleton to stop the 4th AD from attacking Lorient.[57]

In reality the danger was minor as the German infantry was no match for the highly mo• bile armored forces of the 6th AD. Grow simply turned his division around and attacked and destroyed the elements of the 266th to his rear. The Germans were even unaware that the 6th AD stood between them and Brest until they were attacked. However, while this action was going on, farther to the south the German 3d Parachute Division managed to slip into the city, making the garrison much more formidable than it had been previously. While mopping up the Germans to his rear, permanent air courier service was finally established and the 6th AD and Task Force A, to its north, which had had intermittent radio contact with corps, were finally in continuous communications.[58] Events to the east overtook the Brest operation and it was left to the 8th ID and two other infantry divisions transferred from other corps to invest and take the city, which did not fall until 18 September. Grow's 6th AD was, however, dis• patched to replace the 4th AD outside of Lorient and St. Nazaire and along the southern flank of the Third Army along the Loire River until the 83d ID became available with the fall of St. Malo. The VIII Corps' mobile campaign was over.

Poor command and control in the Brittany campaign created almost as much confusion in the American ranks as the breakthrough had created in those of the Germans. The uncertain• ties of the situation allowed contradictory orders, delays in the advance and misunderstand• ings over the tactical situation at both higher and lower levels. These ultimately resulted in the bulk of the German defenders being able to fall back to their fortified port enclaves. There the Germans were either taken by siege, as at St. Malo and Brest, or allowed to languish until the end of the war as at Lorient and St. Nazaire. In any event the greatest fruits of the rapid advance into Brittany— the use of the ports— was denied the Allied forces. While at the time the advance across France overshadowed the need for the ports, the subsequent stabilization of the front on the German border made the failure to take these key logistical hubs very criti• cal as supply difficulties bogged the advance down.

Ironically, the command and control difficulties encountered by the VIII Corps were not considered significant enough to merit changing the structure of the postwar corps headquar• ters. The European Theater general board, which met after the cessation of hostilities, recom• mended no changes to the corps headquarters personnel or equipment related to command

and control. Perhaps memories of subsequent successes dimmed recollections of the problems associated with the Brittany campaign.[59]

The success of mobile armored operations in World War II would provide a springboard for the postwar continuation of the battle command procedures, techniques and organizational structures in the United States Army up to the present day. Armored division organization would remain basically the same in the US Army until 1963 and the new organizations ad•opted that year were based on the former armored division organization and concepts adopted in World War II.

Summary

The internal combustion engine, caterpillar tracks and armored plating combined to form tactical armored vehicles, which ushered in the modern era of mobile operations. When the Germans applied their World War I tactical innovations to massed tank forces, the result was the creation of modern armored operations. Such operations, consisting of hundreds of mov•ing or potentially moving vehicles, operating over great stretches of terrain, were inherently difficult to control. By a combination of the mass deployment of radios and various com•mand techniques, the Germans were able to control such forces. The Germans were the first to use specially designed mobile command posts and command vehicles. One of the German pioneers, Heinz Guderian, not only worked out much of the theory of armored operations, but was one of its most important practitioners. As a key panzer corps commander in the 1940 campaign in France, Guderian's drive from the Ardennes forest to the coast of the English Channel was decisive in the French defeat and British evacuation at Dunkirk. Guderian typi•cally commanded his corps from a modified (with additional radios) infantry half-tracked carrier up forward, communicating primarily via radio and frequent personal contact with subordinates.

Famed German commander Erwin Rommel provided a bridge between the new infantry tactics of World War I, of which he had been one of the most successful practitioners, and the World War II era armored operations. As commander of panzer forces at the division, corps, group and army levels, Rommel, like Guderian, employed a specially designed command vehicle. He tended to stay primarily up front with his subordinate units making on-the-spot decisions. But this style forced his command post staff to often assume battle command func•tions when Rommel was swallowed up by the small picture of a localized tactical situation. Rommel's staff devised systems to account for his command style, and to oversee opera•tions themselves even while the command post moved. While an extreme example, Rommel showed the typical style of battle command exercised by German commanders in mobile operations in World War II—use of austere command posts well forward.

After the success of the German armored attack in France, the German army as a whole and all their opponents, including the United States Army, adopted the concept of armored opera•tions. US Army headquarters for mobile operations were echeloned, with the forward ele•ment (called the command post) focused on current intelligence and operations activities. US armored forces relied on a combination of mission-style orders, battle drills, and extensive use of map overlays to exercise battle command. As with the Germans, radios were fielded lavishly.

The first major mobile armored operation in the history of the United States Army was August 1944's Brittany campaign. In this operation, the VIII Corps sent mobile forces off in three different directions designed to exploit the breakout from Normandy by both cutting the German forces in the Brittany peninsula off while advancing to capture key port facilities. As operations extended as far as 150 miles to the west and 70 miles to the south, and the VIII Corps also commanded infantry forces besieging several key towns, command and control was extremely difficult. VIII Corps commander Troy Middleton lost contact with several of his key subordinate units for extended periods, and several units were halted or jockeyed around unnecessarily. Dependence on couriers and long range radios made Middleton's communications haphazard at best. However, the initiative of his subordinate division commanders and their understanding of their missions played a key role in the success of the campaign. While some German forces managed to occupy most of the ports, these forces were soon cut off and besieged and many more were destroyed or isolated. The first modern American experience of battle command on the move relied on organizational technique for its success over the lack of capability of the communications technology of the day to cope with such an extended advance.

Notes

1.   Heinz Guderian, *Panzer Leader*, Abridged, Constantine Fitzgibbon, tr.(New York; Ballantine, 1972), 21.

2.   Gudmundsson, 144.

3.   Larew, 4.

4.   See Hellmuth Reinhardt, *Size and Composition of Divisional and Higher Staffs in the German Army,* Foreign Military Studies, MS- P-139 (Heidelberg: Historical Division, Headquarters, US Army Europe), 1954, Table 6, p. 67-9; Table 7, p. 70; Table 15, p.78-80; Table 16, p. 81; Table 17, p.82; Table 26, p. 97-8; Table 27, p. 100; Table 31, p. 104-7; Table 32, p.108; Table 37, p. 117-25; Table 38, p. 125, Table 39, p.127. The primary differences are summarized in the following table:

Echelon	Primary Differences between Non-Panzer and Panzer Headquarters
Division	- Panzer division headquarters was more than twice as large as an infantry division headquarters and had an organic motorcycle messenger platoon - In 1944 an escort company was assigned directly to the Panzer and *Panzergrenadier* division headquarters - Panzer division signal battalion completely motorized and contained two armored command vehicles
Corps	- Panzer corps headquarters slightly bigger than non-panzer corps headquarters - Attached signal battalion very similar except panzer corps battalion has two armored command vehicles, extra radio teams and its cable laying teams are heavier
Army	- The replacement of the army radio company in the army headquarters signal regiment with a heavier armored radio company, which included two armored command vehicles and additional motorized radio teams in the panzer army headquarters - Panzer army headquarters equipped with additional motorcycles and trucks

5.   Larew, 4.

6.   David Fraser, *Knight's Cross: A Life of Field Marshal Erwin Rommel* (New York: HarperCollins, 1993), 160.

7.   Guderian, 70.

8.   Ibid., 80-84, 86.

9.   Ibid., 77-9, 85, 87. Guderian was not cautious but he was also not reckless. He did cover his exposed left flank with one of his panzer divisions during his advance. Guderian believed that as long as his command remained in motion and the French could not pin down its location, they would not counterattack him. See Guderian 89.

10.   Guderian, 87-8.

11.   Ibid., 93-6.

12.   Alan Shepperd, *France 1940: Blitzkrieg in the West*, Campaign Series No. 3. (London: Osprey, 1990, 86-7.

13.   Guderian, 86-94, 96. The troops called Guderian 'schneller Heinz,' or 'quick Heinz.'

14.   Ibid., 82, 86.

15.   Timothy A. Wray, *Standing Fast: German Defensive Doctrine on the Russian Front During World War II Prewar to March 1943* (Fort Leavenworth: US Army Command and Staff College, 1986), 148,159.

16.   Siegfried Knappe with Ted Brusaw, *Soldat: Reflections of a German Soldier, 1936-1949* (New York: Dell, 1993), 270; For example in June 1944 the German 352d Infantry Division, defending the sector including Omaha Beach, retained its fusilier battalion as a mobile reserve, 12 miles behind the coast. See Balkoski, 73. For a good fictionalized version of German infantry division defensive concepts late in World War II written by a former German infantry officer, see Willi Heinrich, *Crack of Doom* (New York:Bantam, 1981), 156-9.

17.   Erhard Raus. *Panzer Operations: The Eastern Front Memoir of General Raus*, 1941-1945, Steven H. Newton, tr. (Cambridge, MA: Da Capo Press, 2003), 341-3.

18.   Wray, 65. One author contends that Guderian could have won the war for the Germans if his pan•zer group had not been shifted to the south in August 1941. See R.H.S. Stolfi, *Hitler's Panzers East: World War II Reinterpreted* (Norman, OK: University of Oklahoma Press, 1993).

19.   Ibid., 91-3; Erwin Rommel, *Attacks* (Vienna, VA: Athena Press, 1979), 77-9.

20.   Fraser,162.

21.   Shepperd, 43.

22.   Fraser, 183-5.

23.   F.W. von Mellenthin, *Panzer Battles: A Study of the Employment of Armor in the Second World War*, H. Betzler, tr., L.C.F. Turner, ed (New York: Ballantine, 1984), 53-56.

24.   Ibid., 58-63.

25.   On more than one occasion during World War II, German command posts at the Army and Army Group level were so far forward that they were virtually in the front line. For example, in early January 1943 on the Eastern Front west of Stalingrad, Army Group Don's command post found itself only 12 miles from the nearest Russian forces, which were advancing on the headquarters location and the key city of Rostov farther to the west. The German headquarters responded by scraping together a force of tanks being repaired at maintenance units and headquarters personnel under a junior general staff corps officer to repulse the attack. See HG Don, Ia "KTB, Tagesmeldun Befehlshaber Brückenkopf Rostow," 8 January 1943, 39694/7, National Archives Microfilm Publication T311, roll 270, frame 1076 and Paul Carrell, *Scorched Earth* (New York: Ballantine, 1971), 131-2. Additionally, on 31 July 1944, dur•ing the Normandy breakout, Combat Command B, 4th Armored Division, US Army, passed unknow•ingly within several hundred meters of the German Seventh Army command post near Avranches, forc•ing the evacuation and relocation of that headquarters, disrupting German command and control at a key point in the campaign. See Martin Blumenson, *Breakout and Pursuit*, United States Army in World War II: The European Theater of Operations (Washington, DC: US Army Center of Military History, 1961), 317.

26. Bruce Condell and David Zabecki, trans. and ed., *On the German Art of War: Truppenführung*, (Boulder, CO: Lynee Rienner Publications, 2001), 36-38.

27. US War Department, Adjutant General Office, German Military Documents Section, *The German General Staff Corps: A Study of the Organization of the German General Staff*, April 1946, 175-189; Martin van Creveld, *Fighting Power: German and U.S. Army Performance, 1939-1945*, Contributions in Military History, Number 32 (Westport, CT: Greenwood Press, 1982), 47-51.

28. US War Department, *Field Service Regulations, United States Army, 1923* (Washington, D.C.: War Department, 1923), 28-9.

29. Ibid., 29.

30. The rear echelon of the headquarters was responsible for logistics and administrative activities and was usually located in the rear where it could best control these activities and communicate with similar higher headquarters activities. See US War Department, *FM 100-5, Field Service Regulations-Operations (*Washington, DC: War Department, May 22, 1941)(hereafter *FM 100-5, 1941*), 34.

31. *FM 100-5, 1941,* 33-5:US War Department, *FM 101-5, Staff Officers' Field Manual, The Staff and Combat Orders (*Washington, DC: War Department, August 19, 1940), 30, 139.

32. Johns, 34.

33. *FM 17-10 Armored Force Field Manual: Tactics and Techniques,* March 7, 1942, 8; the drill 'playbook' was *FM 17-5, Armored Force Field Manual: Armored Force Drill*, June 18, 1943.

34. *FM 17 The Armored Force: Employment of Armored Units (The Armored Division)*, undated (probably 1941), 13, 16, 48. 50; Larew, 11.

35. *FM 17-10*, 299.

36. The General Board, United States Forces, European Theater. *The Functions, Organization and Equipment of the Corps Headquarters and Headquarters Company.* Study Number 23, 1945, 8-9 and Figure 15 (hereafter General Board, Corps Headquarters).

37. The General Board, United States Forces, European Theater. *Organization, Equipment and Tacti•cal Employment of the Airborne Division,* Study Number 16, 1945, 7.

38. Ibid., 32.

39. The XV Corps was temporarily disrupted in early August 1944 when several of its assigned divi•sions were switched out for different units and the corps had no wire laid to the new units. See Blu•menson, 429.

40. Blumenson 347-8.

41. Ibid., 350.

42. Ibid., 309, 330.

43. Ibid., 350.

44. Thompson and Harrison, 640; Balkoski, 108.

45. Blumenson, 352.

46. Ibid., 351, 388.

47. Ibid., 351, 369-72.

48. Ibid., 357-8, 378-9.

49. Ibid., 375, 377.

50. Blumenson, 362-3, 375-6.

51. Blumenson, 374-5, 377-9, 391.

52. Ibid., 361-3; Price, 188-9.

53. Blumenson, 363.

54. Ibid., 363-5.

55. Ibid., 366, 385-6.

56. Ibid., 413.

57. Ibid., 377-8, 382.

58. Ibid., 384-7.

59. General Board, Corps Headquarters, 4; in the latter report, communications equipment is not even addressed. See The General Board, United States Forces, European Theater. *Organization, Functions and Operations of G-3 Sections in Theater Headquarters, Army Groups, Armies, Corps and Divisions.* Study Number 25, 1945.

BATTLE COMMAND IN VIETNAM 1965-72

The integration of aircraft into the organic structure of the ground force is as radical a change as the move from the horse to the truck.

—Lieutenant General John J. Tolson[1]

Command and Control by Helicopter

While technology had provided motor vehicles and armored vehicles that enhanced the mobility of ground forces, and communications technology in the form of portable radios to control such mobile forces, the development of the helicopter in the 1950s and early 1960s added a third dimension to ground force operations. In addition to enhancing battlefield mobility, the helicopter also provided a mobile command and control platform from which commanders could control their forces over extended geographical expanses while not being tied down to one force or its close actions.

Unlike fixed wing aircraft, helicopters could both hover over specific points and land without the need for an extensive runway. These characteristics, along with the aircraft's mobility, made it a perfect command and control platform for operations involving several subordinate units with different missions, or extended some distance over terrain from each other.

Figure 17. Lower level command and control, Vietnam 1966.

119

The command and control helicopter allowed the commander at levels from battalion to the highest to control combat operations from a vantage point where a greater part of the battlefield could be observed. The commander could also conduct face-to-face visits with his subordinate commanders and even place himself at a crucial place at the right time. When using the Huey version of the command and control helicopter, a commander could bring along his operations and artillery officer and both modify operations and direct fire support from the aircraft.[2]

The use of the helicopter as a command and control platform had some drawbacks. The most obvious was the frailty of helicopters. Many commanders lost their lives when their helicopters were shot down or crashed. Use of aviation required friendly control of the air and at least a minimal suppression of enemy ground air defense fire. Additionally, even if they did not receive ground fire, the helicopters could give away friendly positions to the enemy.[3]

Some critics of the ubiquitous use of such aircraft cite that its use could often give commanders a false sense of the state of the battle on the ground or a tendency to micromanage down to the lowest unit in contact with the enemy, while flying at 3,000 feet. But even the critics realized the utility of the command and control helicopter when used properly.[4]

Aviation, even the most hardy of tactical helicopters, requires a logistical tail far larger and more complex than that of infantrymen operating on foot. A secure base with maintenance facilities and personnel is required, as well as supply dumps of aviation fuel and the bulk ammunition used by helicopters.

Helicopter availability could also be a drawback. In Vietnam, in units without organic aircraft, helicopter availability was usually at a ratio of roughly one direct support assault helicopter company per brigade and an aviation battalion headquarters per division. From this allocation came the unit command and control helicopters. Additionally, during the Vietnam era, infantry brigades had small aviation platoons with four light observation helicopters and two specially rigged Command and Control (C&C) UH-1 Huey helicopters in them, the use of which for command and control purposes was usually rotated among the subordinate battalions. Therefore, while such assets were always available at brigade and division level, battalion commanders would go without at times.[5]

Aside from its uses as a command and control platform, the helicopter also brought to the infantry and its supporting arms an unparalleled mobility. The maximum effect of this mobility was found in a new specialized unit, the airmobile division. How such a unit fought and was commanded in a mobile campaign will be the subject of the next section.

Operation PEGASUS: Battle Command on the Move
in Airmobile Operations

In the Vietnam War, the extensive employment of the helicopter created unique three-dimensional tactical mobility. However, most of the operations were against enemy forces fighting either as guerillas or in small groups hiding in covering terrain. As in the Indian

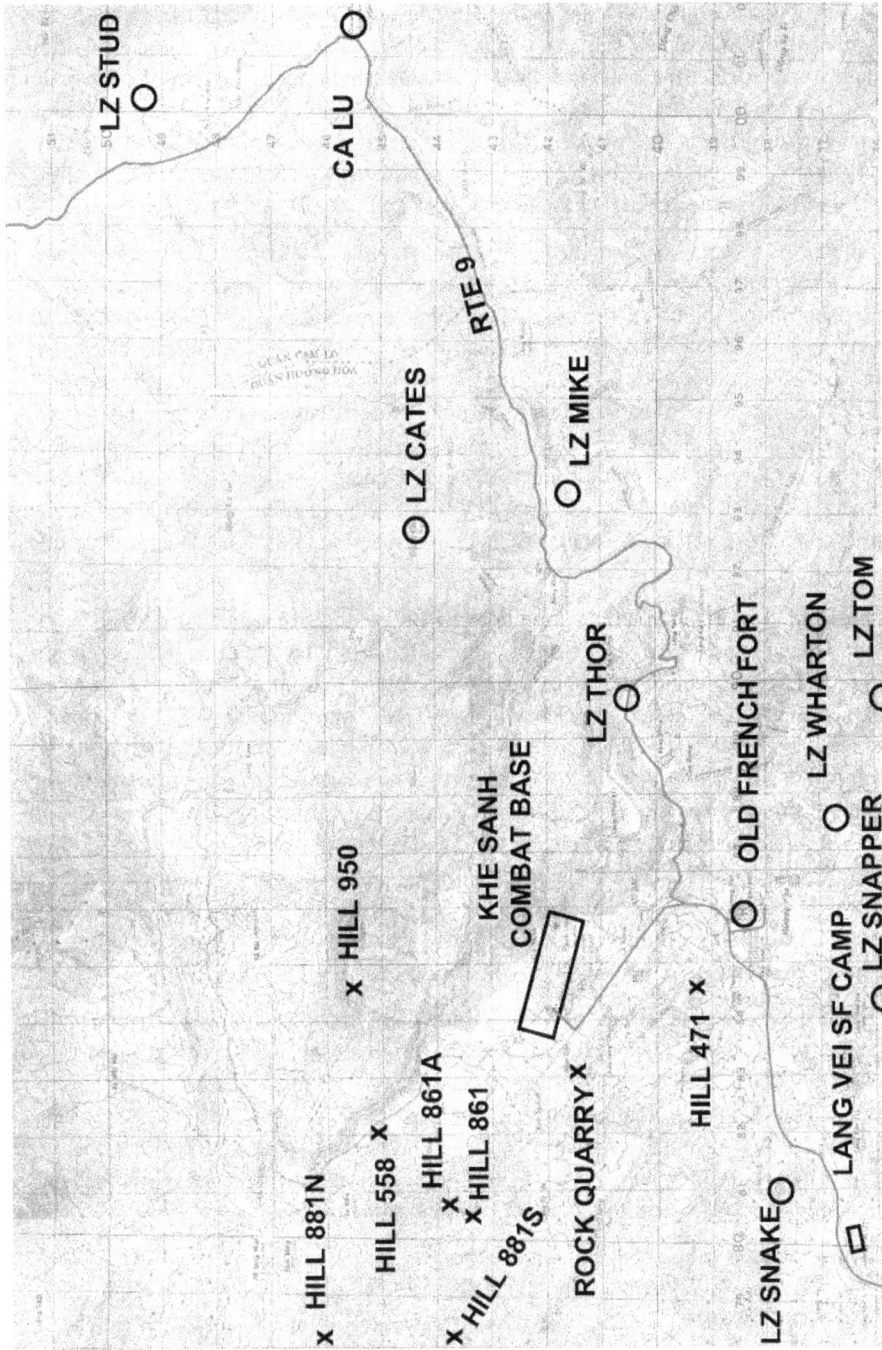

Figure 18. Khe Sanh area, 1968.

121

Wars of the previous century, much mobility was consumed in just finding the enemy. When units got into trouble, mobility was also spent in getting them out of trouble. Pitched battles of a mobile nature were rare in the war. Of the few, one which stands out is 1968's Operation PEGASUS in which the Army's 1st Cavalry Division (Airmobile), augmented with Marine and Republic of Vietnam Army (ARVN) forces, fought a successful mobile campaign against North Vietnamese forces besieging a Marine regiment at the Khe Sanh combat base in the extreme northwestern corner of the Republic of Vietnam.

Operation PEGASUS posed battle command challenges at division, brigade/regiment, and battalion levels. Aside from the third dimension added to operations by the helicopter, the operation was in fact the first division-sized airmobile operation in US Army history and, in addition to the maneuver forces of the 1st Cavalry Division (Airmobile) which were capable of being moved operationally by air and similarly supported, battle command of the force also also involved the coordination of these airmobile forces with stationary ground Marine forces, moving Marine infantry and airmobile ARVN allied forces. These were the challenges faced by the 1st Cavalry Division commander, Major General John Tolson, overall command•er of the US and ARVN forces in Operation PEGASUS. Before going into the details of the operation and how Tolson led his command, a brief discussion of the situational background follows.

Khe Sanh stood on a small plateau surrounded by several higher mountain ridgelines cov•ered with dense jungle vegetation, 15 miles south of the Demilitarized Zone (DMZ) separat•ing North and South Vietnam and about seven miles east of Laos, not far from the extensive Communist supply line known as the Ho Chi Minh Trail. The combat base itself, a former French air strip, measured roughly a mile by a half mile in size and overlooked to the south the Vietnamese National Route 9, the only major east-west highway running from the coastal area to the Laotian border. To the north and east of the base was the Rao Quan river. Beyond the Rao Quan to the north was a small plateau; to the northeast, northwest, and west of the post there was a series of ridgelines that overlooked the post. The combat base was situated 31 miles west of the provincial capital of Quang Tri, easily being the farthest flung large American position in the northern portion of South Vietnam. In fact it was the western anchor of a chain of posts covering the DMZ that US Marines had established in 1967.[6]

The Khe Sanh area had been an active one operationally from the start of American involve•ment in the locality. In April and May 1967, two battalions of the 3d Marine Regiment fought a preemptive battle against elements of the North Vietnamese Army (NVA) 325C Division along the major hill mass four miles northwest of the base which contained Hills 881N and 881S. After a series of battles, prosaically referred to as "the Hill Fights," the Marines, sup•ported by Air Force B-52 strikes, ejected the NVA forces from the ridgeline, leaving behind small outposts to provide security for the Khe Sanh installation.[7]

The siege of Khe Sanh began as a prelude to the January 1968 South- Vietnam-wide Tet Of•fensive and continued on after the Communist defeat in Tet. It was an operation reminiscent of the 1954 Battle of Dien Bien Phu. There the predecessors of the North Vietnamese, the

Viet Minh, besieged a large French force, defeated all attempts at relief and ended up tak•
ing its surrender, which ultimately resulted in the French departure from Indochina. Clearly
the NVA intended to duplicate this success at Khe Sanh, by destroying the garrison, either
outright, or after defeating any relief attempts that would, by geographical necessity, have to
come westward along Route 9.[8]

The enemy situation around Khe Sanh in early 1968 was very threatening. For supporting
fires, the North Vietnamese had assembled long-range artillery that could easily reach the
Khe Sanh area from prepared positions in caves from nearby Laos. Additionally, intelligence
indicated that elements of between two and four NVA divisions, a total of about 22,000
troops, were assembled in and around the combat base. One division, the 304th, was consid•
ered one of the premier divisions of the NVA. Sent down from Laos it was expected to oper•
ate south of the Khe Sanh base along Route 9. North of the base were elements of the veteran
325C Division, which had been fighting Marines in Quang Tri provincial area for several
years. Elements of two other divisions, the 341st and the 324B, were later presumed to have
been employed to hold blocking positions north and south of Route 9 east of Khe Sanh. All
these NVA units were all reinforced with additional antiaircraft and artillery assets.[9]

In January and February 1968 a series of NVA actions had placed the Khe Sanh Combat
Base under a state of siege. First, on the night of 20/21 January 1968, elements of the NVA's
325C Division attacked one of the company-sized hill outposts of the Khe Sanh garrison, Hill
861, located about five miles north west of the combat base. After a fierce fight over several
days, K Company 2/26th Marines repulsed the attack and the position was improved by the
placement of another company on the spur (Hill 861A) from which the Communists had
mounted their attack.[10]

Even as the battle died down atop Hill 861, NVA artillery opened up an intense bombard•
ment of the Khe Sanh base itself. Soon mortars, rockets and automatic weapons joined in,
exploding the base's main ammunition dump.[11] The next night, the 304th NVA Division
joined the operation by executing a bloody assault against indigenous and irregular forces
garrisoning the village of Khe Sanh, a couple of miles south of the post. The village positions
were overrun with the survivors evacuated to the combat base. This action effectively closed
Khe Sanh to ground communications along Route 9 from the east. The NVA bombardment
continued the next night, with American counterbattery fire and air strikes entering the fray.[12]

Even though the garrison had been reinforced in late January with two Marine battalions,
placed, respectively, in outposts to the north and west of the base, and an ARVN ranger bat•
talion, placed in an expanded base perimeter, the enemy continued to close in. While the
Tet Offensive still raged throughout South Vietnam, on the night of 4/5 February, two NVA
battalions attacked the Marine company freshly deployed onto Hill 861A. The attack was
repulsed after hand-to-hand combat and ample fire support.[13]

The next day, the 304th Division commenced a preparatory bombardment against the Lang
Vei Special Forces Camp, located astride Route 9 near the Laotian border, five and a half
miles southwest of the Khe Sanh base. Fifteen days previously, farther down Route 9 in Laos,

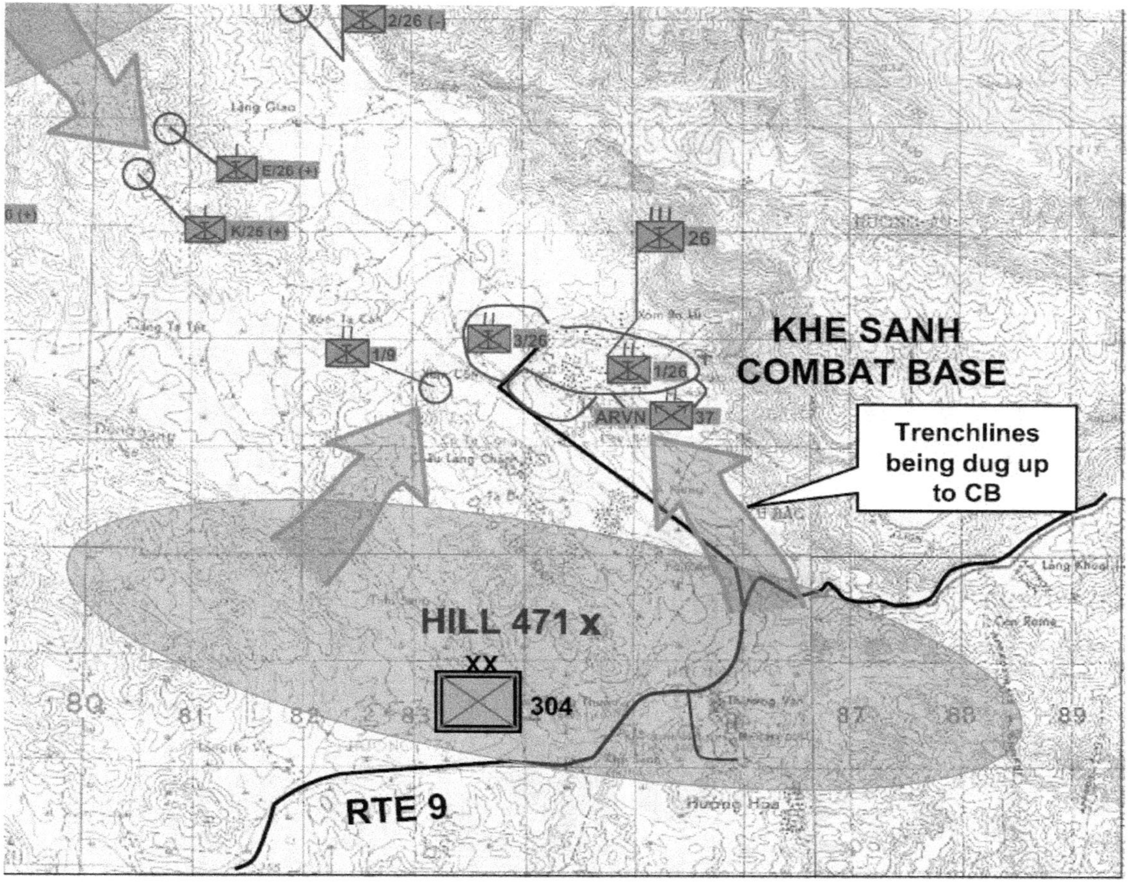

Figure 19. Khe Sanh under siege, January-March 1968.

124

the 304th had destroyed a Laotian border battalion garrison. Now after a day's bombard‧ment, it was Lang Vei's turn. Early on the morning of 7 February, NVA infantry, supported by twelve PT-76 light tanks, attacked the camp's 500 member garrison from three directions. After losing half its strength as casualties, while destroying five of the tanks, the garrison was evacuated by air and foot. The way was clear to concentrate on Khe Sanh itself. With the Tet Offensive still ongoing in the key cities of Hue and Quang Tri, US and ARVN forces were not available to halt the NVA moves towards isolating Khe Sanh.[14]

Two nights after the fall of Lang Vei, an estimated NVA battalion-sized force from the 325C Division attacked a platoon-sized position of the 1st Battalion, 9th Marines, located on the perimeter of a position called the Rock Quarry, just west of the main combat base. After a period of stalemate, the battalion repulsed the attack with a vigorous counterattack.[15]

The vise that the NVA was placing on the Khe Sanh perimeter was demonstrated clearly on 10 February when a Marine C-130 transport aircraft was fired upon with small arms fire while landing at the base airstrip. Aircraft landings were temporarily suspended, although there still was helicopter traffic and the smaller, C-123 transport plane.[16]

In a tactic reminiscent of Dien Bien Phu, the NVA were digging trenches on the south, west and northern flanks of Khe Sanh, and getting closer nightly to the base perimeter, particularly in the south.[17] They broke this patient stranglehold methodology only once, on 29 February, when a battalion of the 304th Division climbed out of its trenches three times and attacked the southeastern section of the Khe Sanh base perimeter held by the ARVN rangers. The rangers were given all available fire support and timely B-52 strikes. The attack was repulsed relatively easily. After this the NVA went back to less direct, but more effective methods, as the siege continued through March.[18]

This semi-defensive posture was forced on the Communists because of their overall situ‧ation. The North Vietnamese had suffered heavy losses in the concurrent Tet Offensive and there are indications that some forces were even withdrawn from the Khe Sanh area to fight elsewhere in the later stages of Tet. Nevertheless the 304th Division planned on making one final grand attack on the base on 23 March. While the usual intense preparatory artil‧lery shelling took place, the attack never happened. Sensors and other intelligence indicators alerted the defenders and B-52 bomber air strikes had broken up the NVA attack before it happened.[19]

Into this operational situation was thrust the forces of the US Army's 1st Cavalry Division (Airmobile) and its commander, Major General Tolson. Even while the siege continued and US forces fought to extinguish the fumes of the Tet Offensive, wheels were rolling for the relief of Khe Sanh. With the relief operation codenamed PEGASUS, Tolson was given free rein to plan and execute the employment of the assembled forces. The operational goals of PEGASUS were the relief Khe Sanh, the clearing of Route 9, and the destruction of as much of the NVA forces arrayed around Khe Sanh and on Route 9 as possible. Counting the Khe Sanh garrison, Tolson's force would be composed of almost 30,000 Army, Marine and ARVN troops.[20]

The major unit involved in Operation PEGASUS was Tolson's 1st Cavalry Division (Air•mobile). This division was a unique organizational mix of the conventional combat arms of infantry and field artillery with the enhanced mobility and firepower of a brigade-equivalent of assigned helicopters. The 1st Cavalry Division in 1968 was organized with three maneu•ver brigades, each normally with three infantry battalions, a special air cavalry squadron equipped with reconnaissance and attack helicopters, and scouts, and an aviation group of three utility aviation battalions capable of carrying simultaneously one third (or a brigade) of the division's maneuver and combat support assets. The division would provide a highly mobile combat force that could operate very flexibly. In support of the infantry the division fielded three artillery battalions equipped with 105mm howitzers, one with 155mm howitzers, and a battalion of rocket-firing helicopters.

In addition to the 1st Cav, the following forces were also available for Operation PEGASUS and at Khe Sanh: the 26th Marine Regiment, reinforced with an extra Marine infantry bat•talion, a Marine 105mm howitzer field artillery battalion, a composite battalion of special•ized troops, a battalion-equivalent of Army artillerymen, Army special forces elements, and the 37th ARVN Ranger Battalion, a total of about 6,000 troops and 40 plus artillery pieces. Apart from the Khe Sanh defenders, Tolson also controlled the 1st Marine Regiment and the brigade-sized 3d ARVN Airborne Task Force, units which directly supported the 1st Cav's advance.

As they awaited relief, the Khe Sanh garrison, under the command of Colonel David Lownds, 26th Marines, held the main base compound and adjacent air strip with two marine infantry battalions, the ARVN ranger battalion, artillery and assorted other support units. Outside the combat base Lownds had used the assets of two more Marine battalions to deploy a series of outposts, most of company size along the hills and ridges to the west and north of the post.

In preparation for operations in the north, the 1st Cav had in early 1968 moved its base camp from An Khe in the central part of South Vietnam to sprawling Camp Evans, located near Route 1—the Vietnamese coastal highway—15 miles south of Quang Tri. From here the division assembled its forces, some of which were still to the south in residual battles of the Tet Offensive. Prior to the kick off of the operation, commanders or American advisors of the attached units, including the ARVN task force, met with Tolson and his staff at the Division TOC at Camp Evans.[21]

Instead of playing into the enemy's hands by conducting a ground campaign along the axis of Route 9, Tolson intended to conduct a mobile campaign using his helicopter assets to overwhelm the NVA defenders swiftly, while retaining freedom of action and flexibility and exploiting tactical surprise.[22]

To lay the groundwork for the campaign, Tolson did three things. First, he visited the Khe Sanh garrison on multiple occasions to get a feel for the situation and to coordinate with Colonel Lownds face-to-face.[23] Second, the 1st Cav commander dispatched the divisional engineers and other supporting forces to build a large staging base at a new landing zone designated as Landing Zone (LZ) Stud. LZ Stud was established on the east side of Route 9 several miles north of Ca Lu, roughly 10 miles east of Khe Sanh. A large airfield complex and artillery support base was constructed and was completed on 25 March, six days before Operation PEGASUS was slated to begin. To facilitate his control of the operation, Tolson relocated his forward headquarters to the LZ Stud base complex on 30 March.[24]

Tolson's last major preparation was his dispatch of the 1st Cav's air cavalry squadron (1-9th Cavalry) to conduct reconnaissance along Route 9 between LZ Stud and the combat base, as well as to direct fire on discovered enemy positions, particularly antiaircraft positions. In five days, the squadron directed over 700 air sorties and strikes against NVA positions. The squadron also selected projected landing zone positions for the subsequent operation.[25]

The plan for Operation PEGASUS included three basic components. First, a supporting ground advance of two Marine battalions along Route 9 followed by an engineer battalion to rebuild the highway. Second, the main attack— the forward air assault movement of the three brigades of the 1st Cavalry Division and the ARVN airborne task force to landing zones successively closer to Khe Sanh and key enemy positions. Once on the ground, the airmobile infantry battalions of the three brigades would move and strike at enemy positions and advance towards Khe Sanh and Lang Vei. The third component was action by the Khe Sanh garrison itself, pushing out aggressively from the base.[26]

To facilitate his control and flexibility, Tolson only designated the initial LZs at the beginning of the operation with fixed times and places. The location and timing of all subsequent air assaults would be based on the enemy or friendly situation. As mentioned above, Tolson depended upon his divisional air cavalry squadron to find follow-on landing zones and discovering the disposition of enemy forces not in direct contact with friendly troops.[27]

The operation commenced on the morning of 1 April 1968. Bad flying weather hindered airmobile operations so the first action was the advance of the two Marine ground battalions from Ca Lu westward along Route 9. The 2d Battalion, 1st Marines, advanced north of the highway, while the 2d Battalion, 3d Marines, advanced south of the highway, both under the control of the commander of the 1st Marine Regiment. Marine engineers followed along the road, improving it as they went. While enemy resistance was meager, the going was tough for the two battalions, as they had to hack their way through thick jungle on both sides of the highway.[28]

Tolson controlled his forces from LZ Stud through a combination of visits to brigade command posts, and through radio communications from both his forward command post at LZ Stud and from his command and control helicopter. As he deployed each of his brigades and the ARVN task force in succession, these units staged through LZ Stud where Tolson could directly impart his intent and an update of the tactical situation to the commanders of the newly committed brigades. To facilitate the employment of the ARVN task force, it was initially controlled by the 1st Cav's 1st Brigade as it staged from its base camp to the east at Quang Tri city.[29] At the division level, Tolson used this combination of face-to-face meetings with his immediate subordinates both before and during the operation, and continual commu‑ nication during the operation.

At 1300 the airmobile forces of the 2d Brigade, 1st Cavalry Division (Airmobile), com‑ manded by Colonel Hubert Campbell, finally entered the fray. Until it redeployed to LZ Stud on the morning of 1 April, the brigade had been operating west of Hue about 50 miles to the southeast. The 5th Battalion, 7th Cavalry (5-7th Cav), an airmobile infantry battalion, and the 3d Brigade headquarters were flown via helicopter into LZ Cates, a jungle hilltop (Hill 950) four and a half miles east of Khe Sanh Combat Base and about the same distance west of LZ Stud. Two other 3d Brigade airmobile infantry battalions, 1-7th Cavalry, followed by 2-7th Cavalry, were air assaulted into LZ Mike, which overlooked Route 9 from the south and east, about five and a half miles southeast of the combat base, and five miles southwest of LZ Stud. A battery of 105mm field artillery howitzers was also airlifted into each LZ. The air cavalry squadron had determined the two LZs were free of enemy opposition before the assault. In one airmobile leap, the 1st Cav was almost halfway to Khe Sanh.[30]

There was only light contact with enemy forces everywhere on this first day of the opera‑ tion. In subsequent days the weather proved to cause more delays to the operation than enemy activities, as the NVA initially refused to make large scale contact. In the following days, the operation continued in the pattern set on D-day, including the seemingly obligatory bad weather in the mornings, which forced delays in airmobile operations. The North Vietnamese remained elusive in the initial phases of the operation.[31]

On 2 April, the 3d Brigade continued its move westward, with 2-7th Cav being airlifted to LZ Thor, on Rte 9 at Ra Co village, about three and a half miles southeast of Khe Sanh and two miles west of LZ Mike, while 1-7 Cav moved south and west on foot from LZ Mike and 5-7 Cav advanced south, west and southeast from LZ Cates. The two Marine battalions con‑ tinued their advance along the axis of Route 9. To assist their advance on the highway, two Marine companies were airlifted to LZ Robin, northeast of the Marine ground advance.[32]

On 3 April, Tolson accelerated his plan by a day by moving up the deployment of his next brigade. The 1st Cav's 2d Brigade, commanded by Colonel Joseph McDonough, entered the operation by air assaulting three battalions into LZs even closer to Khe Sanh. The 1-5th Cavalry air assaulted into LZ Wharton, four miles southeast of Khe Sanh, followed by 1-12th Cav and the 2d Brigade headquarters. 1-5th Cav then advanced to the south, west and north, with the NVA-infested Old French Fort, located at the intersection of Route 9 and the road north to the combat base, as one of its objectives. The 2-5th Cav was inserted at LZ Tom, two miles southwest of LZ Thor, two miles south of Route 9 and five miles southeast of Khe Sanh combat base. From LZ Tom, the airmobile infantry moved on foot west and northwest. The Marines, continuing their ground advance along Route 9, discovered battalion-sized bunker complexes abandoned by the NVA.[33]

Subordinate brigades controlled their battalions from forward landing zones through the use of radios and command and control (C&C) helicopters. Tolson and most battalion command‑ ers also used C&C helicopters throughout the operation to get a feel for the battlefield, con‑

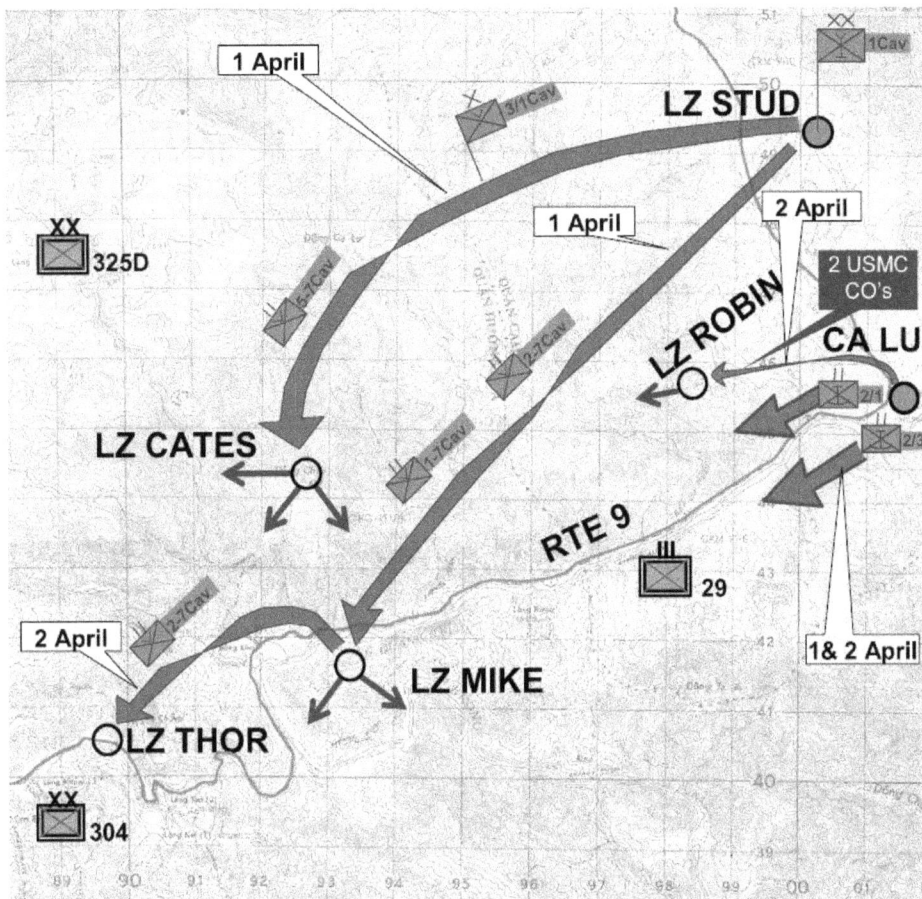

Figure 20. Operation PEGASUS Phase 1, April 1-2, 1968.

trol subordinate units, and provide on-the-spot visits. Despite the dispersed nature of the op•
erations, and the bounding forward by air and ground of more than a dozen combat battalions,
US commanders at all levels were able to control their subordinate forces and coordinate their
actions and operations. Tolson's forward command post at LZ Stud led the way in this, with
each subordinate brigade and Marine regimental headquarters being equally adept at control•
ling their subordinate units and support elements within their own operational spheres.

On the fourth day of Operation PEGASUS (4 April), the Khe Sanh garrison joined in the
offensive operations, with the 1/9th Marines battalion moving from its outpost position at the
Rock Quarry just west of the combat base to assault the NVA stronghold, Hill 471. Hill 471,
located at the end of a ridgeline just two miles southwest of the Khe Sanh Combat Base and
just north of Route 9, the hill overlooked the base. The Marine battalion, with three compa•

129

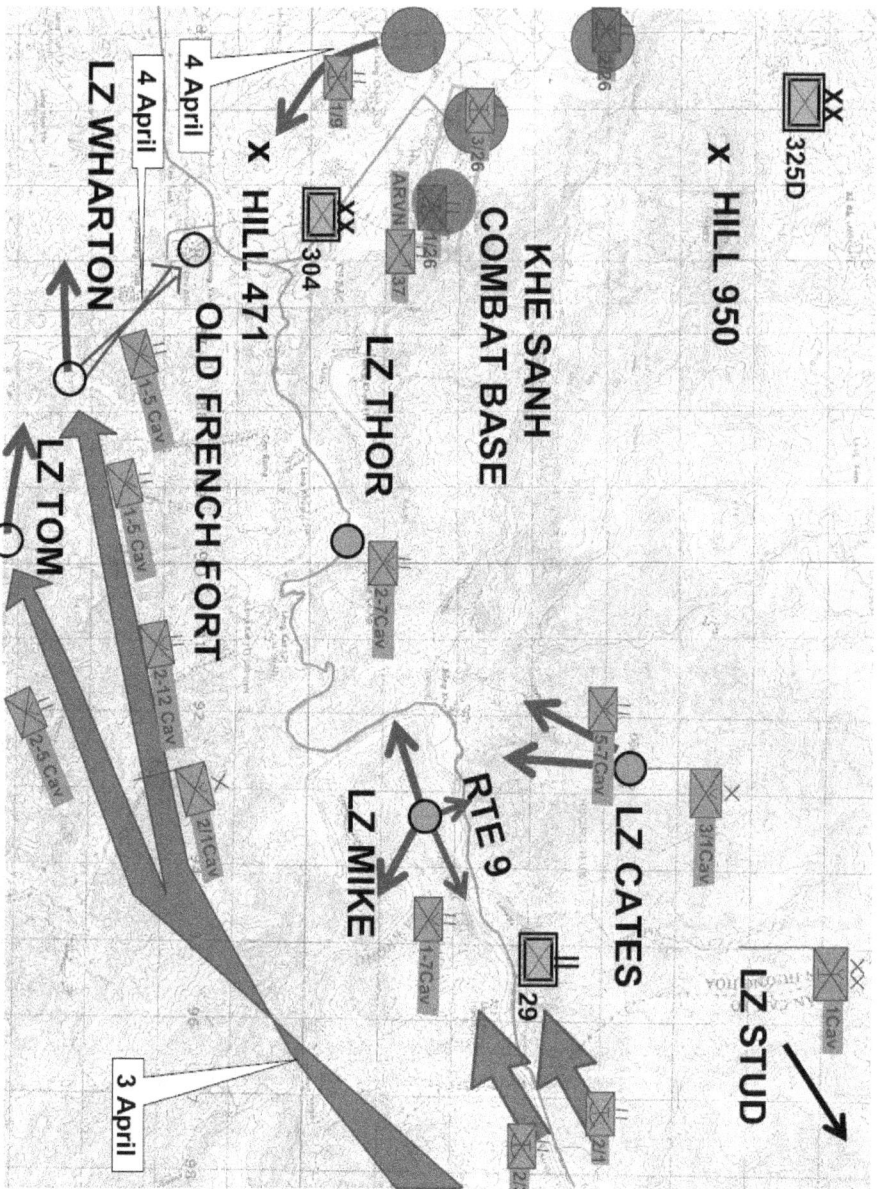

Figure 21. Operation PEGASUS Phase 2, April 3-4 1968.

nies, moved swiftly under the cover of morning fog in an effort to take the hilltop by surprise. However, when the fog cleared, enemy resistance solidified. The Marines had to call in air strikes and artillery before deliberately assaulting the NVA position, capturing the hill by late afternoon. Fighting on the hilltop continued the next day, as the NVA counterattacked in strength, only to be repulsed with great losses. On the next day (6 April), 2-12th Cav was air-lifted from LZ Wharton to relieve the Marines who then turned northwest to secure the rest of the ridgeline, having a big fight at Hill 689 on 16-19 April, after the end of Operation PEGA-SUS.[34] Also on the 4th and just to the southeast, the 1-5 Cav moved up from LZ Wharton via helicopter and attacked enemy units near the Old French Fort. The battalion commander, Lieutenant Colonel Robert Runkle, was killed in action when enemy fire shot down his C&C helicopter as the battalion came up against an estimated NVA battalion defending the area of the fort. The battle continued into the 5th, before the 1-5th Cav withdrew. The 2-5th Cav bat-talion replaced it in the assault, airlifting from LZ Tom to attack from the northeast. The fort held out until 7 April.[35]

On 5 April, as the 2d Brigade continued the fight at the old fort, and the 1/9th Marine bat-talion was fighting off counterattacks on Hill 471, Tolson committed his final brigade, the 1st Brigade, commanded by Colonel John Stannard. Stannard air assaulted his 1-8th Cav battal-ion to LZ Snapper, located four miles due south of Khe Sanh Combat Base and overlooking Route 9. The brigade headquarters and 2-12th Cav battalion then followed. The brigade then sent elements to the north and west.[36]

Action on the 5th placed NVA elements south of the Khe Sanh base in a vise around the Old French Fort, Hill 471 and Route 9 to the east. Nevertheless, the Communists fought hard. The 2-7th Cav battalion, attacking west along Route 9 from LZ Thor, faced strong defensive stands along the highway, which finally evaporated towards the end of the day.[37]

The action of the 2-7th Cav on 6 April is a good demonstration of how battle command was executed by commanders at the battalion level. While the battalion attacked a dug in NVA force of approximately company size along Route 9 several miles southeast of the Khe Sanh Combat Base, battalion commander Lieutenant Colonel Roscoe Robinson controlled his companies from a command and control helicopter hovering over the battlefield. During the course of the all day battle, Robinson had to return to LZ Thor twice to exchange helicopters as his first two became too heavily damaged from enemy fire. In addition he combined sever-al of these runs with the medical evacuation of wounded personnel. Accompanying Robinson in his command aircraft was a small command group including his field artillery fire support officer and several staff officers and radio operators. In his third helicopter of the day, Robin-son managed to return to the sky over the action towards the end of the day as NVA resistance finally slackened and broke. The 2-7th Cav paused for the night ready to finish the push to the combat base the next day.[38]

In a move designed as the initial link up with the Khe Sanh defenders, the 84th Company of the 8th Battalion, ARVN 3d Airborne Task Force, was airlifted to the combat base in the early afternoon of 6 April. The next day Tolson committed the rest of the task force, under com-

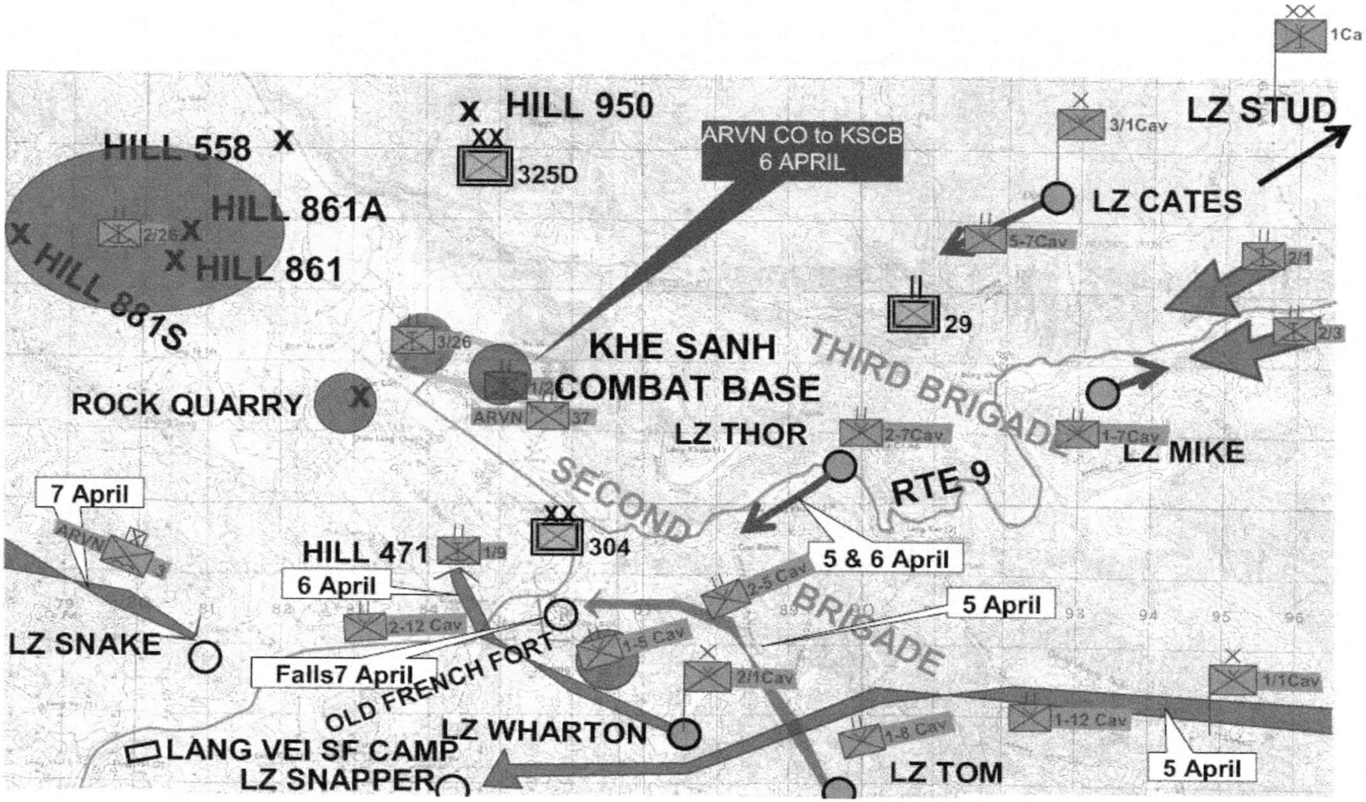

Figure 22. Operation PEGASUS Phase 3, April 5-7 1968.

132

mand of Colonel Nguyen Khoa Nam, to LZ Snake, the most westerly LZ used in PEGASUS. LZ Snake was about three and a half miles southwest of the combat base and a mile north of Route 9 and the abandoned Lang Vei Special Forces Camp. The ARVN troops fought off NVA attacks and then advanced southwest towards Lang Vei and placed blocking positions to disrupt the retreat of NVA forces near Khe Sanh.[39]

By 7 April it was obvious the NVA forces were now attempting to retreat into Laos and PEGASUS became a pursuit operation. Elements of the 3d Brigade, (2-7th Cav) advancing down Route 9, linked up with the combat base garrison on 8 April. The 3d Brigade command post then flew into the formerly besieged combat base and took command of the operations there. Khe Sanh was relieved and the large enemy presence in the area was either destroyed or forced back into Laos.[40]

In the flexibility that was inherent in the 1st Cavalry Division (Airmobile) in Vietnam, the division was diverted from the Khe Sanh area on short notice starting on 10 April. Higher commands wanted the division to operate in the NVA stronghold of the A Shau Valley, just to the south of the Khe Sanh area, before the changing seasons made campaigning there more difficult. Although the 2d Brigade stayed behind for a while at Khe Sanh, within four days the first divisional elements were air assaulting into the A Shau.[41]

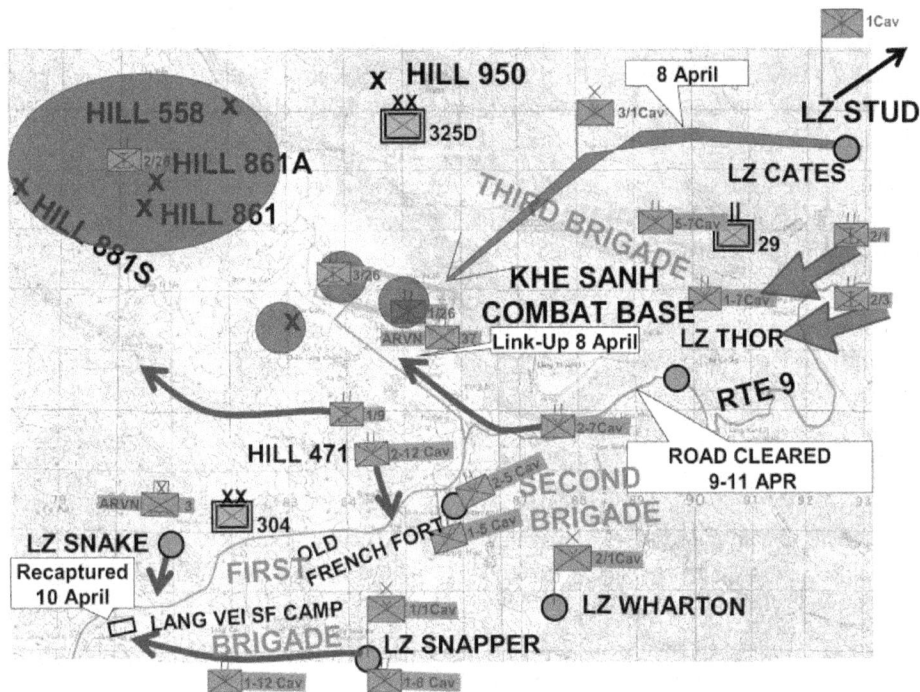

Figure 23. Operation PEGASUS Final Phase.

PEGASUS was the first operation of the Vietnam War where the 1st Cav simultaneously employed all three of its brigades and as many as eight maneuver battalions in an air assault role. Tolson controlled up to 19 maneuver battalions, employing six subordinate headquarters (three Army brigades, two Marine regiments and one ARVN task force) to direct their operations, each with its own specific mission and/or area of operations. Except for the Marines, all units, before they were committed to battle, were staged through LZ Stud, where Tolson's headquarters was. Before the operation commenced, he visited the Khe Sanh garrison several times and coordinated operations from that end.[42]

Tolson faced the challenge of commanding such a varied force through a combination of constant radio communication with subordinate units, personal visits to all major units via helicopter, and locating himself both at the forward base for the operation—LZ Stud—and over the battlefield via command and control helicopter throughout the operation. Despite the unique scale of the operation and its employment of ground and aviation assets from two services and an allied nation, Tolson successfully relieved the Khe Sanh garrison, destroying or pushing away the large force the North Vietnamese had assembled around the Marine combat base.

While providing the commander a unique, new means of battle command, C&C helicopters were not without their drawbacks. As previously mentioned, one commander, Lieutenant Colonel Robert Runkle of the 1-5th Cav, was killed in action when his C&C helicopter was shot down by enemy fire. Other commanders such as Lieutenant Colonel Roscoe Robinson of the 2-7th Cav were luckier than Runkle. As related earlier, Robinson had several helicopters shot out from under him, but continued to vigorously lead his battalion with replacement aircraft as it pushed up Route 9.[43]

The advent of the helicopter made both units and commanders more mobile, and all future US Army divisional organizations included a unit of light observation helicopters available for use as command and control instruments.

However, the expected Cold War face-off against the Soviets and other projected high- or mid-intensity conflicts did not necessarily count on the complete control of the air and the relatively low level of air defense encountered in Vietnam. Therefore the helicopter became just one of several battle command options available.

Summary

The development of the helicopter added a third dimension to ground operations and provided a reliable platform from which commanders could control dispersed forces. Use of the helicopter to move troops operationally around the battlefield and provide immediate firepower created a new kind of mobile operation.

Vietnam provided the major arena for this new kind of mobile warfare and Operation PEGASUS, the 1st Cavalry Division (Airmobile)'s relief of Khe Sanh, provides the classic example of battle command on the move, helicopter-style. In a little more than a week, the airmobile troops and Marine forces had relieved the Khe Sanh garrison and destroyed or pushed away the large North Vietnamese force which had been threatening the extreme northwestern corner of South Vietnam for months.

As in the Little Bighorn campaign a century earlier, large-scale airmobile operations sought to throw converging forces at the enemy in a manner which would destroy him by massing on him. In the case of PEGASUS, the Marine garrison in and around the Khe Sanh combat base acted as a fulcrum upon which the mobile operation was focused. Unlike at Little Bighorn, 1st Cav commander Tolson, as the overall operational commander, had complete control of his dispersed forces and constant communications with them. The helicopter also provided him the operational mobility and flexibility to move forces around the battlefield to where they were most needed or where they could have the most effect. While basically employing command and control organizations common to the United States Army infantry since World War II, these battle command techniques were greatly enhanced by the technological innovation of the helicopter. The helicopter provided the force commander not only with a means to view the battlefield or quickly move to any key locations, but it allowed continuous communications as a mobile radio hub, and provided immediately available troop transportation and direct fire effects.

Notes

1. John J. Tolson, *Airmobility 1961-1971*, Vietnam Studies (Washington, DC: Department of the Army, 1973), vii.

2. David Hackworth and Eilhys England, *Steel My Soldiers' Hearts: The Hopeless to Hardcore Transformation of US Army, 4th Battalion, 39th Infantry, Vietnam* (New York: Simon & Schuster, 2002),155

3. Some brigade commanders preferred their battalion commanders to control their forces entirely from the ground. A good example of this is the case of the 2d Battalion, 28th Infantry, 1st Brigade, 1st infantry Division. Brigade commander Colonel George Newman preferred his battalion commanders to locate themselves on the ground with one of their subordinate units rather than in a command and control helicopter. 2-28th Infantry commander, Lieutenant Colonel Terry Allen was killed in action when two companies of the battalion were ambushed by enemy forces near the Ong Thanh stream, Binh Long province on 17 October 1967. See George L. MacGarrigle, *Taking the Offensive: October 1966 to October 1967*, The United States Army in Vietnam, Combat Operations (Washington, DC: US Army Center of Military History, 1998), 353-61.

4. Hackworth, 159-60; Anthony Herbert, *Soldier* (New York: Holt, Rinehart and Winston, 1973), 266-68.

5. Tolson, 103-4; Hackworth, 106, 155.

6. Tolson, 165; Willard Pearson, *The War in the Northern Provinces 1966-1968*, Vietnam Studies (Washington, DC: Department of the Army, 1975), 3-4, 15-6; Michael P. Kelly, *Where We Were in Vietnam: A Comprehensive Guide to the Firebases, Military Installations and Naval Vessels of the Vietnam War 1945-75* (Central Point, OR: Hellgate Press, 2002), 5-274.

7. Pearson, 17-8; Kelly, 5-236.

8. Tolson, 165, 167.

9. John Prados and Ray W. Stubbe, *Valley of Decision: The Siege of Khe Sanh* (Boston: Houghton Mifflin, 1991), 171, 268-9, 271.

10. Prados and Stubbe , 248.

11. Ibid., 249, 251.

12. Ibid., 258, 263-4.

13. Pearson, 73; Kelly, 5-236; Prados and Stubbe, 304-9.

14. Pearson, 74-5; Prados and Stubbe, 317-9, 327-330.

15. Pearson, 75; Prados and Stubbe, 343, 345-349.

16. Pearson, 75-6; Prados and Stubbe, 375.

17. Prados and Stubbe, 391, 395.

18. Ibid, 409; Pearson, 77.

136

19. Prados and Stubbe, 413-6.

20. Tolson, 169.

21. Kelly, 5-174; The US liaison officer to the 3d ARVN Airborne Task Force, Captain Joseph Kinzer, ended up making key decisions for his ARVN commander because of time restraints. See Kinzer, Joseph, "US Army Oral History Interview VNIT 101, End-of-Tour Interview CPT Joseph W. Kinzer, Advisory Team 163, Liaison Officer, 3d Airborne Brigade, [ARVN] Airborne Division," 11 June 1968. Transcribed copy maintained at US Army Center of Military History, Washington, DC. Also available at http://www.army.mil/cmh-pg/documents/vietnam/vnit/vbit0101.htm, accessed 1 April 2005. Hereaf•ter referred to as VNIT 101.

22. Tolson, 169.

23. Ibid., 169-70.

24. Ibid.,170-1.

25. Ibid.,170-2.

26. Ibid., 170.

27. Ibid., 175.

28. Ibid., 173; Prados and Stubbe, 427-9.

29. VNIT 101.

30. Tolson, 173-4; Prados and Stubbe, 428-9; Kelly 5-95, 5-333.

31. Shulimson, Jack, Leonard A. Blasiol, Charles R. Smith and David A. Dawson, *The Defining Year: 1968*, U.S. Marines In Vietnam (Washington, DC: History And Museums Division, Headquarters, U.S. Marine Corps, 1997), 285.

32. Tolson, 174; Kelly, 5-506.

33. Tolson, 174-5; Kelly, 5-515, 5-547; Prados and Stubbe, 432.

34. Prados and Stubbe, 432-4; Kelly, 5-230, 5-233; Tolson, 176.

35. Tolson, 174; Prados and Stubbe, 432. Runkle was immediately replaced by LTC Clarence Jordan.

36. Kelly, 5-469; Tolson, 175-6.

37. Tolson, 176.

38. Prados and Stubbe, 438.

39. Tolson, 177; Kelly, 5-468; Prados and Stubbe, 437.

40. Tolson, 177.

41. Tolson, 178-180.

42. Tolson, 169-70, 174, 179-80.

43. Tolson, 174; Prados and Stubbe, 438-9.

BATTLE COMMAND IN THE 1973 ARAB-ISRAELI WAR

"In the Armored Corps we take our orders on the move"
—Colonel Arieh Karen, Commander, Israeli 217th Armored Brigade, 1973[1]

In many ways the Israeli Defense Force (IDF) is the latter-day successor to the German World War II practitioners of mobile armored warfare. After fielding a primarily infantry army in their wars with the various Arab states in 1948-9 and 1956, the success enjoyed in the latter war by the relatively small armored portion of the IDF resulted in an army over‧ haul in the years between 1956 and 1967. The result was a force structure giving a more prominent role to the classic blitzkrieg combination of massed armor forces and close air support fighter-bombers. The swift victory in the June 1967 war was won by this combina‧ tion. The IDF that fought the 1973 war was even more organized in this fashion at the start of the war, with emphasis on main battle tanks and jet fighter-bombers. Combined arms coordination only went this far. Self-propelled artillery and mechanized infantry were given lesser roles. Unfortunately for the Israelis, the Egyptians negated the role of close air sup‧ port by fielding a protective umbrella of massed surface to air missiles (SAMs). The main battle tank was also negated by the use of massed Sagger anti-tank guided missile systems and RPG-7 short-range anti-tank rockets carried by light infantry. Without its own infantry to push away the ambushing Egyptian infantry, the Israeli tanks were left to fight off volleys of wire-guided missiles and rockets.

The Egyptian tactical improvements were, however, thinly applied. After the initial canal crossing, the Egyptians were able only to defend with their Saggers and RPGs under their SAM shield. Offensive operations with their armored forces proved to display the same weaknesses seen in past wars. Meanwhile, the Israelis managed to learn from their mistakes and adjust to the new situation by realigning their forces into a better combined arms team and executing an operation that both destroyed the SAM umbrella and made the position of the Egyptian forces dug in along the east bank of the Suez Canal perilous before a ceasefire ended the conflict.

This chapter will analyze two Israeli mobile operations from the 1973 war in terms of command and control. One operation, the 8 October Battle of El Firdan, was a failure. The other, the 15-17 October Battle of the Chinese Farm, though ultimately an Israeli victory, proved to be very challenging from a command and control perspective.

The Battle of El Firdan

On 8 October 1973, a planned coordinated attack by two IDF armored divisions against the Egyptian bridgehead at El Firdan, led by experienced, battle-hardened commanders, resulted in two separate uncoordinated attacks by single tank battalions. Each battalion was virtually

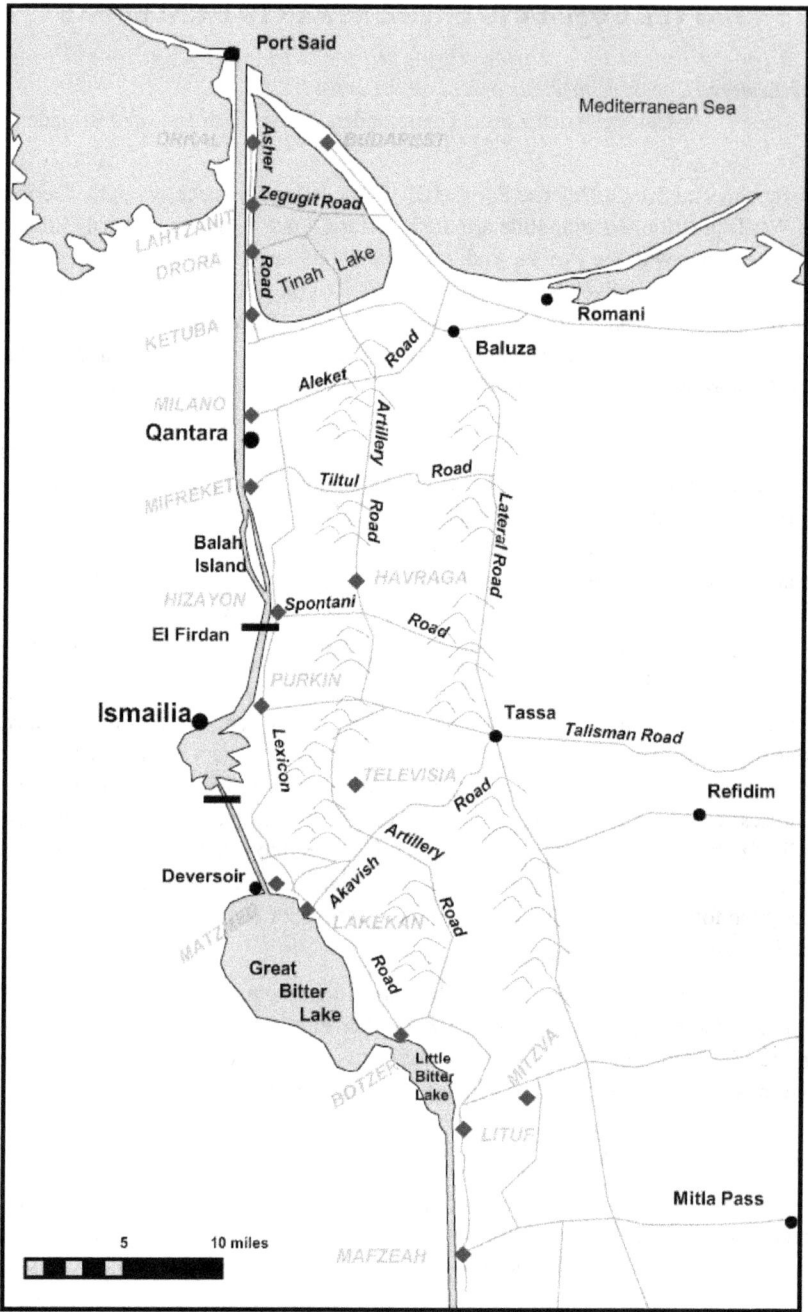

Figure 24. Sinai Canal Front topography 1973.

destroyed within minutes by Egyptian antitank missile and rocket fire. How did this grand failure in mobile operations command happen?

At 2 pm on 6 October 1973, with the western sun in their enemy's eyes, the infantry forces of the corps-sized Egyptian Second and Third Armies conducted an assault crossing of the Suez Canal along its whole length. The Egyptian plan was to cross and occupy a narrow strip of the eastern canal bank out to about 3 miles, covered by the SAM umbrella. For the most part, Israeli defensive fortifications, the so-called Bar Lev Line, would be bypassed to pro•vide bait for the Israeli armor to counterattack. In one of the most successful river-crossing operation in military history, elements of five Egyptian infantry divisions crossed the canal on 6 October and secured the desired bridgeheads.

The Israeli defensive concept was based on defeating local crossings of the canal, not a full-scale crossing along its whole length, an operation they did not think the Egyptians to be capable of executing. Under this concept, the Israelis created and manned 17 strongpoints, the Bar Lev Line, along the 155 miles of the canal, spaced between six and 18 miles apart. These fortifications were manned with small units of infantry and designed to resist the Egyptians until reinforcements in the form of local reserves in each sector of the front, usually a tank battalion, could come forward to counterattack. Above the local sectors was the Sinai ar•mored division, in 1973 the 252d Armored Division commanded by Major General Avraham Mandler, with three armored brigades and supporting arms and services. In October 1973 Mandler had one brigade forward and two in reserve in the center of the canal front.[2]

Behind the Bar Lev Line, the Israelis had built a series of roads designed to enable them to move and maneuver armored forces around rapidly. These roads were essential because the geography near the canal did not favor the use of armored forces off roads. From the canal to the first high ground, a north-south running ridgeline 6-7 miles to the east, the terrain was flat and generally open, but the sand dunes were deep and treacherous for travel by armored vehicles. Along the canal connecting the Bar Lev fortifications ran the Lexicon road in the south and the Asher Road in the north, the latter being in actuality merely a causeway running between the canal and the swampy marshland of Lake Tinah.

Just behind the first ridgeline 7 miles east of the canal, the Israelis built their north-south running Artillery Road. A farther 18 miles to the east ran the Lateral Road, built upon the sec•ond, higher ridgeline east of the canal. Between the ridges and extending eastward from the canal 40 miles into the mountains of central Sinai were deep sand dunes. Additionally, near the ruins of the town of Qantara, could be found swamp marshes covered by a thin layer of sand. Both the dunes and the marshes could restrict the trafficability of not just wheeled but even armored vehicles. In addition to their three parallel north-south highways, the Israelis had built or improved numerous roads running generally east-west between these parallel roads down to the canal.[3]

On the 6th and early part of the 7th, while the Israelis waited for their reserve armored forces to mobilize and move to the Sinai, Mandler defended the Sinai on his own. His for•ward brigade was in action immediately with three tank battalions supporting the Bar Lev fortification defenders.[4] After feeding some of their tank battalions separately into the battle, he then deployed his two other brigades to the north and south respectively.[5]

Under mobilization plans, two reserve armored divisions were earmarked for the Sinai. As these forces arrived, they took over sectors of the front from Mandler. Major General Avraham Adan took over the northern sector with his 162d Armored Division on the morning of the 7th even as his own brigades of freshly mobilized reservists were still arriving. Adan assumed command of Mandler's forces in the north, while his own forces concentrated in an assembly area near Baluza on the coastal road about 12 miles from the Suez Canal.[6]

Adan's lead elements had begun moving to the Sinai within 12 hours of receiving the mobilization order. The canal was 180 miles from the divisional mobilization sites. Most units moved using tractor-trailer tank transports, though some, like the self-propelled artillery, moved cross-country on their own tracks to avoid the traffic on the coastal road. The movement was slow and even hindered at times by Egyptian helicopter-borne commandos.[7]

Major General Ariel Sharon assumed command in the center with his reserve 143d Armored Division. Mandler retained control over the southern sector, giving Sharon the brigade that was covering the central sector while receiving two reservist brigades in the south to replace the regulars given to Adan and Sharon.[8] The three divisions now held a loose front along the Lateral Road with advance outposts on the Artillery Road, containing the Egyptian advance and preparing for counteroffensive operations on the 8th.[9]

As Commander of the IDF Southern Command, Major General Shmuel Gonen was the corps-equivalent theater commander for the Sinai front in early October 1973. Initially Gonen commanded from his peacetime garrison headquarters at Beersheba in southern Israel, but early on the 7th shifted to a forward bunker complex at Umm Hashiba near the Refidim Airbase, about 25 miles west of the Suez Canal, a location central to the canal front.[10] Gonen controlled operations by face-to-face meetings with subordinates at his headquarters and via radio. He did not leave his headquarters during operations. This would soon be reflected in his situational conceptions not being anywhere in synchronization with those of his key subordinate commanders.[11]

With the arrival of the reservist units somewhat stabilizing the front, the Israelis began planning to take the counteroffensive on 8 October to regain the initiative. This planning and subsequent orders would prove to be faulty for the execution of sound armored operations. A clear and concise commander's intent, aside from simply the notion of attacking, was absent. Gonen's goals and intentions would change so much over the hours before and during the attack that his subordinate commanders would have no clear idea of what was expected of them. Time would be wasted, units would stop, awaiting clarification, units would attack without orders. One division would not only *not* support the attack of its neighbor, but would, under orders, depart and leave the attacking unit's flank wide open, ultimately marching around in a big circle and returning to find its previously occupied positions now held by the enemy.

142

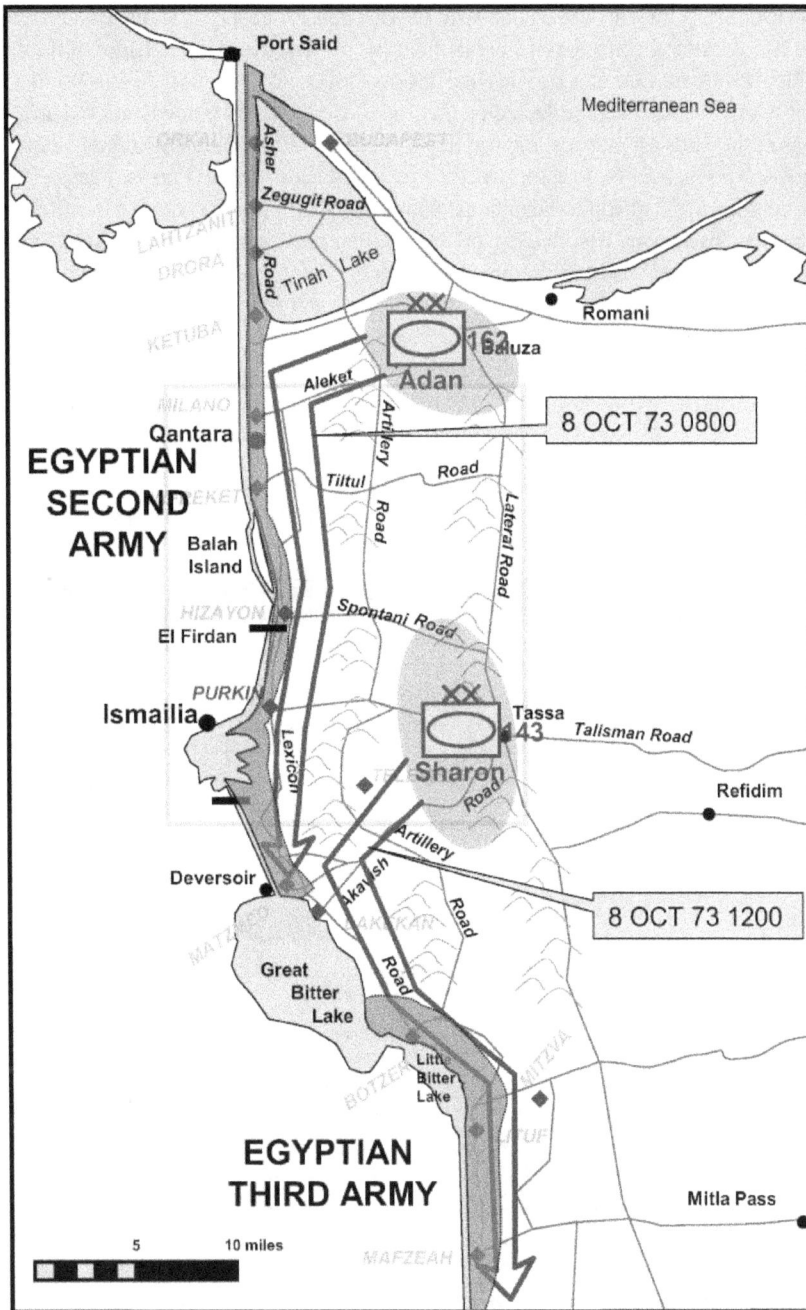

Figure 25. Original Israeli plan for 8 October 1973 counterattack.

On the evening of the 7th, Gonen met with the division commanders at his headquarters to go over the plans for the next day's operations. Also present was the IDF Chief of Staff, Lieutenant General David Elazar, who had final approval over any operational plan. While Gonen was overly optimistic, Elazar reflected on the importance of the two newly arrived armored divisions in the Sinai as, perhaps, the last line of defense for the nation from that quarter and did not want to squander these assets as IDF forces had been the previous two days. Therefore the original plan called for Adan to advance his division west to within two miles of the canal, but no closer, away from the Egyptian antiarmor nests, then to advance south parallel to the canal to the Matzmed strongpoint, located at the point where the Suez Canal empties into the Great Bitter Lake. The purpose of this advance was to prevent any Egyptian attempts to push farther into the Sinai. Mandler in the south would contain the Egyptians. Adan and Sharon would not move their divisions simultaneously, so that one was always available to support the other. The attack would be executed with adequate air and artillery support.[12]

But, under pressure from Sharon, who had missed the meeting and who wanted to immediately relieve three Bar Lev Line strongpoints in his sector, and under a 1967-esque optimism that minimized Egyptian capabilities, Gonen kept changing and revising the basic plan. The table below outlines these changes.

Time and Date	Changes/ Remarks
2100, 7 October	Original Plan- Adan sweeps 2 miles from canal to Matzmed in morning, then Sharon sweeps similarly to the south
0245, 8 October	Written Overlay Plan- Adan to now clear area from canal to Artillery Road, relive Bar Lev forts, and prepare to cross canal, Sharon to do same in southern sector after Adan reaches the Great Bitter Lake.[13]
0354	Adan to link up with Bar Lev Line forts near Qantara and Ismailia and capture Egyptian Bridge at El Firdan or Ismailia and send a brigade across the canal at Ismailia or Deversoir.[14]
c. 0430	Cancelled Adan's instructions to cross anywhere but at Deversoir; mission of linking-up with Bar Lev forts now given to Sharon as an operation preliminary to Adan's movement; Sharon to then move south after Adan's movement and cross canal near Suez city.[15]
0806	Gonen inexplicably reminds Adan not to get too close to the canal, contradicting previous instructions.[16]
0955	Adan ordered to seize a bridgehead at El Firdan with a small force, in addition to other missions.[17]
1005	In mistaken belief that enemy was collapsing, Southern Command ordered Adan to move with all speed and all forces to the south
1015	Adan ordered to destroy enemy forces in Qantara in addition to other missions
1045	Sharon ordered to pull back and move in a big eastern arc to the south
c.1400	Sharon ordered to turn back

Figure 26. Israeli plan changes for 8 October 1973 counterattack.

When Elazar, now back in Tel Aviv, received a copy of Gonen's written order, a map overlay with one page of text, flown in by helicopter, he was busy with events on the Golan front and apparently did not read the plan, presuming it reflected his oral guidance from the meeting several hours before. In the morning, even after talking with Gonen, Elazar still felt the operation being executed was that which he had outlined the night before.[13] The commanders in the field never even saw the overlay order and continued to work from the oral guidance given out at the face-to-face meeting and from radio calls from Gonen.[14]

Aside from confusion as to the continually changing scheme of maneuver, Gonen would also be plagued by some communications problems. He chose to notify his division commanders of the changes via radio instead of going to each commander and discussing things directly. This became problematic when the Egyptians apparently jammed radio signals to Adan and messages had to be relayed to him through another commander who was located at a site with a larger antenna. Eventually Adan had to relocate to a high hilltop to get direct communications with Gonen.[15]

The changes impacted not only the division commanders, but also the brigade commanders as well. Adan had met with his key subordinates as soon as he got back from his meeting with Gonen, dismissing them before he got word of any operational changes. Adan's two available brigades had begun moving into their attack positions at 0400. Gonen downplayed any complications Adan would have communicating the new plan to his subordinates.[16]

162d Armored Division
(Major General Avraham Adan)

460th Armored Brigade
(Colonel Gavriel 'Gabi' Amir)

    Tank Battalion
    (Lieutenant Colonel Amir Yoffe)
    Tank Battalion
    (Lieutenant Colonel Haim Adini)

600th Armored Brigade
(Colonel Nathan 'Natke' Nir)

    Tank Battalion
    (Lieutenant Colonel Assaf Yaguri)
    Tank Battalion
    (Lieutenant Colonel Nathan)
    Tank Battalion
    (Lieutenant Colonel Giora Lev)

217th Armored Brigade
(Colonel Arieh Karen)

    Tank Battalion
    (Lieutenant Colonel Nahum Zaken)
    Tank Battalion
    (Lieutenant Colonel Dan Sapir)
    Tank Battalion
    (Lieutenant Colonel Eliashiv Shimski)

Figure 27. Israeli Defense Force Order of Battle–Battle of El Firdan.

Adan had his division deployed at 6 am for the attack with two brigades on line facing southwest towards the canal.[17] On the right was Colonel Gavriel Amir's regular army 460th Armored Brigade, with only two tank battalions and 25 tanks. Amir's brigade, though originally earmarked for Adan's division, had been deployed to reinforce Mandler on the day before the Egyptian attack and had fought in the northern sector during the initial Egyptian operations.[18] One of the brigade's battalions was Amir's only remaining organic regular tank battalion, commanded by Lieutenant Colonel Amir Yoffe. Mandler had dispatched Amir's other battalions separately to the central and southern sectors. After road marching 60 miles from Refidim to the northern canal front, Yoffe had seen his battalion beat up by the Egyptians on the 6th around Qantara. When he subsequently fell under Adan's command, he only had nine available tanks. His new division commander had Yoffe pull back, regroup and recover any tanks he could. Through ingenuity and hard work, Yoffre recovered 18 Centurion and seven Patton tanks from his own battalion and the battalion from Mandler's forward brigade, which had been decimated on the 6th before Amir's brigade had gotten to the scene. Amir's other battalion, a reserve battalion commanded by Lieutenant Colonel Haim Adini, had originally been assigned to Adan's mechanized infantry brigade. When the mech brigade was detached from the division to cover the coastal road, Adan sent its tank battalion to Amir.[19]

Colonel Nathan Nir's reservist 600th Armored Brigade of three tank battalions and 71 tanks was on the left facing Qantara.[20] Nir's brigade, though freshly mobilized, had already seen combat. After the brigade's first tank battalion, commanded by Lieutenant Colonel Assaf Yaguri, had been offloaded from its heavy equipment transporters near the coastal locality of Romani, Egyptian commandos who had landed by helicopter ambushed his second battalion, led by Lieutenant Colonel Natan, as it off-loaded. Yaguri's battalion attacked and disbursed the Egyptians after a tough fight. A short while later the Egyptians returned and attacked one of Adan's reconnaissance units, which had counterattacked and destroyed the enemy force, capturing its commander.[21]

Adan's third armored brigade, the 217th commanded by Colonel Arieh Karen, was still arriving in the theater. Accordingly, Adan had designated Karen as the reserve to move behind the other two brigades. Karen had three tank battalions and 62 tanks.

Gonen had promised Adan air and artillery support for the attack. But on 8 October Israeli air assets were concentrated on the more critical Golan front. Air support was limited and Gonen's headquarters insisted on controling it, resulting in several fratricidal incidents. Adequate artillery had not also arrived yet as Adan was supported only by the two batteries and ten artillery tubes that had been supporting Amir's brigade before his arrival. A shortage of tank transporters had forced the bulk of his self-propelled guns to move cross-country over their own tracks and they would not arrive until after the counterattack was over.[22]

While Adan's division was envisioned in mobilization plans, in many ways it was an ad hoc organization. Since 1967 the Israeli armored corps had grown to two and a half times its pre-1967 size. In 1967 the armored division, or *ugda* in modern Hebrew, had operated more as a task force than a permanent unit. This mindset still held in the IDF in 1973 where, with the much larger size of the armored corps, meant a lot more *ugdas* would be needed to control the increased number of armored and mechanized brigades.[23] Adan's peacetime job was as commander of the IDF armored corps. Under a more orderly scenario of mobilization, he was to take his armored corps headquarters staff with him to be the divisional staff. But in this situation, the armored corps staff would still be needed to mobilize and organize the armored units. Accordingly, Adan had split his staff in half leaving part to oversee the armored corps mobilization under a former deputy while he took his current deputy and went about prepar•ing his armored division for war.[24]

By dawn of the 8th, the defending Egyptians had been across the canal for over 40 hours and were firmly established on the far side. At Qantara part of their 18th infantry Division was dug in around the ruins of the town, supported by the freshly arrived 15th Armored Bri•gade with its T-62 tanks. South of Qantara, the 2d Infantry Division held a narrow bridgehead centered on a 60-ton metal bridge placed across the canal at El Firdan. The 23d Mechanized Division on the west bank was preparing to cross over the canal. Between Ismailia and the Great Bitter Lake, the 16th Infantry Division held a bridgehead. This division was ordered to advance and secure the high ground in its sector, called Missouri by the Israelis, on 8 Octo•ber, thus allowing the 21st Armored Division to cross over bridges near Ismailia out of range of Israeli artillery. Each of the Egyptian infantry divisions were augmented with extra anti•tank units, Sagger missiles and RPG-7 rocket launchers. All the Egyptian units had a general mission for 8 October of expanding the bridgehead eastward out to the line of the Artillery Road.[25]

Adan commanded during the operation by moving with his tactical command post, consist•ing of his operations, intelligence and communications officers, and three M113 armored personnel carriers (APCs) and two half tracks.[26] He initially moved in a position between the two forward brigades, trying to coordinate and establish physical contact between the flanks of each unit. Then, as they moved into the attack, located himself on a high dune from which he could observe the action.[27] When possible, he moved around his command in a jeep while his staff remained in the APCs, both constantly monitoring the radio nets of both the brigade and the higher command.[28]

Adan's two forward brigades began the attack at 6 am with a westerly move towards the canal, shifting to a north-south axis just before 8 o'clock. On the right, Nir's 600th Brigade became engaged with the Egyptian armored forces defending Qantara. Adan left Nir to destroy the Qantara forces and become the new divisional reserve. He ordered Amir's 460th Brigade on the right to execute the southern advance moving between the Lexicon and Artil•lery Roads. He had already ordered up Karen's reserve brigade to advance to the left (east) of Amir, utilizing roads in Sharon's sector, the use of which having been coordinated in advance. After the Egyptian tanks near Qantara disengaged and disappeared into the city, Nir started proceeding to the south as well.[29]

Except for almost continuous artillery fire, and occasional infantry hunter-killer teams, Amir's advance south was unopposed, as the Egyptians had not advanced this far east yet.[30] Gonen and his Southern Command staff were monitoring Adan's radio nets and surmised from the lack of opposition that the Egyptians were about to collapse as they had in 1967. Gonen, therefore, began issuing overly optimistic orders to Adan and Sharon. Adan was to advance to the south with his whole force as quickly as possible and Sharon was to disen•gage and withdraw to the east to advance in a roundabout route to the southern end of the canal where he was to try crossing. Chief of Staff Elazar, back in Tel Aviv, tacitly approved these revised orders as he felt that Gonen, as the commander in the field, had a better pulse on the situation.[31] However, Elazar was unaware that Gonen had not left his bunker and that his estimates of the enemy situation were based purely on assumptions not reflected in any battlefield realities.

Even as these orders were being issued, Adan's lead elements were encountering their first real resistance of the day. As his brigade neared El Firdan, Amir had come into contact with heavy artillery, missile and tank gun fire, while Nir, trying to move away from Qantara, was again involved in action with the Egyptian 15th Armored Brigade. Feeling the higher com•mand must know something he did not, Adan attempted to comply, withdrawing Nir from Qantara while leaving behind a tank battalion (commanded by Lieutenant Colonel Giora Lev) and moving south with his other two.[32]

Amir's two battalions had slowed their advance awaiting close air support that never came, approaching the area east of El Firdan at around 9 o'clock. While under enemy artillery fire, his tanks tarried for two hours, moving around to avoid being hit. With the revised orders to force a crossing at El Firdan, Amir balked—his brigade had been repulsed nearby the day be•fore and he only had two small battalions and needed reinforcements. On high ground to the west sat Lieutenant Colonel Ami Morag's tank battalion from the 421st Brigade of Sharon's division. Amir tried to get that battalion attached to his brigade for the attack. Adan got Gonen's approval for the attachment, but, for disputed reasons, Sharon never gave the order and instead, Morag's battalion withdrew to the west with the rest of Sharon's division.[33]

Per his latest instructions, at 11 o'clock Adan was still trying to concentrate his forces for a coordinated attack and get adequate support for the attack. Amir sat before Firdan without reconnaissance, mortar or artillery support. Nir was moving to the right and north of Amir towards the Firdan area, closer to the canal. Adan's third brigade, under Karen, was east of Amir with two battalions (Lieutenant Colonel Nahum Zaken's with 22 tanks, and Lieuten•ant Colonel Dan Sapir's with 15 tanks) advancing in column westward down the Talisman Road towards Ismailia and one tank battalion to the north (commanded by Lieutenant Colonel Eliashiv Shimshi) being held in divisional reserve at the junction of the Artillery and Spon•tani Roads. Sharon formerly held Adan's left (southern flank), but was withdrawing, leav•ing Karen's brigade holding the left and a void of key high ground into which the Egyptians would now be able to advance unhindered.[34]

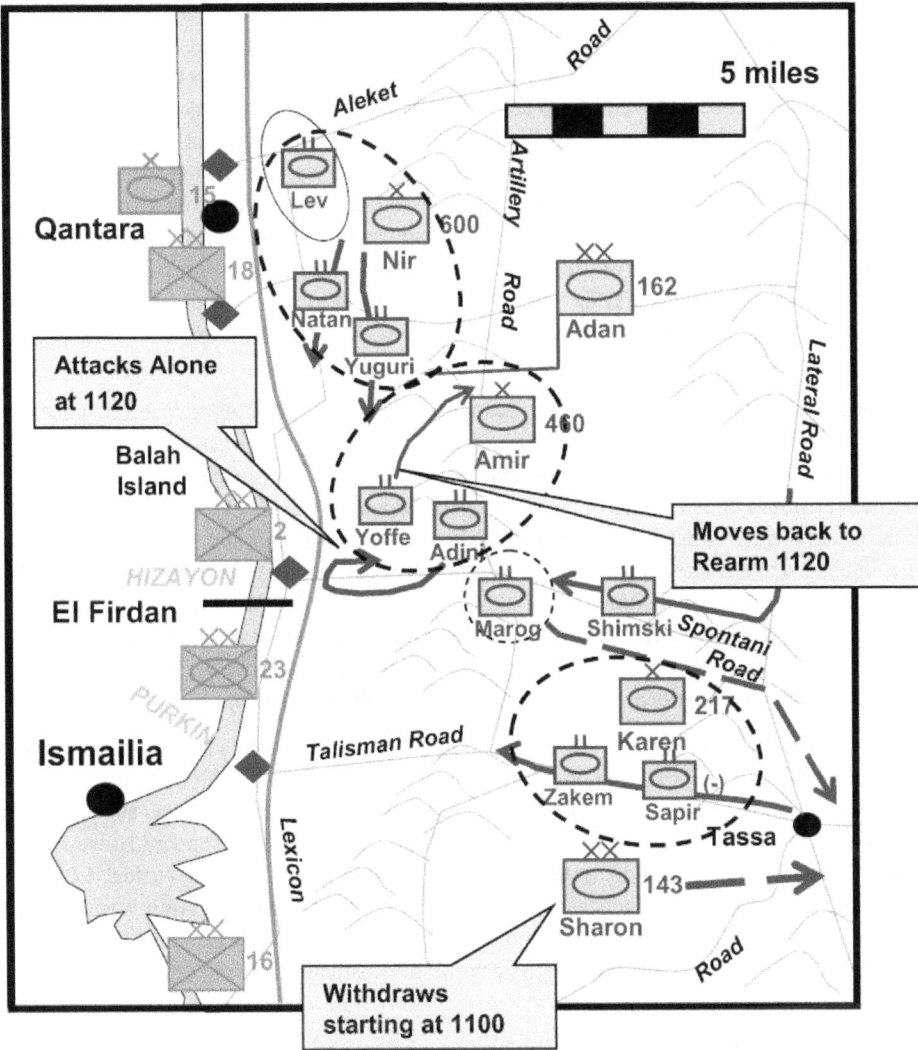

Figure 28. Israeli attack situation late morning 8 October 1973 counterattack.

At 11 o'clock Amir's two battalions before El Firdan were Yoffe's ad hoc battalion on the right and Adini's reservist battalion on the left. Yoffe's unit had been engaged in a long-range engagement with Egyptian tanks and antitank missiles, and by this point was short of am• munition and fuel. Yoffe asked permission to fall back to refuel and rearm. With the expected attack still delayed, Amir and Adan approved the request, leaving Adini's battalion alone op• posite El Firdan.[35]

In a confusing sequence of events, Amir now lost contact with his subordinate units and higfor Amir sought to move away from his battalions to higher ground to gain better com•munications and to better see the battlefield, leaving his deputy, Lieutenant Colonel Shilo Sasson behind with Adini. Switching to the division radio frequency with Amir out of contact, Adini apparently heard the reiteration of higher orders to seize the bridge at El Firdan. He, his artillery officer, and Sasson could clearly see the canal to the west and Israeli artillery and air•craft bombing unseen Egyptian positions near it. Sasson, very frustrated at the two-hour delay under enemy artillery fire, and now apparently seeing friendly fire support in play, decided on his own initiative to order the two battalions forward to take the bridge. The bridge seemed ripe for the picking. However, Yoffe, low on fuel and ammunition, had already begun to retire to resupply. Adini, nevertheless, advanced with his 25 tanks alone. Neither Adan nor Amir, the division and brigade commanders had ordered the attack.[36]

At roughly 11:20 am, Adini's battalion advanced towards the El Firdan bridgehead, a one battalion-sized division attack. As soon as he started to advance, the Israeli air support he ob•served had stopped. It was not being coordinated for him. As Adini advanced, Egyptian tank fire from positions on both sides of the canal opened up on him as he got to within 800 yards of the canal. Sagger missiles fired in massed salvos promptly hit four tanks. The rest of the tanks managed to advance an additional 300 yards. By then, Egyptian infantry had popped out of concealed fighting positions and at close range began volley firing RPG rockets at the tanks; quickly disabling three more tanks and damaging half of the rest. Wounded himself, Adini ordered a hasty retreat. The shattered battalion left seven tanks on the battlefield and had only seven left operational as it fell back away from the ambush.[37]

Though located on a high dune five miles east of the canal, with good visibility, Adan could not see the action of Adini's battalion. His radio nets were jammed, but through fragmentary radio calls, he soon became aware that Amir's brigade was in trouble, that it had attacked pre•maturely before Adan had assembled a larger force and coordinated fire support. However, he was not immediately aware of the extent of the disaster, and made following tactical decisions based on a more optimistic understanding of the events. On the battlefield, Amir was stunned to learn about the unordered attack. He immediately appealed to Morag again but that officer had already begun to move out, and when he requested instructions through his own chain of command, was told to continue.[38]

Adan was determined to attack now with his two available brigades. He ordered Nir, whose two battalions were coming up from the north, and Amir to coordinate the positioning of their two brigades for the attack. Unfortunately, without their commander present in person, each brigade commander had wrong impressions of the operation. Nir thought both brigades would attack, while Amir, still licking his wounds, thought Nir would attack while he him•self supported by fire. Adan in fact did not intend anyone to attack until he had arranged adequate close air support. Amir also did not share the fate of Adini's battalion with his peer. Adan, meanwhile, reinforced Amir with Shimshi's battalion, his divisional reserve, which was nearby. With Yoffe rearming and Adini's battalion reorganizing its remnants, Shimshi became, effectively, Amir's only battalion.[39]

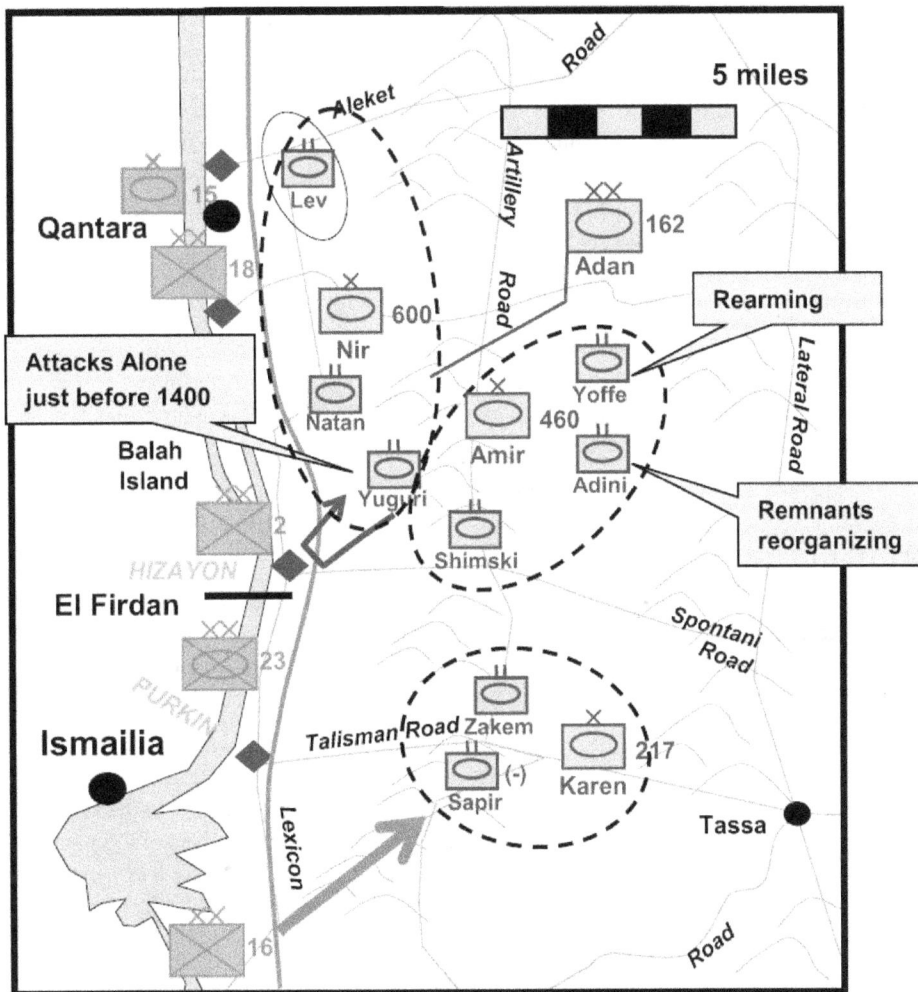

Figure 29. Israeli attack situation mid-afternoon 8 October 1973 counterattack.

Shortly after 2 pm, as soon as he returned from his coordination meeting, Nir commenced his advance with Yaguri's battalion advancing on his left. An Egyptian tank and Sagger nest in a palm grove delayed the advance of his right battalion, Natan's. Natan was to join the attack as soon as he shook off the enemy strongpoint, initially by providing covering fire. As in the morning, a single, unsupported tank battalion was now conducting a coordinated divisional attack.[40]

Unlike Adini, Yaguri and his officers had no illusions about the ferocity of the Egyptian defenses, but rumors of Israelis already across the canal and trust in the chain of command's judgment drove his battalion forward. Yaguri advanced with his three companies abreast, dispersed as widely as possible. Nir initially followed and had his first inkling that something was wrong when he noticed Shimski's battalion not moving forward as well and angrily protested over the radio to Amir. Meanwhile the Egyptians were even better prepared this time and began their ambush of Yaguri's force a mile from the canal. The defenders included two infantry brigades from the 2d Infantry Division on the flanks, and a mechanized infantry brigade from the 23d Mechanized Division in the center. Yaguri immediately realized he was attacking a far superior force and radioed his command to fall back. It was too late. In short order, the battalion was nearly annihilated, losing 16 of 25 tanks, with Yaguri being captured and later paraded on Egyptian state television.[41]

As the remnants of Yaguri's command pulled back, they met their brigade commander who was vainly trying to reach Yaguri on the radio. Immediately recognizing the extent of the disaster, Nir radioed Adan with the news. This time Adan found out almost immediately that another subordinate battalion had attacked without orders from him and been decimated.

The destruction of Yaguri's battalion may have ended Israeli offensive action on the 8th, but the Egyptians commenced their own attack designed to expand their bridgehead out to the Artillery Road and the ridgeline in front of it.

Adan took prompt action, calling his two forward brigade commanders together to confer about what to do next. Adan already had bad news about Egyptian pressure against Karen when his brigade commanders were summoned back to their units that were now themselves under attack.[42]

Since a little after noon, five miles to the south, Karen had been fighting small groups of Egyptian tanks in the area vacated by Sharon's brigades. He deployed his lead battalion (Zakem's) to the north side of the Talisman Road and his other battalion (Sapir's) to the south. Even as they were leaving, Sharon's units reported sightings of large numbers of Egyptian tanks crossing the canal at El Firdan and moving southward toward the sector they were vacating. Despite these reports, Adan ordered Karen to move forward to support the afternoon's two-brigade attack.[43]

Around the time Yaguri's command was being destroyed, a large force of infantry from the Egyptian 16th Infantry Division, supported by tanks, approached the position of Sapir's battalion south of the Talisman Road. Fearing that that road could be cut, Karen requested permission from Adan to move Zakem's battalion from its key position north of the road to support Sapir. After a break in communications caused by artillery shelling his headquarters, Adan re-contacted Karen to discover that Sapir's battalion had already been forced from its position after almost being overrun.[44]

Since the loss of the position threatened the whole Israeli line, Adan and Karen were determined to counterattack. Needing reinforcements, Adan took Yoffe's ad hoc small battalion from Amir's brigade and sent it to Karen. Once it arrived at about 3:30 pm, Karen counterattacked to the southeast with his three battalions, with Zakem supporting by fire while Sapir

152

and Yoffe attacked. Sapir was killed at the beginning of the action and his battalion was stopped cold. Yoffe, however, closed with the Egyptians and in bitter fights, lost seven out of 12 tanks, retreating back to the Talisman Road at dusk. In the distance to the east he could see reinforcements arriving. Sharon was returning.[45]

While Karen fought to retake key terrain, to the north before El Firdan the Egyptians were now advancing against Nir and Amir's depleted brigades with two full strength mechanized brigades reinforced with tanks and Saggers, and supported by heavy volleys of artillery. Observing the action from a high vantage point, Adan could not control the disorganization

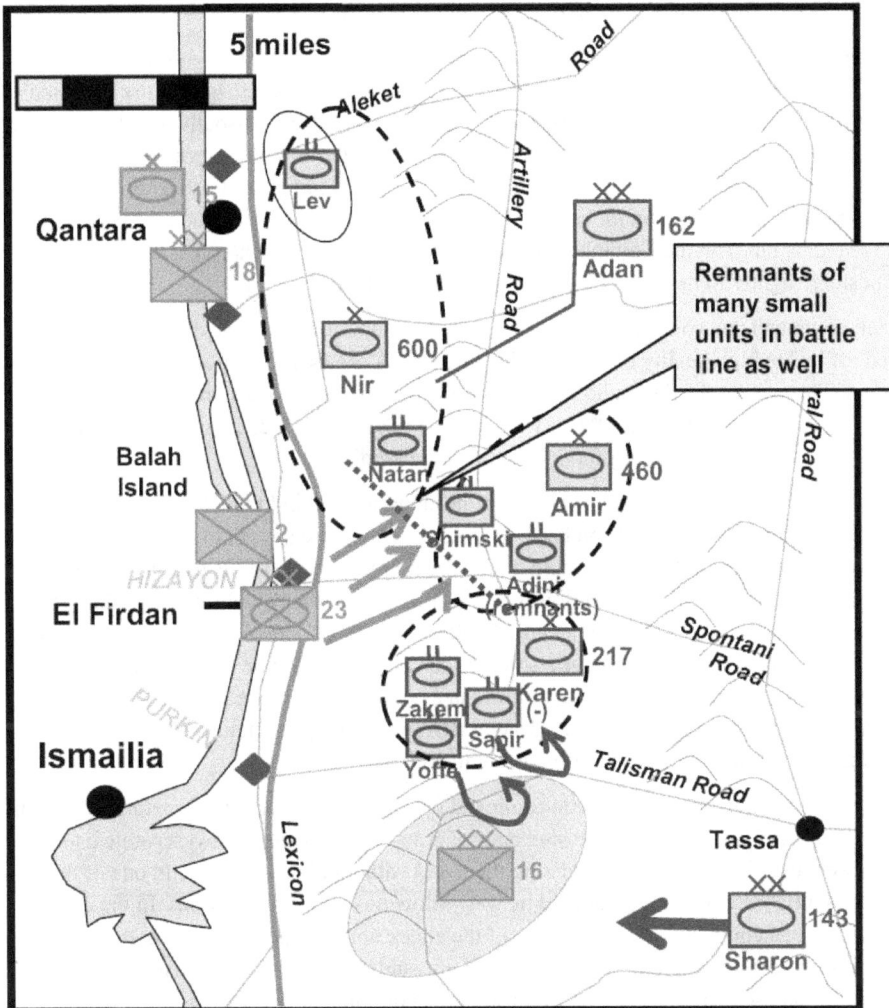

Figure 30. Egyptian counterattack situation late afternoon 8 October 1973.

he saw even though he had radio contact with his subordinate commanders. He finally had to dispatch his operations officer to personally organize straggler tanks and met himself with the commanders as mentioned above. Adan did not want to order a retreat, but the pressure on his depleted and disrupted forces left him with little alternative. Then Sharon's operations officer called to announce that Sharon was returning. Instead of ordering a retreat, Adan asked his troops to hold on until Sharon arrived. As the sun set, a mishmash of 50 Israeli tanks from all units of Adan's division turned the tables on the Egyptian attackers, transforming the Firdan plain into a tank gunnery range. The Egyptian attack had been repulsed. After darkness set in, Adan had his brigades withdraw to regroup and refit, leaving a reinforced reconnaissance bat•talion borrowed from Mandler's division to provide security in the sector.[46]

Sharon had departed in the late morning and headed east then south to the Giddi Pass.[47] He was to pause there for additional orders that would direct him to attack against the Egyptian Third Army bridgehead at the southern end of the canal from north-to-south or south-to-north. While he was there, Gonen realized the folly of the move after monitoring radio reports from Adan's units. So three hours after Sharon had moved, Gonen sent a staff officer by helicopter to personally turn Sharon around. Initially Sharon was to attack towards and cross the canal south of Adan, but with the Egyptian pressure on Adan, Gonen had Sharon assume a defen•sive posture slightly to the rear of Adan's left (southern flank).

Israeli command and control on 8 October 1973 was poor and complete disaster was only staved off by the high quality of individual soldiers, tank crews, and junior officers and com•manders. Throughout the day radio communications were terrible and unreliable, primarily due to Egyptian jamming efforts.[48] But when communications failed, commanders often did not compensate for it by moving forward to the critical point.

Gonen, the theater commander, never left his headquarters behind the front during the whole day and his estimate of the situation became progressively more a work of fantasy as the day went on. A simple trip to the front would have shown him the folly of his overly optimistic orders. The withdrawal of Sharon's division, exposing Adan's flank right when the Egyp•tian 16th Division was poised to attack that flank, was, perhaps, the biggest error of the day. Gonen had trouble controlling Sharon, which became critical when he allowed Sharon to ignore orders to attach Morag's battalion to Adan's command.[49] Gonen's intent was usually only known to his subordinates in very general terms and changed often, with each change not being communicated to all subordinate commanders.

Gonen was not alone in having battle command problems. At several key junctures, division commander Adan was not present, losing control of his subordinates as two separate battalion attacks were executed without his ordering them and without his knowledge. In one of these attacks, the brigade commander thought he was following Adan's instructions. In the other, even the brigade commander was unaware of the attack until too late. Adan's control was further impacted when shelling of his forward command post at a key time disrupted his com•munications and scattered his staff.[50] Because of the communications difficulties, he often lost positive control of one or more of his brigades, ultimately having to meet with two of the commanders face-to-face, a meeting abruptly ended by a sudden Egyptian attack.

Reports from lower to higher were often poor. Adan did not discover the extent of Adini's losses in his morning attack until after the battle. Gonen did not realize the tough situation Adan was in from his reports, which emphasized the positive and downplayed the negative.

Coordination between units on the battlefield was weak in this operation, as was coordination for fire support assets. Gonen at the theater level controlled close air support, making its use restrictive, untimely and uncoordinated. During the attacks, units on the battlefield did not support each other. A battalion from Sharon's division sat and watched while one of Adan's weakened brigades prepared an unsupported attack. Sharon's whole division abandoned positions without new units taking their place. Within Adan's division, one brigade attacked while another watched.

After the bad offensive maneuvers of the morning and early afternoon, the Israeli commanders rebounded as the Egyptians counterattacked. Gonen brought Sharon's division back. Adan and his brigade commanders managed to scrape together a 50-tank battle-line from numerous wrecked units. And the Israelis managed to coordinate their small unit actions to defeat a larger enemy force before they could be overwhelmed themselves.

The Battle of the Chinese Farm/ Suez Crossing

In an epic turnaround a week after the failure at El Firdan, many of the same commanders and units successfully executed a far more ambitious mobile operation against the same tough Egyptian defenders. Why such a drastic change? There were many factors involved, but the most telling was the placement of retired Lieutenant General Haim Bar Lev as unofficial theater commander over Gonen, who became Bar Lev's de facto chief of staff late on the 9th. Chief of Staff Elazar was disappointed both with Gonen's performance on the 8th and with his inability to control Sharon. On the 9th, Sharon had disobeyed orders to stay on the defensive and moved his tanks forward. Bar Lev replaced organizational chaos with a more orderly and effective control over the subordinate divisions. And, unlike Gonen, he made frequent trips to the command posts of his division commanders to get a feel for the situation on the ground.[51]

One of Bar Lev's first decisions was to halt the uncoordinated, piecemeal offensive actions that had marked Israeli operations in the Sinai before his arrival. After the defeat on 8 October, the Israelis licked their wounds and reorganized, learning from their defeat and adjusting to the new Egyptian tactics. Mandler still held the southern sector, Sharon the center, and Adan the north. On the extreme north a new division, the 146th Composite under Brigadier General Kalman Magen, was organized from the task force that controlled a variety of brigades sent or retained in the north to secure that vital flank. On the 9th the front had remained relatively quiet except for vain Egyptian attempts to push out on both the northern and southern ends of the line. Now Bar Lev planned to continue the containment operations while gathering strength for an eventual counter-crossing of the canal.[52]

Except for the Quay position (Masrek) in the extreme south and Budapest in the extreme north, only three Israeli garrisons still held out in Bar Lev Line forts: Hizayon opposite El Firdan, Purkin opposite Ismailia, and Matzmed opposite Deversoir where the canal flowed into the Great Bitter Lake. The garrison of Hizayon was captured late on 8 October as the survivors attempted to exfiltrate out. The 35-man garrison of Matzmed held off a large infantry assault on the 8th, but a shortage of ammunition resulted in the fort's surrender on the morning of the 9th. The garrison at Purkin exfiltrated during the night of 8/9 October. They linked up with troops from Sharon's division on the morning of the 9th.[53]

Bar Lev decided, after a meeting with his staff and key subordinates, that the command would remain on the defensive. This pause would allow the building up of strength with personnel replacements and repaired tanks, the gathering of intelligence, and the preparation of detailed plans to resume the offensive. Offensive action would only be resumed when the situation was right. Additionally, as the Egyptians continued to attack while attempting to expand their bridgeheads, Bar Lev hoped to wear down their strength.[54]

During this period the Israelis reorganized their forces to adjust to the new Egyptian tactics, placing armored infantry with tank units and bringing forward supporting artillery. For example, Adan ensured each of his tank battalions had a small armored infantry unit attached to it, with the infantry mounted in the modern M113 armored personnel carriers (APCs) which could keep up with the tanks rather than antiquated World War II era half-tracks. Bar Lev attached a parachute infantry battalion to both Sharon's and Adan's divisions, primarily for use to conduct nighttime security operations, but also to shore up the infantry element in those primarily tank organizations. An additional mechanized infantry battalion was also assigned to Adan's division from the replacement pool.[55]

However the primary source of infantry for the upcoming action would be paratrooper battalions attached to the divisions. Paratroopers were the elite of the IDF's infantry troops. Unfortunately such troops, despite their status, had limited experience working as armored infantry and would be made into ad hoc mechanized infantry by attaching half tracks or M113 APCs to their units.[56]

The Egyptians continued to move tanks over to the east bank of the canal, with over 800 across by the end of the 9th, and 1000 by the 13th. On that day Mandler was killed by artillery fire while sitting in his command vehicle talking on the radio after visiting one of his brigades.[57] Magen, who had originally been designated as his successor, took over the division, with Brigadier General Sassoon Yzhaki taking over Magen's command in the north.

While Egyptian plans originally did not call for a large-scale offensive action into the Sinai, a combination of new confidence from the successes of 6-8 October, and a need to apply pressure to support a faltering Syria, changed this. The Egyptians now planned a massive attack for the 14th, building up and deploying their forces for three days in advance.[58]

The Israelis did not want to try to cross the canal until after the Egyptians attacked. But even with the noticeable preparations, they were not sure if an attack was in the offing. Therefore,

Bar Lev determined that the crossing operation would begin on the evening of 15 October if the Egyptians did not attack or right after their attack was defeated otherwise. Time consuming preparations, such as the pulling of Adan's division out of the line, therefore, took place starting on the 13th.[59]

The Egyptians attacked with a force of about 1000 tanks on five main axes. In the north from Qantara towards Baluza; in front of El Firdan (the 8 October battlefield); against the ridgeline called Missouri by the Israelis between Ismailia and the Great Bitter Lake; towards the Giddi Pass; and a double pincer attack at the south end of the Israeli lines. The five thrusts were all repulsed with about 260 Egyptian tank losses to 40 Israeli (of which only two were not repairable).[60]

Adan's division had been pulled out of the line to be in reserve for the follow-on canal crossing operation and Adan had to reinsert a brigade into the line before El Firdan to repulse the attack of an Egyptian armored brigade.[61] The stage was now set for the second Israeli offensive in the Sinai: the creation of a bridgehead on the opposite side of the Suez Canal at Matzmed-Deversoir.

Planning for this operation had commenced almost as soon as Bar Lev took command.[62] On the evening of the 9th, Sharon's divisional recon battalion, commanded by Lieutenant Colonel Yoav Brom, had discovered a gap between the two Egyptian bridgeheads, that of the Second Army in the north and the Third Army in the south. The right flank of the former was located at the intersection of the north-south Lexicon Road and the east west Tirtur Road about two miles east of the canal, and a mile north of where it flowed into the Great Bitter Lake near the now abandoned Matzmed fortification. The Third Army's bridgehead began 25 miles to the south below the lake. This left a gap along the lake itself and an unguarded gap of a mile along the bank of the canal itself. In an instance of military serendipity, this gap was centered on the Matzmed area, where the Israelis had built a preplanned crossing site.[63] The Tirtur Road itself, which led right down to Matzmed, had been built and graded to specifically allow the passage to the canal of a unique roller bridge designed to allow tanks to cross to the far bank. Once this gap was discovered, Israeli canal crossing planners worked to exploit it, hoping to get a large body of troops to and across the canal without a serious fight.

During the preparation phase, the IDF had to assemble the necessary river crossing equipment. For this mission were available four types of specialized bridging equipment. The first were inflatable, man-portable rafts capable of ferrying across light infantry. Elite paratrooper infantry and engineers would initially cross the canal using 60 of these and secure the far side.[64] The second piece of equipment was a unique modular ferryboat called Gilowa, capable, when three were linked together, of carrying tanks. The Gilowas, basically glorified rafts, could travel on their own wheels, but the rubber belts that made them float were vulnerable to artillery fire. In addition to the rafts, the IDF also fielded two bridges, a pontoon bridge and a steel roller bridge. The pontoon bridge, like the Gilowas, was modular and once assembled, could support tanks and span the canal. This bridge was a lot more durable than the Gilowas, but each section required a tank to tow it to the canal.[65]

The roller bridge was a unique piece of equipment designed by the IDF's senior engineer to provide a sturdy, ready to use assault bridge that could support tanks. The bridge consisted of 100 sections of floatable rollers with a bridge frame on top, which, when put together extend• ed 200 yards. Once assembled, a task that took three days, the bridge was bulky and with its weight of 400 tons, needed 12 tanks to tow it and four to act as brakes.[66]

Such an unwieldy structure also required a gently graded road with few curves in it. In this respect, the discovery of the gap in the Egyptian lines played into the hands of the Israelis. They had modified the natural geography of this sector in the period before the war to facili• tate a potential crossing operation. In particular during the prewar period Israeli engineers had built two east-west roads leading down to the canal from the Artillery Road, to a pre-planned crossing site next to the Bar Lev Line fortification Matzmed. On the south, the paved Akavish Road led down to the coast of the Great Bitter Lake at the evacuated fortification of Lakekan and the canal east shore route, Lexicon Road. About a mile north of Akavish Road and paral• lel to it was the improved dirt Tirtur Road that was built specifically to allow passage of the roller bridge down to the crossing point at Matzmed. Branching off from Tirtur and run• ning down to the canal roughly parallel and several miles north of it was another key lateral road—the Shick Road.

The Matzmed crossing site was located just north of where the canal flowed into the Great Bitter Lake, providing natural flank protection from the south. Across the canal was the old World War II era airbase complex of Deversoir. A small body of water, the Sweetwater Canal, paralleled the Suez Canal and produced a narrow belt of fertile land west of the canal. Be• yond this was a chain of Egyptian SAM sites. The destruction of the SAM sites was an Israeli priority, so that their air support could then operate unhindered. To the east of the crossing site, astride the junctions of the Akavish, Tirtur and Lexicon Roads, was a complex of easily fortifiable irrigation ditches in IDF parlance known as the Chinese Farm. Possession of the Chinese Farm would be essential to any Israeli canal crossing operation as its possession by the enemy would block the key arteries into the crossing site both for the bridging equipment, and for the units moving to cross the canal.

For the crossing operation, Bar Lev intended to mass his armored forces. He used one divi• sion (Sharon's) to force the crossing and secure the crossing site, and two divisions (Adan's and Magen's) to exploit and expand the bridgehead. Surprise and exploiting the gap between the two Egyptian armies were key. While one of his armored brigades attacked the Egyptian defenders frontally, Sharon would send another armored brigade, reinforced with additional tanks, recon troops, engineers and paratroopers mounted in half tracks, through the gap to secure the crossing site, and push any Egyptian defenders away from it. The tanks would also push up Akavish and Tirtur from the back to clear those routes for the bridging equipment and remove the crossing site from Egyptian artillery range. With those routes cleared, an at• tached parachute brigade, the 243d commanded by Colonel Danny Matt, would immediately move to the crossing site and cross on the rafts. The Gilowas and part of Sharon's remaining armored brigade, the 421st commanded by Haim Erez, would move down and cross next. The rest of the 421st would follow bringing the pontoon bridge down the Akavish road and

IDF CHINESE FARM ORDER OF BATTLE

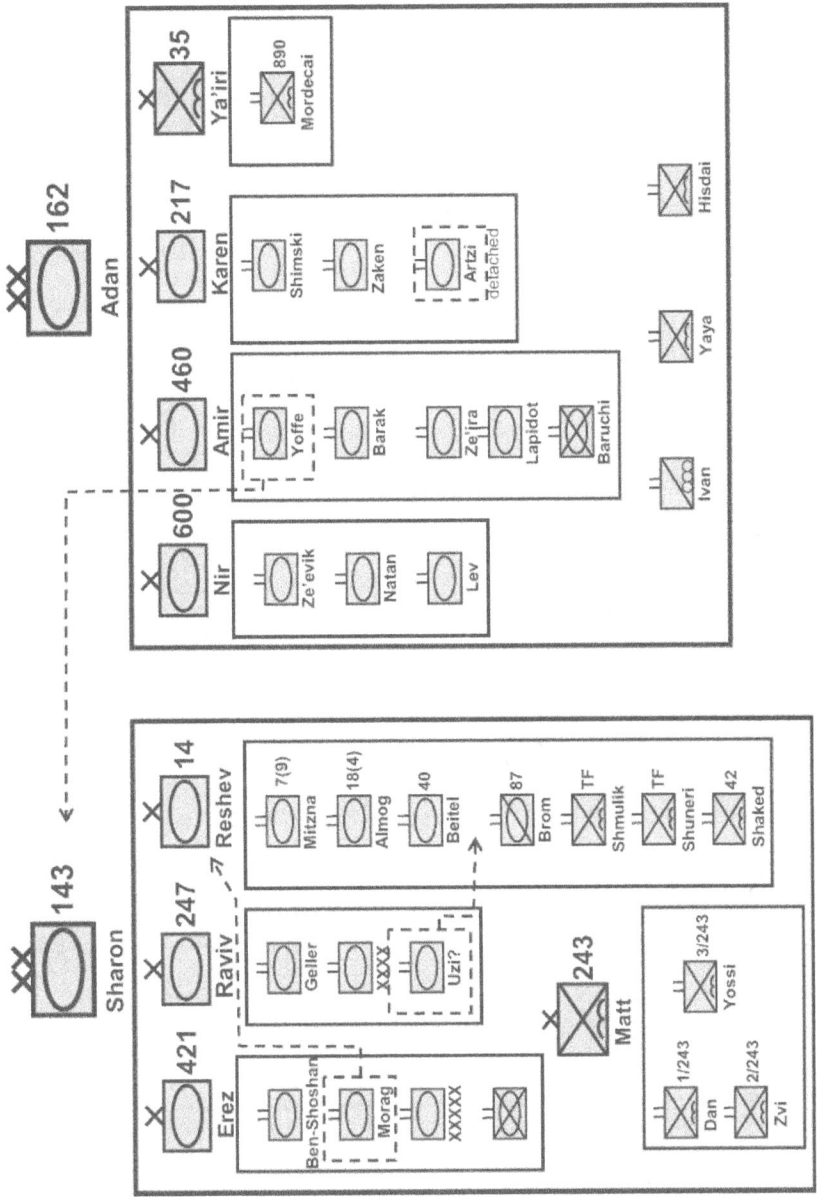

Figure 31. IDF initial Chinese Farm Order of Battle.

159

Southern Command
Lieutenant General (ret.) Haim Bar Lev [representative of Chief of Staff]
Major General Shmuel Gonen

143d Armored Division
(Major General (ret). Ariel "Arik' Sharon
    421st Armored Brigade
    (Colonel Haim Erez)
      Tank Battalion
      (Lieutenant Colonel Shimon Ben-Shosan)
      Tank Battalion
      (Lieutenant Colonel Ami Morag)
      Tank Battalion
      (Commander Unknown)
      Separate Armored Infantry Battalion

    247th Armored Brigade
    Colonel Tuvia Raviv
      Tank Battalion
      (Lieutenant Colonel Yehuda Geller)
      Tank Battalion
      (Commander Unknown)
      Tank Battalion
      (Lieutenant Colonel Uzi)
    14th Armored Brigade
    (Colonel Amnon Reshev)
      7th Tank Battalion
      (Lieutenant Colonel Amran Mitzna)
      18th Tank Battalion
      (Lieutenant Colonel Avraham Almog)
      40th Tank Battalion
      (Major Shaya Beitel)
      87th Armored Reconnaissance Battalion
      (Lieutenant Colonel Yoav Brom)
      Task Force Shmulik
      (2 paratrooper companies)
      (Lieutenant Colonel Shmulik)
      Task Force Shuneri
      (2 paratrooper companies)
      (Major Natan Shuneri Shmulik)
      42d Parachute Infantry Battalion
      (Major Shaked)
    243d Parachute Brigade
    (Colonel Dani Matt)
      Parachute Infantry Battalion
      (Lieutenant Colonel Dan)
      Parachute Infantry Battalion
      (Lieutenant Colonel Dan Zvi)
      Parachute Infantry Battalion
      (Lieutenant Colonel Yossi Yoffe)

162d Armored Division
(Major General Avraham 'Bren' Adan)
    600th Armored Brigade
    (Colonel Natan 'Natke' Nir)
      190th Tank Battalion
      (Major Ze'evik)
      Tank Battalion
      (Lieutenant Colonel Natan)
      Tank Battalion
      (Lieutenant Colonel Giora Lev)
    460th Armored Brigade
    (Colonel Gavriel 'Gabi' Amir)
      Tank Battalion
      (Lieutenant Colonel Amir Yoffe)
      Tank Battalion
      (Lieutenant Colonel Ehud Barak)
      Tank Battalion
      (Major Ze'ira)
      Tank Battalion
      (Lieutenant Colonel Lapidot)
      Armored Infantry Battalion
      (Lieutenant Colonel Baruchi)
    217th Armored Brigade
    (Colonel Arieh Karen)
      Tank Battalion
      (Lieutenant Colonel Eliashiv Shimski)
      Tank Battalion
      (Lieutenant Colonel Nahum Zakem)
      Tank Battalion
      (Lieutenant Colonel Artzi)
    35th Parachute Brigade
    (Colonel Uzi Ya'iri)

      890th Parachute Infantry Battalion
      (Lieutenant Colonel Yitzhak Mordecai)

    Motorized Reconnaissance Battalion
    (Major Ivan)
    Parachute Infantry Battalion
    (Lieutenant Colonel Yaya)
    Parachute Infantry Battalion
    (Lieutenant Colonel Ya'acov Hisdai)

Figure 31 (continued). IDF initial Chinese Farm Order of Battle.

160

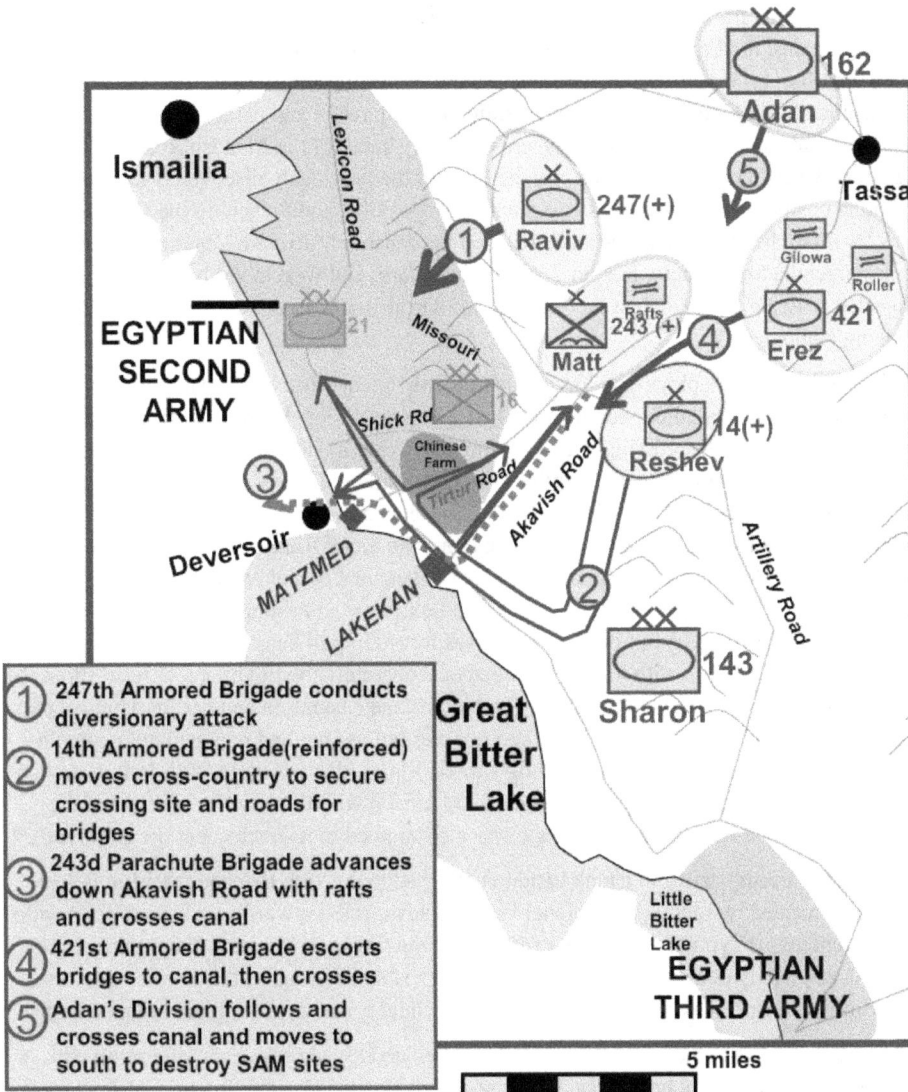

Figure 32. Israeli plan to cross the Suez Canal.

the roller bridge down the Tirtur Road. Once these bridges were set up, the rest of the 421st would cross followed by Adan's reinforced division, and then Magen's (formerly Mandler's) division.

The crossing operation began at 5 pm on 15 October with Israeli artillery firing a front-long barrage onto the Egyptian positions. The two battalions of Colonel Tuvia Raviv's 247th

Armored Brigade from Sharon's 143d Armored Division then began the diversionary attack frontally against the Egyptian 21st Armored and 16th Infantry Divisions, holding positions along the Missouri ridgeline. An hour later, Sharon's spearhead, the 14th Armored Brigade, commanded by Colonel Amnon Reshev, reinforced with recon and parachute troops, commenced its advance to the left of Raviv, cross-country south of the Akavish Road towards the Great Bitter Lake.[67] As this area was the heart of the previously discovered gap in the Egyptian positions, Reshev advanced against no opposition, soon reaching the shore of the lake. By 9 pm, he had swung north and reached the canal at Matzmed. Leaving the recon and some parachute troops there, Reshev sent his tanks north and west to secure the flank of the projected crossing site and clear the Akavish and Tirtur Roads from behind for the follow-on bridging equipment.

In the midst of this deployment, Egyptians suddenly opened fire from nearby dug-in positions. The 7th Tank Battalion, commanded by Lieutenant Colonel Amran Mitzna, had been sent northward from the crossing site along the left (western) side of the Lexicon Road to capture an Egyptian bridge (near Ismailia) intact, encountered heavy resistance from tanks of the Egyptian 21st Armored Division at the Shick-Lexicon road junction. After inconclusive fighting, the 16 surviving tanks formed a line along the Shick Road. To the south, however, in Mitzna's rear, the 18th Tank Battalion led by Lieutenant Colonel Avraham Almog—which had sent to secure the right (eastern) flank of the Lexicon road in support of Mitna—lost ten tanks at the Tirtur-Lexicon road junction and was forced to pull back northward along the Lexicon Road joining up with Mitzna's remnants. Apparently the Egyptians were so surprised to see Israeli tanks in their midst that they had let Mitzna's battalion and half of Almog's pass the Tirtur-Lexicon intersection unfired upon minutes before, but had regained their composure in time to fire upon the bulk of Almog's force. Major Shaya Beitel's 40th Tank Battalion which was following the other two battalions up Lexicon with the mission of securing the Tirtur Road for the roller bridge's passage was also stopped in its tracks near the crossroads.[68]

Meanwhile a company from a tank battalion attached to the 14th Brigade from Raviv's brigade, commanded by Lieutenant Colonel Uzi, had advanced eastward up Akavish Road without encountering Egyptian resistance, except for some fire from the north.[69] Egyptian forces were not physically occupying Akavish, but were capable of firing on it from their positions on Tirtur Road. But Akavish was open for the parachute brigade carrying the inflatable rafts.[70]

Starting at 11:30 pm, therefore, Matt's 243d Parachute Brigade began moving south with the rafts along the road in halftracks, led by an attached tank company from Erez's brigade.[71] As Matt did not have enough half-tracks for his whole brigade, only one battalion would go forward at first, followed by the second when the half-tracks could come back for them. Upon reaching the end of the road, the brigade detoured around the fighting now taking place along Lexicon Road by following the coast of the Great Bitter Lake. Despite the nearby firefight, the paratroopers reached the canal virtually unscathed. The first parachute troops, from Lieutenant Colonel Dan's battalion and a company of engineers, begin crossing the canal in the rubber rafts at 1:25 am on the 16th, about five and a half hours behind schedule.[72]

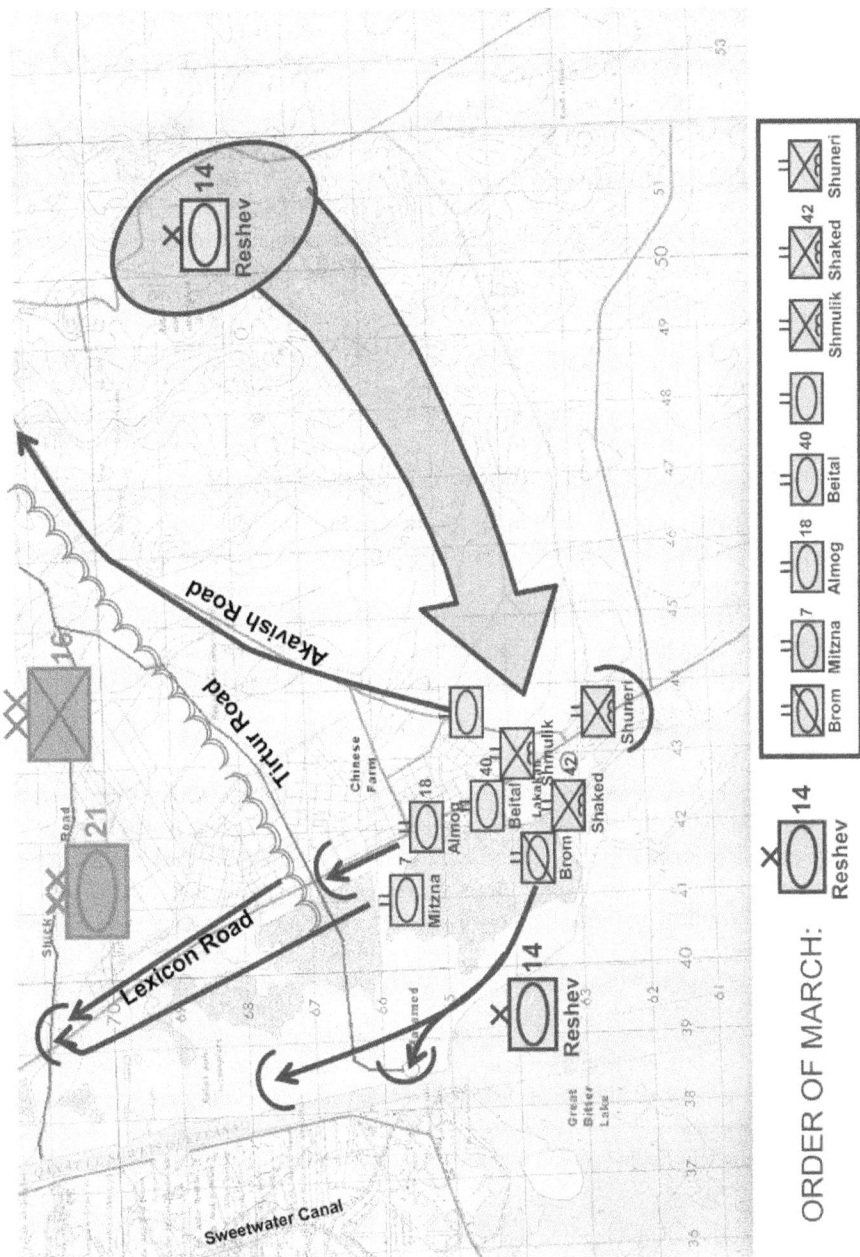

ORDER OF MARCH:

Figure 33. Chinese Farm initial operations, 15 October 1973.

By 3 am, Dan's entire battalion and Matt's 243d Brigade headquarters, 750 troops in total, were across the canal and had established a bridgehead two miles northward from the Great Bitter Lake. Matt's second battalion, commanded by Lieutenant Colonel Dan Zvi, however, was unable to immediately come forward as the Egyptians would block the Akavish Road by the time the half-tracks were bringing the battalion forward.[73]

Upon arrival at the canal, at about 12:20 am, Matt had dispatched the parachute brigade's attached tank company up the Lexicon Road to secure the brigade's flank while it was cross·ing the canal. The freshly arrived unit, unfamiliar with the situation, advanced between the remnants of two of Reshev's tank battalions and Egyptian infantry and tanks dug-in near the Tirtur-Lexicon crossroads promptly destroyed every tank in the company.[74]

The Israeli attackers had run into the right flank defenders of the Egyptian 16th Infantry Division, its 16th Infantry Brigade, apparently anchored on the Tirtur Road and running east·ward almost to its intersection with the Artillery Road. Several miles north of Tirtur, along the Shick Road were the rear installations of the 16th Division as well as several units of the Egyptian 21st Armored Division, which were in reserve, some after being bloodied in the Egyptian offensive on the 14th. Reshev's brigade had ridden into this hornet's nest.[75]

Mitzna, though isolated, found himself in the logistics hub of two Egyptian divisions and took advantage of the situation until the Egyptians recovered from their surprise. Soon Mitz·na's tank crewmen were fighting for their lives. To the south, but still north of the intersec·tion, Almog found himself, with the remnants of his battalion, in a similar situation. Brigade commander Reshev, with his forward command post consisting of his command tank and two half tracks, was in the midst of the action at the crossroads from the start. On Reshev's shoul·ders, however, rode the success of the entire operation. He could not give up while the enemy controlled key terrain.[76]

Therefore at 2 am the 14th Armored Brigade mounted another attack against the Egyptians holding the Tirtur-Lexicon crossroads. Reshev called on his reserve force, a battalion task force of two parachute infantry companies of recalled veterans mounted in half-tracks un·der the command of Major Natan Shuneri. To this force he also attached the company-sized remnants of Beitel's 40th Tank Battalion, now under the command of Captain Gideon Giladi. As Reshev watched from nearby, the badly coordinated attack was repulsed with most of the tanks being knocked out and Giladi killed, though the Egyptians took heavy tank losses as well.[77]

An hour later, at 3 am, the brigade tried again, this time attacking with two companies of the recon battalion, which had initially secured the crossing site. Attacking from west to east along Tirtur, the attackers were again repulsed with heavy losses, with the battalion com·mander, Yoav Brom, being killed when a volley of RPGs blew up his tank within 30 yards of the crossroads.[78]

In another hour, Reshev, believing that the Egyptians were withdrawing, tried again with his half-track infantry and the remnants of the 40th Battalion, now under the command of the

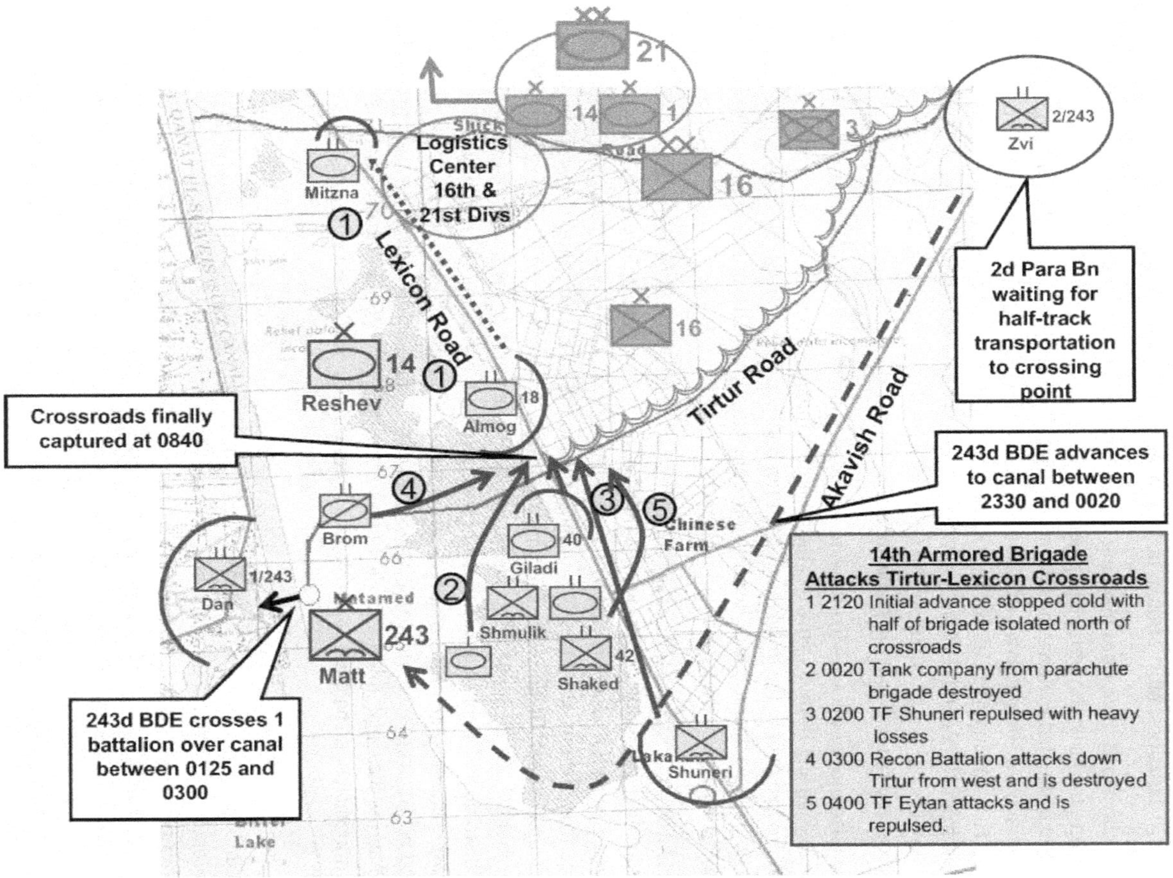

Figure 34. Israeli assaults on the Tirtur–Lexicon crossroads, night of 15/16 October 1973.

The following text labels appear within the figure:

14th Armored Brigade Attacks Tirtur-Lexicon Crossroads
1. 2120 Initial advance stopped cold with half of brigade isolated north of crossroads
2. 0020 Tank company from parachute brigade destroyed
3. 0200 TF Shuneri repulsed with heavy losses
4. 0300 Recon Battalion attacks down Tirtur from west and is destroyed
5. 0400 TF Eytan attacks and is repulsed.

2d Para Bn waiting for half-track transportation to crossing point

243d BDE advances to canal between 2330 and 0020

Crossroads finally captured at 0840

243d BDE crosses 1 battalion over canal between 0125 and 0300

Akavish Road

Tirtur Road

Lexicon Road

Chinese Farm

Logistics Center 16th & 21st Divs

QANAT UL-SUWEIS SUEZ CANAL

Great Bitter Lake

165

deputy brigade commander, Lieutenant Colonel Eytan. An antiarmor ambush destroyed all but two of the vehicles as the crossroads remained firmly in Egyptian hands. After another failed attempt, the brigade had through the night suffered 120 soldiers killed in action with a total of 190 casualties, most of them tank crewmen, and lost over 60 tanks.[79]

Behind the Israeli lines, poor planning and geography had resulted in a massive traffic jam surrounding the heavy bridging equipment.[80] A conference at Israeli Southern Command headquarters decided to move the Gilowa wheeled ferry vehicles out of the jam to get them to the crossing site before dawn so that tanks could cross the canal as soon as possible. After moving cross-country, the Gilowa ferries reached the crossing site by 4 am, escorted by the battalion from Nir's 600th Brigade of Adan's division commanded by Giora Lev. Soon the boats were operational. At 6:30 am the Gilowas ferried the first ten tanks (from Lev's battal• ion) across the canal to join the paratroopers.[81]

Sharon had moved out with his forward command post (five APCs) with the Gilowas down to the crossing site from his previous location near the upper portion of the Akavish Road. Sharon crossed over to the bridgehead and then returned to the Matzmed crossing site from where he directed operations of his division, concentrating on the crossing aspects of his mis• sion at the expense of the road clearing aspects.[82]

Meanwhile on the Akavish Road, in the traffic jam, the roller bridge broke a connection, jeopardizing the crossing operation. The tank battalion from Sharon's reserve, the 421st Armored Brigade (-), commanded by Colonel Haim Erez, which was towing the bridge, was released from the mission and sent to join Reshev at the canal. En route the battalion, led by Lieutenant Colonel Yitzhak Ben-Shoshan, escorted Zvi's battalion of Matt's parachute bri• gade, mounted on half-tracks. Sagger fire from positions astride the nearby Tirtur road forced the vulnerable half-tracks back. But the tanks continued, bypassing the roadblock by mov• ing cross-country south of the road, reaching the crossing site at midmorning. Erez with his forward brigade command post and Ben-Shoshan's 21 tanks and seven APCs were promptly ferried across the canal, joining Lev's 14 and a company of APC-mounted infantry. The tanks were immediately dispatched to attack SAM sites throughout the rest of the morning of the 16th.[83]

With the Tirtur Road—essential to moving the heavy bridge to the crossing site—still blocked, Sharon committed his reserve, Erez's remaining battalion, commanded by Lieuten• ant Colonel Ami Morag, placed under control of Reshev's brigade, to clear that road from the east. Part of Uzi's battalion, which had earlier cleared Akavish for Matt's brigade, supported the attack by fire. Though Morag managed to penetrate almost all the way to the Lexicon intersection, infantry dug-in near the Chinese Farm repulsed his attack with antitank missiles fired in salvoes. Through the clever maneuvering of his tanks and constant suppressive fires, Morag managed to suffer no fatal casualties. Before he retreated, he also managed to rescue survivors from Shuneri's abortive attack.[84]

To the west Reshev assembled a scratch force, to attempt once again to clear the Lexicon-Tirtur crossroads, this time in daylight. After making initial headway, the attack was again

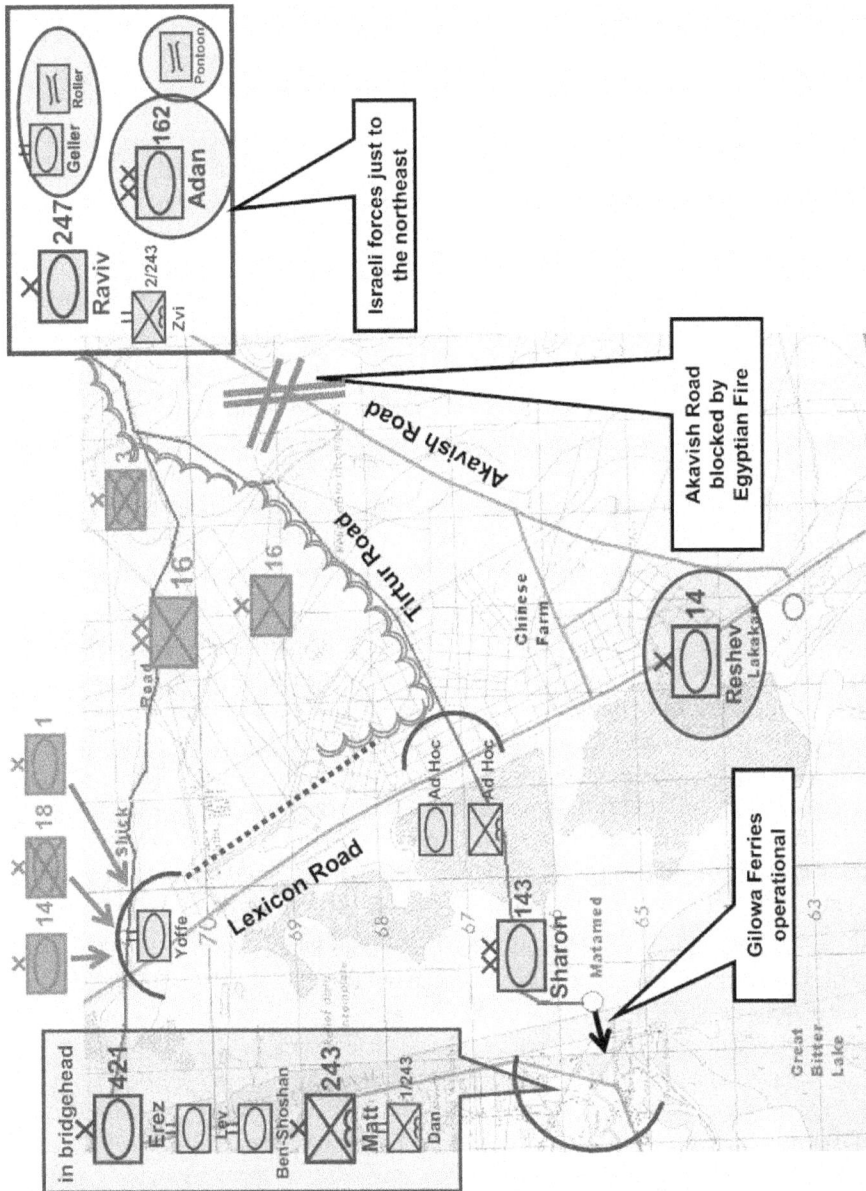

Figure 35. General situation, midday 16 October 1973.

repulsed. The troops had become exhausted. Nevertheless, Reshev sent them in again. This time 22 tanks attacked from the north and east. They were forced back by Egyptian armor after losing three tanks. Several minutes later, Reshev scraped together 13 tanks from the 40th Battalion led by Captain Gabriel Vardi, infantry and recon troops for one more try. The Egyptian fire began to slacken as they too had also taken heavy losses. Under the pressure of Israeli tank fire, the Egyptians fell back, some offering up white flags. By 9 am the critical Tirtur-Lexicon junction was finally in Israeli hands.[85]

On the morning of the 16th, Adan sent a tank battalion from Amir's 460th Brigade to relieve Reshev, who was down to a strength of 27 tanks. The battalion, led by Lieutenant Colonel Amir Yoffe, had originally been earmarked to cross the canal, but Reshev's desperate situa•tion forced it into action on the east bank instead. Yoffe took over the Shick line while Reshev moved his depleted battalions back to the vicinity of Lakekan to reorganize. Yoffe fought off Egyptian counterattacks from the 1st and 14th Armored Brigades and the 18th Mechanized Brigade of the Egyptian 21st Armored Division all day.[86]

While the Tirtur-Lexicon crossroads was now in Israeli hands, both the Tirtur and Akavish Roads remained blocked. After Ben-Shoshan's battalion joined Lev's on the far bank, Bar Lev refused to allow any more troops to cross the canal on the Gilowas or rafts until the roads were cleared and more permanent bridges could be brought down. Despite the fact that his division was barely holding open the line of communications to the far bank, and now would have to rely on Adan to finish the job, the decision outraged Sharon.[87]

At noon Southern Command ordered Sharon to take the Chinese Farm from the west, while Adan's division would now enter the fight clearing the Akavish and Tirtur Roads and bring up the pontoon bridges.[88] But Adan's attack, executed by two battalions from Nir's brigade, was quickly brought to a halt. Nir then assumed defensive positions when dust clouds in the distance indicated the approach of a large Egyptian armored force. But the force turned back before Nir could engage it. Several other armored forces approached through the afternoon but were engaged only by artillery. Adan guessed that the Egyptians were trying to bait him into sending his tanks forward so the Egyptian infantry could destroy them with Saggers. He did not take the bait and instead spent the rest of daylight waiting for infantry support prom•ised him in the guise of a parachute battalion. The battalion arrived via planes and bus.[89]

At 2 am on the 17th, Lieutenant Colonel Yitzhak Mordecai's 890th Parachute Battalion attacked the Chinese Farm from the east, along the six-mile trace of the Tirtur Road. Mor•decai's parent brigade, the 35th Parachute under Colonel Uzi Ya'iri, controlled the opera•tion. Ya'iri deployed three infantry companies forward under Mordecai and followed with an infantry company and the battalion's heavy weapons company under his personal com•mand. One company would advance north of Tirtur, one between Tirtur and Akavish and one south of Akavish. Once enemy locations would be found, the battalion would consolidate. A battalion of tanks from Amir's 460th Brigade (Adan's division), commanded by Lieutenant Colonel Ehud Barak, later prime minister of Israel, would support, though it would not join the advance. The paratroopers were soon pinned down and artillery fire, because of fratricidal

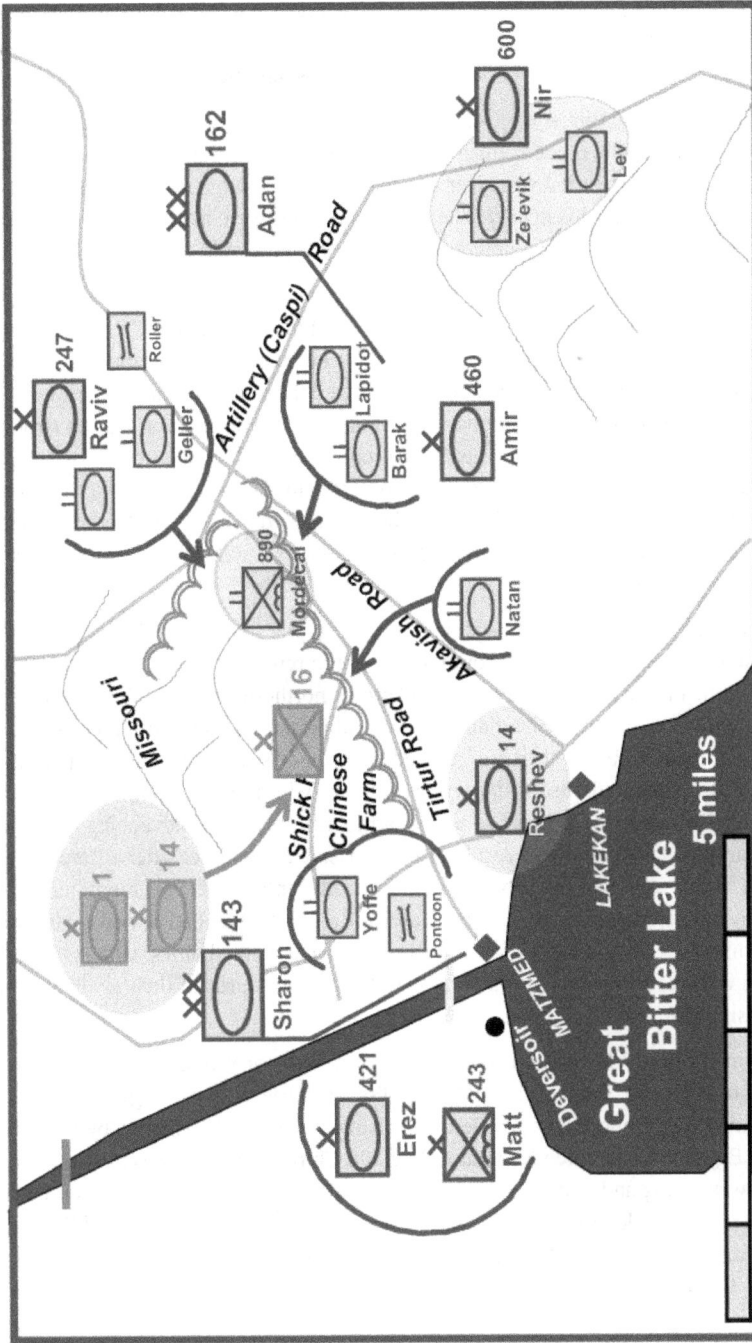

Figure 36. 17 October 1973, coordinated attack on the Chinese Farm.

169

concerns, was ineffective. The operation soon became a rescue mission for the wounded. At first light, Barak's tanks were sent in to help the paratrooper resume their attack. The now familiar Saggers, however, quickly knocked out five tanks, ending the effort.[90]

During the night, the fighting at the Chinese Farm distracted Egyptian attention from the Akavish area. Adan sent the recon company from Amir's brigade down Akavish in its APCs. These scouts discovered the road was clear and the division commander promptly sent out the pontoons with escorts under his deputy. The pontoon bridges were able to reach the crossing site. By 8 am they were being put together, though the bridge would not be operational until 4 pm.[91]

At dawn on the 17th Adan prepared to throw every available tank at the Chinese Farm. Finally the IDF had massed enough battalions to make an irresistible, coordinated attack. Natan's battalion from Nir's 600th Brigade had followed the pontoons and was now in posi•tion to advance on the Egyptian Tirtur positions from the southwest. Amir's 460th Brigade would attack from the east with Barak's battalion reinforced with another battalion (com•manded by Lieutenant Colonel Lapidot's). Nir's brigade (minus Natan's battalion) was held in reserve to the southeast. Karen's brigade had been detached to Southern Command reserve but Raviv's 247th Brigade was now attached from Sharon. Raviv, with two battalions, would move in from the northwest.[92]

The attack turned into a meeting engagement as the Egyptian 1st and 14th Armored Bri•gades were simultaneously advancing south to attempt to reblock the Akavish Road. West of this attack zone on the Shick Road holding Sharon's northern flank, Yoffe's battalion had successfully repulsed numerous Egyptian armored and infantry attacks with no losses to his own force. Additionally, Reshev had reorganized his brigade's remnants and was preparing to reinforce Yoffe. Yoffe had observed Egyptian infantry withdrawing from the Chinese Farm area to his east. But while the infantry retreated, armored forces were advancing to face off with Adan's arrayed tank battalions, resulting in a massive tank battle. After a fierce five-hour seesaw battle, Adan secured a line along the Tirtur Road, capturing the southern third of the Chinese Farm and permanently secured the Akavish Road. The tide had turned clearly to the Israelis as, while the IDF had lost between 80 and 100 tanks in the battles, tank losses now favored them with the Egyptians losing at least 160, over two-thirds of their available tanks near the crossing site.[93]

In the morning of the 17th a conference was held at Adan's forward command post, includ•ing Adan, Sharon, Gonen, Bar Lev, and IDF Chief of Staff Elazar. On-the-spot decisions were made concerning future operations. While the crossing site was being shelled by Egyptian artillery, and Egyptians had defended tenuously at the Chinese Farm, it was obvious that that defense was weakening and, with the arrival of the pontoon bridge, the tide had turned and offensive operations could continue with Sharon holding the bridgehead open while Adan would then cross and exploit on the west bank.[94] First, however, Adan would have to take care of a new threat.

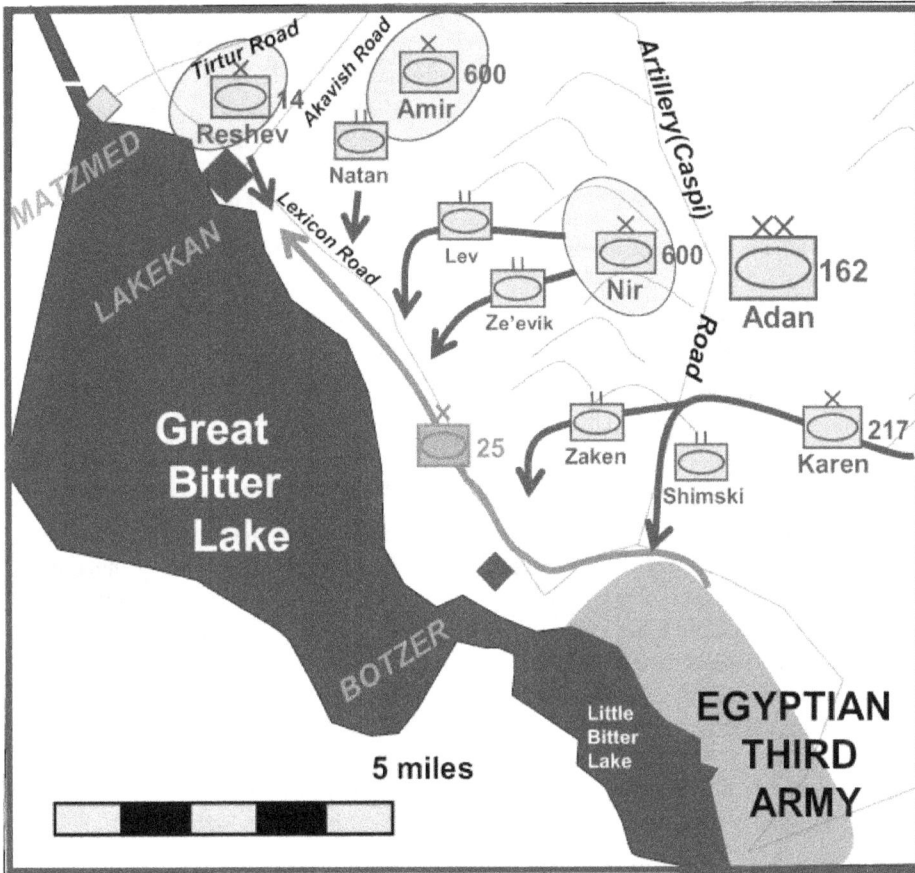

Figure 37. 17 October 1973, Adan destroys the Egyptian 25th Armored Brigade.

In the afternoon, even as the battle of the Chinese Farm still went on, Adan was forced to redeploy his forces to stop the advance of the Egyptian 25th Armored Brigade. This brigade was moving in column from the south up the Lexicon Road along the shore of the Great Bit‧ ter Lake out of the bridgehead of the Egyptian Third Army. This movement was supposed to be in coordination with the attacks of the two armored brigades from the north and could, if not stopped, take the units fighting at the Chinese Farm in the rear. Instead, Adan moved his forces to create a large anti-armor ambush. Southern Command released back to Adan Karen's two-battalion brigade, which he immediately moved down the Lateral Road south of Tasa. Then Karen swung to the west to attack the rear of the Egyptian column. Nir, al‧ ready located along the Artillery (Caspi) Road with two battalions, moved west to attack the center of the column. Amir with Natan's battalion and Reshev from Sharon's division would block the front of the column and attack it from the north. With the ambush set, Adan let the

171

Egyptians fall into it, holding artillery and tank fire until the entire 10-mile long column was within range of Israeli weapons. When the Egyptian vanguard fired on Reshev near Lakekan, Adan sprung his trap. While Karen sealed the southern escape route, Nir attacked the flank of the column. The ambush was a complete success. By late afternoon the Israelis had com• pleted the annihilation of the Egyptian force, destroying between 60 and 86 vehicles while losing only four tanks, (two to mines). Only a handful of Egyptian vehicles, including that of the brigade commander, survived by fleeing into the abandoned Bar Lev fort of Botzer.[95]

At 9 pm, with the pontoon bridge in place, Adan's Division started crossing the canal. Sharon took over the portion of the Tirtur front held by Adan's units and the next morning (18 October), pushed the Egyptians completely out of the Chinese Farm.[96] This allowed the deployment of the roller bridge. It was operational the next day.

Once across, Adan, followed by Magen's division, between the 19th and 23d, advanced south along the west side of the Great Bitter Lake to isolate the Egyptian Third Army around Suez city. Through hard fighting, Adan and Magen managed to cut off the Egyptians, though Suez city itself was not captured. Several ceasefires and an eventual peace treaty followed.

The Battle of the Chinese Farm showed Israeli mobile operations and battle command at its best, and at its worst. While the Israelis had no complete picture of the enemy situation, their intelligence was far superior than on 8 October. Planning and coordination, while clearly superior to that of the El Firdan attack, still showed flaws. The IDF often replaced good staff work with good, though possibly unnecessary, improvisation. The traffic jams, span of control problems and task organization difficulties could all have been resolved up front with good planning and staff work. It took two days of failed, piecemeal, uncoordinated attacks on the Chinese Farm position before a massed, coordinated attack was finally employed. While battle command on the move requires an inherent flexibility and capability to improvise, good planning and staff work can reduce greatly the requirement for improvisation.

Nevertheless battle command in the Chinese Farm operation was greatly improved from that of the El Firdan battle. The theater level command team of Bar Lev and Gonen made frequent visits to their subordinates and, despite Sharon's claims to the contrary, actually had a far better situational awareness than on 8 October. At all times commanders knew their highers' intentions and plans were changed based on the enemy situation, not on whimsy or unbridled optimism or pessimism. For matters important enough, Bar Lev was even capable of talk• ing directly to battalion commanders, as he did with one of the first units across the canal, to which he personally gave the mission of destroying Egyptian surface-to-air missile sites under instructions from the Air Force.[97]

The Israeli divisional and brigade commanders led from the saddle, using forward command posts and usually collocating with either their lead subordinate unit or their reserve element. Radio communications allowed a span of control over units that were separated by enemy forces or great distances. While this allowed great situational awareness and responsiveness, this up-front style of leadership was a double-edged sword. Commanders so far forward often ended up in close combat that hindered their ability to control their unit. This happened to Re•

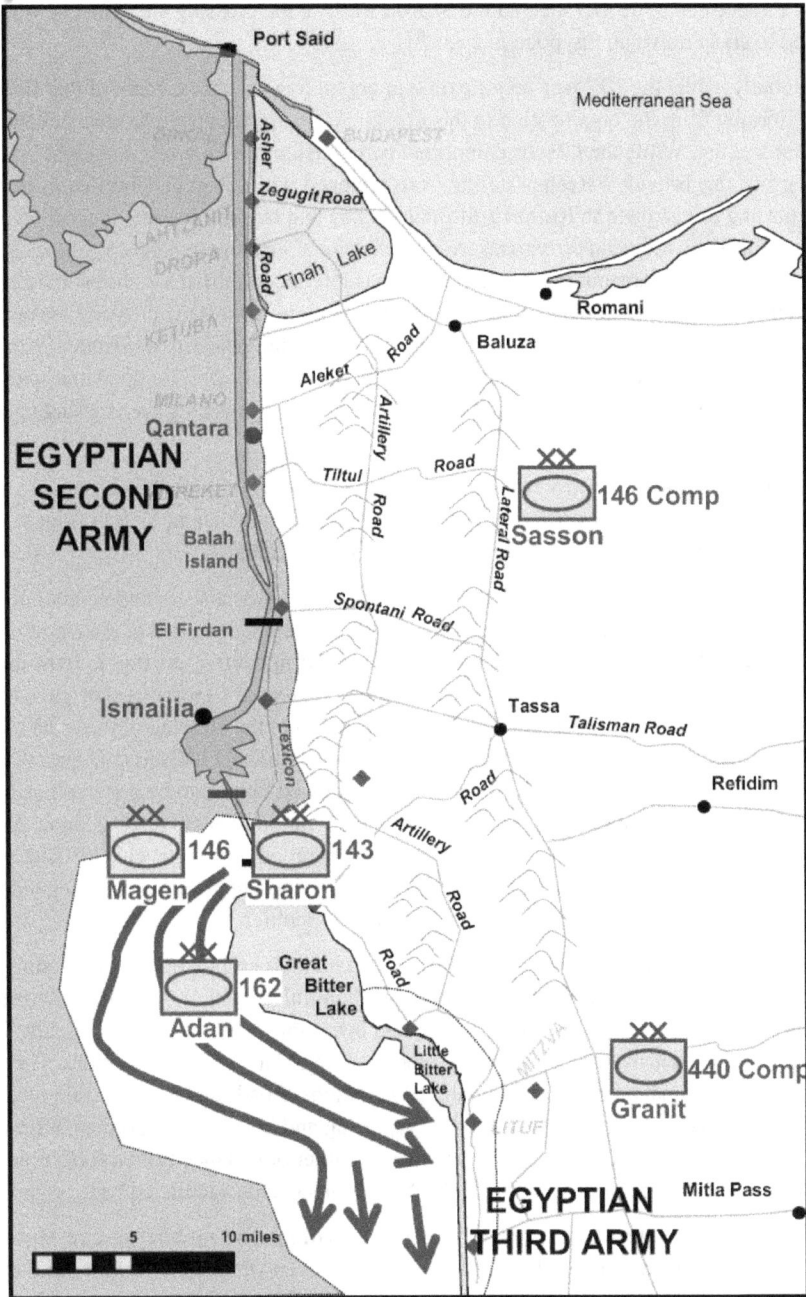

Figure 38. Post-crossing operations.

shev on the evening of 15 October, and to Sharon while at the crossing site when he person•ally tried to shoot down an Egyptian aircraft.[98]

Additionally, while the IDF was very flexible in organizing its forces, some of that flexibil•ity was missing from the organization in this operation. Span of control and ease of control was often lacking. While the Israelis committed two division headquarters and eight brigade headquarters, one brigade—Reshev's 14th—was strapped with seven battalion-equivalent units reporting to it. Added to Reshev's difficulties was that he soon became embroiled in combat at the Tirtur-Lexicon crossroads. Adan's divisional headquarters, led by the most ex•perienced armored commander in the operation, was left uncommitted for almost the first 24 hours of the operation. Meanwhile Sharon was attempting to control the crossing operation, Reshev's battle, and, on the other side of the enemy's blocking position, a brigade towing the bridging equipment, and another executing a diversionary attack. Despite this large span of control, Sharon essentially spent most of his time personally overseeing the crossing opera•tion.[99]

At the other extreme when only two battalion-equivalents were across the canal, there were also two brigade headquarters controlling them (Matt's and Erez's), and Ya'iri's brigade con•trolled only Mordecai's battalion in its night attack on 17 October.

While there was no effort to balance spans of control, there was also no appreciation for the personalities of the subordinate commanders. Bar Lev and Gonen had to realize Sharon was a difficult subordinate who would, if not kept under firm control, attempt to twist their intent into whatever it was he wanted to do. Knowing he favored a crossing, they gave him a key role in it. However, Sharon paid inadequate attention to the clearing of the route to the crossing site, leaving that to an overextended subordinate, while he himself concentrated on the crossing itself. Additionally, Bar Lev and Gonen allowed Sharon to be geographically separated from direct contact with higher headquarters with predictable results: vague reports and frequent unavailability. With such a complicated operation, placing such a difficult sub•ordinate, who believed in improvisation over planning, out where he could act independently, created unnecessary stress and command and control difficulties.[100]

The Israelis used many standard techniques to facilitate their mobile operations. A small forward command post, usually consisting of only a handful of vehicles, was their standard for commanders with units conducting fast moving operations. Operations were greatly facili•tated through the extensive use of overlays, overlay-style orders, and map graphics. The IDF had organized the Sinai on maps to facilitate its operations. Roads and major terrain features were given codenames. Unit locations, both in reporting and in positioning orders, were given in relation to the road's codename and its kilometer marker or distance from a fixed point. As in all modern mobile operations, the use of such shortcuts greatly facilitated battle command.

After initial setbacks, the Israelis proved to be masters of modern mobile warfare. However, they also proved how difficult such operations could be, even when there is clear radio com•munication and leaders at all levels display high initiative. Improvisation is not necessarily a good substitute for planning and routine staff work.

174

Summary

The operations of the Israeli Defense Force in the Sinai in 1973, much like Grant's two cam•
paigns discussed earlier, show a sharp contrast between ineffective battle command on the
move in the Battle of El Firdan and the same commanders effectively leading mobile forces
in the subsequent Battle of the Chinese Farm.

The Battle of El Firdan, the first theater-wide Israeli counterattack, failed primarily be•
cause of command failures. Theater commander Gonen was unable to effectively control
his forces, leaving his division commanders Adan and Sharon to operate independently and
without coordination. Gonen never left his headquarters in the rear and had a poor apprecia•
tion for battlefield realities. The orders he gave were constantly changing and conflicting. At
El Firdan, confusion, lack of understanding of the enemy situation and a brief loss of control
caused by subordinate initiative in Adan's division, resulted in two divisional attacks being
reduced to two separate tank battalion attacks. In each, the battalion was quickly annihilated.
Meanwhile, Sharon's division marched around in a big circle during the day and failed to
support Adan when help was most needed.

A week later the Israeli command coordinated its operation far more successfully in the
Battle of the Chinese Farm, the operation where the Israelis crossed large armored forces
over to the west bank of the Suez Canal. This operation was complicated by the need to move
specialized bridging equipment down certain roads, astride which the Egyptians had placed
dug-in infantry. While this operation had some command and control problems, primarily
concerned with massing adequate forces to eject the Egyptians from the Chinese Farm area,
overall the Israelis achieved their objective of opening a crossing site at the canal.

Even though many of the commanders were the same as those present at the El Firdan bat•
tle, Bar Lev had succeeded Gonen in overall command and this experienced officer controlled
his forces far better than Gonen had. He did so through a combination of personal visits,
radio communications and periodic conferences. Planning for the operation was done in great
detail, rather than improvised on the fly as had been the case a week earlier. While Egyptian
resistance proved tougher than expected and their troop deployments came as a surprise, this
time the Israelis were ready for the unexpected.

Despite the overall success of the Chinese Farm operation, there were some organizational
problems on the Israeli side. The leading force from Sharon's division suffered from a span of
control problem, with one brigade commander given control of too many subordinate ele•
ments, each with different missions. This situation was compounded when that commander
was soon cut off behind enemy lines in running battles with Egyptian armored forces. How•
ever, the extensive preparations paid off as each separate Israeli unit commander knew the
intent of the operation and were able to continue with the mission even when not under any
superior's direct command and control.

Sharon had his division actually deployed on two fronts with a large Egyptian force between
them and a forward element across the Suez Canal. Bar Lev alleviated this difficulty by giv•

ing Adan control over Sharon's forces facing the Egyptians from the east. The IDF command was under such good control in the later phases of this operation that Adan was able to easily respond to an enemy threat from a new direction and set up a trap and then destroy an Egyptian armored brigade.

Israeli success was based primarily on superior command and control techniques. While technology in the form of armored vehicles and radios was a factor, the big difference between El Firdan and Chinese Farm was the refinement of battle command techniques made in the period between the two battles. Despite some difficulties primarily associated with the command techniques of the dynamic Sharon, the Israelis were able to respond to the tactical situation with swift battle command adjustments.

Notes

1.   Abraham Rabinovich, *The Yom Kippur War: The Epic Encounter that Transformed the Middle East* (New York: Schocken Books, 2004), 468.

2.   Avraham Adan, *On the Banks of the Suez: An Israeli General's Personal Account of the Yom Kippur War* (London: Arms and Armour Press, 1980), 17, 25.

3.   Adan, 18.

4.   Chaim Herzog, *The War of Atonement: October, 1973* (Boston: Little, Brown and Company, 1975), 158.

5.   Adan, 25, Herzog, 159, 161, 165.

6.   Adan, 10, 17.

7.   Ibid., 10, 13-4.

8.   Trevor Dupuy, *Elusive Victory: The Arab-Israeli Wars 1947-1974* (Fairfax, VA: HERO Books, 1980), 612; Herzog, 158, 182, Rabinovich, 138.

9.   Adan, 92. 109. Sharon, of course later became Israeli prime minister, a position he still holds as of the publication of this work (2005).

10.   Ibid., 31, Rabinovich, 120.

11.   Rabinovich, 242-3.

12.   Rabinovich, 224-5; Herzog 184; Adan, 98-99.

13.   Ibid., 115.

14.   Rabinovich, 233: Adan 107.

15.   Adan, 112.

16.   Ibid., 112-3.

17.   Ibid., 118.

18.   Ibid., 5.

19.   Ibid., 37, 39-40.

20.   Nir's last name is sometimes listed as Baram instead of Nir. See Dupuy, *Elusive Victory*, 612.

21.   Adan, 35, 38-9; Rabinovich, 133-4, 137. Natan's full name is never indicated in any available sources. He was later wounded on 18 October and evacuated.

22.   Adan, 95, 119. 121-2.

23.   Adan, 6.

24.   Ibid., 6-7, 13.

25.   John J. McGrath, "The Battle of El Firdan" *Armor* (May-June 1983), 10; Adan, 118.

26.   Adan, 102.

27.   Ibid., 103, 119.

28.   Ibid., 15-16, 120.

29.   Ibid., 119.

30.   Some sources claim that Amir mistakenly advanced too far to the east as he moved southward (Herzog, 185, George W. Gawrych, *The 1973 Arab-Israeli War: The Albatross of Decisive Victory,* Leavenworth Paper No. 21 (Fort Leavenworth: Combat Studies Institute, 1996), 46.) However, in his memoirs, Adan does not indicate such an error. See Adan, 120. It seems much more likely that Amir, advancing on the left of the original divisional attack, was following the guidance of the original order.

31.   Rabinovich, 242.

32.   Adan, 123.

33.   Ibid., 126-7, 135-6.

34.   Ibid., 132-3, 135.

35.   Ibid., 136.

36.   Rabinovich, 243-4; Adan, 135-6; Gawrych, 46.

37.   Adan, 136; Rabinovich, 244.

38.   Adan, 136-7; Rabinovich 244-5.

39.   Adan, 137-9: Rabinovich, 245-7.

40.   Adan, 139; Rabinovich, 247.

41.   Rabinovich, 248-9; Adan, 140-3; Gawrych, 49.

42.   Adan, 140-1, 143-4; Rabinovich, 249.

43.   Adan, 137-9.

44.   Ibid., 142.

45.   Adan, 147; Rabinovich, 251-2.

46.   Rabinovich, 249-50; Adan, 144-6, 152. Adan's own recon battalion was fighting in the north under a detached command.

47.   The Giddi Pass is just off the eastern edge of the map in Figure 25 on the east-west road south of Refidim.

48.   Adan, 141.

49.   Ibid., 124, 126-7.

50. Ibid., 142.

51. Rabinovich, 327-8, 330; Adan, 215, 227.

52. Adan, 219.

53. Rabinovich, 271-4.

54. Ibid., 331.

55. Adan, 196, 221, 227, 229.

56. Ibid., 207-210.

57. Herzog, 204-5.

58. Saad el Shazly, *The Crossing of the Suez* (San Francisco: American Mideast Research, 1980), 245-8; Rabinovich, 346-8.

59. Adan, 231, 236.

60. Rabinovich, 353, 355; Adan, 239.

61. Adan, 239.

62. Ibid., 218.

63. Rabinovich., 282-3.

64. Herzog, 217.

65. Ariel Sharon, with David Chanoff, *Warrior: The Autobiography of Ariel Sharon* (New York: Si• mon and Schuster, 1989), 312-3; Simon Dunstan, *The Yom Kippur War 1973 (2); The Sinai*, Campaign series (Oxford: Osprey, 2003), 70-2; Rabinovich, 359-60.

66. Ibid.

67. Sources conflict on the composition of the infantry and recon components of Reshev's task force. However it seems to have consisted on three small infantry battalion task forces, consisting of para• chute troops in half-tracks and some tanks. However, one source claims (see Dupuy, 496) that one of the battalions was the mechanized infantry battalion from the 421st Armored Brigade and another was a separate mechanized infantry battalion. The recon battalion was apparently Sharon's divisional unit reinforced with additional tanks. For the best discussion of Reshev's order of battle, see Frank Chad-wick and Joseph Bermudez, "Historical Notes and Scenarios Booklet," *Suez '73: The Battle of the Chinese Farm: October 15-22, 1973* (Normal, IL: Game Designer's Workshop, 1981), 5.

68. Rabinovich, 368-9; Herzog, 211-2,214; Adan, 263-4, 266.

69. The rest of this battalion was divided up as follows: one company sent to unsuccessfully clear the Tirtur Road, and the last company to join the brigade reserve force near Lakekan, Task Force Shuneri. See Chadwick and Bermudez, 5. Uzi's complete name is not given in available sources (Herzog, 222).

70.   The tank company followed the paratroopers back down Akavish and joined the rest of its bat•talion south of the Tirtur-Lexicon crossroads. Adan, 267.

71.   The tank company came from Ami Morag's battalion. See note 78 below.

72.   Rabinovich, 362, 364; Adan, 267. Available sources do not indicate Dan's complete name.

73.   Rabinovich, 374: Adan, 264. See note 87. Zvi's battalion would not get across until the 17th. Sometimes Zvi's name is given as Ziv.

74.   Dupuy, *Elusive Victory*, 499; Rabinovich, 374, 385-6; the tank company came from Lieutenant Colonel Ami Morag's tank battalion in Erez's brigade. While most sources claim all tanks in the com•pany were destroyed at the crossoads, Rabinovich claims only four of the company's seven tanks were destroyed.

75.   Chadwick and Bermudez, 5; Herzog, 212;Sharon, 315.

76.   Rabinovich, 369-70.

77.   Ibid., 376-7; Adan, 267-8.

78.   Rabinovich, 375; Herzog, 216.

79.   Herzog, 216-7; Adan, 269; Rabinovich, 381. The infantry probably came from either TF Schmu•lik or TF Shaked (possibly really designated as the 42d Parachute Infantry Battalion), both of which were with the brigade but whose actions are not mentioned in most sources. The tanks probably came also from Uzi's tank battalion borrowed from Raviv's brigade.

80.   Herzog, 218; Sharon, 313.

81.   Rabinovich, 379-80, 388; There's some confusion about Lev's battalion as sources seem to indicate it was in two places at once: 14 tanks across the canal and a battalion under Nir with Adan's division to the east. Probably the battalion had been split into two task forces, a common IDF practice.

82.   Rabinovich, 379; Sharon, 316; Adan, 268.

83.   Rabinovich, 378, 385, 388-9; Adan, 276.

84.   Rabinovich, 382, 385-8; Herzog 222; Adan, 269. Morag's battalion had been providing security for the roller bridge.

85.   Rabinovich, 382-3; Herzog, 221-2.

86.   Adan, 277-8, 293.

87.   Rabinovich, 391-3; Sharon, 317-320.

88.   Rabinovich, 373, 393; Adan, 278.

89.   Adan, 279-81, 284-5.

90.   Ibid., 286-8, 291; Rabinovich, 396-8.

91.   Adan, 290-1; Rabinovich, 399, 412.

180

92. Adan, 292-3; Lapidot's complete name is not given in available sources.

93. Gawrych 63; Adan, 293; Rabinovich, 403-4; Chadwick and Bermudez, 6-7.

94. Adan, 298-9; Rabinovich, 409-10.

95. Adan, 301-3; Herzog, 228; Rabinovich, 411-2.

96. Rabinovich, 426.

97. Sharon, 319; Adan 277, Herzog, 223; Rabinovich, 389.

98. Sharon, 321, 323-4.

99. Adan, 268; Gawrych, 60.

100. Adan, 277; Rabinovich, 406-8; Sharon, 321.

THE SOVIET APPROACH TO MOBILE BATTLE COMMAND

"Fas est et ab hoste doceri."
It is right to learn even from the enemy.
—Ovid[1]

The Red Army of the former Soviet Union, while deploying large numbers of armored forces, both in World War II and during the Cold War period, developed a completely different approach to battle command than the US Army and its allies, including the new German Army. These forces depended on the initiative of subordinate leaders to accomplish missions when either battlefield realities conflicted with the plan, or the unit was out of effective communications. The Soviets, however, approached the same circumstances with a dependence on following pre-arranged plans, using well-practiced drills, and turning the concept of maneuver on its head by employing artillery as an offensive weapon supported by the other arms, rather than the other way around. The Soviet approach, ideal for a force of semi-poorly trained conscripts with little or no NCO corps, was also adopted by many of the Soviet client states and nations which used Soviet equipment and advisors. Many of these nations and, perhaps even Russia itself, the Soviet successor state, still depend on the former Soviet system, making it still relevant in the post-Cold War era.

Battle Command on the Move By the Numbers

After the Second World War, the Soviet Union retained a very large military force and then motorized and mechanized almost all of it. Therefore command and control of mobile operations would naturally be of primary importance to the Soviets. Additionally, in the latter half of World War II the Red Army had overwhelmed the Germans with a series of swift offensives, then pushed the Japanese out of Manchuria in the last days of the war with a large mobile campaign. Mobile campaigns were part of the Soviet heritage.

However, mission-type orders, individual initiative, and tactical flexibility were not part of the Soviet heritage. And the placing of infantry into armored vehicles had the added advantage of making them easier to control—they had to go wherever the vehicle went. Soviet soldiers were trained based on rote memorization and practice of drills. The Russians had adopted old style battlefield drill to an army composed of armored and wheeled vehicles. These drills covered the basic movements and assault formations. Under this system platoon leaders, and company and battalion commanders were merely there to ensure their echelons carried out their drill as part of the larger unit, much as similar positions were in pre-1914 armies.[2]

Instead of mission orders, the Soviets depended on pre-arranged planning, the result of centralized decision-making. Emphasis was on strict obedience to orders. Instead of initiative, lower level commanders were expected to look for word from above in new situations, or in those not covered by orders.[3] The large mass army the Soviets maintained allowed them to accept a certain amount of inflexibility tactically—numbers would allow recovery from mistakes made in blindly following plans which may have no longer made sense at the tactical level. While Soviet doctrine stressed a certain amount of flexibility, initiative and imagination at the operational levels above regiment and division, employing multiple attack echelons and deep striking forces (operational maneuver groups), the inherent inflexibility at the tactical level would naturally impact significantly on those operations.[4]

The use of radios is a good example of the difference in the Soviet system. Although radios were distributed virtually universally in all armored fighting vehicles, as in western armies, all but those in company command and higher command vehicles would be set to a listening only mode. Typically all the vehicles in a battalion would be tied into a single battalion command network, with all vehicles hearing all traffic, but only the company commanders and battalion commander are able to talk. Another variant was the company net being tied into the battalion commander, and battalion chief of staff, forcing the company commander to have to go through the battalion to request fire support, or talk to neighboring companies.[5]

The Soviet concept of a high-speed armored offensive consisted basically of three types of operations, each with its own version of battle drill: the meeting engagement, the breakthrough attack, and the pursuit. The meeting engagement was the most common offensive operation and was used when the enemy situation was vague, or the enemy was moving forward. The breakthrough attack was utilized when the enemy was stationary in a defensive posture. The pursuit was executed when the enemy was moving away from the Soviet force.

For example, the drill used to execute an attack at the regimental level would see the regiment break up into battalion columns about eight to ten kilometers from the forward enemy positions. Between four to six kilometers out, the battalion columns split into company columns. From about 2 to 3 kilometers away from the enemy the company columns split into platoon columns and about 1000 meters from the enemy forward positions, the platoon columns shifted into assault lines. A motorized rifle (mechanized infantry) battalion with its usual attached tank company would normally be given an assault sector of about two to three kilometers width, with the attack formation taking up about 1.5 kilometers of that space, if only two infantry companies were in the first assault line. The tanks would advance in front of the infantry carriers about 300 meters and be extended across the whole battalion front. The motorized rifle companies would be on line behind the tanks. If the third company was used as a second echelon attacking force, it would be located between one and four kilometers behind the lead echelon, with the battalion command group roughly one kilometer behind the lead assault line.[6]

Attacking units were given geographically designated battalion and regimental sectors and objectives. Battalions were given immediate objectives about two to four kilometers in the enemy rear. Battalion subsequent objectives, located about five to six kilometers into the enemy rear were components of the regiment's immediate objective. The regiment would also have a subsequent objective about eight to twelve kilometers deep into the enemy position.[7]

184

An example of the drill used to take a motorized rifle (mechanized infantry) regiment from an assembly area to attack formation is illustrated below.

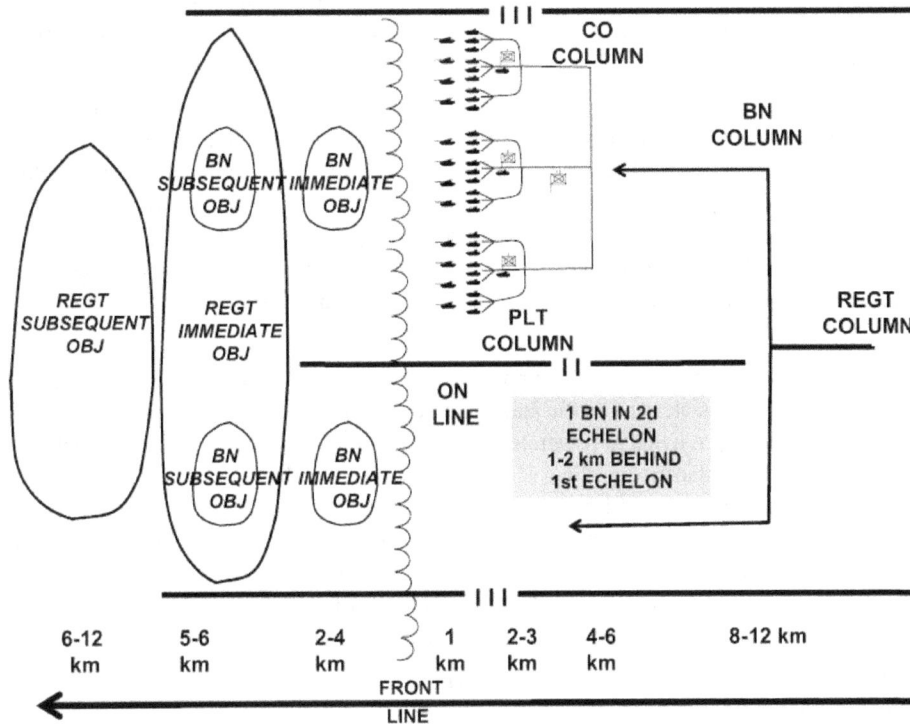

Figure 39. Motorized Rifle Regiment attack drill.

Artillery Offensive

In addition to the traditional forms of maneuver, Soviet doctrine also recognized what it called the artillery offensive. In this type of operation, the maneuver forces supported the artillery rather than the other way around. The field artillery, and all other means of fire support including infantry mortars and rockets, are massed in regimental, divisional, and army artillery groups—all controlled by the corps-sized army's artillery chief. This chief planned the artillery fires. Artillery battery and battalion commanders observed the fire, adjusting it per the plan if necessary. The artillery fires were designed to destroy or suppress enemy defenses, with the maneuver forces maneuvering in the wake of the fires to occupy the ground or otherwise take advantage of the effects of the fires. Artillery offensives could also be executed as a component of an attack by the ground forces.[8]

185

The Soviet Approach in Other Armies

Many national armies in the world have adopted, or formerly used, the Soviet approach to command and control of mobile operations, particularly those in the Arab world formerly supplied with Soviet materiel. Except for non-mobile operations in Afghanistan, the Soviet army was never in combat. To look for examples of the use of its rigid command and control protocols, one must look to its use by Arab armies in the wars with Israel or Iran.

The classic example of this system in action was the attack of the Syrian army against a relatively weak Israeli defense on the Golan Heights in October 1973. Spurred on by up to 3,000 Soviet advisors, the Syrians drew up a breakthrough attack plan, with three infantry di• visions mounted in BTR-50 or BTR-60 wheeled armored personnel carriers and supported by tanks leading the assault, followed by the equivalent of three armored divisions.[9] The Israeli defense was initially only two armored brigades (one being held in reserve) and an infantry brigade whose personnel were strung out in small, localized fortifications arrayed along the Syrian border.

Despite the disparity in numbers, the Syrian attack failed. While the Israelis were caught by surprise, border obstacles and traffic jams hindered performance. In the northern sector, the original assault force failed to penetrate the Israeli forward defenses.[10] After the initial assaulting motorized infantry division was beaten back on 6 October by one Israeli tank bat• talion, both sides reinforced; the Israelis with their elite 7th Armored Brigade, and the Syrians with an armored division. On 7 October the Syrians formed their infantry division on line and assaulted the Israeli lines, being repulsed. Over the next three days the Syrians repeatedly as• saulted, reinforcing their assaulting echelons with tanks. Each time they were repulsed either by long range Israeli tank fire or local counterattacks.[11]

In the southern sector of the Golan front, the Syrians had their only limited success. At• tacking a portion of the defending Israeli armored brigade, the Syrians managed to mass against a gap in the Israeli lines and push through it. However, while trying to capitalize on this success, the Syrian commander gave one brigade a new mission not part of the original plan, which called for it to attack northern Israeli positions from behind. When not executing preplanned operations, however, the brigade faltered, allowing a handful of Israeli tanks to destroy 40 out of 45 of the brigade's tanks. Similarly, where the Syrians had broken through, small groups of Israeli tanks ambushed and slowed down the Syrian advance. Nevertheless, the Syrians managed to bludgeon their way forward and were reinforced on the morning of 7 October with an additional armored division. The commander of this reinforcing unit then turned the southern advance from a northwest axis to a westerly one, hoping to capture the strategically important bridges across the Jordan River. However, instead of continuing to ad• vance, the Syrians stopped when harassed by small Israeli units, eventually halting just short of the bridges for the night. The pause was crucial as the Israelis used it to rush reinforce• ments to the southern Golan front, halting the Syrian advance on the 8th and mounting their own Golan-wide counterattack on the 9th.[12]

186

The tactical inflexibility of the Syrian battle command clearly showed. The complete tactical flexibility of the Israeli defenders allowed them to take advantage of every opportunity to halt the advance, while the Syrian forces missed many opportunities to overwhelm the small Israeli forces and ultimately led to the Syrians trying to bludgeon their way through to a breakthrough. This tactic was stymied more by Syrian inflexibility than by direct enemy action.

The weaknesses of the Iraqi military, which also employed its own variant of the Soviet system, are well documented. While at the operational and strategic level, Iraqi planning and, to some extent, execution—particularly in armored, mechanized, and Republican Guard units—showed a certain effectiveness ineptitude at the tactical level negated any advantages. In 1991 Iraqi planning called for vigorous frontal armored counterattacks against coalition penetrations.[13] Leadership at all levels below division showed little initiative and an inability to respond quickly (or sometimes at all) to changes in the tactical situation.[14] When faced with the overwhelming firepower, air superiority and maneuverability of Western forces in both 1991 and 2003, Iraqi forces failed miserably at mobile operations.

During Operation DESERT STORM in 1991, when various Arab contingents were part of the coalition to free Kuwait from the Iraqi invaders, the contrast between the rigid Soviet system and the more initiative-based system used by the Western contingents was readily apparent. One Arab ally force failed to reach its objectives even when advancing virtually unopposed, and executed scheduled artillery fires even though intelligence clearly indicated the Iraqis had already fled the positions the fire was planned on. The lack of initiative at the tactical level was evident when a large unit halted for ten hours at a minor Iraqi obstacle that could have easily been breached.[15]

Without masses of troops, and massive firepower, the Soviet system of rigid command and control has, historically, proven to be an ineffective method of executing battle command of modern armies in mobile campaigns. While not always ultimately successful, armies using decentralized techniques—mission-style orders; the initiative of junior leaders; the use of the commander's intent as the guiding principle for response to a changing situation—have displayed a tactical flexibility that increased the odds for success. Forces using decentralized techniques were able to succeed even when outnumbered, surprised or less well equipped. Decentralization gave armies the ability to quickly take advantage of every battlefield opportunity. Tactical flexibility has also proven to be a necessary prerequisite for operational level success. Moving large units around on the battlefield that cannot fight at the point of the spear requires overwhelming numbers or firepower to be even marginally successful.

Summary

The Soviet Union and its Red Army took a different approach to battle command on the move than most other military forces (except those modeled after the Soviets themselves). The Soviets emphasized centralization: the preparation and rote following of elaborate plans, the stereotyped use of complicated battle drills and the minimal use of initiative at all levels from division on down. The inherent centralization and inflexibility of Soviet mobile operations resulted in an emphasis on firepower over maneuver. To gain the firepower advantage, the Soviets intended to mass their forces and assault in several attack waves or echelons, defeating the enemy defense through brute force. Accordingly, the Soviets planned to use artillery as a firepower sledgehammer, with the maneuver forces following up its effects. In essence, the tank and motorized infantry forces would be supporting the firepower of the artillery with their maneuver. The Soviet systems seems, however, to be incompatible with the successful execution of modern mobile operations. The inherent uncertainty of the modern battlefield requires a certain amount of initiative and flexibility at all levels that even large numbers of soldiers and massive firepower cannot overcome.

Many non-Soviet armies employed the Soviet system, providing in some cases, the only practical example of the system being used in actual combat operations. For example, in 1973 the Syrian Army, used the Soviet system in their assault against defending Israeli armored forces on the Golan Heights. The Syrian attack's ultimate failure hinged largely on its inherent inflexibility, even after they managed to batter a penetration into the Israeli positions. The Iraqi military also espoused the Soviet system with poor results in 1991 and 2003.

Notes

1. Heinl, 98.

2. David Isby, *Weapons and Tactics of the Soviet Army* (London, Jane's, 1988), 99, 103; Steven Zaloga, *Red Thrust: Attack on the Central Front: Soviet Tactics and Capabilities in the 1990s* (Novato, CA: Presidio Press, 1989), 65, 68.

3. Isby, 103.

4. Zaloga, 254.

5. Isby, 480-1.

6. Ibid., 58-61.

7. Ibid., 58.

8. Ibid., 225, 228-9.

9. Kenneth M. Pollack, *Arabs at War: Military Effectiveness, 1948-1991* (Lincoln, NE: University of Nebraska Press, 2002), 481, 485-7.

10. Ibid., 486-7.

11. Ibid., 399-401.

12. Ibid., 487-9.

13. G2, VII Corps, *The 100 Hour Ground War: How the Iraqi Plan Failed*, Redacted Version (hereaf• ter G2, VII Corps, US Army, 1991), 9, 12.

14. Pollack, 265.

15. Ibid., 140-2.

MODERN US ARMY BATTLE COMMAND AND COMMAND POST THEORY AND ORGANIZATION

"The TOC [Tactical Operations Center] is neither a formal military organization nor a separate echelon of command. It is formed from resources of the command solely as an op•erating element to accomplish timely staff actions on matters concerning current operations at the echelon of employment."
—FM 101-5, June 1968[1]

Command Post Theory versus Actual Organization

Since World War II, US Army forces at each tactical level above company have orga•nized their headquarters companies into forward command posts and rear headquarters. The forward portion of the operations (G/S-3) and intelligence (G/S-2) sections have over time organized themselves into an element called the tactical operations center (TOC). The organization of TOCs was formalized in the June 1968 edition of FM 101-5. The manual, however, stressed that the TOC was "not a formal organization or separate agency or ech•elon," but was to be formed from the current organization. TOC organization was to be a commander's prerogative.[2] At each level of command a variety of command posts were set up using unit assets. As in World War II, almost all units (battalion and above) established rear and forward command posts. After World War II, this number gradually increased, with the forward command post usually being split into a main command post (usually called the TOC at the brigade and battalion levels) and an even more forward command post called the tactical command post (TAC), which originally consisted of the commander and a small group of key assistants, but eventually evolved into a fully operational headquarters element on its own.

Generally speaking, the parts of the staff sections not immediately needed for combat operations were placed either in the rear or main headquarters. The rear headquarters, usu•ally centered around the command's logistical headquarters, was usually overseen by either a deputy commander, the logistics commander, or the logistics or personnel staff officer. The main headquarters was usually led by the unit's chief of staff (or equivalent), or deputy commander, assisted by the unit's headquarters company commander. The forward com•mand post/ TOC typically contained the bulk of the operations (G/S3) and intelligence (G/S2) sections from the unit's staff. Originally the commander posted himself here, but over time most commanders developed a battle command style that required an even smaller headquarters to accompany him when he went forward. This developed into the TAC, which usually included the minimal number of people necessary for the commander to exercise command. Typically this included the unit operations officer, the fire support coordinator, and some communications and security soldiers. Sometimes commanders operated indepen•dent even of the TAC in command vehicles or command and control helicopters.

Since command post theory, as defined in doctrinal literature, was not reflected in unit tables of organization and equipment, the latter retaining the typical staff system in use since World War I, actual command post organization could vary to some extent from unit-to-unit, or command-to-command depending on the command style of the unit commander. Specific examples of command post organization will be outlined in the next chapter.

The ad hoc organization of command posts for combat operations continued to be the stan‐ dard procedure in the United States Army up into the new millennium. However, in the early 1960s, the Army introduced its first armored vehicles designed exclusively for use as com‐ mand posts for mobile operations, the M577 and the M114.

Command and Command Post Vehicles

After World War II, where the primary armored vehicle used by infantry and command‐ ers was the armored half-track, the Army developed a series of increasingly improved fully tracked and closed armored personnel carriers (APCs), culminating in the M113 APC which was fielded after 1960.[3] The M577, also initially fielded in 1960, was built on the M113 chas‐ sis. It resembled the M113 except that it had a taller, 12 foot rear compartment and mounts for a generator to power the bank of radios. The M577 was the first true command post vehicle. It was designed to provide a ready-made mobile command post for US army units at the divi‐ sion-level and lower. The vehicle came with a tent extension, which could be attached to tent

Figure 40. M577A2 Light Tracked Command Post Vehicle.

extensions from one or more additional M577s to quickly create the workspace for a mobile command post. The M577 (along with the M113) was modified with a diesel engine (instead of the previous gasoline one) and designated the M577A1 in 1962. A total of 944 M577s and 2,693 M577A1s were fielded by the US Army starting in the early 1960s. The M577 fleet was later all upgraded to A1s. Later the M577A1 was modified into an A2 version currently still found in the US Army inventory and an A3 version in the 1990s, with an A4 version being currently developed.[4]

While the M577 was a command post vehicle, at the same time as it was fielded, the US Army also fielded a unique command vehicle, the M114. The M114 was similar in appear·ance to the M113, except it was smaller with a lower silhouette. The M114 could carry four men including the driver and vehicle commander. When used as a reconnaissance vehicle in armored cavalry units, the other two-crew members were observers or scouts. As a com·mand vehicle, the M114 provided a unique vehicle for commanders of mechanized infantry platoons, companies, and battalions to command their units. With the original vehicle being gasoline powered, a diesel version, the M114A1, was fielded in 1962. All together the Army purchased 3,710 M114s, of which 615 were M114, the rest being M114A1s. The M114 sys·tem had problems with cross country mobility and proved to be unreliable. Its unique silhou·ette marked it as a command vehicle as well, making it a big target. Therefore, the M114 was phased out in the late 1960s, early 1970s, being replaced with M113s. For many years after, M114 hulks could be found being used as targets on Army live fire ranges worldwide.[5]

Figure 41. M114 Armored Command And Reconnaissance Carrier.

Figure 42. M1068 Standard Integrated Command Post System Carrier.

After the demise of the M114, Army mobile commanders used M113 APCs and its successor, the M2/3 Bradley Infantry Fight‐ing Vehicle, both equipped with extra radio mounts, as a command vehicle. Tank battalion and com‐pany commanders used a tank as their command vehicle. The M577 remained the basic command post vehicle. In the 1990s, after the Gulf War, the Army commenced a pro‐gram called Force XXI, designed to use the technological revolution in digitalization and apply it to Army command and control. As part of this process, the Army first developed a modified version of the M577 called the M1068 Standard Integrated Command Post System Carrier. The M1068 was designed to be equipped with the new Army digital communications computer system, the Army Tacti‐cal Command and Control System (ATCCS). The deployment plan for the M1068 included two for the divisional tactical command Post, two for the maneuver brigade's tactical com‐mand post, three for its main command post and one for rear command post. Each armored or mechanized infantry battalion would receive three, and each armored cavalry squadron receiving four. The Army also developed a new prefabricated command post tent, the Modu‐lar Command Post System. This CP tent could be set up as a separate element or as a tent extension to the M1068.[6]

Figure 43. The Modular Command Post System attached to an M1068.

As a follow-on to the M1068, the Army developed a completely new command post vehicle, the M4 Command and Control Vehicle (C2V). The C2V was built on the same chassis as the M993 Multiple Launcher Rocket System (MLRS). The system contained four workstations with ATCCS computers. However, after initial testing, the vehicle was discovered to have a limited capability unless it was in a stationary mode, and the radios and systems integrated into it had limited ranges of 25 to 30 kilometers (15 to 24 miles). The system was designed to replace the M577/M1068 in the tactical operations center role at brigade and battalion levels. Despite the initial limitations, the Army ordered 25 C2Vs in 1997.[7]

Figure 44. M4 Command and Control Vehicle (C2V).

However, after this initial order was produced, the Army cancelled the program as part of its shift to the Stryker medium wheeled vehicle system in 1999. The contractor, United De- fense, placed the C2Vs in storage for possible foreign military sales. In 2002, in preparation for ground combat operations in Iraq, 15 of the CV2s were fielded to the Army units slated to fight, with the remainder designated for spare parts. V Corps headquarters received three vehicles, as did the 3d Infantry Division and 1st Armored Division. The 1st Cavalry Division received four and the 3d Armored Cavalry Regiment two systems. The systems were upgrad- ed with a suite of the new Army Battle Command System (ABCS) hardware and software.[8]

In addition to working on command post vehicles, the Army also worked on command ve- hicles in the 1990s as part of the Force XXI program. Work was done to convert the Bradley Fighting Vehicle into a command vehicle. The Bradley Commander's Vehicle (BCV) was used by the Force XXI test unit, the 4th Infantry Division (Mechanized), as a brigade com- mand vehicle. The basic Bradley was modified to contain three workstations and set up to ac- cept a variety of digitalized devices. Five such systems were ultimately deployed in the 2003 Baghdad campaign.[9]

Summary

Since World War II, US Army commanders at all levels have had to reorganize their unit headquarters elements (headquarters company at all levels above company) into elements useful for field operations. Doctrinal manuals provided guidance for this reorganization, the details of which could vary depending upon the battle command style of respective com- manders. Headquarters were, however, usually reorganized into four elements, a rear head- quarters for administrative/ logistical activities, a main headquarters to conduct the com- mand's detailed staff work and planning, a forward command post/tactical operations center to facilitate the execution of current and projected tactical operations and a tactical command post from which the commander could lead tactical operations with the minimal necessary staff elements available to him. In addition to these four headquarters, commanders could also chose to move about the battlefield in command vehicles, usually either tracked vehicles with extra radios or command and control helicopters.

After World War II the US Army developed a series of increasingly more sophisticated command post and command vehicles, specially equipped with additional communications and power generation assets and tent extensions. During the 2003 Baghdad campaign this culminated in the fielding of several modified Bradley fighting vehicles used as a digitalized command vehicle and the C2V command and control vehicle, which proved to be the first ever fully mobile and digitalized command and control vehicle.

Notes

1.   US Department of the Army, *FM 101-5, Staff Officers' Field Manual, Staff Organization and Procedure* (Washington, DC: Department of the Army, 13 June 1968) L-1.

2.   Ibid.

3.   Fred W. Crismon, *US Military Tracked Vehicles* (Osceola, WI: Motorbooks International, 1992), 254, 256. The Army fielded its first true armored personnel carrier, the M75 between 1952 and 1954, and the M59 in 1954-60. See Christopher Foss, ed, *The Encyclopedia of Tanks and Armored Fighting Vehicles: The Comprehensive Guide to 900 Armored Fighting Vehicles from 1915 to the Present Day* (San Diego: Thunder Bay Press, 2002), 67.

4.   Crismon, 259; The M577A3 and A4 are discussed at "M577A3 Command Post Carrier" http://www.fas.org/man/dod-101/sys/land/m577.htm, (accessed on 24 November 2004).

5.   Crismon, 254-5.

6.   For information on the M1068 see http://tacom.army.mil/tardec/m113/m1068a3.htm, (accessed 27 November 2004) and http://www.fas.org/man/dod-101/sys/land/docts/bnB007AA.htm; for the Modu•lar Command Post System see http://ct.dscp.dla.mil/ctinfo/basecamp/mcps/mcps.htm, (accessed 27 November 2004).

7.   "M4 Command and Control Vehicle (C2V)", http://www.fas.org/man/dod-101/sys/land/c2v.htm, (accessed 27 November 2004); Scott R. Gourley, "Command on the Move: New Mobile Systems Untether the Commander from the Command Post While Maintaining Situational Awareness," *MIT [Military Information Technology] E-nnouncement* (Volume 8, Issue 5, July 9, 2004), http://www.mit•kmi.com/archive_article.cfm?DocID=526 (accessed on 26 November 2004).

8.   Ibid.; Rebecca Morley and Joseph Kobsar, "Battle Command on the Move," paper presented at the 9th Annual Command and Control Research and Technology Symposium, San Diego, CA, 15-17 June 2004, http://www.dodccrp.org/events/2004/CCRTS_San_Diego/CD/papers/225.pdf accessed on (26 November 2004), 2.

9.   Morley and Kobsar, 2; Gourley.

MOBILE BATTLE COMMAND IN MODERN
US ARMY OPERATIONS 1991-2003

"Battle command is decision making. The commander will visualize the present friendly and enemy situations, then the situation that must occur if his mission is to be achieved at least cost to his soldiers, and then devise tactical methods to get from one state to the other."
—General Frederick Franks[1]

Of all the US Army campaigns in the post-Vietnam era—all of which were of a mobile, expeditionary nature—only two involved a significant number of American troops and were mobile operations at the operational and tactical levels. This chapter discusses battle command in these two actions, the 1991 Gulf War and the 2003 Baghdad Campaign.

The 1991 Gulf War

The 100 hour 1991 DESERT STORM ground campaign was a highly mobile operation in which all the US Army forces employed were armored or mechanized, except for the air assault elements of the 101st Airborne Division (Air Assault), which was mobile through the use of helicopters, and the airborne infantry battalions of the 82d Airborne Division, which were augmented with reserve component truck units to make them motorized.[2]

Lieutenant General Frederick Franks, DESERT STORM commander of the VII Corps, has outlined his approach to battle command in the fast moving 1991 campaign in his memoirs of the war, *Into the Storm*. Franks commanded the largest single tactical mobile force ever used in combat by the US Army. His corps contained 1,584 tanks and over 50,000 vehicles of all types. And almost all were on the move.[3]

To control the corps, Franks operated multiple command posts. The rear command post remained stationary at a location along the main supply route (MSR) and next to an airfield to the right (southeast) rear of the corps sector, 18 miles east of the town of Hafar Al Batin. The corps main command post (MAIN CP), led by the chief of staff and where the bulk of the corps headquarters staff was located, also remained stationary at a location 25 miles south of the Iraqi-Saudi Arabian border in the center of the corps sector. The main command post consisted primarily of two large general purpose (called GP Large in the Army) tents hooked together, with ancillary tents located around the periphery of the main tents. The main command post area was both a working area and a briefing area.[4]

In addition to these command nodes, which would not move during the actual operation, Franks employed three mobile command posts. The Tactical Command Post (TAC CP), initially located about 30 miles northwest of the MAIN CP, usually headed by the corps operations officer (G-3), was slated to move forward starting on the second day of the offensive right behind the 3d Armored Division, in the center of the corps sector. Additionally there were two Jump TAC CPs, one initially located right behind the 1st Infantry Division (Mechanized) on the right of the corps sector, the other up front with the 3d Armored Divi-

199

Dennis M. Giangreco

Figure 45. The VII Corps TAC linking up with a Jump TAC in DESERT STORM.

sion. The former Jump CP, under the leadership of the deputy corps commanding general, was positioned to oversee the 1st Infantry Division's breach operation, while the latter was positioned to communicate easily with the corps left wing enveloping force consisting of the 1st and 3d Armored Divisions and the 2d Armored Cavalry Regiment.[5]

Franks felt it would be difficult for him to command the corps from a moving armored vehicle, so he planned to position himself either at the TAC CP or at one of the Jump TAC CPs. He planned to be as close to the corps main effort as possible, using his lieutenant colonel executive officer as a twice-daily courier between his location at one of the Jump TACs and the TAC CP, whenever he was not at the latter. In this way he would be able to stay current while being forward. Franks would move around the battlefield in a Blackhawk utility helicopter specially configured with map boards and communications equipment, and meet daily face-to-face with subordinate commanders, while keeping in communications with his staff, his superiors and other subordinate units through the use of recently fielded tactical satellite (TACSAT) radios and telephones. TACSATs provided an almost unlimited communications range.[6]

The VII Corps Tactical Command Post consisted of three M577s with connected tent extensions. Within the extensions was a workspace of roughly 20 by 15 feet with a seven-foot ceiling. Field desks—small wooden, collapsible tables and cabinets with attached stools—were set against the walls of the tented area. The field desks contained field telephones linked into the corps communications network. Near his G3 officer's M577, Franks had his own field desk, opposite which was a large-scale situation map hanging from the tent wall. TAC staffers constantly updated the information on the map by hand, using small acetate stickers. The

200

TAC CP communicated with subordinate units through the use of short burst radio messages, with longer messages being sent via SAT phones.[7]

Third Army and Central Command (CENTCOM) required a daily written SITREP covering corps operations in the previous 24 hours and projected operations for the next 24 hours as of midnight. Franks' MAIN CP completed that requirement. Whenever Franks was at the TAC CP, he required a short briefing at 6 am.

In this mobile campaign, the armored and mechanized infantry divisions were the striking power of the VII Corps. These units organized for command and control in a similar manner. Each had a tactical command post up forward, composed of several M577s and part of each divisional staff section. A brigadier general, the division's assistant commander for maneuver, usually headed the TAC CP. The TAC CP's ascribed mission was to provide control for the close battle of the divisional elements with the enemy.[8]

The division main command post and tactical operations center was typically located farther to the rear. The MAIN CP at this level consisted of a combination of expandable vans on 5-ton truck chassis, and smaller vans and tents. The mission of the TOC portion of the MAIN CP was to control the deep battle while monitoring the close battle, and to plan for future operations and direct service support operations. A colonel, the division's chief of staff, usu‑ ally headed the MAIN CP. In highly mobile operations, the TOC would typically split in half, sending a small party, forward as a Jump TOC to run operations while the rest of the TOC and MAIN CP relocated. In DESERT STORM, however, while the campaign moved quickly, it lasted only four days and no MAIN CPs relocated.[9]

The divisions also organized a rear command post under the assistant division commander for support, a brigadier general. Usually located with the headquarters of the division support command, the REAR CP normally managed divisional combat service support activities and was an emergency back-up command post for tactical operations.[10]

In addition to these command posts, the division commanders personally directed operations through a command group, a small group of staff officers and assistants who accompanied the commander. Each division commanding general tailored this group to his own specifications, but it almost always included representatives from the operations (G3) staff section (if not the G3 officer himself), the intelligence (G2) section, a signal expert and a fire support officer from the division artillery command. The divisional commanders chose different methods of moving their command group, some from Blackhawk helicopters, others from M1A1 Abrams tanks or armored personnel carriers. Most, like Franks, moved among their subordinate com‑ manders and based themselves at the division's TAC CP or at an even more forward slice of the TAC CP called the Jump TAC.[11]

The maneuver brigades in each division fielded smaller versions of similar headquarters, with each brigade command post being roughly the size of the division TAC CP. The armored cavalry regiment (ACR), which operated directly under the corps, was in actuality a min‑ iaturized division with its own organic aviation and field artillery. Even its company-sized

troops had the capability of running their own TOCs out of a M577, unlike tank or mechanized infantry companies. For DESERT STORM, the VII Corps' 2d ACR organized a MAIN
CP/TOC, headed by the regimental XO, and a TAC CP under the regimental S3 officer. The
MAIN CP consisted of a number of military vans on 5-ton truck chassis, some M577s and
liaison and augmentee detachments from supporting units. The TAC CP consisted of two
M577s (S3 and Fire Support Element section vehicles), a former 2 1/2 ton truck maintenance
van converted for use as a command and control vehicle, and several M113 armored personnel carriers acting as security. The regimental commander stayed with the TAC CP, but
frequently formed a small command group to accompany him about the battlefield, which
usually included the S3 and the field artillery fire support officer.[12]

As part of the larger CENTCOM plan to eject the Iraqis from Kuwait and destroy their offensive military capability in the process, Franks' VII Corps was the main effort. His corps'
objective was the destruction of the Iraqi's Republican Guard Forces Command (RGFC), a
collection of the best armored and mechanized divisions in the Iraqi armed forces which was
deployed in reserve positions along the northwestern corner of Kuwait and in adjacent Iraq.
The VII Corps was slated to commence offensive operations at 0600 on G+1, the day after

Figure 46. 2d ACR Tactical Command Post in action during DESERT STORM.

the ground offensive started. This staggered start was designed to enable the Marine forces directly facing the entrenched Iraqis in southern Kuwait to initiate the offensive and, hope• fully pin the Iraqis in place so the more westerly flank attacks by the Arab allied Joint Forces Command North (JFC-N), VII Corps, and XVIIII Airborne Corps could then outflank the committed Iraqi forces, envelop and destroy them.

Franks' corps was in the center of the CENTCOM deployment, in a sector roughly 100 miles wide, extending from a little east of the north-south Iraqi-Kuwait frontier out into the desert. To the corps' left was the XVIII Airborne Corps. This corps consisted of a French light armored division, the 82d Airborne Division mounted on trucks, the 101st Airborne Division (Air Assault) and the 24th Infantry Division (Mechanized). The XVIII's mission was to use the French and 101st to isolate the Kuwaiti theater from the rest of Iraq. These forces would move at the same time as the Marines on G-Day. The 24th Mech would move in concert with the VII Corps offensive and provide a heavy armored force to isolate the Kuwaiti theater and provide flank support to the VII Corps operations against the Republican Guards. JFC-N on Franks' right, was also supposed to move in concert with the VII Corps, covering the flank of both the VII Corps and the Marines to their right. Behind JFC-N, the CENTCOM com• mander, General Norman Schwarzkopf, retained his reserve, the 1st Cavalry Division, a two-brigade-sized armored division, which was also tasked with feinting the Iraqis into thinking it was the main effort.

In the VII Corps sector, Franks and his operations staff devised a plan to carry out the corps mission of attacking in sector and destroying the RGFC. His plan was based on the enemy situation and was designed to be flexible in order to respond to any enemy reaction to the initiation of the offensive. The Iraqi troops formed into a frontline defensive belt of infantry divisions defending with two brigades forward, and one slightly to the rear in reserve. The extensive Iraqi defensive line stretching westward from the Persian Gulf along the Kuwait-Saudi Arabian border and the Iraqi-Saudi frontier extended roughly halfway across the sector assigned to the VII Corps 60 miles west of the Kuwaiti-Iraqi-Saudi border triangle. In this defensive line were positioned the one-third remnants of four Iraqi infantry divisions (east to west, the 27th, 25th, 31st, 48th). The 27th, 25th and 31st Infantry Divisions were heavily entrenched around the Wadi al Batin, a wide gully leading north from Saudi Arabia along the Kuwait-Iraq border. This wadi the Iraqis saw as the most probable lane for the US attack. To aid this conviction, the 1st Cavalry Division, the theater reserve force, conducted a series of feints up the wadi, both before and after G-Day. A fourth Iraqi infantry division, the 26th, covered the western flank of the Iraqi defensive line with its two forward brigades holding frontages of ten miles each and its third brigade located 25 miles to the rear. The division's frontage refused its right flank towards the north. Beyond this refused flank to the west was unoccupied until the positions of the 45th Infantry Division were reached far to the west in the XVIII Airborne Corps Sector.[13]

Behind the front line infantry, the Iraqi 7th Corps commander, who controlled all the front line troops on the Iraqi western flank, deployed the 52d Armored Division in positions between three to six miles behind the frontline brigades, roughly behind the right (east) side of Franks' sector.[14] Farther back were two concentrations of Iraqi armored forces that were the VII Corps' goal. The corps-sized Republican Guard Forces Command (RGFC) was the Iraqi theater operational reserve and consisted of, from west to east, the Tawakalna Mechanized Division, and the Medina and Hammurabi Armored Divisions deployed in a semicircle behind the 7th Corps and the adjacent (to the east) 4th Corps in southern Iraq just north of the Kuwaiti border. To the north and northeast of these divisions near Basra were four more Republican Guard divisions, the Al Faw, Nebuchadnezzar, and Adnan Motorized Infantry Divisions, and the Republican Guard Special Forces Division. Southwest of the RGFC concentration was the Jihad Corps, consisting of the 10th and 12th Armored Divisions. This corps' mission was as a tactical level reserve for the frontline forces. The 12th Armored Division had the particular mission of deploying forces to halt coalition penetrations in the western part of the Iraqi 7th Corps sector. Its location, however, meant that unless it moved, the US VII Corps would eventually encounter it.[15]

The destruction of the three heavy Republican Guard divisions was Franks' primary objective. To do so he had a force consisting of two armored divisions, a mechanized infantry division, an armored cavalry regiment and a British armored division. Additionally, the theater reserve, a two-brigade armored division, was also slated to be released to his control sometime during the operation. The plan Franks and his staff drew up had two phases. In the first phase, in the eastern portion of the corps sector, the 1st Infantry Division (Mechanized), supported by extra field artillery and engineers, would conduct a breaching operation against the defensive line of the Iraqi 48th and 26th Divisions, then open a gap for the British 1st Armoured Division to move through. The British would then advance to the northeast and destroy the Iraqi 52d Armored Division, while the US 1st Division would do the same to the Iraqi 48th and 26th Divisions. The British division would continue to the east towards the Persian Gulf as the extreme right (or southern) flank of the corps' maneuver. In the western part of the corps sector, with the 2d Armored Cavalry Regiment in the lead, the 1st Armored Division on the left and the 3d Armored Division on the right would advance around the Iraqi right flank northeast towards the RGFC. During this advance, the 3d Armored Division was also designated as the corps reserve as it was in the center of the corps movement. The phase one advance would end when the corps units were on a line 90 miles inside of Iraq. At this line, Phase Line Smash, Franks would then decided which one of several previously drawn up courses of action, packaged as fragmentary plans (FRAGPLAN), that he would adopt to deal with the Republican Guards. His choice would depend on the enemy situation and the condition of the VII Corps troops. Franks intended to pivot his corps 90 degrees to the east and hit the RGFC with a tight fist of three heavy divisions (FRAGPLAN 7), the third division being either the 1st Cavalry Division out of theater reserve or the 1st Mech Division if it was done with its breach mission. If a third division were not available, Franks intended to use the armored cavalry regiment as a substitute. After the destruction of the RGFC, the VII Corps would push east to block the retreat of Iraqi army forces out of Kuwait.[16]

To facilitate command and control of this operation, the VII Corps operational staff established a series of graphic control measures. Each division was assigned a specific sector.

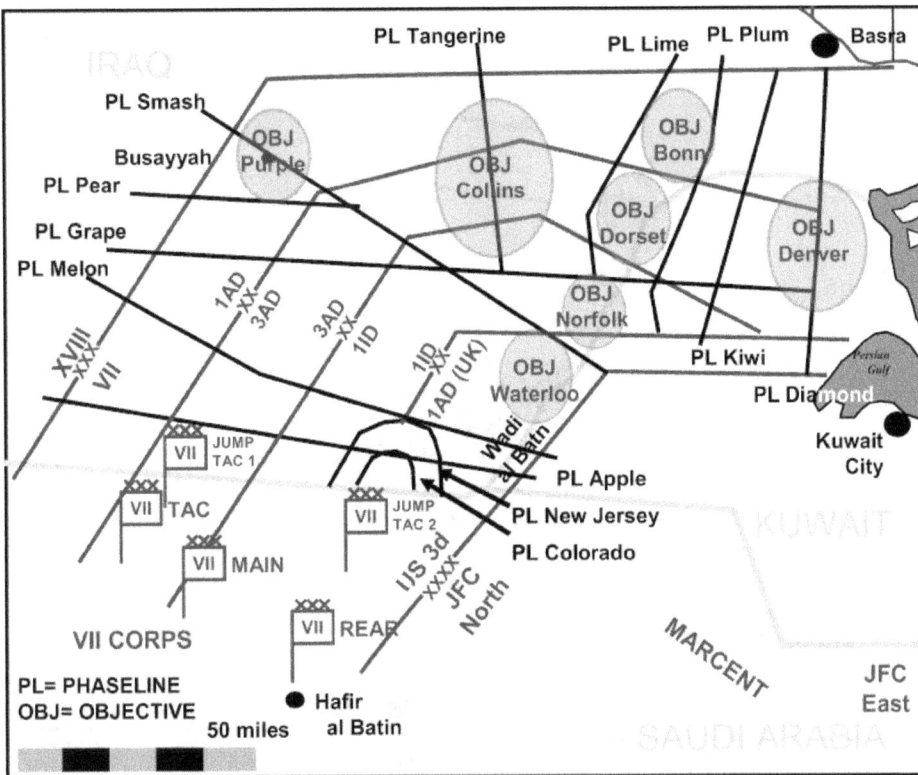

Figure 47. VII Corps DESERT STORM operational graphics, 1991.

Phase lines were drawn perpendicular to the sector boundaries to help control the advance. Franks intended that his forces advance abreast of each other and attack as a concentrated force. In addition to phase lines, geographical objectives were established to help coordinate the advance. Objective COLLINS, the major corps objective, was the expected location of the RGFC.[17]

As planned, Franks started out on G-Day, 24 February 1991, at the corps TAC CP, located near the TAC CP of the 3d Armored Division. The corps was slated to begin operations at 6 am on G+1, but, as the Marines attacked the Iraqis in southern Kuwait early on G-Day, the Iraqi defenses quickly began to collapse. With things moving faster than expected, the VII Corps attack was moved up to 3 pm on G-Day. Franks received a warning of this potential change early on G-Day and was prepared. The corps launched 15 hours early.[18]

In the east of the corps sector, the 1st Mech Division successfully executed its breach opera- tion, and advanced fifteen miles to Phase Line Apple, its objective line by darkness on G-Day. In the western portion of the corps sector, the 2d ACR and the 1st Armored Division's organic cavalry squadron (1-1st Cav) streaked ahead almost 40 miles to Phase Line Grape, with the

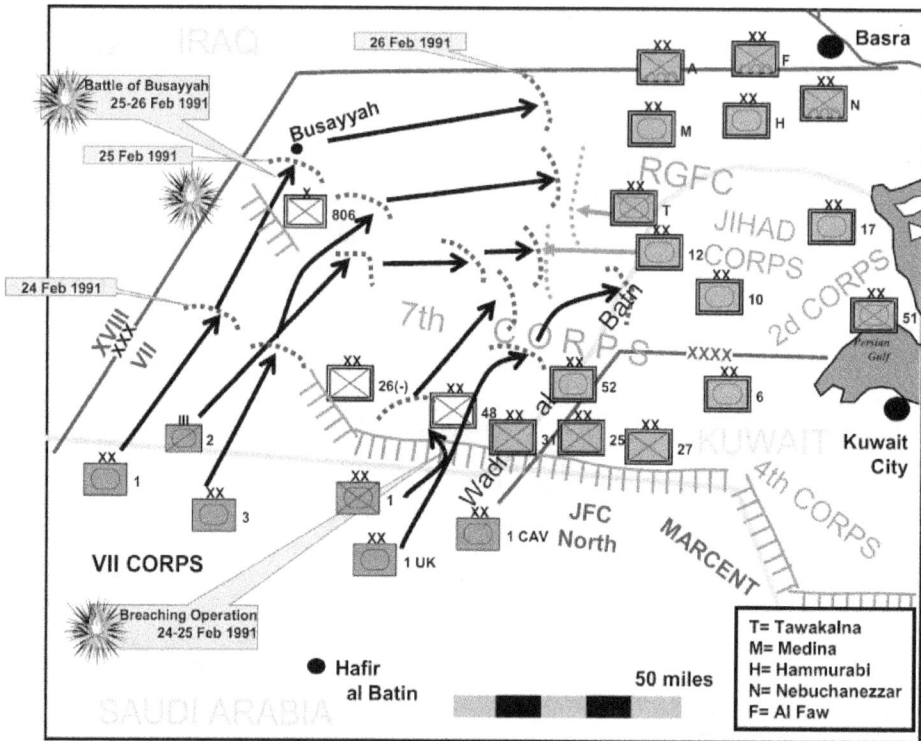

Figure 48. The VII Corps attacks 24-26 February 1991.

bulk of the two armored divisions following while arraying into attack formation, reaching Phase Line Melon roughly 20 miles behind the advance cavalry elements. The 1-1 Cavalry also was tied in with units on its left from the XVIII Airborne Corps. A patch of rough desert terrain that the Iraqis considered impassable for armored vehicles had slowed the initial ad•vance of the 1st Armored Division. But the division's maneuver elements had gotten through the rough area and were in more open terrain by the end of daylight.[19]

With this success, Franks chose to halt his corps for the night. He felt a night advance would create more problems than the ground gained would justify.[20] As there were not indications of a RGFC retreat or movement, the corps would recommence the advance at first light, advanc•ing to Phase Line Smash while the 1st Armored Division captured an Iraqi supply installation (Objective PURPLE) at the desert town of Busayyah, and the UK armored division destroyed the Iraqi 52d Armored Division. The taking of Objective PURPLE would threaten the north•west flank of the RGFC concentration.[21]

Franks planned to make his decision on how to attack the RGFC on the second day of the advance (G+1, 25 February 1991). He expected to reach the Republican Guard's positions on the third day. Because of the large size of his subordinate units, Franks preferred to issue

206

orders that would direct operations for at least the next twelve hours and to issue such orders at least 24 hours in advance of their execution. The corps commander also tried as much as possible to let his subordinates run their own units. Even though he had daily face-to-face meetings with all his subordinate commanders, he still presumed they were in a better posi•tion to make most tactical decisions about their commands.[22]

As G+1, 25 February, dawned, the Iraqi command, fragmented by communications de•stroyed by the air campaign, started to recognize the importance of the American armored advance on the western flank of their Kuwait position. They responded by moving up part of the 12th Armored Division from the Jihad Corps to positions astride the projected American advance, and having the neighboring Tawakalna Mech Division (to the north) deploy into positions in advance of the rest of the RGFC. The main attack was still expected at the Wadi al Batin, and poor communications meant that the Iraqi front line infantry divisions continued to hold their positions facing south even after the VII Corps had ripped open their right flank. The speed of the VII Corps advance would stun the Iraqis.[23]

The VII Corps advance continued. At the breach site, the 1st Division was through and had knocked out of action two brigades of the Iraqi 26th Division, and a third from the 48th Divi•sion. The British armored division started moving through the gap for its enveloping attack against the Iraqi forces facing south covering the Wadi al Batin avenue of approach. The Brit•ish would spend the rest of the campaign advancing eastward and destroying Iraqi units that were facing the wrong direction and capturing headquarters.[24]

The Iraqi 12th Armored Division tried to deploy two brigades in blocking positions about 20 miles southeast of Busayyah, but air strikes destroyed one brigade while it was moving to the new positions and the 2d ACR overran the other by midday. In front of the Iraqi 7th Corps lo•gistics base at Busayyah, the 1st Armored Division encountered the remaining brigade of the 26th Infantry Division, dug in before and in the town. After destroying the forward units, the 1st Armored was to attack the town with one brigade while the other two passed around to the south and swung east to advance onto Objective Collins, the location of the RGFC defensive line.[25]

The fight at Busayyah would take longer than expected. As darkness fell on G+1, the 1st Armored Division's 1st Brigade had finally reached the outskirts of the heavily defended town. The division commander, Major General Ronald Griffith, wanted to wait until morn•ing to finish the action. Franks approved as long as the bulk of the division would make it to its prescribed positions to press the attack on the RGFC. Griffith left behind a mech infantry battalion task force to finish the fight. The task force cleared the town early on the morning of G+2.[26]

Elsewhere during the previous day, with the 2d ACR already into the RGFC security zone and the Iraqi heavy divisions remaining in position, Franks decided to commit to the 90-de•gree turn to the east. The operation, originally mapped out as FRAGPLAN 7, required only minor adjustments for implementation, the primary of these being the use of the 1st Mech Division, once cleared of the breach, as the third division in his projected corps attack. Franks promptly issued oral orders and revised map overlays to place the two forward divisions and the 2d ACR on line to attack the Iraqis on G+2. The 2d ACR would initially attack, but once it came up, the 1st would then pass through and take the 2d ACR's place in the attack. Franks had expected to get the theater reserve force, the 1st Cavalry Division as his third attacking division. But the success of the 1st Division made it available. This substitution of large units made on the fly precluded detailed staff work and the specific time and place for the relief of the 2d ACR by the 1st Division was left up in the air depending on when the division started its movement, how long it took to go the roughly 60 miles to the vicinity of the 2d ACR, and where exactly the ACR was by that time.[27]

On G+2, the Iraqi mission changed. Instead of defending, the RGFC and units of the Jihad Corps were now tasked with covering the retreat of the Iraqi army out of Kuwait. Meanwhile, leading the US VII Corps advance, the 2d ACR was already deep into the security zone of the RGFC's most forward division, the Tawakalna. With the 3d Armored Division follow-ing behind and moving to the ACR's left and the 1st Armored Division moving up farther on the left from Busayyah, Franks directed the cavalry to keep pressing the enemy and conduct reconnaissance as to the extent of his positions in front of the corps.[28]

As the 2d ACR complied with these orders, the VII Corps attack developed in the afternoon of G+2 (26 February). The cavalry advanced about 14 miles through the Tawakalna security zone, expecting to encounter the main defensive position at about mile ten. But it was four miles farther to the east. Around 4 pm the two forces collided in what has since been called the Battle of 73 Easting, a reference to the north-south map gridline, which roughly demarked the Iraqi defensive line. The US forces continued to advance even though the action took place during a rainstorm/sandstorm. Within several minutes all three attack elements—from south to north: the 2d ACR, 3d Armored Division, and 1st Armored Division—were engaged against two brigades of the Tawakalna Mechanized Division. The 2d ACR quickly destroyed the entire Iraqi force to its front. Farther to the north the two armored divisions fought through the night, as the Iraqis used the increasingly worsening weather to funnel in rein-forcements and a brigade of the adjacent Adnan Motorized Division fought the 1st Armored Division before withdrawing into the sector of the XVIII Airborne Corps.[29]

On the morning of G+3 (27 February), after the Battle of 73 Easting, the 1st Infantry Divi-sion (Mechanized) passed through the 2d ACR to continue the attack against remaining ele-ments of the Tawakalna and the 12th Armored Division, giving Franks his three division fist at last. The Iraqis fought tenaciously but by the end of the day the attacks of the 1st Mech and 3d Armored Divisions overran the defensive positions of the Iraqi Tawakalna and 12th Ar-mored Divisions. The 3d Armored continued east, overrunning reserve positions of the Iraqi 10th Armored Division as the attack became a pursuit.[30]

Farther to the north, the Iraqi Medina Armored Division was positioned in reserve slightly to the right rear of the Tawakalna Division in front of the advance of the 1st Armored Division. Despite the battles to the southwest, the Medina's commanders did not expect the advance to reach them soon. At midday on G+3, however, the 1st Armored Division's advance elements

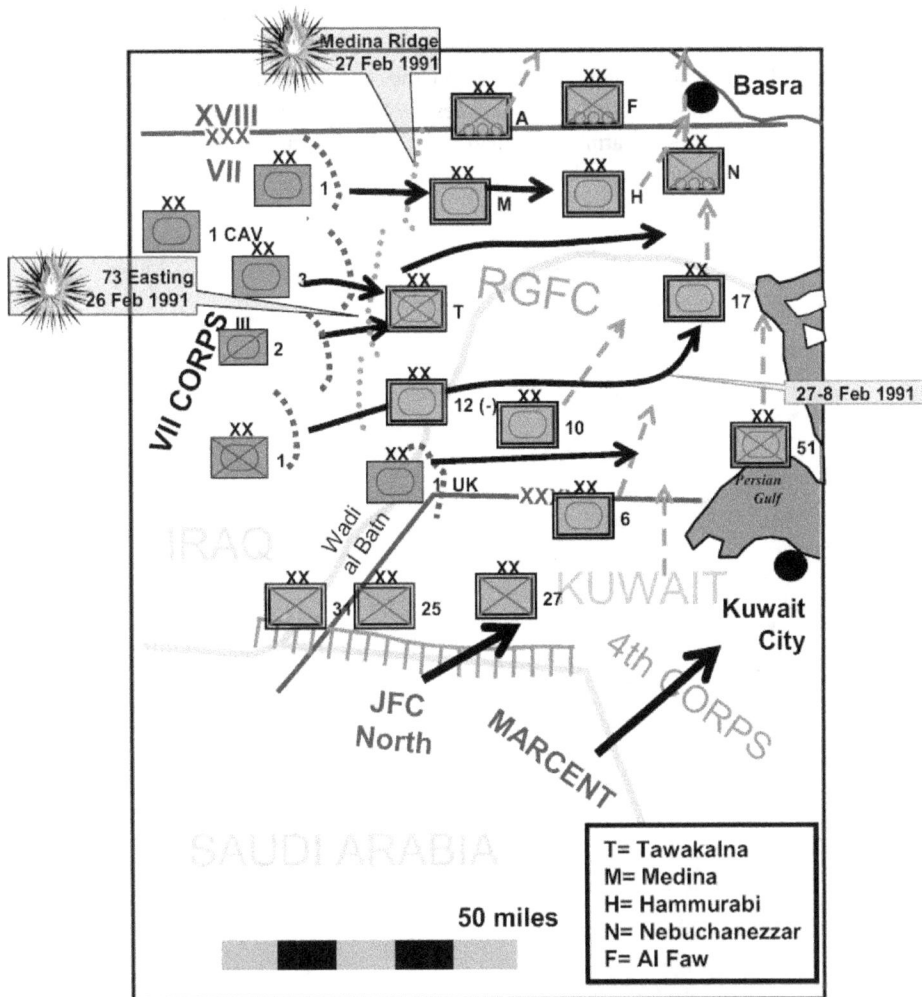

Figure 49. The VII Corps attack 26-28 February 1991.

caught one of the Medina's armored brigades at lunch and destroyed over 100 vehicles in ten minutes, while the rest of the American division was overrunning other Medina units to the south.[31]

After this engagement, called the Battle of Medina Ridge, the remaining intact Iraqi units began a general withdrawal everywhere. The US 24th Infantry Division (Mechanized), in the neighboring (to the north) XVIII Airborne Corps sector, destroyed some of the withdrawing Republican Guard elements as they attempted to flee from the VII Corps towards Basra and across the Euphrates River.[32]

For the remainder of G+3 and on into G+4, the 1st Mech and 1st UK Armoured Divisions pursued the routed Iraqi remnants up into eastern Kuwait and to the shore of the Persian Gulf, with few Iraqis left in front of their advance, before the ceasefire ended active operations. In four days of mobile combat, the VII Corps had destroyed one armored and six infantry divisions of the Iraqi 7th Corps, an armored division of the Jihad Corps, and two of three heavy divisions of the Republican Guards Forces Command.[33]

Figure 50. M577 from 2d ACR on move with FM radio antennas still in upright position.

Franks commanded his corps as he had planned. He initially based himself out of his tactical command post, but once the operation started, this headquarters was stuck back in the mael• strom of vehicles and he primarily based himself out of a small Jump TAC CP located with the 3d Armored Division's TAC CP. Though his command consisted of thousands of vehicles, his control headquarters ended up consisting of two M577s and his Blackhawk command and control helicopter.[34]

Franks used various techniques to command his corps while he was up forward. He had key staffers come forward from the MAIN CP and TAC CP. Jump TAC key staffers from Main came forward.[35] In his helicopter, after getting a short morning briefing at his CP location, Franks spent most days touring the battlefield and meeting with subordinates. From the air, the corps commander was able to see how his units were deployed and exactly where they were. The Blackhawk had a specially designed map-stand in the back of it and Franks was most frequently accompanied only by his aide, a noncommissioned officer (NCO) to oper• ate his portable TACSAT radio, and another NCO to provide security when they were on the ground. While the TACSAT radio had long-range power, it could only be operated on the ground. While in the air, Franks was restricted to an FM radio with the relatively short range of 12 to 18 miles.[36]

Communications were a problem for Franks. This was partially a trade-off for his desire to be up front. On several occasions he had to use the radios of his subordinate units to substitute for the relatively weak communications of his Jump TAC, particularly during the heavy rain of the evening of G+1/G+2. The main command post of the Third Army, which controlled both the VII and XVIII Corps, was located over 360 miles to the south in Riyadh. Although the army had established a tactical CP a good bit closer, Franks usually needed to talk to his superior, Lieutenant General John Yeosock, who remained at the main command post. Yeosock maintained a liaison officer at the VII Corps TAC CP, whose job was to keep him informed of the activities of the corps.[37]

Operating with large armored units in open desert terrain allowed the VII Corps and subor• dinate units to employ simple battle formations as a control method. The units practiced and choreographed these drills before the ground offensive and were able to shift between forma• tions to great effect during the four-day campaign. In addition, this campaign also saw the first use of digital land navigation aids such as Ground Positioning Satellites (GPS), which not only aided units in knowing where they were in trackless deserts, but allowed command• ers to be confident that units were where they said they were.[38]

Franks had an unusually large span of control, which, with the addition of the 1st Cavalry Division late in the operation, ended up being six major subordinate maneuver units. How• ever, excellent communications, control measures and Franks' ability to rotate personal visits to each subordinate commander's location facilitated the control of so many units. Addition• ally, the nature of the operations simplified span difficulties as well. Never were all six major elements in operations at the same time. Initially the corps forces in contact included one division in the breach zone and the armored cavalry regiment in the envelopment maneuver zone, followed by the two armored divisions. Later, when the British were committed, the division in the breach was out of contact and in reserve. In the final phases of the operation, the 1st Cavalry Division and the 2d ACR were in reserve out of contact. For most of the action, Franks only had four major elements in contact. And, unlike the case of Middleton in Brittany in 1944, who actually had a tough time controlling five major subordinate elements with far less capable communications technology, Franks' forces were not spread out and advancing in several different directions at the same time, but were basically moving on a single axis shoulder-to-shoulder.

While the VII Corps conducted its mobile campaign, the army and theater commanders remained in Riyadh far from the front. Early on in the campaign, theater commander General H. Norman Schwarzkopf was concerned about the speed (or tempo) of the VII Corps' advance, fearing the Iraqis in Kuwait would escape the trap. Twice Franks stopped his corps at night so that his units could attack the RGFC as a three-division entity. While Franks' immediate superior, Third Army commander John Yeosock, approved each halt, Schwarzkopf was still unhappy with the pace of the corps advance. However, this was never voiced directly to Franks who remained unaware of the criticism for almost a year. Naturally, Franks later admitted in his memoirs, if he had realized the theater commander wanted to emphasize speed over mass, he would have complied immediately, even if he felt such a maneuver to be somewhat risky.[39]

The Baghdad Campaign, 2003

The 2003 Baghdad campaign again saw US armored and airmobile forces face off against the military forces of Iraq in a high speed, long distance campaign of some 300-350 miles.[40] While, overall, the campaign lasted 20 days, there were actually two mobile phases. The first was the march of armored forces from Kuwait to the area around the city of Najaf and lasted from 20 to 24 March. After a five day pause, the second phase took US mechanized forces into downtown Baghdad, lasting from 30 March to 8 April. In this mobile campaign, the 3d Infantry Division (Mechanized), commanded by Major General Buford Blount, spearheaded a single division advance on Baghdad. To the east, the partially mechanized 1st Marine Division also advanced towards Baghdad along an axis ultimately paralleling the Tigris River.

The 3d Division's advance emphasized forward progress over concern about flanks or enemy strongpoints. Nests of Iraqi resistance, primarily the cities of Nasiriyah, Samawah, Najaf and Karbala, were bypassed and screened. Ultimately follow-on forces of the 101st Airborne Division (Air Assault) and the 82d Airborne Division cleared these cities.

The initial advance from Kuwait was in two main columns advancing across open, trackless desert. The right (eastern) column, consisted of two brigades and was aiming at securing the key Tallil Air Base complex south of Nasiriyah and roughly 85 miles north of the Kuwaiti border, and an important highway bridge across the Euphrates west of Nasiriyah. Tallil and the bridge were important for securing the lines of communication for following support troops and the Marine advance. The other column, on the left (west), consisting of the divi•

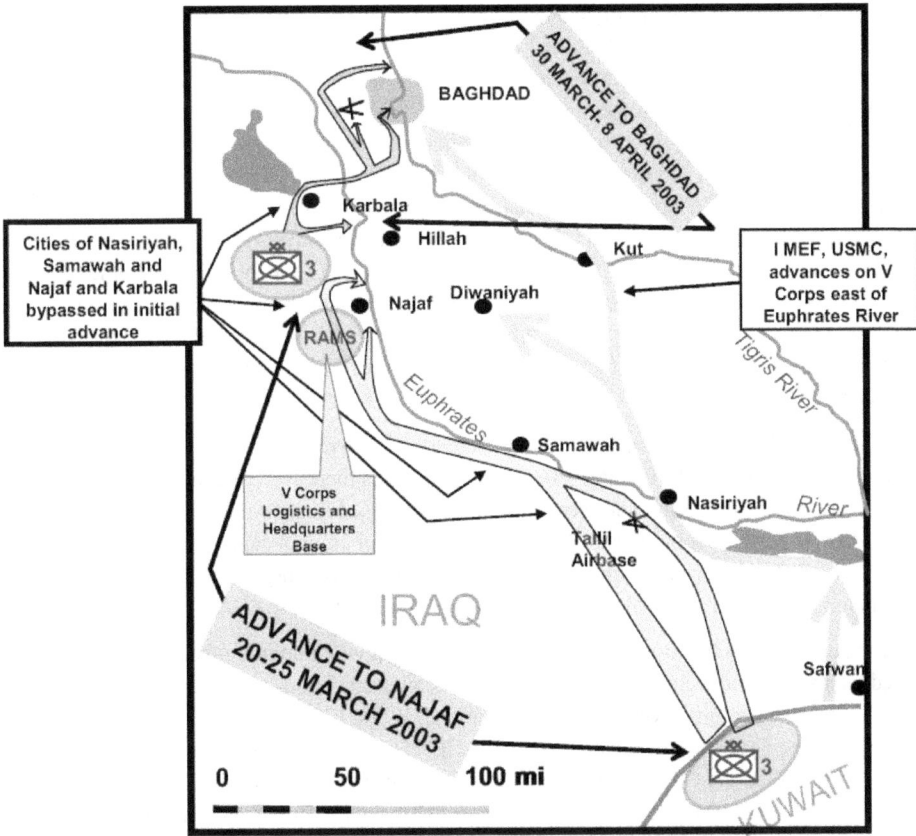

Figure 51. The Baghdad Campaign, 2003: Mobile Operations.

sional armored cavalry squadron and a brigade, pushed through the desert a little over 100 miles to the city of Samawah on the Euphrates, 60 miles northwest of Nasiriyah. While the cavalry isolated Samawah, the brigade swung around the city to the north and continued the advance 50 miles to the northwest to the city of Najaf where it secured Objective RAMS, the projected site for the corps and divisional command and control and logistics hub. After being relieved of duties guarding Nasiriyah and Samawah, the rest of the division isolated Najaf, and then began preparing for the next phase of the operation—attacking around the city of Karbala, crossing the Euphrates, and moving on to Baghdad.

After the operational pause that saw the establishment of RAMS, and the consolidation of the 3d Division south of Karbala and north of Najaf, the second phase commenced on 30 March with several preparatory operations. Because of terrain restrictions, during this ad• vance US forces had to pass through a narrow two mile-wide strip of passable land between the city of Karbala on the east and a large lake, called the Salt Sea by the Iraqis, to the west.

213

US forces expected to fight a pitched battle with heavy forces of the Republican Guard in the gap and farther to the east when the Euphrates would be crossed. Firepower, particularly airpower, ensured that no real battle with the Republican Guard took place in the gap. After advancing through the gap on the night of 1/2 April, the 3d Mech's 1st Brigade continued the advance up to the Euphrates at Musayyib, where it promptly crossed on some highway bridges captured intact, and then beat off the only major armored counterattack of the cam‑ paign. On 3 April the 2d Brigade established a base just south of Baghdad and on the same evening, the 1st Brigade moved up and captured the Baghdad airport. The division's 3d Brigade, relieved of screening duties at Karbala, then established a cordon around the north‑ ern part of Baghdad while the 2d Brigade conducted a raid into the city. The success of the raid prompted a larger advance into the downtown district on 7 April, which resulted in the collapse of conventional forces there and the ultimate transformation of the campaign into an extended stability operation.

The speed of the advance stunned the Iraqi defenders. When the first troops arrived in the area of RAMS, southwest of Najaf, a small force of Iraqis there were prepared to defend against an airborne operation and were completely surprised to see American armored ve‑ hicles that far north so soon. Similarly, on 5 April, an Iraqi colonel captured south of Baghdad was shocked to run into a column of US tanks and Bradley fighting vehicles. The colonel was so stunned that he literally drove his vehicle into a Bradley.[41]

Battle command on the move in the Baghdad campaign was a unique mix of long estab‑ lished techniques and technology, and new digital communications technology. Army forces used a relatively straightforward chain of command. While Central Command (CENTCOM) had overall responsibility for the operation, the CENTCOM commander, General Tommy Franks, established the Combined Forces Land Component Command (CFLCC), under Lieu‑ tenant General David McKiernan. McKiernan used his own Third Army headquarters, greatly augmented, to support joint (US Marines) and combined (British Army forces) operations. Under CFLCC's relatively decentralized method of command, aside from small forces oper‑ ating in northern and western Iraq, were the Army's V Corps and the I Marine Expeditionary Force (I MEF). I MEF controlled Marine air assets as well as the 1st Marine Division, the 2d Marine Expeditionary Brigade, and the British 1st Armoured Division, which remained around Basra. During the Baghdad campaign, the V Corps, commanded by Lieutenant Gen‑ eral William Wallace, commanded the 3d Infantry Division (Mechanized), the 101st Airborne Division (Air Assault), the headquarters and 2d Brigade of the 82d Airborne Division, and miscellaneous elements from the 3d Brigade, 1st Armored Division. While World War II era army corps had had little logistical functions, the 2003 corps played a key role in service support for its subordinate units. The divisions functioned to integrate and synchronize the operations of their assigned and attached maneuver forces. These maneuver forces were di‑ rectly controlled by brigade headquarters—the brigades not being fixed structures, but being designed by mission and the situation. In the Baghdad campaign, brigades showed great flex‑ ibility in managing the actions of maneuver battalions often dispersed over great distances.[42]

Commanders such as McKiernan and Wallace balanced directing their subordinates through the use of digital management and communications tools, and personal up-front contact. Wallace, like Franks before him in DESERT STORM, sought to visit all his subordinate division commanders at least once a day. McKiernan, though controlling the campaign from distant Qatar, came forward to talk to his corps commanders at critical points. 3d Division commander Blount commanded from up front at the Baghdad airport even as his forces moved into downtown Baghdad.[43]

While McKiernan organized his staff into multifaceted functional areas and used a staff assessment briefing focused on problem solving rather than the traditional, chronologically based staff update briefing, most operational commands employed a daily battle update briefing (BUB). The traditional division of command posts into a forward tactical CP, a main CP, and a rear CP was also maintained with some revisions based on new technology. Often the campaign moved too fast for commanders to operate out of Main or Tactical CPs, which took time to set up; so often commanders operated out of what Franks called a Jump TAC in 1991, but was now called an Assault Command Post (ACP).[44]

While the V Corps established main and tactical command posts, corps commander Wallace primarily operated out of his assault command post, composed principally of three M4 C2Vs. The corps ACP was usually located near and slightly to the rear of and separate from the tactical command post of the 3d Infantry Division (Mechanized). The use of the M4 C2V in the Baghdad campaign has already been mentioned in this work. The issue of these systems to the V Corps headquarters, and the 3d Infantry Division (Mechanized) was designed to

US Army

Figure 52. V Corps Assualt Command Post, 2003

provide these commands with the ability to create a digitalized command post. For use in Iraq the C2V prototype was upgraded to include broadband satellite suites that allowed commands to be well forward and command on the move, though the system required short halts to work optimally.[45]

Wallace organized the V Corps ACP using one M4 C2V as his own personal command and control vehicle, a second as an intelligence vehicle, the third a fires vehicle, controlling coordination with supporting field artillery and close air support assets. The whole corps ACP staffing consisted of about 80 soldiers, including a 43-man mechanized infantry platoon detached from the 2-6th Infantry battalion (1st Armored Division), and two military police squads, both of whom provided security, and only three signals specialists to troubleshoot the ACP digital communications systems.[46]

Wallace's command rhythm during the mobile operations phase was similar to Franks, twelve years earlier. Wallace usually spent his nights at the corps ACP. Because of weather conditions caused by desert dust, he preferred not to travel by air after darkness. In the morn‑ing he would receive a battle update briefing, then sit down with his staff to issue planning guidance and talk to the corps chief of staff far to the rear with the corps main CP. After this, the V Corps commander would then spend the bulk of the day in battlefield circulation, flying via Blackhawk helicopter to visit each division commander. After returning at dusk to the ACP, Wallace would receive another battle update briefing. After that, he'd follow the battle via digital means until he went to bed to end the day.[47]

Similar to the V Corps, the two mechanized divisions deployed first to Iraq, the 3d Infantry Division (Mechanized) and the later arriving 4th Infantry Division (Mechanized), did not use the ACP as a temporary Jump TAC equivalent. Instead the ACP was made permanent and built around specially redesigned and deployed M4 C2Vs or Bradleys. The 3d placed its three M4s at the Division TAC CP (DTAC), the Main CP (DMAIN), and the rear CP (DREAR). The DTAC M4 was sometimes used with the ACP. Due to the limited issue of the vehicle, there were no C2Vs below division level.[48]

While maneuver unit command posts in the Baghdad campaign were echeloned through the reorganizing of headquarters' formal organizational structure into the one used in the field in the US Army since World War II, command posts were now all networked into digitalized networks which will be discussed in more detail later in this section. Despite this network‑ing and its inherent long range communications capabilities, the echeloned CPs were given traditional functions based more on geographical or special considerations when the new technology may have allowed for possible different approaches based on the enhanced ability to command up front.[49]

During the Baghdad campaign's two mobile phases, the 3d Division had at least one, and usually two or three, of its maneuver brigades and most of its command and control elements moving at all times. Accordingly the division had to depend upon its ability to communicate on the move using secondary communication means or recently issued articles of digital equipment instead of the primary means—mobile subscriber equipment (MSE), which was designed to be mobile only within relatively short distances of about 10 miles. At one point, the division moved over 350 miles in three days with all of its command posts moving, and used an augmented engineer brigade headquarters CP to control the division's movement.[50]

The forces in the Baghdad campaign used the traditional graphic control measures common to most armored advances since World War II. With only one division in the advance, sectors were not initially assigned. Axes of advance, code-named routes, and phaselines were used to control movements; and commanders used code-named geographical objectives to key unit movements and missions. Many of these objectives subsequently became logistical or operational bases. Sectors, usually delineated by numbers, were later used to divide up the close quarters of Iraq's major cities. In the follow-on city fights, commands used both geographic sectors and unit sectors.[51]

In the interval between DESERT STORM and 2003, the Army made a deliberate effort to improve the technology of command and control. This program, called Force XXI, used the 4th Infantry Division (Mechanized) at Fort Hood, Texas, as its test organization for digitalizing communications and command and control functions in the Army division. By 1997, the 4th ID had validated the digitalized division concept and some of the organizational concepts adopted by the division, including smaller maneuver battalions and the addition of reconnaissance troops to each brigade, were then adopted Army-wide. But only the 4th ID had the specialized package of Force XXI equipment, though by 2002, the other division at Fort Hood, the 1st Cavalry Division, had begun receiving it as well. Neither the 4th Infantry Division nor the 1st Cavalry Division participated in the Baghdad campaign.[52]

Starting in October 2002, however, the Army began supplying the units deployed for the Baghdad campaign with Battle Command on the Move (BCOTM) vehicles (the M4 C2V), satellite telephones at lower levels, and digital systems such as Blue Force Tracker and voice tactical satellite (TACSAT) radios down to brigade level. These digital systems provided communications across vast distances, thus augmenting pre-existing FM radios (with a line-of-sight range of 18-30 miles), and MSE.[53]

Blue Force Tracker was part of the Force XXI Battle Command Brigade and Below (FBCB2) component of the Army Battle Command System (ABCS). ABCS was a digitalized suite of software and hardware components that had coalesced together from all the digital systems the Army developed since 1991. ABCS consisted of eleven major subsystems that enabled digital command and control and coordination of various battlefield functions. These components are illustrated in Figure 53. While not all units had all ABCS components, commanders who had most of the key packages could see their forces, plan and execute supporting field artillery and army aviation fires digitally, produce and print digital maps, and visualize terrain in relation to units widely dispersed. With this system commanders could fight their spread out units effectively.[54]

V Corps and the 3d Division successfully substituted a locally developed package, C2PC (Command and Control for the Personal Computer) in lieu of the unissued Maneuver Control System (MCS) module. Although this meant digitalization modules were not standardized

217

ARMY BATTLE COMMAND SYSTEM COMPONENTS

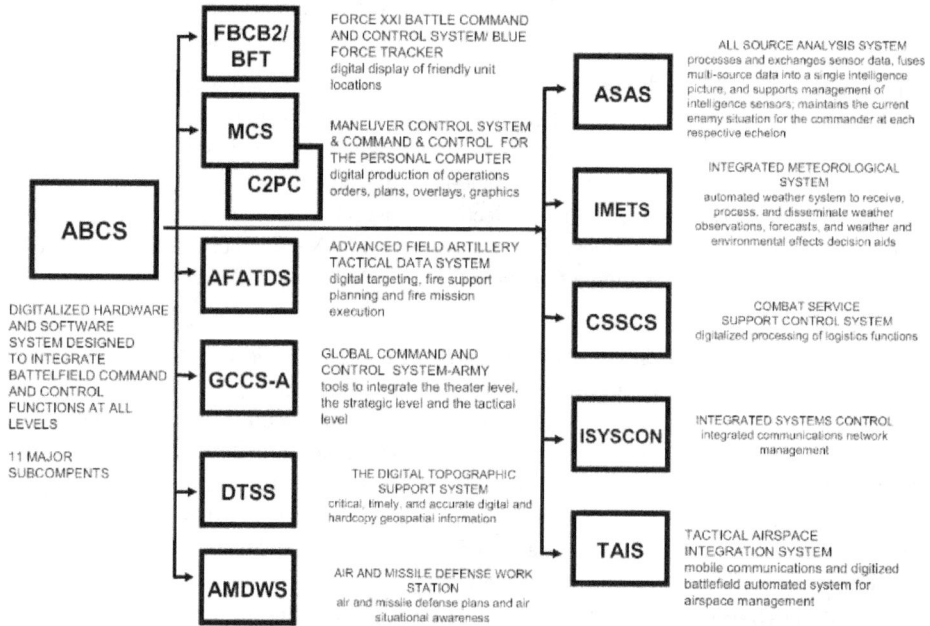

ABCS

DIGITALIZED HARDWARE AND SOFTWARE SYSTEM DESIGNED TO INTEGRATE BATTLEFIELD COMMAND AND CONTROL FUNCTIONS AT ALL LEVELS

11 MAJOR SUBCOMPENTS

FBCB2/ BFT
FORCE XXI BATTLE COMMAND AND CONTROL SYSTEM/ BLUE FORCE TRACKER
digital display of friendly unit locations

MCS
C2PC
MANEUVER CONTROL SYSTEM & COMMAND & CONTROL FOR THE PERSONAL COMPUTER
digital production of operations orders, plans, overlays, graphics

AFATDS
ADVANCED FIELD ARTILLERY TACTICAL DATA SYSTEM
digital targeting, fire support planning and fire mission execution

GCCS-A
GLOBAL COMMAND AND CONTROL SYSTEM-ARMY
tools to integrate the theater level, the strategic level and the tactical level

DTSS
THE DIGITAL TOPOGRAPHIC SUPPORT SYSTEM
critical, timely, and accurate digital and hardcopy geospatial information

AMDWS
AIR AND MISSILE DEFENSE WORK STATION
air and missile defense plans and air situational awareness

ASAS
ALL SOURCE ANALYSIS SYSTEM
processes and exchanges sensor data, fuses multi-source data into a single intelligence picture, and supports management of intelligence sensors; maintains the current enemy situation for the commander at each respective echelon

IMETS
INTEGRATED METEOROLOGICAL SYSTEM
automated weather system to receive, process, and disseminate weather observations, forecasts, and weather and environmental effects decision aids

CSSCS
COMBAT SERVICE SUPPORT CONTROL SYSTEM
digitalized processing of logistics functions

ISYSCON
INTEGRATED SYSTEMS CONTROL
integrated communications network management

TAIS
TACTICAL AIRSPACE INTEGRATION SYSTEM
mobile communications and digitized battlefield automated system for airspace management

Figure 53. The Army Battle Command System.

with those outside of V Corps, C2PC was used more effectively in the campaign overall than MCS. Similarly, the core ABCS intelligence component, ASAS (All Source Analysis System) was not used because of system limitations, being replaced by the more flexible Movement Tracking System (MTS) already in use within the corps. Combat service support (CSS) units also primarily used MTS in lieu of the CSS module in ABCS, though MTS lacked the long-range communications capabilities of the ABCS module.[55]

For battle command on the move, Blue Force Tracker (BFT) was the key component of ABCS. BFT-equipped vehicles carried a transponder that both transmitted the vehicle's location to other BFT-equipped vehicles, and received similar signals from other BFT vehicles and nodes via satellite communications. These locations were posted to a digital map, which, along with other components of ABCS, helped provide a common operational picture and situational awareness and the swift creation of operational graphics on digital maps.[56]

In the 3d Infantry Division (Mechanized), BFT was issued down to the company level in maneuver units. While the situational awareness aspects of BFT was important to battle command, almost as important were the long-range communication capabilities of the software. The e-mail capability of BFT, tied into the satellite communications system, enabled BFT units with only short range FM radio capability otherwise, to communicate over great distances. Accordingly, BFT soon replaced the less mobile MSE data systems as the primary

218

communications means for passing down operational fragmentary orders (FRAGOs) while the division was conducting mobile operations.[57]

One weakness of BFT and the ABCS suite in general was a system of updating information on the enemy situation that depended on immobile communications nodes, particularly at lower levels. While BFT started operations with preset intelligence information, updates depended on MSE communications that was unavailable once the units were on the move.[58]

Another weakness of ABCS was its joint capability. While Army air defense, field artillery and aviation fires were all tied into ABCS, Air Force close air support was not, requiring special techniques and handling. Similarly, special arrangements also were required when operating with or near US Marine forces.[59]

Aside from the communications capabilities inherent in BFT, almost all maneuver units down to brigade level had satellite communications separate from BFT in the form of tactical satellite (TACSAT) radios. These TACSATs allowed brigades and divisions to talk to each other even at long ranges. Below brigade, maneuver units employed short-range FM radios and, when stationary, MSE. The big communications divide was, however, between maneuver units with BFT and TACSATs, and the many combat support and combat service support organizations that depended on MSE even to get into the Army Battle Command System. These units, therefore, had a far weaker digital and long-range communications capability. To assist in communications flexibility in the V Corps, the corps signal brigade established bands of signal nodes within specified geographic areas that allowed command posts within the band's range to tie effortlessly into long-range communications. However, this system was obviously ineffective for use by units on the move forward.[60]

The V Corps commander, Lieutenant General William Wallace, successfully utilized digital technology from his assault command post during the Baghdad campaign. When operating from the ACP, Wallace worked out of his own M4 C2V, which contained six workstations. Aside from having a workstation for the corps commander's own use, the other workstations were used by intelligence, fire support, and operations personnel. The first two were Wallace's link to the fires and intelligence C2Vs which also were part of the ACP. The intelligence representative also provided timely intelligence updates. The operations officer assisted Wallace in monitoring the battle via the use of FBCB2. Wallace's own workstation consisted of a laptop computer which used C2PC and which he operated directly himself. During ACP movement, FBCB2 was the only available system that worked well; even with short halts, Wallace had almost all digital packages and video feeds available. Despite the availability of various types of communications mediums, the V Corps ACP primarily used TACSAT radios to communicate.[61]

While the 4th Infantry Division (Mechanized), the Army's only fully capable digitalized division in 2003, was unavailable for the Baghdad campaign, the division did arrive in the theater and began operations immediately afterwards. As the Force XXI testbed unit, the 4th ID was at the forefront of the development of new technology to the application of battle command. The division was given the opportunity to test these applications when it was given tactical responsibility for clearing and occupying a section of Iraq north of Baghdad centered on the former Iraqi military complex at Taji. The primary innovations the 4th ID brought to Taji were a technological innovation: the Battle Command on the Move (BCOTM) vehicle and an organizational innovation—the digitalized assault command post.[62]

The BCOTM vehicle was a modified Bradley fighting vehicle. The vehicle was refitted at Fort Hood to place the digital hardware and software packages and communications equip‑ment into the vehicle essential for the division command to operate while not at the division's TAC CP. The redesignated M7 BCOTM-Bradley included TACSAT capability, and radio equipment to operate and monitor three FM networks at the same time, and a message-pro‑cessing unit capable of operating the components of ABCS. The division fielded four M7s.[63]

Because the M7 soon became cramped with all this equipment, the division also refitted several M1068 command post vehicles, to include Blue force Tracker, which was not used by the 4th ID, but would be needed for compatibility with other commands in Iraq. The M1068, coupled with an M7 was the heart of the division's new assault command post organization. The ACP was also augmented with two tanks and a Bradley with an infantry squad to provide local security, a small military police element mounted in HMMWVs (High-Mobility Multi‑purpose Wheeled Vehicle), a communications team, and two Blackhawk helicopters.[64]

In the field the 4th ID's ACP concept was highly successful. The ACP was able to set up and be operational in 15 minutes. The division commander successfully orchestrated division operations from the ACP alone when the other division CPs were on the move or stuck in traffic jams. It also proved flexible and mobile, moving several times in the course of tactical operations, and still allowing the division commander to communicate with large parts of the division over 400 miles away.[65]

In addition to operations at the division-level, the 4th's three brigades were able to operate independently as separate digital units or as part of the larger division while executing tactical operations. With the developing nature of stability operations in Iraq, this capability proved very helpful.[66] In later phases of the stability operations portion of Operation IRAQI FREE‑DOM (OIF), the Army deployed other digital units, including the 1st Cavalry Division, and a Stryker medium motorized infantry brigade, which had been designed from inception to be completely digital in function.[67]

Despite the relative small size of the force employed, 2003's Baghdad campaign proved to be the US Army's most successful mobile campaign in terms of distances traveled and deci‑sive results. New technology—coupled with proven and new techniques and organizational structures—allowed for effective battle command and command and control over widely dis‑persed units executing a variety of complicated, simultaneous missions. Sometimes, however, in spite of the role of technology and multiple command posts, command and control came down to simply placing a map on the hood of a HMMWV and conferring with subordinates about combat operations.[68]

Summary

This chapter discussed two major mobile campaigns in terms of battle command on the move, VII Corps's 1991 operations against the Iraqi Republican Guard, and 2003's Baghdad campaign. These campaigns were marked by fast movement, large number of armored vehicles, and relatively complicated battle command considerations.

In the 1991 campaign, Lieutenant General Frederick Franks commanded the VII Corps through the use of multiple command posts. The Rear and Main command posts stayed behind in Saudi Arabia and really did not play a large role in the short, four day campaign. Franks primarily commanded through his tactical command post, and two Jump Tactical Command Posts which were usually collocated with the command posts of subordinate units. He would typically move throughout the day between his subordinate unit command posts via helicopter and spend the evening at the TAC CP, or one of the Jump TACs. Each of his subordinate units likewise echeloned their command posts.

VII Corps's mission was to destroy the Iraqi Republican Guard. To do so the corps units had to advance northeast through roughly 100 miles of formidable desert, then pivot to the east and strike the defending Iraqis. Franks controlled his advance through the use of phase lines, divisional sectors, and objectives. While his command and control element ended up being two M577s and a Blackhawk helicopter, Franks employed various techniques to augment this small force such as bringing forward key staffers at various times, and relaying communications through subordinate headquarters. Franks was able to effectively synchronize a corps attack where three plus divisions struck the Republican Guard simultaneously, shattering the Iraqi defenses. Operating in a broad sector of open desert, the subordinate divisions employed simple battle formations to ease command and control.

In the 2003 Baghdad campaign, basically one mechanized infantry division advanced on a narrow front in a rapid campaign over 350 miles from Kuwait to Baghdad in two mobile phases, the first lasting four days and the second nine days. In this advance, the 3d Infantry Division (Mechanized) commander, Major General Blount, emphasized forward progress over concern about flanks or enemy strongpoints. Forces he left behind to guard various bypassed Iraqi cites were soon relieved by follow-on forces from the 101st and 82d Airborne Divisions and the Marines. For battle command of this mobile campaign, extensive use was made of both digital communications equipment and traditional techniques of echeloning command posts and graphics control measures.

Extensive use of digital packages, primarily components of the Army Battle Command System, particularly the friendly unit locator and messaging system Blue Force Tracker, facilitated the commander's situational awareness and capability to communicate with subordinate commanders. Additional systems, such as satellite telephones and the limited fielding of specialized command and control and command vehicles greatly enhanced the ability of commanders to control forces without having to be physically with them. Nevertheless, command and control often still came down to command meetings with a map spread on the hood of a vehicle.

Notes

1.   Tom Clancy, with Fred Franks, Jr., *Into the Storm: A Study in Command* (New York: Putnam, 1997), 504.

2.   Charles Lane Toomey, *XVIII Airborne Corps: From Planning to Victory* (Central Point, OR: Hellgate Press, 2004), 303.

3.   Clancy and Franks, Jr., 261.

4.   Ibid., 252-3, 257.

5.   Ibid., 255, 257; The XVIII Airborne Corps had an additional command post called the Assault Command Post, which was a small cell of 75 staff officers commanded by a brigadier general, which was designed to be an early arriving control headquarters. See Toomey, 48-9. This concept would be universalized in 2004.

6.   Ibid., 255-6; Stephen Bourque, *Jayhawk: The VII Corps in the Persian Gulf War* (Washington, DC: Department of the Army, 2002), 97, 177.

7.   Clancy and Franks, 260, 290-2.

8.   Bourque, 213-4.; Clancy and Franks, 298.

9.   Bourque, 214; Clancy and Franks, 298.

10.   Ibid.

11.   Ibid., 176, 214.

12.   Author's interview with MAJ (ret) Kendall Gott, Assistant Regimental S2, 2d ACR, 1991, 30 November 2004.

13.   G2, VII Corps, US Army, 1991, 16-7, 73, 79, 91, 94-5; Toomey, 184, 302. Most of these Iraqi infantry divisions were down to about a third of their full strength.

14.   John J. McGrath, "Iraqi Army Order of Battle." Unpublished Manuscript prepared as a fact sheet for the US Army Center of Military History, Washington, DC, 2001,updated 2003.

15.   G2, VII Corps, US Army, 1991, 16, 21-3, 98; McGrath "Iraqi Army Order of Battle."

16.   Clancy and Franks, 280, 285. 297.

17.   Ibid., 277.

18.   Ibid., 287.

19.   Ibid., 285, 293, 298-9; Bourque, 225-7,229.

20.   Clancy and Franks, 288.

21.   Ibid., 285-6, 298; G2, VII Corps, US Army, 1991, 95-6.

22.   Clancy and Franks, 289-92.

23.   G2, VII Corps, US Army, 1991, 98-9, 101-2; Bourque 229-30, Clancy and Franks 294.

24.   G2, VII Corps, US Army, 1991, 102, 106-7, 113, 116, 127; Clancy and Franks, 304-5, 319.

25.   G2, VII Corps, US Army, 1991, 103, 105-6, 109, 117; Clancy, 299, 306.

26.   Clancy and Franks, 300, 318, 334-5; G2, VII Corps, US Army, 1991, 115-6.

27.   Clancy and Franks, 298, 300-1., 304, 306, 309-13, 330. A written copy of the fragmentary order implementing FRAGPLAN 7 did not reach most units until very early in the morning of 26 February.

28.   G2, VII Corps, US Army, 1991, 112-3; Clancy and Franks, 309-11, 331-2, 335-7.

29.   Clancy, 309; G2, VII Corps, US Army, 1991, 117, 119-21.

30.   G2, VII Corps, US Army, 1991,128-30, 133.

31.   Ibid., 132-3.

32.   Ibid., 134-6, 139.

33.   Ibid., 139-40.

34.   Clancy and Franks, 301, 313.

35.   Ibid., 313, 320.

36.   Ibid., 302, 307.

37.   Ibid., 294, 315, 321, 329-30.

38.   Ibid., 324-5; Tom Clancy, *Armored Cav: A Guided Tour of an Armored Cavalry Regiment* (New York: Berkley Books, 1994), 175.

39.   Clancy and Franks, 322-3, 338-340, 344-7.

40.   COL (ret) Gregory Fontenot, LTC E.J. Degan and LTC David Tohn. *On Point: The US Army in Operation Iraqi Freedom* (Fort Leavenworth, KS: US Army Combat Studies Institute Press, 2004), 147.

41.   Fontenot, 162; John Diamond and Dave Moniz, "Iraqi Colonel's Capture Sped Up taking of City," *USA TODAY*, 9 April 2003; David Zucchino, *Thunder Run: The Armored Strike to Capture Baghdad* (New York: Atlantic Monthly Press, 2004), 34-5.

42.   Fontenot, 42, 391, 396-7.

43.   Ibid., 393: Zucchino, 67; Lieutenant General William Wallace. Videotape of briefing to and inter•view by Staff Ride Team, US Army Combat Studies Institute, April 14, 2005. (Hereafter Wallace, April 14, 2005)

44.   Fontenot, 394.

45.   Wallace, Apr 14 2005; Morley, 2; Fontenot, 395. The V Corps MAIN CP did not deploy into Iraq until the conclusion of the campaign. The corps TAC CP moved forward to the vicinity of RAMS at the

beginning of the operational pause. During the pause/sandstorm, Wallace remained with the TAC CP. Upon renewal of mobile operations, he stayed with the ACP again for the remainder of the campaign. The ACP moved to the Baghdad airport on 9/10 April 2003 and was soon joined there by the TAC CP.

46.   Wallace, April 14, 2005.

47.   Ibid.

48.   Morley, 2; 3d Infantry Division (Mechanized), *Operation Iraqi Freedom After Action Report*, Final Draft, dated 12 May 2003 (hereafter 3d ID AAR), 17-3, 26-3; Fontenot, 394.

49.   Fontenot, 395.

50.   3d ID AAR, 1-5, 1-6.

51.   A good depiction of these graphic control measures can be found in Fontenot, 542-3.

52.   Fontenot, 14. The changes to the non-digital divisions was called Limited Conversion Division (LCD).

53.   Ibid., 58-9, 62.

54.   Ibid., 60-2, 394.

55.   Ibid., 417; 3d ID AAR, 8-4.

56.   Fontenot, 60, 63.

57.   Ibid., 62, 395; 3d ID AAR, 8-2.

58.   Fontenot, 395.

59.   Ibid., 417.

60.   Ibid., 62, 395.

61.   Wallace, April 14, 2005.

62.   Lieutenant Colonel Edward J Erickson, and Major General Raymond T. Odierno. "The Battle of Taji and Battle Command on the Move." *Military Review* July-August 2003, 4.

63.   Ibid.

64.   Ibid., 4-5.

65.   Ibid., 7-8.

66.   Fontenot, 417.

67.   Ibid., 418.

68.   Ibid., 220.

BATTLE COMMAND IN THE AGE OF THE MODULAR ARMY

"Today's operations require Army forces to respond rapidly with forces that move quickly and commence operations immediately upon arrival in distant theaters of operations."
—Army Comprehensive Guide to Modularity, 2004.[1]

As the US Army reorganizes in the early twenty-first century, battle command on the move is reflected in both emerging technology and organization, and in the lessons of recent operations.

Lessons From Iraq

While very effective in the Baghdad and subsequent campaigns, the technology and organization of battle command on the move in Iraq was fragmented and not standardized. The systems used needed both improvements and tweaks, and a much greater proliferation. Lack of proliferation showed the weaknesses of communications systems dependent on essentially immobile MSE (mobile subscriber equipment) networks. Additionally, while ABCS (Army Battle Command System) was on paper a standardized system, in actuality its fielding was hit or miss and some of its components were completely different.[2] Only Blue Force Tracker (BFT) worked well on the move as most of the rest of the systems required MSE.[3]

BFT was the success story of the Baghdad campaign. BFT enabled commanders at higher levels to have an unprecedented understanding of the location and activities of their units. Additionally, the satellite e-mail feature allowed a 'back-door' long range communications capability for battalion and company-sized maneuver units operating beyond the ranges of their organic FM radios and MSE networks. BFT proved to be the only true system capable of operating on the move. The ad hoc fielding of BFT meant that at lower levels, only certain vehicles had the system and combat support and combat service support (CSS) units often did not have it at all. This uneven level of fielding, while not impacting greatly on operations in 2003, could—if not corrected—have an impact on the sustainment and support of mobile operations. Moreover, CSS unit convoys with better situational awareness would be less likely to fall into ambushes along unsecured routes, and would be better able to extract themselves as the chain of command would be instantly aware of their situation.

One inherent weakness of BFT in Iraq in 2003 was an inability to tie into enemy situation updates at a level comparable to the friendly situation updates. Separate modules of the ABCS provided intelligence data and these, at certain echelons, often depended on immobile communications means like MSE.

The ABCS package also requires a better tie into joint operating forces, particularly the Marines and the supporting fixed wing aviation elements. While US Army fire support (field artillery, mortars, air defense) and combat aviation was tied into the network digitally, US Air Force close air support required a separate system, both for planning and execution. In addition, for US forces operating with friendly foreign armed services, a tie-in to the digital

225

packages used by those forces or a method of giving such forces US comparable-capability, even if on a temporary basis, may be required to facilitate battle command across such com- bined elements.

The 3d Infantry Division (Mechanized) estimated that over 90 percent of divisional com- mand and control took place on the move using broadband TACSAT radios, BFT, and the digital fire support system (AFATDS). To do this, commanders in Iraq often used Bradley fighting vehicles with reconfigured communications packages as command vehicles or recon- figured helicopters. The M4 C2V, deployed as a command post vehicle, while having many advanced technological features, was unable to operate on the move, as many of the long-range voice and data systems of the ABCS required a stationary set-up to operate effectively. The M4 could only fully operate after a short halt of 30 minutes and often had durability problems during the fast paced campaign.[4]

Both the 3d and 4th Infantry Divisions (Mechanized) also strove to streamline their head- quarters at all levels, making them smaller, more mobile, survivable, and functional on the move. In the case of both divisions, the commanders were frequently up front with small headquarters elements (assault command post) while the divisional command posts lagged behind. TACSATs enabled both to command units operating over extended frontages or in two or three different remote places at the same time.[5]

In late 2003, the US Army implemented a study of command and control in the Baghdad campaign. This committee, headed by a lieutenant general, incorporated many of the lessons into an already ongoing project designed to transform the Army into a force more appropri- ate for the post-Cold War era. This project ultimately became known as the Modular Army, a plan aimed at a decade-long reorganization of the Army into a flexible, responsive force. Incorporating, as part of its command and control structure, the best available digital and communications technology into units organized to provide the best technique to command and control combat operations using this technology.[6]

Modularity

By 2004, the US Army was in the midst of transforming into a new brigade-based structure called modularity. The crux of the concept was the creation of modular brigade-sized units, which, capitalizing on digital technology, would have greater firepower through greater com- mand and control of their assets. The units would be modular in the way that all units of the same general type would be organized in a similar fixed organizational structure, so that they could fit under any controlling headquarters requiring a unit of that type, and be replaced by a similar unit.[7] A parallel initiative would create a unit manning system based on stabilizing the tours of soldiers assigned to specific brigade combat teams (BCTs) for the projected 36 month operational cycle of the unit.[8]

Organizationally the modular concept included the repackaging of higher-level Army head- quarters units into two configurations, UE_y and UE_x. Unit of Employment Y (UEy) would be the theater/operational headquarters, equivalent of higher commands such as armies, component commands, theater commands and in some cases corps operating in a joint environment. UE_x would be a primary tactical headquarters generally equivalent to the division echelon of command, but sometimes equivalent to the corps. UE_x and UE_y headquarters would be tailored and augment for the specific theater or operation. The basic maneuver unit in this reconfiguration would be the BCT, organized as a stand-alone combined arms organization consisting of several maneuver battalions and all the primary support assets they would need contained in one organization.[9]

The creation of standardized brigade-sized units and higher-level headquarters units provides the first battle command organization reflecting actual practice in the history of the US Army. At the UE_y (theater command) level, by organization the command would contain four command and control organizations. The Mobile Command Group (MCG) would contain command and control helicopters for use by the UE_y commander. The Operational Command Post (OCP) provides a forward control command post roughly equivalent to the former tactical command post. The Early Entrance Command Post (EECP) is the part of the OCP that would deploy first to a theater by aircraft under a deputy commanding general, to run the early part of a theater operation. In addition to these command posts, there will also be a Main Command Post, which would normally operate from a fixed location, either home station or a secure base forward in the theater area.[10]

The UE_x headquarters, usually a divisional command, will be organized around four command post elements illustrated in Figure 54. The UE_x commander will center his activities on

UNIT OF EMPLOYMENT X (UE_x) MODULAR HEADQUARTERS

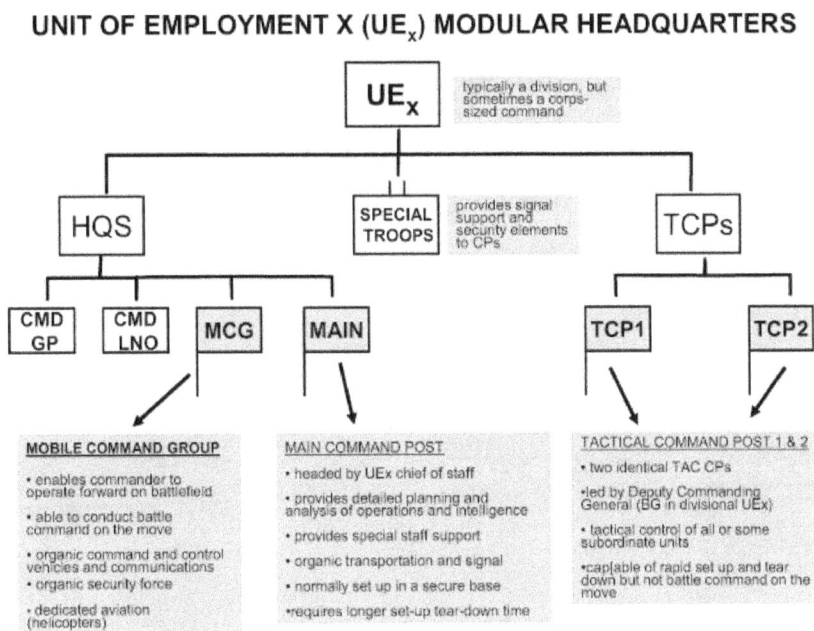

Figure 54. Unit of Employment X (UE_x) Modular Headquarters.

the Mobile Command Group (MCG). With its own aircraft and specially designed command vehicles, this will be the only UE_x command element capable of true battle command on the move. This allows the commander, accompanied only by two or three key staff officers, the ability to move about the battlefield and between subordinate units, exerting his personal influence and obtaining personal situational observation.[11]

In addition to the MCG, the new UE_x organization will also include two identical tactical command posts (TAC1 and TAC2), each headed by a deputy commanding general. These TAC CPs are designed to be rapidly set up and torn down, though they must be static to optimize their command and control capabilities. Flexibility is added with the dual capabil•ity. One can always be operational while the other is moving or they could each have specific roles in an operation.[12]

The UE_x will also contain a Main Command Post (MAIN). The MAIN, headed by the UE_x chief of staff, would contain the bulk of the UE_x staff, and provide detailed planning and analysis of operations, intelligence, and special staff support. It would normally be set up in a secure base and have its own transportation and signal support. The MAIN, by its nature, would require longer set-up and tear-down time than the other UE_x CPs.[13]

Unlike the mission-tailored organization of UE_y and UE_x headquarters, the new modular maneuver brigade combat team is a fixed organization coming in three basic variations, heavy (armored/ mechanized infantry), medium (equipped with Stryker wheeled armored fighting vehicles) and light (infantry). The basic organization of the heavy BCT is illustrated in Figure 55. The BCT includes two maneuver combat battalions; each with two companies

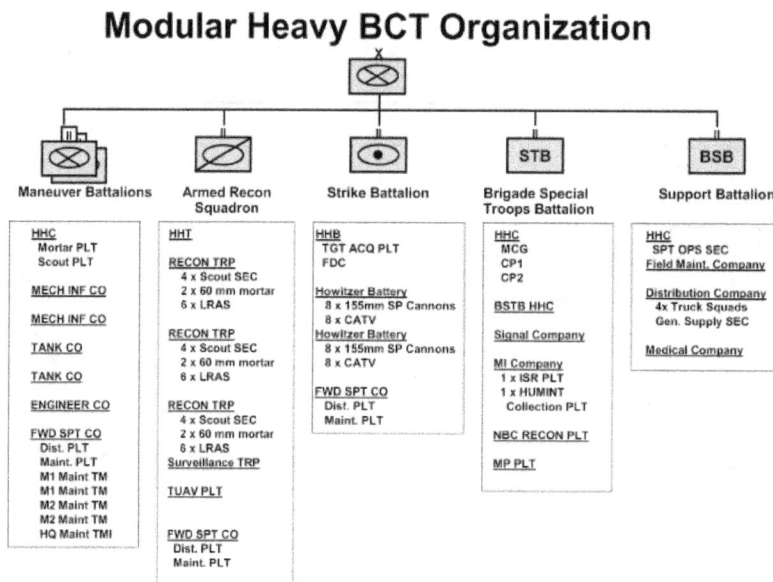

Figure 55. Modular BCT Organization.

228

of mechanized infantry, two companies of tanks, a cavalry reconnaissance squadron, a field artillery "strike" battalion, and a support battalion. The new organization consolidates most of the smaller units formerly reporting directly to the brigade headquarters into a special troops battalion. Included in this battalion are the elements of battle command for the brigade, including the brigade staff, supporting elements from the brigade headquarters company (HHC), and signal support troops. In the brigade, HHC are the components that make up the command posts of the BCT.

A key component of the modular design of the new BCTs is that its headquarters and subor‑ dinate battalions are designed similarly to allow mission versatility. Administrative support, and command and control functions are organized in the same way in all types of BCTs, and in the subordinate battalions. This allows 'plug and play' reorganization, as well as command and control at all levels, and between combat, combat support, and combat service support elements.[14]

As with the UEx, the BCT would also be organized with functional command posts and a mobile command group (MCG). The MCG, equipped with a battle command on the move capability, would allow the brigade commander to operate forward on the battlefield and be at critical places at critical times, without losing control over the rest of the brigade. Two func‑ tional command posts, CP1 and CP2, are also part of the modular BCT design. CP1 fulfills the role of the former tactical command post. It is small, mobile, and primarily responsible for controlling the current battle. It can function as the sole brigade CP for limited periods of time when CP2 is moving. The modular BCT now has a newly authorized deputy commander who

MODULAR BRIGADE HEADQUARTERS

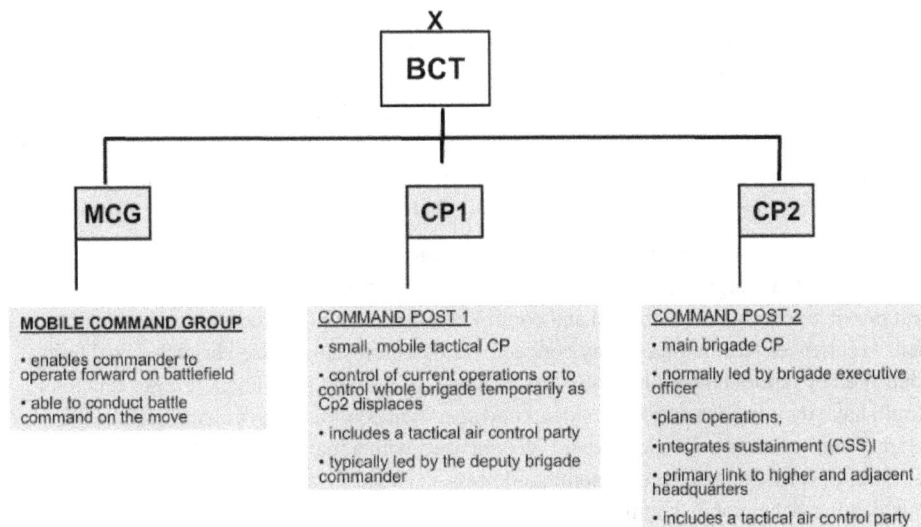

MOBILE COMMAND GROUP

• enables commander to operate forward on battlefield

• able to conduct battle command on the move

COMMAND POST 1

• small, mobile tactical CP

• control of current operations or to control whole brigade temporarily as Cp2 displaces

• includes a tactical air control party

• typically led by the deputy brigade commander

COMMAND POST 2

• main brigade CP

• normally led by brigade executive officer

•plans operations,

•integrates sustainment (CSS)l

• primary link to higher and adjacent headquarters

• includes a tactical air control party

Figure 56. Modular BCT Headquarters.

would normally run CP1. CP2 is the brigade's main CP. The BCT's de facto chief of staff, the executive officer, normally runs CP2. This CP plans future operations and integrates combat service support activities into current operations. Both CPs include an Air Force tactical air control party to assist in providing close air support.[15]

To support the new modular concept, improved command and control equipment technology is envisioned for future development. But as the modular Army is organized in the present, the reorganized force will be issued a digital package to every BCT, with Blue Force Tracker down to company-level and improved internal and external long range communications centered on an upgraded version of the ABCS (Army Battle Command System) digital package. MCGs will be given a battle command on the move capability by placing the ABCS package, along with long-range communication devices, into selected vehicles and aircraft for the use of commanders at BCT and above levels.[16]

The modular reorganization of the US Army in the early twenty-first century indicates a philosophy that smaller units—if placed under better command and control—can provide greater flexibility, firepower and versatility than prior organizations with older information systems. Characteristics of the new organization—higher leader-to-led ratios, greater use of more experienced staffs, and enhanced information systems—are expected to allow BCT commanders and their staffs to employ their units better than their counterparts in the past.[17]

Summary

Many battle command on the move lessons came out of the Baghdad campaign and follow-on operations. The issue of digital communications packages was not standardized and not available across the board. Blue Force Tracker proved to be the only digital system capable of operating effectively on the move. The digital packages also were weak on providing information about the enemy situation, and tying in with friendly joint and allied forces. The 3d Infantry Division performed most of its battle command functions while on the move, using not only BFT, but also tactical satellite telephones and the digitalized fire support system. The preferred command vehicle was a modified Bradley fighting vehicle. Most commanders operated with a streamlined command post—the assault command post—up forward, while other command posts lagged behind in traffic jams or other delays.

In response to these lessons and other considerations, the Army initiated the modular Army concept, a reorganization program established to provide, among other things, the best possible redesign of command and control structure using new technology and battlefield experience. The modular Army concept was based on standardized brigade-sized units controlled by tailored higher headquarters elements (UE$_x$ and UE$_y$). Each of these echelons would have their headquarters redesigned into specified command post elements. The UE$_x$, roughly equivalent to a division, would be organized with a main command post headed by the chief of staff, and two tactical command posts, each led by a deputy commander. A new organization—the mobile command post—would provide a small element, including a battle command on the move capability, to support the commander up forward. The modular BCTs would be similarly organized with two command posts; one being the main element, and the second one being the smaller, mobile tactical element. As with the UE$_x$, the BCT will have a small mobile command group element giving the commander battle command on the move capability. The battle command on the move capability at both UE$_x$ and BCT levels is based on the fielding of the ABCS digital package and long range communication devices into selected vehicles and helicopters. Digital packages as a whole will be fielded as quickly as possible to where they are most needed.

Notes

1.   Task Force Modularity, US Army Training and Doctrine Command, *Army Comprehensive Guide to Modularity, Version 1.0* (Fort Monroe, VA: US Army Training and Doctrine Command, 8 October 2004)(hereafter *Guide to Modularity*), 1-1.

2.   Fontenot, 394.

3.   3d ID ARR, 26-2.

4.   Ibid., 26-3.

5.   Ibid., 26-1, 26-3; Erickson and Odierno, 4-5.

6.   *Guide to Modularity*, 1-6, 7-2.

7.   For a more detailed discussion of this organizational shift, see John McGrath, *The Brigade: A History* (Fort Leavenworth: CSI Press, 2004), 131-138.

8.   "Worth Fighting For," PowerPoint presentation given to all Army personnel as part of a briefing on the *Army Campaign Plan* in April 2004.

9.   *Guide to Modularity*, viii, ix.

10.   Ibid., 4-4 to 4-6.

11.   Ibid., 5-8 to 5-9.

12.   Ibid., 5-9.

13.   Ibid., 5-9 to 5-10.

14.   Ibid., 8-3, 10-20.

15.   Ibid., 7-1 to 7-2.

16.   Ibid., 7-2, 10-1.

17.   Ibid., 10-4.

CONCLUSION

"In war we must be speedy."
—Silius Italicus[1]

Battle Command on the Move has always been a balancing act between the technology and technique. The technology available to the field commander to communicate with his subordinates has varied over time. Techniques of organization and command are designed to optimize the probability that the commander's intent would be followed—even in the absence of direct guidance. Due to a historic lack of adequate technology to communicate in real time with distant elements—a characteristic of mobile operations by their nature—successful battle command on the move has depended more on technique than technology.

Mobility required the effective use of organizational and command techniques to make up for the commander's lack of personal presence at certain times and places. In the era before electronic communications, organizational command technique in mobile operations had to depend on either the use of only one main force controlled directly by the commander, or the use of multiple forces. Experienced commanders would work under the general plan but once separated from direct communications with their superiors, would work under their own initiative.[2]

ASPECTS OF BATTLE COMMAND ON THE MOVE

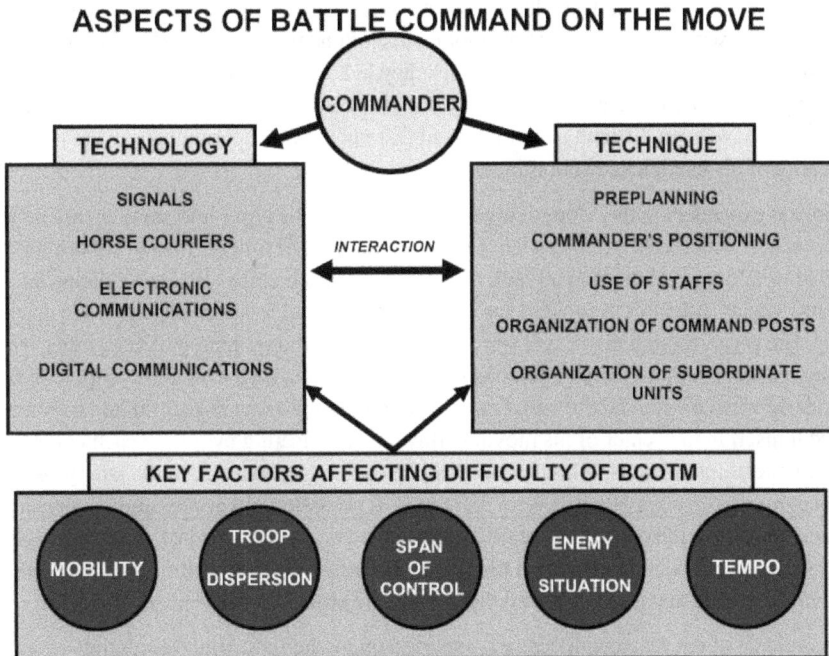

Figure 57. Aspects of Battle Command on the Move.

233

Up until the late nineteenth century available communications technology consisted of the commander personally commanding soldiers within the sound of his voice and vision, or using signal flags, smoke, or messengers mounted on horses. Commanders typically used horses themselves to move around the relatively short distances between their units. With this limitation on communications, commanders of mobile forces had to develop organizational techniques to maximize their ability to control their forces. The most crucial decision a commander had to make was his own location. This he usually keyed to where he expected the key action or series of events to take place.

After determining his own location, the next key decision for the commander was the organizing of his forces. Generally this meant the division of the force into more than one column or to keep it as a whole. In the case of several columns, the commander would lose direct and immediate control over any column he was not with. For this reason, Alexander the Great preferred to use a single column in his campaigns, except when geography restricted movements. If a commander divided his force, he had to depend on preplanning and the ability of subordinate commanders to understand his intentions when he was not there to tell them.

However, the effect of various columns in a mobile campaign converging from different or unexpected directions could be devastatingly decisive. This was the effect Mongol leader Genghis Khan desired, particularly when facing a numerically superior enemy. Genghis had a team of key subordinates and, after placing himself with what he considered the column with the most decisive role, he set his forces in motion while only effectively controlling the column he was with. The success of his mobile operations was directly related to the quality of his subordinate commanders and the troops they led. Additionally, Genghis' reliance on a purely light cavalry force gave him mobility not available to most of his adversaries. Such a force would have been difficult, if not impossible, to command operationally were it not for the quality of his handpicked subordinates.

Napoleon expanded on the Mongol model by organizing his army into smaller forces, army corps, each of which could fight by itself for a short period of time. A trusted subordinate, who had usually earned the special rank of marshal, led each corps. Typically, facing an unknown enemy situation, Napoleon spread his corps out in the initial phases of his maneuvering. The corps, though dispersed, were all within several days march of each other. The baffling maneuvers of the corps often had devastating effects on the enemies Napoleon faced, particularly when he massed the corps upon determining the exact enemy situation. Napoleon located himself in the center of his moving army, communicating by giving each corps commander general instructions to last for several days unless superseded. In the later years of the Napoleonic wars, groups of corps were organized as separate field armies and maneuvered in a manner similar to the corps in the earlier part of the era. Even in his last campaign, Waterloo, Napoleon almost outmaneuvered his British-Prussian adversaries through the speed of his advance, before key errors allowed the two enemy armies to combine against him.

In the middle of the nineteenth century—spurred on by the Industrial Revolution—electronic communications developed first with the telegraph, then with the telephone. While these inventions had a great effect on battle command in general, their effectiveness was most telling in static situations. Mobile operations were less able to effectively use these electronic communication means that were tethered to lines of wire. The 1876 campaign against the Sioux clearly shows the limitations that still existed. Several columns of US Army troops were near each other and near a large force of Indians. The Indians were able to attack one column then another, destroying a large part of the latter, without the other columns interfering.

In addition to communications technology, transportation technology, in the form of the railroad, also developed. Railroad management allowed armies to be moved rapidly from one theater to another, or one front to another behind the lines. This gave the defender a great strategic advantage that would become most apparent in the stalemated battles of World War I. Except for initial deployments or responding to enemy mobile attacks in friendly rear areas, railroads at this point had little impact on mobile operations.

In 1806 Napoleon had shattered the Prussian Army at Jena-Auerstädt and the following mobile pursuit. As a result, the Prussians developed the staff system, which became their general staff system. This system was an organizational technique that gave Prussian, and later German, units a professional staff capable of executing the operational intent of its commanders. With the development of industry later in the same century, the German general staff applied its collective brain to mobile operations and the use of railroads to deploy mass conscript armies to crucial points to fulfill the provisions of complicated war plans. In this age, most armies adopted staff systems of similar types. In the opening campaign in Western Europe in August 1914, the Germans used railroads to deploy their armies for their envisioned move to outflank the French forces' from the north through Belgium. The ensuing mobile operation saw the Germans march their infantry hard to get around the Franco-British left flank. After initial success, the speed and length of the advance hindered the German command system where eight individual armies all reported to a distant general headquarters. Depending on the shaky new technology of radio, German command and control broke down, allowing disjointed attacks and retreats to take place—collectively known as the First Battle of the Marne. Using railroads and taxicabs, the French rushed troops to cover Paris and counterattack. The French reinforcements alone were not enough to stop the German advance. But a combination of the uncertainty caused by the reinforcements and the breakdown of German command, resulted in a German retreat to thwart a threat that was perceived to be greater than it actually was.

Just as communications technology was starting to advance for the first time in history, the same industrial revolution that had developed the telegraph and telephone also developed improved weaponry such as the machine gun and heavy artillery capable of being fired indirectly. For centuries one of the best means of control available to commanders was the use of well-practiced drills at the tactical level. Soldiers were arrayed shoulder-to-shoulder and fire and movement commands were conveyed verbally, making a large body of soldiers relatively easy to control. But the lethality of the new weaponry made close order tactics suicidal. The infantry had to spread out and fight in small groups in order to survive and, ultimately, succeed on the offensive. But a dispersed force is much harder to control than a compact one. Originally adopted by the Germans in World War I, these dispersed 'infiltration tactics' were in use by all armies by World War II and were soon applied to armored forces as well as infantry.

The development of new technology in the form of the radio (greatly improved by the time of World War II) and the motor vehicle would make dispersion somewhat easier to control in mobile operations in World War II and after. But the 1944 Brittany campaign still shows the limitations of the radio as a means of communication. VIII Corps commander Troy Middleton, while himself remaining tethered to a telephone wire to his higher headquarters, practically lost control of his subordinate armored forces when they moved beyond effective radio range.

The radio did, however, make practical the massed use of armored vehicles. With a radio in every tank and supported by a combined arms team of infantry, artillery and supporting arms all also mounted in armored or motorized vehicles, true mobile operations came of age in World War II. The application of infiltration tactics to massed forces of armored vehicles controlled via radio communication resulted in the advent of modern armored warfare. Since World War II, armored warfare has developed progressively, although many features of the World War II era are still of use in the modern one.

Aside from the extensive use of the radio, mobile armored warfare also saw the development of standardized techniques and organizational structures which enhanced the ability to command and control fast moving operations. These included the streamlining of the combat orders process, the development of military symbology, the extensive use of maps and graphical overlays using the symbology and the issuing of fragmentary orders centered on map overlays and brief descriptions of the commander's intent for the operation.

The complications of modern warfare saw the increased swelling of staffs at all levels in order to manage information, intelligence, logistics, and operations. These staffs worked out of headquarters command posts. But to keep up with the pace of mobile operations, headquarters were echeloned with small command posts, focused solely on current combat operations, being pushed forward. Meanwhile the larger more traditional staff headquarters, with their village of tents and trucks, fell behind and was only functional once mobile operations ended and the situation became more static. In several recent American conflicts main, and even tactical command posts, remained static for the duration of entire mobile campaigns while the commander and several key assistants (usually the operations officer and fire support coordinator) moved forward either by a specially fitted command vehicle or helicopter, and ran mobile unit operations through this small command group.

The battlefield positioning of such World War II commanders as Guderian, Rommel, and Patton had presaged the development of such command groups. Their use allowed the commander to place himself on the battlefield where he could immediately affect and observe key operations. However, until the development of satellite communications, the general lack of reliable communications often left the forward commander out of touch with much of his unit. The tactical command post was originally developed to maximize command and control for commanders up front. But as even these headquarters could not sometimes keep up with the pace of operations, a smaller headquarters, the Jump TAC, later called the Assault Command Post, was developed. With the evolution of satellite communication digital packages since 1991, a commander can now be equipped with an assault command post, which could set up very quickly and have almost immediate reliable long-range communications capability. The commander himself, particularly in the 2003 Baghdad campaign and in projected organizational designs for the modular Army, is equipped with command vehicles and aircraft which can communicate over great distances while on the move. Army digital packages can give the commander in his specialized vehicle immediate situational awareness of his entire command while he is moving with the command in a rapid advance or placing himself with a key subordinate unit. Technology has now allowed the commander to be at one particular place without losing effective control over the rest of his command, or effectively delegating it to a more junior staff officer.

Commanders at all levels since the development of portable radios, have long suffered command and control problems centered around radio reliability and range. Technology-wise, longer-range radios were too large or consumed too much power to be practical at lower levels. At higher levels, such radios made the headquarters owning them less mobile to effectively use them to control rapidly moving operations. Commanders had to devise techniques to overcome the limitations of communications technology. Some, like Patton, established units of couriers. Most commanders, particularly at higher levels, developed a routine of issuing advance guidance for specified time periods (24 or 48 hours) and then visiting the key subordinate units during the day to get a clear feel of the situation before issuing new guidance in the evening for the next time interval. The development of digital packages, using satellite technology, particularly the backdoor long range communications e-mail feature of Blue Force Tracker, have given units down to company level the ability to communicate far beyond the typical range of the units' organic FM radios.

In addition to mobile armored operations, the development of the helicopter has resulted in a special type of mobile operation built around that aircraft—the airmobile (or air assault) operation. In several key operations in Vietnam, and in the 1991 Gulf War, division-sized airmobile operations were conducted over great distances, adding a third dimension to the concept of battle command on the move. Aside from providing a means of transportation for maneuver combat troops and immediate fire support for them in the form of the attack helicopter, the helicopter also supplied an ideal command and control platform. It allows commanders at all levels to see their forces at a glance, even when widely dispersed, and communicate with them or move between them relatively quickly. Examples in this work of the use of the helicopter as a means of mobile battle command can be found in 1968's Operation PEGASUS, and in Lieutenant General Frederick Franks' use of the helicopter to command the VII Corps in Operation DESERT STORM in 1991.

While the interplay between technology and technique is the essence of successful battle command on the move, there are several key factors that can increase or decrease the effectiveness of this interplay. The mobility of the force the commander is leading directly affects his ability to control the force. A marching infantry army, even if it is all in motion, will move slower than a force entirely of horsemen or armored vehicles. A mixed force where one part is more mobile than another creates particular difficulties for the operational commander. In France 1940, higher-level German commanders wanted to slow up the armored advance because the infantry divisions to the rear were falling behind. Fortunately for the Germans the tempo of the operation made this point moot very quickly. But in western Russia in 1941 it became a critical problem.[3]

Tempo is related to mobility. How fast an operation unfolds is not just related to the mobility of the commander's force. It is also related to the enemy's mobility, the geography of the area of operations, and the goal of the operation. In DESERT STORM in 1991, US and coalition forces had the goal of destroying the offensive capabilities of the Iraqi army while ejecting that army from Kuwait. The operational tempo increased when it became apparent the Iraqis were trying to withdraw from Kuwait and escape the trap. The faster the tempo, the more difficult it is to exercise battle command on the move.

Span of control is another key factor. The number of subordinate units the commander was able to control was originally based on how far his voice could carry orders or he could see. Beyond a certain level, said to be seven by some scientists, human perception is unable to control the complication of too many subordinates, particularly in high tempo military operations.[4] A high span of control would force the engorgement of staffs, thereby slowing the tempo of mobile operations accordingly. Therefore, despite the revolution in long-range digital communication and situational awareness, the US Army has chosen in its modular Army reconfiguration to decrease the span of control in maneuver brigade units, while at the same time simplifying the span by adopting the formerly temporary structuring of combined arms forces at the brigade and battalion levels.

The enemy situation affects the difficulty of executing battle command on the move. An enemy army defending from static positions, for example, will be a lot easier to control the fight against than another force fighting a mobile battle itself. An enemy using nonlinear tactics increases the complexity of a mobile operation by extending the depth of the battlefield into the rear areas of the force.

Troop dispersion has already been mentioned. The more dispersed geographically, the more difficult it is to control a force. But in modern warfare, relative dispersion is often the key to success. Enhanced digital communications will improve the ability to command dispersed forces, although geography and time will still hinder the commander's ability to see his subordinates' situation for himself.

In mobile operations there is no substitute for the personal presence of the commander at the critical time and place, either to reiterate his intent to tired troops, or to change that intent after discovering a shift in battlefield conditions. Human misinterpretation or misunderstanding of information is common enough in everyday life but can be accelerated when one or both communicators are involved in the high stress of mobile combat operations. At Petersburg neither Grant nor Meade were on the battlefield at the key time to impress a sense of urgency on tired troops and commanders, an urgency that probably would have pushed the Confederate defenders out of that key city. In the 1973 Battle of El Firdan, Israeli division commander Adan knew some of the orders from his superior did not make sense from the situation as he saw it, but he presumed he knew less about the overall situation than his superior, Gonen, did. Gonen, however, was receiving reports from the field but did not have a good situational awareness. Were he to have gone to the front he could have seen the situation as his commanders saw it, and not given orders that resulted in the immediate destruction of a large part of Adan's division.

By the same token, a commander needs to command his whole force and not get self-involved with only the portion of it with which he is positioned. In the past this has been a juggling act that most commanders resolved by conducting regular visits to the command post or forward positions of all their units, while placing themselves where they could support subordinates executing key portions of operations.

While large staffs allow for the processing of mountains of information, the size of the command post staff itself, particularly in mobile operations, negates the advantages of obtaining the information. The digital revolution may allow the processing of information and administrative minutia from secure bases or semi-permanent field locations, leaving much smaller headquarters to concentrate on combat, combat support, and logistics operations. These smaller command posts could be designed to simply provide the information the commander needs immediately to command and control current operations. Such lithe CPs would be able to keep up with the operation, thus maintaining their utility better than similar command posts in previous campaigns. Proposed modular Army concepts provide for just such smaller command posts with enhanced communications techniques.

Historically, effective battle command on the move has been based on the successful interaction between the available communications technology and techniques developed both to overcome the limitations of the technology and to enhance the ability of the commander to control his forces. Modern digital technology gives commanders the capability to remain continuously in communication with all parts of their force. Even with complete communications, however, commanders still must decide from where they can best exercise this capability. This decision should be based on the commander's belief in what, where, or who it is best for him to see face-to-face. While in the past commanders had to trade off between being able to communicate and being able to see things for themselves, the ability to continuously communicate with distant portions of one's command and staff, even while moving between key subordinates or critical points, is the future of battle command on the move—made possible by technological and organizational developments of the present.

Notes

1. Heinl, 305.

2. Van Creveld contends that armies rarely operated except as one entity in what he calls the "Stone Age of Command." See Van Creveld, *Command in War*, 25.

3. A good discussion of this may be found in Stolfi.

4. See George A. Miller, "The Magical Number Seven, Plus or Minus Two: Some Limits in Our Capacity for Processing Information," *Psychological Review* 63 (1956), 81-97.

APPENDIX A
SELECTED MOBILE OPERATIONS OF THE PAST

Selected Historical Campaigns	Technology	Technique	Key Factors 1. Mobility 2. Troop Dispersion 3. Span of Control 4. Enemy Situation 5. Tempo
Mongol Army Genghis Khan-Campaign against the Khwarizm Empire, 1220.	-Visual -Signals -Messengers on horseback	-Multiple columns -Well-trained subunits -Trusted sub-commanders -Prepared plan	1. Horseback 2. Troops dispersed into multiple columns 3. One subordinate; Genghis with most important column 4. Primarily static 5. Progressively faster as columns reached their objectives
French Army Napoleon-Ulm Campaign, 1805	-Visual -Signals -Couriers on horseback	-Long range plans -Trusted subordinates (marshals) -Multiple columns controlled by couriers/ messengers -Maintained control through organization (army corps system) and preplanned concentration of forces -Good staff work	1. Marching infantry 2. Up to 8 separate corps; 3. 1-8 subordinates; Napoleon with center column/ most important column 4. Primarily stationary enemy force 5. Fast marching infantry columns
French Army Napoleon-Jena Campaign, 1806	-Visual -Signals -Couriers on horseback	-Long range plans -Trusted subordinates (marshals) -Multiple columns controlled by couriers/ messengers -Good staff work	1. Marching infantry 2. Up to 8 separate corps; 3. 1-8 subordinates; Napoleon with left wing force at Jena; in pursuit with column headed to Berlin; lost control and knowledge of activities of forces not directly under his personal control, particularly at Jena 4. Hard marching retreating enemy columns 5. Pursuit tempo fast on both sides

Selected Historical Campaigns	Technology	Technique	Key Factors 1. Mobility 2. Troop Dispersion 3. Span of Control 4. Enemy Situation 5. Tempo
US Army Washington-Yorktown Maneuver, 1781	-Couriers on horseback -Ships	-Detailed planning -Trusted subordinates -Deception plan	1. Marching infantry/shipboard infantry 2. Force initially concentrated, then dispersed to march or board ships, then concentrated again 3. One subordinate;-Washington remained with the moving column, then controlled the concentrated force at Yorktown 4. Two static enemy forces 5. Relatively slow- marching infantry, but faster than enemy was able to respond
US Army Scott- Advance on Mexico City, 1847	-Visual -Signals -Couriers on horseback	-Well trained and led professional army -Emphasis on logistics -One primary column	1. Marching infantry 2. Troops concentrated in the mobile phase 3. 1 to 3 subordinates; one column with subordinate commanders 4. Large, poorly led force 5. Fast marches separated by a long pause
US Army Grant- Advance on Petersburg, 1864	-Telegraph -Messengers on horseback	-Multiple columns moving -Planning -Force organized into armies and corps -Rear command	1. Marching infantry 2. Force dispersed into 5 corps under two army commanders in mobile phase moving by boat, ferry and bridge. 3. Two (army commanders); Grant remained at City Point in rear with telegraph during key part of action 4. Small, well-led and trained enemy forces 5. Tempo started fast but fizzled out due to exhaustion and no overall battlefield commander at key times and places
US Army Grant-Appomattox Pursuit, 1865	-Telegraph -Messengers on horseback	-Multiple columns- one direct pursuit, one trying to outflank enemy, one covering pursuing force's flank -Separate commanders for each force -Forward command	1. Foot infantry supported by horse cavalry 2. Three columns 3. Three (army commanders usually in separate columns); with column on telegraph line 4. Well led smaller enemy force 5. Campaign of two fast marching infantry armies supported by cavalry, marching around the clock

242

Selected Historical Campaigns	Technology	Technique	Key Factors 1. Mobility 2. Troop Dispersion 3. Span of Control 4. Enemy Situation 5. Tempo
US Army Terry and Crook-Sioux Campaign, 1876	-Messengers on horseback -Riverboat	-Multiple columns -Large supply train -Small staff	1. Primarily horse cavalry supported by marching infantry 2. Dispersed into multiple columns hard to control; one column defeated in detail while other columns not in action 3. No overall commander; three converging columns (two under Terry, one under Crook) had to try to coordinate operations without being in contact with each other 4. Massed light cavalry and camp followers 5. Sluggish and slow as columns bogged down with logistics
German Army von Moltke-Advance into Belgium and France, 1914	-Radio -Telephone/telegraph -Messengers on horseback or with motor vehicles	-Extensive staff work and planning -Staffs and command posts at operational levels -Rear command	1. Marching infantry 2. Dispersed along long front with 7 armies in France and Belgium 3. Eight separate subordinate armies controlled from distant large headquarters 4. Infantry army with reinforcements moved by railroad and motor vehicles 5. High tempo on both sides as one army tried to outflank the other which was trying to prevent the maneuver
German Army Guderian-France, 1940	-Radio -Armored vehicles	-Extensive staff work and planning -Decentralized execution -Trusted subordinate commanders -Forward command	1. Armored forces supported by motorized forces and marching infantry 2. Armored forces initially massed in small area, disperse as part of advance deep into enemy rear areas 3. Guderian controlled between 2 to 4 units during the operation 4. Disorganized defenders, mostly trying to respond to German actions 5. Fast paced operation across France to the Channel
US Army Middleton- Brittany, 1944	-Radio -Wire -Armored vehicles -Trucks	-Rear command -Armored divisions organized into mission-oriented task forces -Infantry motorized with truck unit attachments	1. Armored forces supported by truck-mounted infantry forces 2. Force dispersed in three different directions as it advanced 3. Middleton controlled two armored divisions an armored task force and two infantry divisions 4. Weak enemy forces trying to concentrate into ports 5. Very fast for armored forces

Selected Historical Campaigns	Technology	Technique	Key Factors 1. Mobility 2. Troop Dispersion 3. Span of Control 4. Enemy Situation 5. Tempo
US Army/US Marines Khe Sanh 1968	-Helicopters -Radio	-Forward command -Specialized airmobile division organization	1. Infantry and artillery moved around battlefield by helicopter and supported by attack helicopters 2. Airmobile forces dispersed within supporting distance of each other 3. Tenacious defending infantry in covering terrain 4. Massed infantry with some armored forces 5. Fast during airmobile phase
Israeli Defense Force Gonen/Adan-El Firdan, 1973	-Radio -Armored vehicles	-Forward command at lower levels -Excellent subunits -Lack of combined arms units	1. Armored forces 2. Troops dispersed and sometimes out of contact with highers 3. 3-4 subordinates 4. Combination of static infantry and armored forces. 5. High tempo- too fast for commanders
Israeli Defense Force Bar Lev/Sharon-Chinese Farm, 1973	-Radio -Armored vehicles	-Forward command at lower levels -Excellent subunits	1. Armored forces 2. Troops dispersed on battlefield in various directions and concentrated to cross canal and clear route to canal 3. 3-4 subordinates; at one point one of Sharon's brigades controlled forces attacking or defending in three different directions simultaneously 4. Combination of static infantry and armored forces. 5. High tempo at points which was crucial to success of operation
US Army Franks-Gulf War VII Corps, 1991	-Radio -Armored vehicles -Satellite telephones	-Extensive planning -Excellent subunits and leaders	1. Armored force 2. Force dispersed in large sector 3. Five divisions and an armored cavalry regiment 4. Armored forces and static infantry with low morale and losses from air campaign 5. High speed tempo with operation starting early
US Army 3d Infantry Division (Mechanized) Baghdad Campaign, 2003	-Radio -Armored vehicles -Satellite telephones -Digital info systems	-One primary route of advance -Extensive planning -Excellent subunits and leaders	1. Armored force 2. Concentrated force punched through along single axis; had to disperse to cover bypassed places 3. Three brigades, aviation forces, artillery force, engineer forces, logistic forces 4. Weak large enemy regular and irregular forces 5. Two very fast phases with a short pause in between

APPENDIX B
THE DEVELOPMENT OF BATTLEFIELD COMMAND
AND CONTROL MEASURES, GRAPHICS AND SYMBOLOGY

A Short History of Military Symbols and Control Measures

Control measures and military map symbols did not really develop before World War I. Prior to then, when military operations were less complicated, with less staff work, and often poor maps without an easily used system of location coordinates, unit symbols were simple. For the maneuver combat arms of infantry and cavalry, the symbols represented how these units were deployed on the battlefield, both in size and deployment.[1] The US Army used blue (the traditional color of the Army's infantry) for friendly forces and red for enemy forces. Other nations used different colors, the British, for example, used red for friendlies (red was the traditional color of the British infantry) and blue for enemy forces. Infantry was represented as a colored rectangle, sized to the unit's size, with a long length for infantry in line (battle formation) and a long width for a unit in column formation (movement formation). Cavalry was represented similarly to infantry, but with the rectangle being bisected by a diagonal line with only the portion of the rectangle above the diagonal being filled in with shading. Artillery was represented as an overhead view of a wheeled cannon. This could represent a single gun or several batteries. Skirmishers, small groups of soldiers out in front of units were represented by a series of colored dots and fortifications were depicted as thick angled lines representing their exact shape on the ground. Figure 58 depicts these basic symbols.[2]

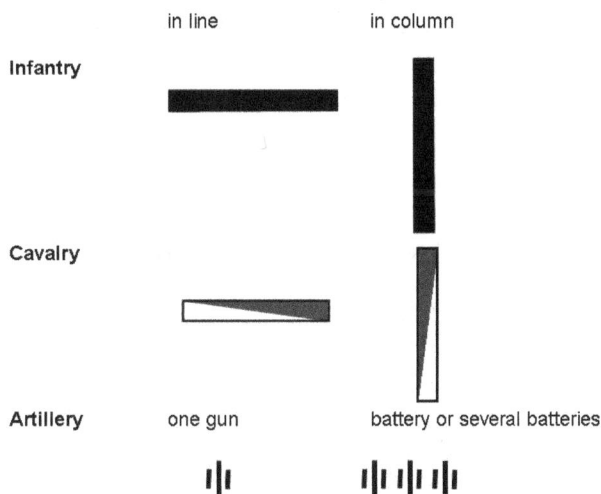

Figure 58. Nineteenth Century Military Symbology.

As modern war became more complicated in World War I, all the major combatants devised systems of military map symbols, or expanded previous limited systems to help graphically depict the different branches of the service, echelons of command, and their locations, bound‐aries between units, and various important weapons. Symbols remained non-standardized be‐tween the combined forces of different nations—even when allied together—as most armies retained uniquely national systems until the members of the North Atlantic Treaty Organiza‐tion (NATO) adopted a modified version of the relatively easy to use United States system in 1949. Each national system and the subsequent NATO system will be discussed separately below. Figure 59 contains a comparison between national systems.

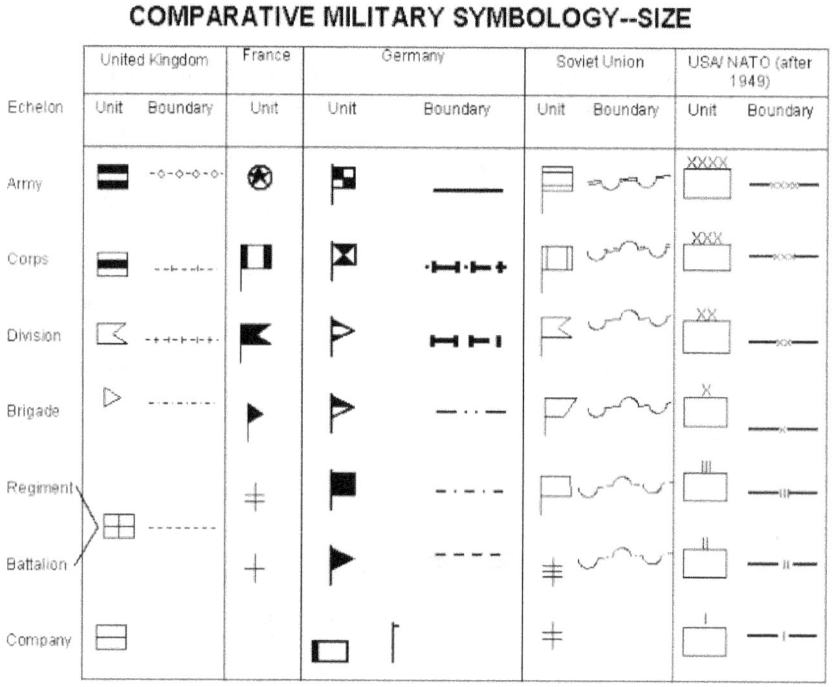

COMPARATIVE MILITARY SYMBOLOGY--SIZE

Figure 59. Comparative Military Symbology.

COMPARATIVE MILITARY SYMBOLOGY--TYPE

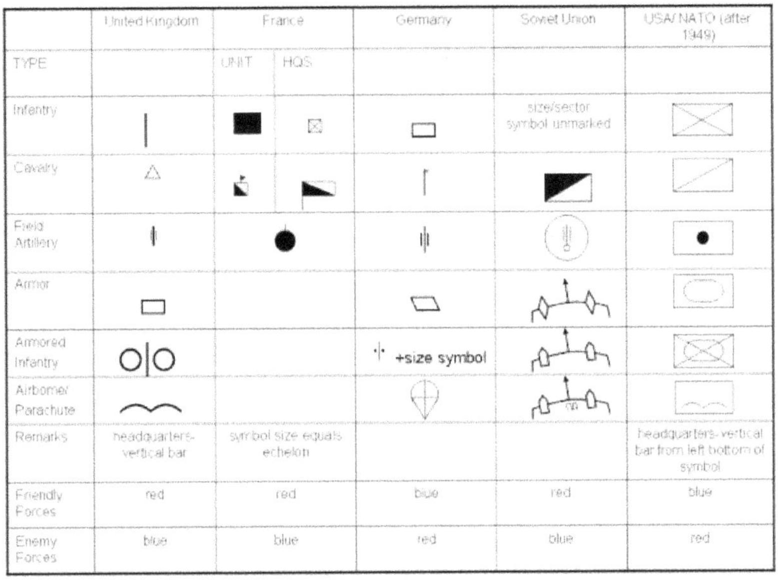

	United Kingdom	France		Germany	Soviet Union	USA/ NATO (after 1949)
TYPE		UNIT	HQS			
Infantry					size/sector symbol unmarked	
Cavalry						
Field Artillery						
Armor						
Armored Infantry	O|O			·|· +size symbol		
Airborne/ Parachute						
Remarks	headquarters-vertical bar	symbol size equals echelon				headquarters-vertical bar from left bottom of symbol
Friendly Forces	red	red		blue	red	blue
Enemy Forces	blue	blue		red	blue	red

COMPARATIVE MILITARY SYMBOLOGY-EXAMPLES

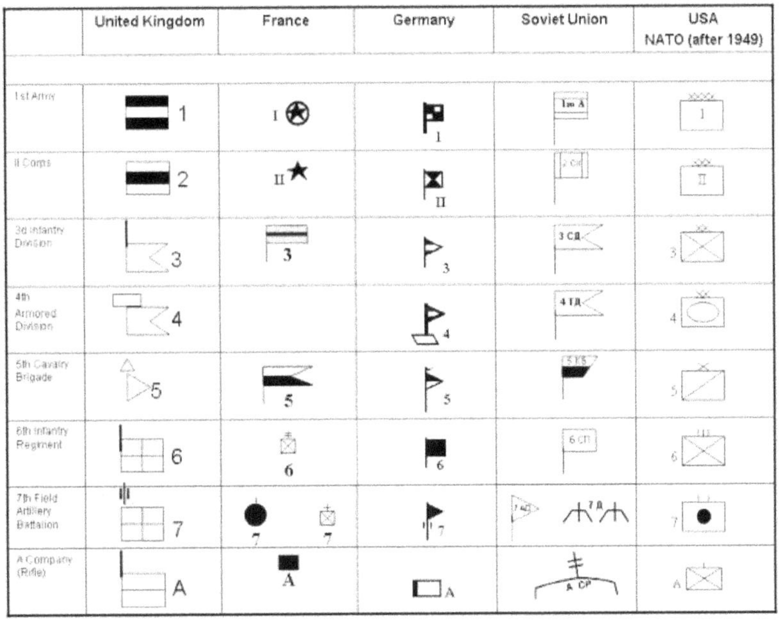

	United Kingdom	France	Germany	Soviet Union	USA NATO (after 1949)
1st Army	1	I	1	1m A	1
II Corps	2	II	II	2 CK	II
3d Infantry Division	3	3	3	3 CД	3
4th Armored Division	4		4	4 ТД	4
5th Cavalry Brigade	5	5	5	5 KБ	5
6th Infantry Regiment	6	6	6	6 сп	6
7th Field Artillery Battalion	7	7 7	7	7 ТД	7
A Company (Rifle)	A	A	A	A CP	A

Figure 59 (continued). Comparative Military Symbology.

247

British and French Military Symbols.[3]

As close World War I allies, the British and French adopted very similar systems of military symbology during that war, primarily by additions to the simplistic system in general use by most European-style armies in the previous century. Both nations used the color red for friendly forces and the color blue for enemy forces, with virtually the same symbols for the various branches, types, and sizes of units. A sampling of the French system in 1918 is found in Figure 60.

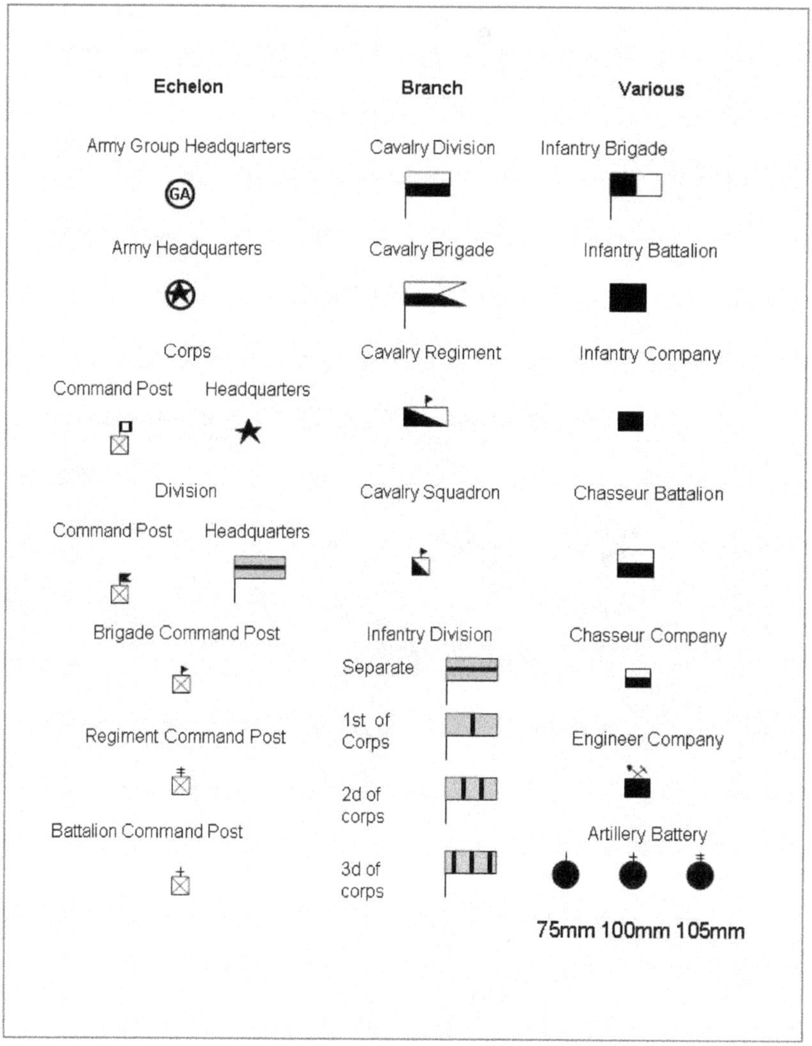

Figure 60. French Military Symbology, 1918.

The British retained the World War I system into the 1920s, and with additional revisions, as late as 1943. In 1943 they introduced a far more ambitious and complicated system than the previous one, which used many of the principles found in the American system (discussed below) but using, for the most part, completely different symbols, or arranging them differently. For example, while the US system used unit type or branch as the basic component, and applied different size symbols to the branch symbol, the British system used the size symbol as the basic symbol (with different symbols for each sized-unit), and added branch or type symbols to this. A sample of this later British system can be found in Figure 61. The British adopted the American system as part of the NATO alliance in 1949.

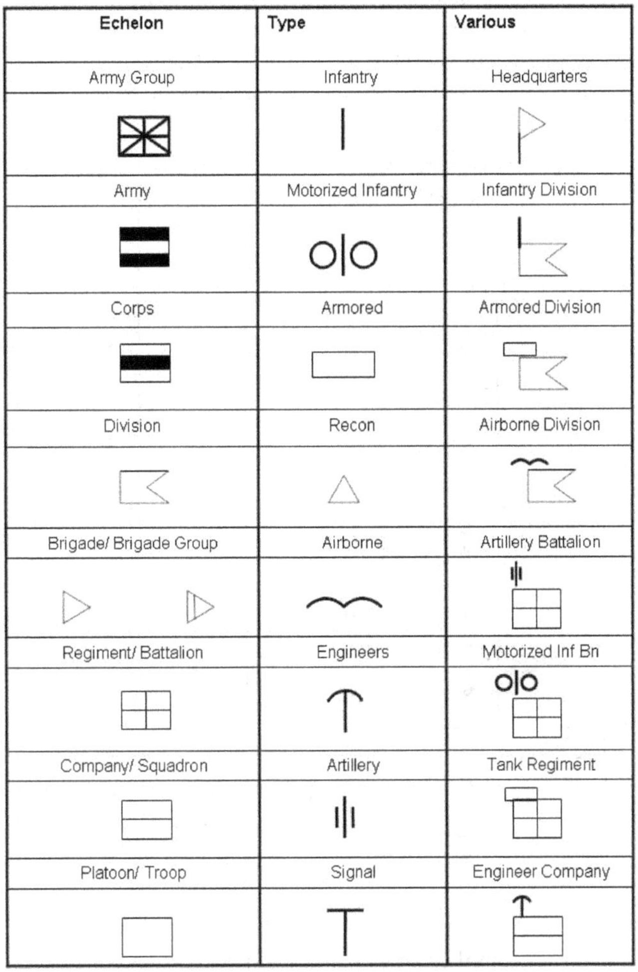

Echelon	Type	Various
Army Group	Infantry	Headquarters
Army	Motorized Infantry	Infantry Division
Corps	Armored	Armored Division
Division	Recon	Airborne Division
Brigade/ Brigade Group	Airborne	Artillery Battalion
Regiment/ Battalion	Engineers	Motorized Inf Bn
Company/ Squadron	Artillery	Tank Regiment
Platoon/ Troop	Signal	Engineer Company

Figure 61. British Military Symbology, 1945.

German Military Symbols.[4]

The German Imperial Army and its successors up to 1945 developed easily the most com•
plicated and comprehensive system of military symbology. The Germans used their symbol•
ogy not just on maps, but also on tactical signs, vehicles, command pennants on vehicles, and
on organizational charts and tables. The modern German Army, the *Bundeswehr*, now using
the American-based NATO system of symbols, has retained many of these additional uses.
By World War II, the German system was so complicated that it had to be simplified several
times, in November 1942, February 1944, and in 1945. The German system combined four
basic elements into a scheme of basic and supplemental symbols. The elements were unit
size, branch, major weapons system the unit was equipped with, and the mobility capabil•
ity of the unit (none, horse-drawn, half-track, truck, or fully tracked). Inherited from the era
when armies were primarily composed of foot soldiers, in German symbology, despite its
complications, a symbol unmarked for branch was considered to be infantry. A brief outline
of the former German symbology is found in Figure 62.

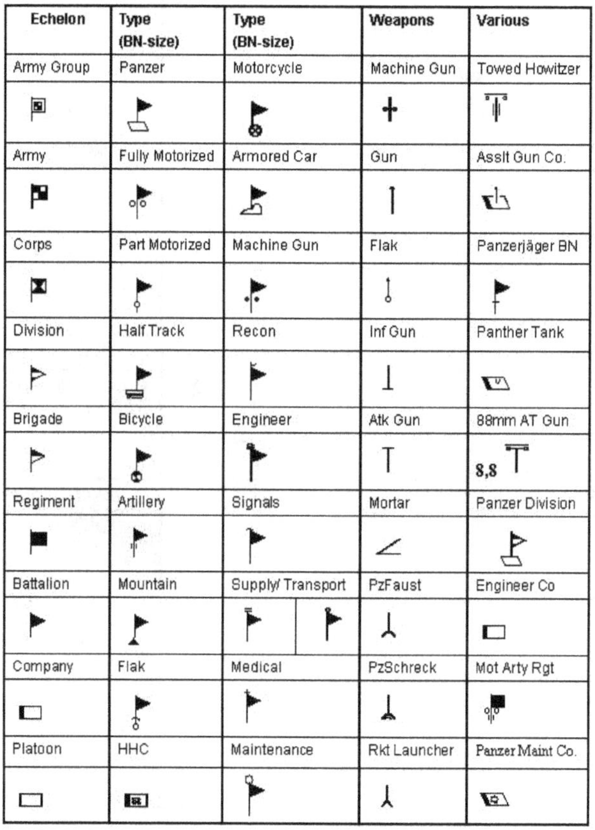

Echelon	Type (BN-size)	Type (BN-size)	Weapons	Various
Army Group	Panzer	Motorcycle	Machine Gun	Towed Howitzer
Army	Fully Motorized	Armored Car	Gun	Asslt Gun Co.
Corps	Part Motorized	Machine Gun	Flak	Panzerjäger BN
Division	Half Track	Recon	Inf Gun	Panther Tank
Brigade	Bicycle	Engineer	Atk Gun	88mm AT Gun
Regiment	Artillery	Signals	Mortar	Panzer Division
Battalion	Mountain	Supply/ Transport	PzFaust	Engineer Co
Company	Flak	Medical	PzSchreck	Mot Arty Rgt
Platoon	HHC	Maintenance	Rkt Launcher	Panzer Maint Co.

Figure 62. German Military Symbology, 1945.

250

Soviet Military Symbols.[5]

Developed parallel to the complicated system of symbols used by the Germans, the Soviet system of military and map symbols consisted of a number of basic and supplementary sym•bols used either alone or in combination with other symbols and alphanumeric abbreviations to indicate headquarters, units, weapons systems, equipment, and tactical control measures in a relatively complicated scheme. This system showed the Soviet emphasis on formations and centralized control. Instead of using abstract symbols to indicate a unit, except for headquar•ters locations, Soviet-style symbology stressed the deployment formation and frontages of units on both the attack and defense.

The Soviet system was also used by the Soviet allies in the Warsaw Pact and other nations allied with or associated with the Soviet bloc. Since the end of the Cold War, however, many of these nations have adopted the NATO symbology. A brief outline of Soviet symbology is found in Figure 63.

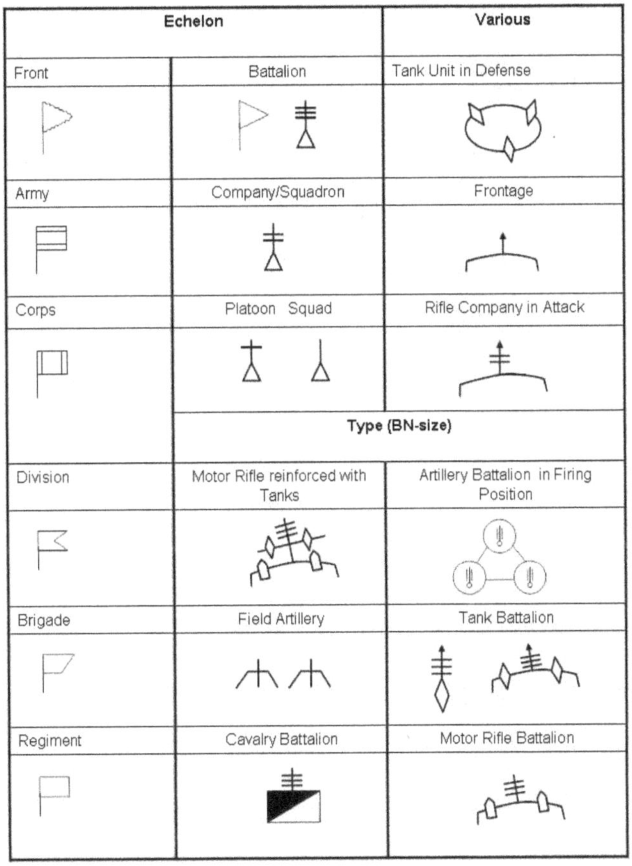

Figure 63. Soviet Military Symbology.

American Military Symbols.

The United States Army entered World War I as a member of the Franco-British dominated Allied coalition. While the US forces were equipped with French and British equipment and helmets, and adopted a version of the French staff system, the Army's Corps of Engineers—then responsible for military topography—developed a system of map symbols which were uniquely American, a system the US Army has used ever since, with continual modifications over the years. In 1949 this system was also adopted by the NATO alliance.

Sharing the same nineteenth century roots as the symbology of the European nations, the US Army developed a relatively straightforward system. The symbology was also initially based on representations of the basic branches it depicted, with the crossed bandolier straps of the infantry being adopted in the X pattern infantry symbol. The saber strap of the cavalry was used to represent the cavalry, a cannonball represented the artillery, and an extended cross represented medical units. Later a stylized tank tread was used to represent armored forces. While the symbols representing engineers and signal originally were simply the rectangular unit symbol with the first letter of the branch inside it; after World War II, a bridge and a zig-zagged line symbolic of a radio wave were adopted to universalize the symbols.

While originally codified in Corps of Engineer documents, the Army soon codified the system in *Field Manual 21-30*, which was has been periodically updated since before World War II up to 1970. When the 1970 manual was revised ten years later, it was renumbered as *Field Manual 101-5-1* as it was combined with a new dictionary of Army operational terms. The latest edition of *FM 101-5-1* was issued in 1997. A new version, renumbered in accordance with a revised Army numbering scheme for field manuals as *FM 1-02* was published in September 2004. Figure 64 depicts the US symbology as used in the volumes of the Army's official history of World War II.

Since 1949, US symbology, though unique in certain features, is also expected to comply with NATO standardization, as agreed to in a series of NATO standardization agreements (STANAGs), with Appendix 6, "Military Symbols for Land-Based Systems" (APP 6) of STANAG 2019 being the basic NATO reference document. As part of the Department of Defense since 1947, Army symbology is also expected to comply with those used by the other branches of the US armed forces, particularly in relation to joint operations with those forces. The basic reference document for the US joint aspects of symbology is DOD's *MIL-STD-2525B, Department of Defense Interface Standard: Common Warfighting Symbology*, published in 1996.

The only major development in US symbology since World War II has been the adoption of the diamond as the characteristic shape for enemy units. This change was first seen in the 1996 MIL-STD-2525B and the Army's subsequent 1997 edition of FM 101-5-1. While enemy forces had previously been depicted in red (with friendly forces in blue), the same symbol set had been used otherwise for units on both sides. When overlays and symbols were not used in color, enemy forces had been depicted with double-lines around their borders.

The 1996 MIL-STD-2525B and the latest version of NATO's APP 6 have obviously been drawn up with digital command and control systems, such as Blue Force Tracker in mind. In addition to unique shape-based symbology for enemy forces, a square shape and the color green was adopted to depict friendly forces and a unique circular four-sided symbol in yellow was adopted for forces whose hostile status was unknown.

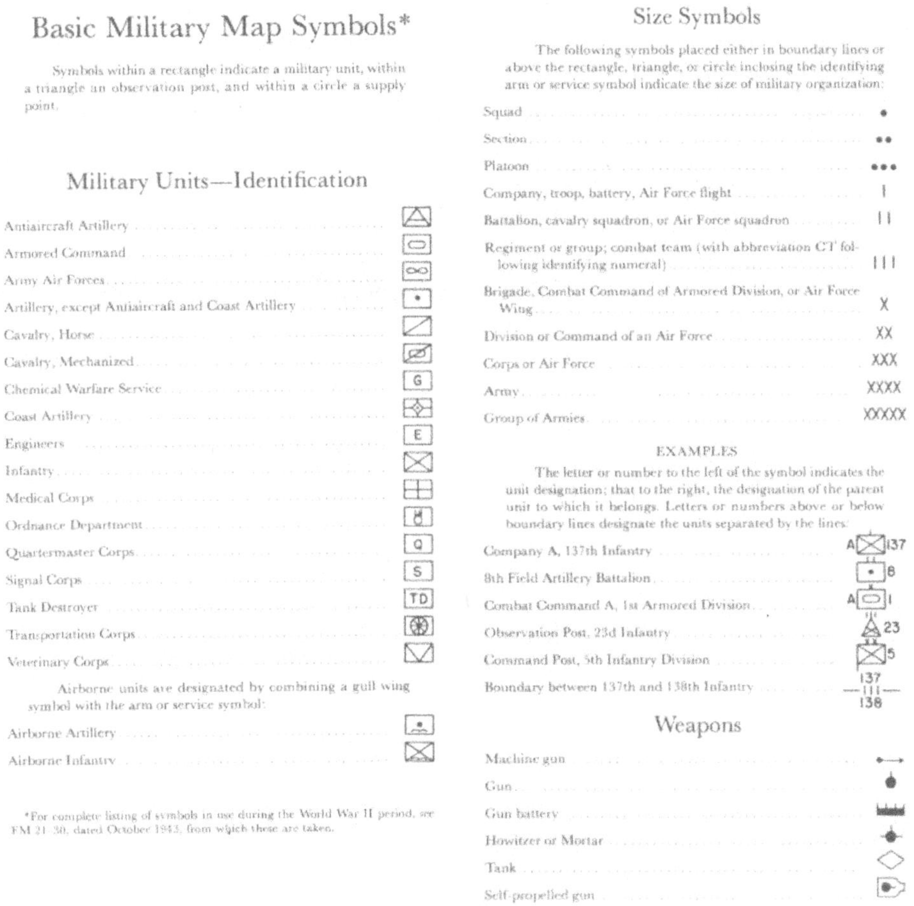

Basic Military Map Symbols*

Symbols within a rectangle indicate a military unit, within a triangle an observation post, and within a circle a supply point.

Military Units—Identification

Antiaircraft Artillery

Armored Command

Army Air Forces

Artillery, except Antiaircraft and Coast Artillery

Cavalry, Horse

Cavalry, Mechanized

Chemical Warfare Service

Coast Artillery

Engineers

Infantry

Medical Corps

Ordnance Department

Quartermaster Corps

Signal Corps

Tank Destroyer

Transportation Corps

Veterinary Corps

Airborne units are designated by combining a gull wing symbol with the arm or service symbol:

Airborne Artillery

Airborne Infantry

*For complete listing of symbols in use during the World War II period, see FM 21-30, dated October 1943, from which these are taken.

Size Symbols

The following symbols placed either in boundary lines or above the rectangle, triangle, or circle inclosing the identifying arm or service symbol indicate the size of military organization:

Squad .... •

Section .... ••

Platoon .... •••

Company, troop, battery, Air Force flight I

Battalion, cavalry squadron, or Air Force squadron ... II

Regiment or group; combat team (with abbreviation CT following identifying numeral) ... III

Brigade, Combat Command of Armored Division, or Air Force Wing ... X

Division or Command of an Air Force ... XX

Corps or Air Force ... XXX

Army ... XXXX

Group of Armies ... XXXXX

EXAMPLES

The letter or number to the left of the symbol indicates the unit designation; that to the right, the designation of the parent unit to which it belongs. Letters or numbers above or below boundary lines designate the units separated by the lines:

Company A, 137th Infantry

8th Field Artillery Battalion

Combat Command A, 1st Armored Division

Observation Post, 23d Infantry

Command Post, 5th Infantry Division

Boundary between 137th and 138th Infantry

Weapons

Machine gun

Gun

Gun battery

Howitzer or Mortar

Tank

Self-propelled gun

Figure 64. American Military Symbology.

Standardized NATO Military Symbology.[6]

With the creation of the North Atlantic Treaty Alliance (NATO) in 1949, standardization in the use of military symbology became imperative as most of the members of the alliance used incompatible systems, where similar symbols could sometimes mean completely different things. For example, the British symbol for a battalion-sized unit was identical with the American symbol for a medical unit. Additionally, some nations did not have all echelons of command or used the same name for different-sized units. A British regiment, for example, equated to an American battalion, and a British troop equated to an American platoon, while a British squadron equated to an American troop. Common size symbol symbols decreased confusion (a British troop and an American platoon would use the same size symbol despite the different designations) and provided a full set of echelon symbols to use when depicting enemy forces.

The standard NATO set of symbols, while still allowing for specialized symbology used by unique units of alliance members, provided standard symbols used in combined operations of forces from different nations. Other nations, such as Israel, the British Commonwealth nations, and the former states of the Warsaw Pact have also adopted versions of the NATO symbol set for their own use.

Figure 65 is a series of tables illustrating a sampling of the most common NATO symbols.

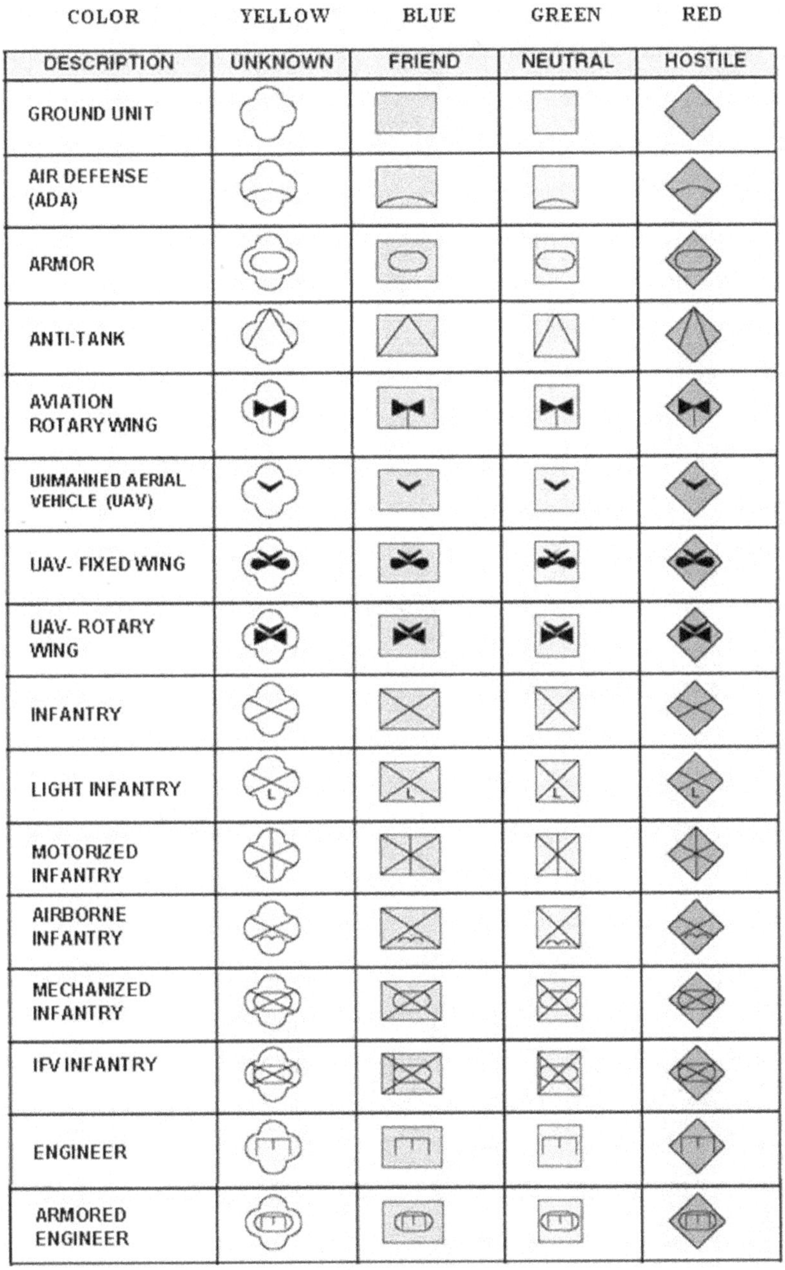

COLOR	YELLOW	BLUE	GREEN	RED
DESCRIPTION	UNKNOWN	FRIEND	NEUTRAL	HOSTILE
GROUND UNIT				
AIR DEFENSE (ADA)				
ARMOR				
ANTI-TANK				
AVIATION ROTARY WING				
UNMANNED AERIAL VEHICLE (UAV)				
UAV- FIXED WING				
UAV- ROTARY WING				
INFANTRY				
LIGHT INFANTRY				
MOTORIZED INFANTRY				
AIRBORNE INFANTRY				
MECHANIZED INFANTRY				
IFV INFANTRY				
ENGINEER				
ARMORED ENGINEER				

Figure 65. NATO Military Symbology.

255

COLOR	YELLOW	BLUE	GREEN	RED
DESCRIPTION	UNKNOWN	FRIEND	NEUTRAL	HOSTILE
FIELD ARTILLERY				
SELF PROPELLED ARTILLERY				
LIGHT FIELD ARTILLERY	L	L	L	L
RECON/ CAVALRY				
ARMORED CAVALRY				
MOTORIZED CAVALRY				
AIRBORNE RECON				
LIGHT RECON	L	L	L	L
INTERNAL SECURITY FORCES	SEC	SEC	SEC	SEC
COMBAT SUPPORT	CS	CS	CS	CS
NBC				
MILITARY INTELLIGENCE	MI	MI	MI	MI
SIGNALS INTELLIGENCE	MI	MI	MI	MI
ELECTRONIC WARFARE	EW	EW	EW	EW
MILITARY POLICE	MP	MP	MP	MP
CIVILIAN LAW ENFORCEMENT				
SIGNAL				

Figure 65 (continued). NATO Military Symbology.

COLOR	YELLOW	BLUE	GREEN	RED
DESCRIPTION	UNKNOWN	FRIEND	NEUTRAL	HOSTILE
COMBAT SERVICE SUPPORT (CSS)	CSS	CSS	CSS	CSS
ADMINISTRATIVE (ADMIN)	ADM	ADM	ADM	ADM
JUDGE ADVOCATE GENERAL (JAG)	JAG	JAG	JAG	JAG
POSTAL				
FINANCE (FIN)				
PERSONNEL SERVICES (PERS SVCS)	PS	PS	PS	PS
MORTUARY/GRAVES REGISTRY				
RELIGIOUS/ CHAPLAIN (CHAP)	REL	REL	REL	REL
PUBLIC AFFAIRS (PA)	PA	PA	PA	PA
REPLACEMENT HOLDING UNIT (RHU)	RHU	RHU	RHU	RHU
LABOR				
MORALE, WELFARE, RECREATION	MWR	MWR	MWR	MWR
MEDICAL (MED)				
SUPPLY (SUP)				
SUBSISTENCE (RATIONS)				
QUARTERMASTER SUPPLY				
POL				

Figure 65 (continued). NATO Military Symbology.

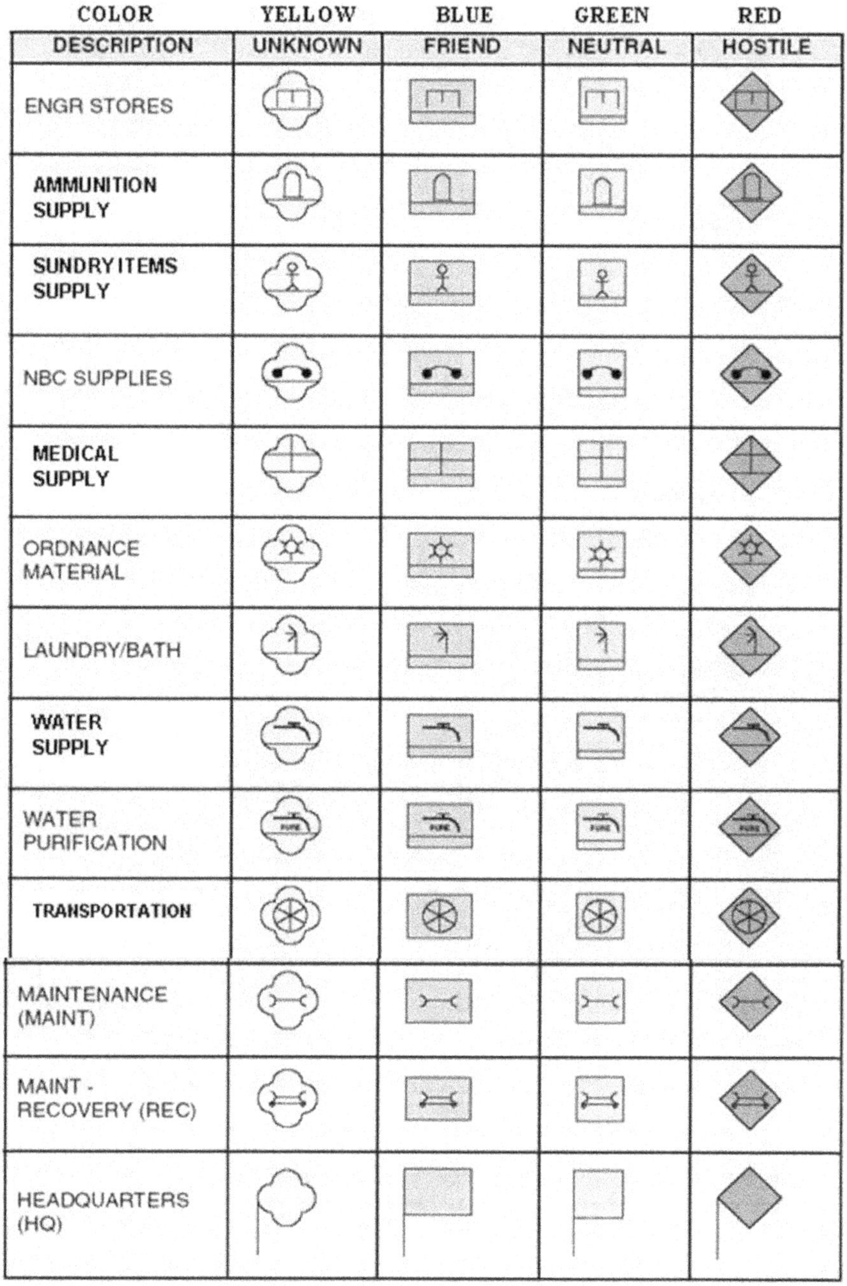

COLOR	YELLOW	BLUE	GREEN	RED
DESCRIPTION	UNKNOWN	FRIEND	NEUTRAL	HOSTILE
ENGR STORES				
AMMUNITION SUPPLY				
SUNDRY ITEMS SUPPLY				
NBC SUPPLIES				
MEDICAL SUPPLY				
ORDNANCE MATERIAL				
LAUNDRY/BATH				
WATER SUPPLY				
WATER PURIFICATION				
TRANSPORTATION				
MAINTENANCE (MAINT)				
MAINT - RECOVERY (REC)				
HEADQUARTERS (HQ)				

Figure 65 (continued). NATO Military Symbology.

Mobile Operations Control Measures.[7]

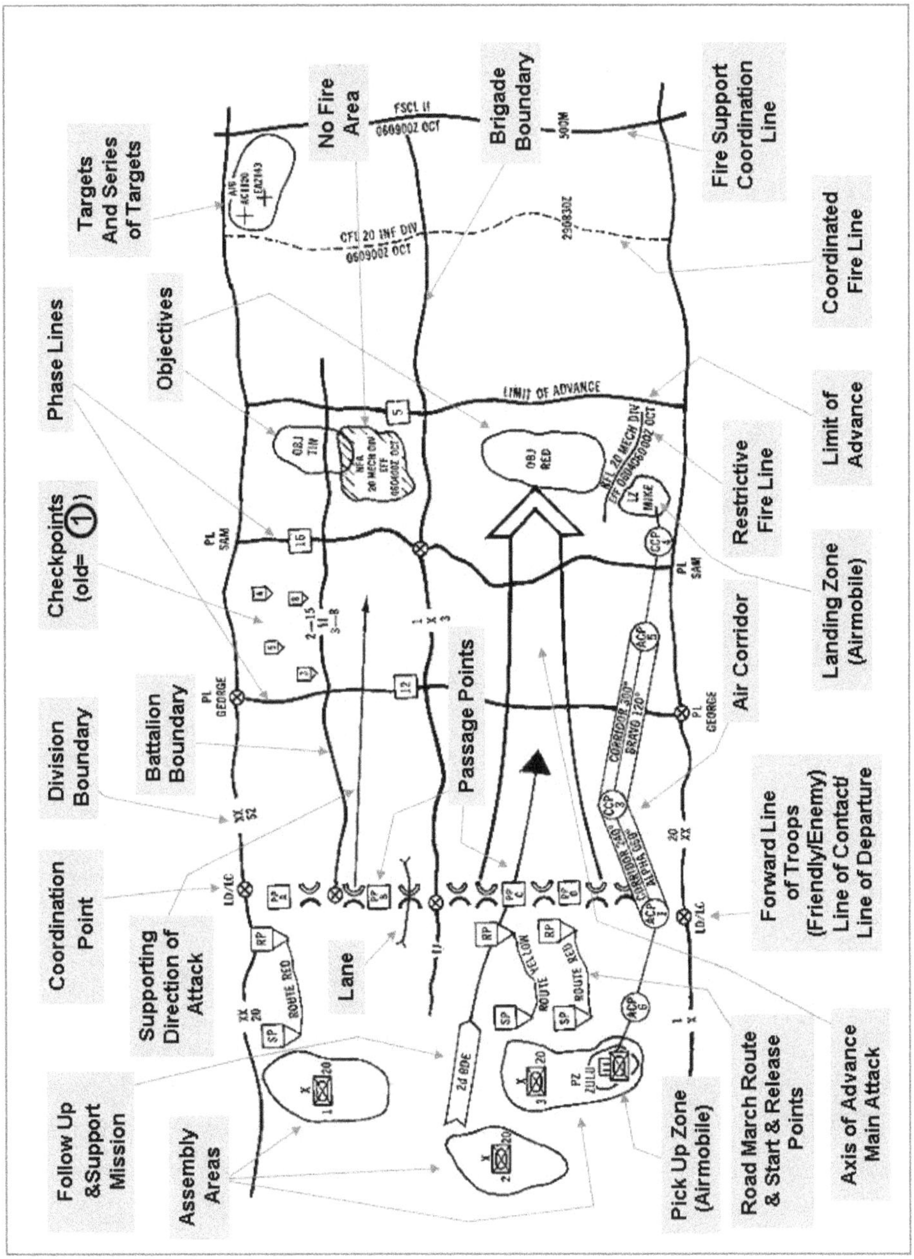

Figure 66. Typical Mobile Forces Control Measure.

Air Corridor

graphic depiction of airspace reserved for the movement of aviation/airmobile forces designated to prevent fratricide and contain• ing air control points (ACP) at each direc• tion change in the flight route and a com• munications checkpoint (CCP) where serial leaders are required to report to the overall mission commander.

Assembly Areas

geographical areas behind the front line trace where units refit and prepare for future operations.

Axis of Advance Main Attack

axis of advance depicts a general route of advance for a military force, in this instance for the force designated as the main attack

Boundaries-Division, Brigade, Battalion

linear control measures that designate the left and right limits of a unit's sector (area of responsibility); within its sector a unit could ordinarily maneuver without close coordination with other units.

Checkpoints (CP)

reference points on the ground used to control friendly movement but not to report enemy locations

Coordinated Fire Line (CFL)

linear control measure usually drawn per• pendicular to a unit's advance beyond which ground fires can be executed without prior coordination.

Coordination Point

point on a boundary where the adjacent units must physically coordinate; usually located along a phase line.

Fire Support Coordination Line (FSCL)

Linear control measure usually drawn per• pendicular to a unit's advance beyond which air and other attacks do not require prior coordination with the ground force com• mander

Follow Up and Support Mission	graphic feature depicting a unit designated to follow up and support the mission of another unit, usually the main attack; follow on and support missions include attacking bypassed enemy forces, or taking over the mission of the unit being supported.
Forward Line of Troops (Friendly/ Enemy)/ Line of Contact/ Line of Departure	frontline trace between friendly and enemy forces. The line of contact (LC) is this line; the line of departure is the linear control measure the crossing of which indicates the commencing of a tactical operation; usually the LC is the LD, often requiring the mov• ing unit to pass through the unit holding positions on the LC.
Landing Zone (Airmobile) (LZ)	place where helicopters land to disembark troops or equipment.
Lane	a designated clear route through an obstacle
Limit of Advance	a linear control measure beyond which at• tacking forces are not to advance.
No Fire Area	a designated area on the ground, like a mosque, into which no fires are to be di• rected.
Objectives	a defined geographical area which is to be reached or captured by military forces
Passage Points	geographical points where one unit coor• dinates and physically passes through the positions of another unit
Pick Up Zone (Airmobile) (PZ)	place where troops are picked up by heli• copters to commence an airmobile opera• tion.
Phase Lines	linear control measures usually perpendicu• lar to a unit's sector boundaries designated to assist in the reporting and control of movements, particularly between various units at a higher level.

261

Restrictive Fire Line	a linear control measure established be‑tween converging forces not permitting each force to fire across in order to preclude fratricide.
Road March Route and Start and Release Points	a road march is an administrative (as op‑posed to a tactical) movement of a military unit with a designated start point (SP) and end point called a release point (RP)
Supporting Direction of Attack	a direction of attack is a linear control mea‑sure directing a restricted route of advance, in this case for the supporting attack of an operation.
Target and Series of Targets	A target is a point at which fire is pre‑planned on; a series of targets is a number of targets or groups of targets that are to be fired upon in support of a specific maneuver phase of an operation.

Notes

1.   The sizing of unit symbols based on the size of the unit on the map and facing it based on line or column was retained as late as the 1941 edition of FM 21-30, then the Army's military symbols manual, See US War Department, *FM 21-30, Basic Field Manual: Conventional Signs, Military Sym•bols and Abbreviations* (Washington, DC: War Department, November 26, 1941), 22.

2.   The best series of examples of these symbols in use is in the maps of the atlas produced to accom•pany the *Official Records of the Civil War*. See Major George Davus, Leslie Perry, and Joseph Kirkley, *The Official Military Atlas of the Civil War* (New York: Gramercy Books, 1983), reprint of 1891 edi•tion.

3.   Sources for British symbology are primarily from a three part article by John Armatys "British Map Symbols 1914-1949: A W.D. A Rough Guide" appearing in *The Nugget*, the journal of British-based Wargames Development: "Part I- 1914-1920's," Issue 106 (December 1995), 31; "Part II- 1929•1943," Issue 107 (February 1996), 15; "Part III- 1943-1949," Issue 108 (March 1996), 19-20. Informa•tion on French symbology is primarily culled from the American Expeditionary Force, General Staff, Second Section (Topography), *List of Conventional Signs and Abbreviations in Use on French and German Maps* (France: Base Printing Plant, 29th Engineers, US Army, 1918).

4.   Sources for German military symbology are US War Department, Military Intelligence Service, *German Military Symbols* (Washington, DC: War Department, January 1943) *and* US War Department. Military Intelligence Service, *German Military Symbols* (Washington, DC: War Department, January 1943).

5.   The primary source for Soviet map and military symbology is Charles R. Taylor, DDB-2680•41-78 Handbook of Soviet Armed Forces Military Symbols (Washington, DC: Defense Intelligence Agency, 1978).

6.   Material in this section is primarily based on US Department of Defense, *Department of Defense Interface Standard MIL-STD-2525B: Common Warfighting Symbology* (Washington, DC: Department of Defense, 30 January 1999) and British Army, *Land Component Handbook (App-6A Map Symbol•ogy)*, Issue 1.0, April 2001.

7.   The primary source for this section is US Department of the Army, *FM 101-5-1 Operational Terms and Symbols* (Washington, DC: Department of the Army, October 1985). The later version,US Department of the Army. *FM 101-5-1 Operational Terms and Symbols* (Washington, DC: Department of the Army, 30 September 1997) does not contain such an example. A revision of FM 101-5-1, redes•ignated as FM 1-02.

GLOSSARY

ABCS	Army Battle Command System
ACP	Assault Command Post
ACR	Armored Cavalry Regiment
AFATDS	Advanced Field Artillery Tactical Data System
air assault	military forces which are organized to move about the battle-field by helicopter; also called airmobile
airmobile	military forces which are organized to move about the battle-field by helicopter; also called air assault
AMDWS	Air and Missile Defense Work Station
APC	Armored Personnel Carrier
armored	a military force organized primarily of fully tracked vehicles usually built around units of tanks
AM	Amplitude Modulation radio frequencies
ARVN	Army of the Republic of Vietnam
ASAS	All Source Analysis System
ATCCS	Army Tactical Command and Control System
BAV	Bavarian
BC	Before Christ
BCOTM	Battle Command on the Move
BCT	brigade combat team
BCV	Bradley Commander's Vehicle
BEF	British Expeditionary Force
BFT	Blue Force Tracker
khawk	UH-60 utility helicopter used primarily for carrying troops
BN	battalion
BSB	brigade support battalion
BUB	battle update briefing
C&C	command and control

C2	command and control
C2PC	Command and Control for the Personal Computer
C2V	M4 command and control vehicle
CAV	cavalry
CENTCOM	Central Command
CFLCC	Coalition Forces Land Component Command
chariotries	the chariot force of an ancient army
CO	company
column	a military force advancing along one route
combined	a force or operation consisting of elements from various na•tions
COMP	composite
CP	command post
CSS	combat service support
CSSCS	Combat Service Support Control System
department	former US Army geographical administrative command usually led by a brigadier-general
DMAIN	division main command post
DREAR	division rear command post
DTAC	division tactical command post
DTSS	Digital Topographic Support System
EECP	Early Entrance Command Post
FBCB2	Force XXI Battle Command Brigade-and-Below
field marshal	in some European armies, the highest grade of general officer
flank	the sides and rear of a military force; left and right flanks are given in perspective to the direction the military force is facing (usually towards the enemy force)
FM	field manual
FM	Frequency Modulation radio frequencies
FR	French

FRAGO	fragmentary order
FRAGPLAN	fragmentary plan
G2	in US Army and some NATO units, the intelligence officer and section on staffs division-level and above
G3	in US Army and some NATO units, the operations officer and section on staffs division-level and above
GCCS-A	Global Command and Control System-Army
G-Day	the day the ground campaign begins in a operation with a separate air phase
General der Kavaller‐ ieGeneral der Panzer‐ truppen	literally general of cavalry, general of armored troops; grade of general officer rank in the German army roughly equivalent to a US Army lieutenant general; the grade indicated the officer's specific branch affiliation with cavalry and panzer being the example here.
Generalmajor	literally major general; the lowest rank of general officer in the German Army; typically commanded a brigade or division; roughly equivalent to a US Army brigadier general.
Generaloberst	literally colonel general; the second highest (next to field marshal) rank of general officer in the German army; typically commanded the highest commands in the German forces- armies, army groups, theaters of war; roughly equivalent to a US Army four-star general.
group	military force usually of brigade or battalion-size
HHC	headquarters and headquarters company
HMMWV	High-Mobility Multipurpose Wheeled Vehicle
Huey	utility helicopter; predecessor to the Blackhawk
Ia	operations section of German Army staffs before 1949
IIa	administrative section of German Army staffs before 1949
IDF	Israeli Defense Force
IFV	infantry fighting vehicle (also called the Bradley)
IMETS	Integrated Meteorological System
Jaxartes River	central Asian river now called the Syr Darya

JFC-E	Joint Forces Command East- Corps-sized Arab allied force in DESERT STORM 1991
JFC-N	Joint Forces Command North- Corps-sized Arab allied force in DESERT STORM 1991
joint	a force or operation consisting of elements from more than one branch of the armed forces
jump CP	small command post that 'jumps' forward to be able to continue CP operations while the bulk of the CP is moving
kilometer	1000 meters; unit of measure equivalent to one-sixth of a mile
legion	Roman military organization composed of similarly organized subunits designed to be able to fight tactical battles with mini•mal direction from the force commander
LTC	lieutenant colonel
LZ	landing zone
M577	US Army command post vehicle
marshal	Highest grade of general officer in the French Army; in the Napoleonic era, a space grade of rank and honor bestowed on the commanders of corps
MCG	mobile command group
MCS	Maneuver Control System
mech	mechanized
mechanized	a military force equipped with tracked vehicles
MEF	Marine Expeditionary Force
MLRS	multiple launcher rocket system
motorized	a military force equipped with wheeled vehicles
MSE	mobile subscriber equipment
MSR	main supply route
MTS	movement tracking system
NCO	noncommissioned officer
NVA	North Vietnamese Army

OBJ	objective
OCP	operational command post
OHL	*die Oberste Heeresleitung*; the German high command field headquarters in World War I, titularly headed by the German emperor (Kaiser), but actually led by the chief of the German General Staff.
OIF	Operation IRAQI FREEDOM
organic	an element of a military unit which is by organization a part of the unit intrinsically
Oxus River	central Asian river now called **Amu Darya.**
panzer	German term for tanks and armored forces
Panzergruppe	literally panzer group; a German command echelon above corps and below army level; in 1942-3 all panzer groups were converted to panzer armies
Panzerarmee	literally panzer army; a German command echelon of army-size equipment with specialized capabilities to command armored operations
phalanx	ancient Greek formation of tightly packed armored soldiers equipped with long spears
PLT	platoon
POL	petroleum, oil and lubricants
REGT	regiment
RGFC	Republican Guard Forces Command
RPG	rocket-propelled grenade
S2	in US Army and some NATO units, the intelligence officer and section on staffs below division-level
S3	in US Army and some NATO units, the operations officer and section on staffs below division-level
SAM	surface to air missile
SdKfw	*Sonderkraftwagen*, a German World War II-era half-track armored vehicle
SITREP	situation report
squadron	in US Army cavalry units, a unit of battalion size

STANAG	Standardization Agreement
STB	special troops battalion
symbology	a system of symbols
SYSCON	Systems Control
TAC CP	tactical command post
TACSAT	tactical satellite (telephone or radio)
TAIS	Tactical Airspace Integration System
TF	task force
TOC	tactical operations center
TO&E	table of organization and equipment
tuman	Mongol army unit consisting of 10,000 riders
XO	executive officer
UEx	Unit of Employment X (divisional-sized modular Army headquarters)
ugda	Israeli Defense Force task force of division size
wire	telegraph or telephone communications dependent on lines of wire strung along the ground between the various points of communication

SELECTED BIBLIOGRAPHY

3d Infantry Division (Mechanized). *Operation Iraqi Freedom After Action Report*. Final Draft, dated 12 May 2003.

101st Airborne Division (Air Assault). *Lessons Learned Part I, Operation Iraqi Freedom*, dated 30 May 2003.

Adan, Avraham . *On the Banks of the Suez: An Israeli General's Personal Account of the Yom Kippur War*. London: Arms and Armour Press, 1980.

American Expeditionary Force, General Staff, Second Section (Topography). *List of Conventional Signs and Abbreviations in Use on French and German Maps.* France: Base Printing Plant, 29th Engineers, US Army, 1918.

Antal, John F. "Combat Orders: An Analysis of the Tactical Orders Process." MMAS Thesis, US Army Command and General Staff College, Fort Leavenworth, KS, 1990.

Bailey, Jonathan B.A. *Field Artillery and Firepower*. Annapolis, Naval Institute Press, 2004.

Balkoski, Joseph. *Beyond the Bridgehead: The 29th Infantry Division in Normandy*. Harrisburg, PA: Stackpole, 1989.

Bearss, Ed and Chris Calkins. *The Battle of Five Forks*. Virginia Civil War Battles and Leaders Series. 2d ed. Lynchburg, VA: H.E. Howard, Inc., 1985.

Blumenson, Martin. *Breakout and Pursuit*. United States Army in World War II: The European Theater of Operations. Washington, DC: US Army Center of Military History, 1961.

Bourque, Stephen. *Jayhawk: The VII Corps in the Persian Gulf War.* Washington, DC: Department of the Army, 2002.

British Army. *Land Component Handbook (App-6A Map Symbology).* Issue 1.0, April 2001.

Caesar, Gaius Julius. *The Gallic War*. Loeb Classical Library. H.J. Edwards, trans. 1994 ed. Cambridge, MA: Harvard University Press, 1917.

Calkins, Chris M. *The Appomattox Campaign: March 29- April 9, 1865.* Great Campaigns. New York: Da Capo Press, 2001.

Calkins, Chris M. *Lee's Retreat: A History and Field Guide.* Richmond: Page One History Publication, 2000.

Carrell, Paul. *Scorched Earth*. New York: Ballantine, 1971.

Cavanaugh, Michael A. and William Marvel. *The Battle of the Crater "The Horrid Pit." June 25- Au•gust 6, 1864.* The Petersburg Campaign. Virginia Civil War Battles and Leaders Series. 2d ed. Lynch•burg, VA: H.E. Howard, Inc., 1989.

Center for Army Lessons Learned, *The Battalion and Brigade Staff.* Newsletter No. 93-3. Fort Leaven•worth, KS, July 1993.

Center for Army Lessons Learned, *Tactical Decision Making: Abbreviated Planning.* Newsletter No. 95-12. Fort Leavenworth, KS. December 1993.

Center for Army Lessons Learned. *The Battalion and Brigade Staff.* Newsletter No. 93-3. Fort Leaven•worth, KS, July 1993.

Center for Army Lessons Learned. *Transforming the Tactical Staff for the 21st Century: Tactics, Tech•niques and Procedures.* Special Study No. 04-1. Fort Leavenworth, KS, March 2004.

Chadwick, Frank and Joseph Bermudez. "Historical Notes and Scenarios Booklet." *Suez '73: The Battle of the Chinese Farm: October 15-22, 1973.* Normal, IL: Game Designer's Workshop, 1981.

Chamberlain, Joshua. *Bayonet Forward: My Civil War Reminiscences.* Gettysburg, PA: Stan Clark Military Books, 1994.

Chamberlain, Joshua. *The Passing of the Armies: An Account of the Final Campaign of the Army of the Potomac Based Upon Personal Reminiscences of the Fifth Army Corps.* New York: G.P. Putnam's Sons, 1915; reprint New York: Bantam, 1993.

Chambers, James. *The Devil's Horsemen: The Mongol Invasion of Europe.* New York: Atheneum, 1979.

Chandler, David G. *The Campaigns of Napoleon.* New York: Scribner, 1966.

Chun, Clayton K.S. *US Army in the Plains 1865-91.* Battle Orders series. London: Osprey, 2004.

Clancy, Tom. *Armored Cav: A Guided Tour of an Armored Cavalry Regiment.* New York: Berkley Books, 1994.

Clancy, Tom, with Fred Franks, Jr. *Into the Storm: A Study in Command.* New York: Putnam, 1997.

Condell, Bruce and David Zabecki, trans. and ed.,*On the German Art of War:Truppenführung*, Boulder, CO: Lynee Rienner Publications, 2001.

Connelly, Owen. *Blundering to Glory: Napoleon's Military Campaigns.* Wilmington, Delaware: Schol•arly Resources, 1987.

Crismon, Fred W. *US Military Tracked Vehicles*. Osceola, WI: Motorbooks International, 1992.

David, Daniel. *The 1914 Campaign: August-October, 1914*. The Great Campaigns of History. New York: Military Press, 1987.

Davis, Burke. *The Campaign that Won America: The Story of Yorktown*. Washington, DC: Acorn press, 1979.

Diamond, John and Dave Moniz, "Iraqi Colonel's Capture Sped Up Taking of City," *USA TODAY*, 9 April 2003.

Drews, Robert. *The End of the Bronze Age: Changes in Warfare and the Catastrophe CA. 1200 B.C.* Princeton: Princeton University Press, 1993.

Dunniga, James and Daniel Masterson. *The Way of the Warrior: Business Tactics and Techniques from History's Twelve Greatest Generals*. New York: St. Martin's Grif• fin, 1997.

Dunstan, Simon. *The Yom Kippur War 1973 (2); The Sinai*. Campaign series. Oxford: Osprey, 2003.

Dupuy, R. Ernest and Trevor N. *The Encyclopedia of Military History: From 3500 B.C. to the Present*. Revised Edition. New York: Harper and Row, 1977.

Dupuy, Trevor. *Elusive Victory: The Arab-Israeli Wars 1947-1974*. Fairfax, VA: HERO Books, 1980.

Epstein, Robert M. "The Creation and Evolution of the Army Corps in the American Civil War," *Jour• nal of Military History*, 55, (January 1991), 21-46.

Epstein, Robert M. "Patterns of Change and Continuity in Nineteenth-Century Warfare," *Journal of Military History*, 56, (July 1992), 375-88.

Erickson, Lieutenant Colonel Edward J. and Major General Raymond T. Odierno. "The Battle of Taji and Battle Command on the Move." *Military Review* July-August 2003, 2-8.

Eshel, David. "Counterattack in the Sinai: 8 October 1973." *Military Review* November 1993, 54-66.

Esposito, BG Vincent J., and COL John R. Elting. *A Military History and Atlas of the Napoleonic Wars*. New York: Praeger, 1968. Arms and Armour press Reprint 1978.

Evans, Paul W. "Strategic Signal Communication—A Study of Signal Communication as applied to Large Field Forces, Based on the Operations of the German Signal Corps During the March on Paris in 1914," *Signal Bulletin* 82 (January-February 1935), 24-58.

Fontenot, COL (ret) Gregory, LTC E.J. Degan and LTC David Tohn. *On Point: The US Army in Opera•tion Iraqi Freedom.* Fort Leavenworth, KS: US Army Combat Studies Institute Press, 2004.

Foote, Shelby. *The Civil War: A Narrative: Red River to Appomattox.* New York: Vintage Books, 1988.

Foss, Christopher ed. *The Encyclopedia of Tanks and armored Fighting Vehicles: The Comprehensive Guide to 900 Armored Fighting Vehicles from 1915 to the Present Day.* San Diego: Thunder Bay Press, 2002.

Fraser, David. *Knight's Cross: A Life of Field Marshal Erwin Rommel.* New York: HarperCollins, 1993.

Frazier, Donald S., ed. *The United States and Mexico at War: Nineteenth Century Expansionism and Conflict.* New York: MacMillan Reference USA, 1998.

Gawrych, George W. *The 1973 Arab-Israeli War: The Albatross of Decisive Victory.* Leavenworth Paper No. 21. Fort Leavenworth: Combat Studies Institute, 1996.

G2, VII Corps (US Army). *The 100 Hour Ground War: How the Iraqi Plan Failed,* Redacted Version. G2, VII Corps, US Army, 1991.

The General Board, United States Forces, European Theater. *Organization, Equipment and Tactical Employment of the Infantry Division.* Study Number 15, 1945.

The General Board, United States Forces, European Theater. *Organization, Equipment and Tactical Employment of the Airborne Division.* Study Number 16, 1945.

The General Board, United States Forces, European Theater. *The Functions, Organization and Equip•ment of the Corps Headquarters and Headquarters Company.* Study Number 23, 1945.

The General Board, United States Forces, European Theater. *Organization, Functions and Operations of G-3 Sections in Theater Headquarters, Army Groups, Armies, Corps and Divisions.* Study Number 25, 1945.

Gott, Kendall D. *In Glory's Shadow: In Service with the 2d Armored Cavalry Regiment during the Persian Gulf War 1990-1991.* Unpublished manuscript, 1997, copy in the archives of the Combined Arms Research Library, Fort Leavenworth, KS.

Gourley, Scott R. "Command on the Move: New Mobile Systems Untether the Commander from the Command Post While Maintaining Situational Awareness" *MIT[Military Information Technol•ogy] E-nnouncement* (Volume 8, Issue 5, July 9, 2004), http://www.mit-kmi.com/archive_article. cfm?DocID=526 (accessed on 26 November 2004).

Grant, Ulysses S. *Personal Memoirs of U.S. Grant.* Cleveland: World Publishing Company, 1952; reprint, E.B. Long, ed. New York: Da Capo Press, 1982.

Gray, John S. *Centennial Campaign: The Sioux War of 1876.* Norman, OK: University of Oklahoma Press, 1988.

Griffiths, William R. *The Great War.* West Point Military History Series. Wayne, NJ: Avery, 1986.

Guderian, Heinz . *Panzer Leader.* Abridged. Constantine Fitzgibbon, tr. New York; Ballantine, 1972.

Gudmundsson, Bruce I. *Stormtroop Tactics: Innovation in the German Army 1914-1918.* New York: Praeger, 1989.

Hackworth David and Eilhys England. *Steel My Soldiers' Hearts: The Hopeless to Hardcore Transfor•mation of US Army, 4th Battalion, 39th Infantry, Vietnam.* New York: Simon & Schuster, 2002.

Heinrich, Willi. *Crack of Doom.* New York: Bantam, 1981.

Herbert, Anthony. *Soldier.* New York: Holt, Rinehart and Winston, 1973.

Herzog, Chaim. *The War of Atonement: October, 1973.* Boston: Little, Brown and Company, 1975.

Howe, Thomas J. *The Petersburg Campaign: Wasted Valor June 15-18, 1864.* Virginia Civil War Battles and Leaders Series. 2d ed. Lynchburg, VA: H.E. Howard, Inc., 1988.

Isby, David. *Weapons and Tactics of the Soviet Army.* London, Jane's, 1988.

Johns, Glover S., Jr. *The Clay Pigeons of St. Lo.* Mechanicsburg, PA: Stackpole, 1958; reprint, New York: Bantam, 1985.

Johnson, John D. "Mission Orders in the United States Army: Is the Doctrine Effective?" MMAS The•sis. US Army Command and General Staff College, Fort Leavenworth, KS, 1990.

Katz, Randy. *Napoleon's Secret Weapon: The Optical Telegraph.* April 2, 1997. http://http.cs.berkeley.edu/%7Erandy/Courses/CS39C.S97/optical/optical.html. (accessed February 23, 2005).

Kelly, Michael P. *Where We Were in Vietnam: A Comprehensive Guide to the Firebases, Military In•stallations and Naval Vessels of the Vietnam War 1945-75.* Central Point, OR: Hellgate Press, 2002.

Kennedy, Frances, ed. *Civil War Battlefield Guide.* 2d ed. The Conservation Fund. Boston: Houghton Mifflin, 1998.

Kennelly, A.E. "Advances in Signaling Contributed During the War" in *The New World of Science: Its Development During the War*, Robert M. Yerkes, ed. New York: Century Co, 1920.

Kennett, Lee. *The French Forces in America, 1780-1783.* Westport, CT: Greenwood, 1977.

Kluck, Alexander von. *The March on Paris and the Battle of the Marne, 1914.* New York: Longmans, Green and Co., 1920.

Knappe, Siegfried, with Ted Brusaw. *Soldat: Reflections of a German Soldier, 1936-1949.* New York: Dell, 1993.

Larew, Karl G. "Signaling the American Blitzkrieg." Unpublished manuscript. Copy at Office of the Command Historian, U.S. Army Signal Center, Fort Gordon.

Lemelin, David J. Jr. "Command and Control Methodology: A Sliding Scale of Centralization." MMAS Thesis. US Army Command and General Staff College, Fort Leavenworth, KS, 1996.

Lupfer, Timothy T. *The Dynamics of Doctrine: The Changes in German Tactical Doctrine During the First World War.* Leavenworth Paper No. 4. Fort Leavenworth: Combat Studies Institute, 1981.

Lyman, Theodore. *With Grant and Meade from the Wilderness to Appomattox.* George R. Agassiz, ed. Lincoln: University of Nebraska Press, 1994.

MacGarrigle, George L. *Taking the Offensive: October 1966 to October 1967.* The United States Army in Vietnam. Combat Operations. Washington, DC: US Army Center of Military History, 1998.

McGrath, John J. "The Battle of El Firdan." *Armor* (May-June 1983), 9-13.

McGrath, John J. *The Brigade: A History.* Fort Leavenworth: CSI Press, 2004.

McGrath, John J. "Humiliation in Victory: The Relief of General Warren at Five Forks." MA Thesis, University of Massachusetts at Boston, 1997.

McGrath, John J. "Iraqi Army Order of Battle." Unpublished Manuscript prepared as a fact sheet for the US Army Center of Military History, Washington, DC, 2001. Updated 2003.

Meade, George. *The Life and Letters of George Gordon Meade, Major-General, United States Army.* Vol. II. New York: Charles Scribner's Sons, 1913.

Mellenthin, F.W. von. *Panzer Battles: A Study of the Employment of Armor in the Second World War.* H. Betzler, tr., L.C.F. Turner, ed. New York: Ballantine, 1984.

Meyer, Bradley John. "Operational Art and the German Command System in World War I." PhD diss., Ohio State University, 1988.

Miller, George A. "The Magical Number Seven, Plus or Minus Two: Some Limits in Our Capacity for Processing Information." *Psychological Review* 63 (1956), 81-97.

Morley, Rebecca and Joseph Kobsar, "Battle Command on the Move," paper presented at the *9th Annual Command and Control Research and Technology Symposium*, San Diego, CA, 15-17 June 2004, accessed at http://www.dodccrp.org/events/2004/CCRTS_San_Diego/CD/papers/225.pdf (accessed on 26 November 2004).

Mountcastle, LTC John W. "On the Move: Command and Control of Armor Units in Combat." *Military Review* (November 1985), 14-39.

Napoleon. *Napoleon's Art of War*. General Burnod, ed. Lieutenant General Sir G.C. D'Aguilar, CB, trans. New York: Barnes and Noble, 1995.

National Archives Collection of Foreign Records Seized, 1941- , Record Group 242, *Records of Heeresgruppe Don*, Microfilm Publication T311, Roll 270.

Ney, Virgil. *Evolution of the US Army Infantry Battalion 1939-1968*. CORG Memorandum CORG-M-343. Fort Belvoir, VA: Combat Operations Research Group, 1968.

Pearson, Willard. *The War in the Northern Provinces 1966-1968*. Vietnam Studies. Washington, DC: Department of the Army, 1975.

Pollack, Kenneth M. *Arabs at War: Military Effectiveness, 1948-1991*. Lincoln, NE: University of Nebraska Press, 2002.

Prados, John and Ray W. Stubbe. *Valley of Decision: The Siege of Khe Sanh*. Boston: Houghton Mifflin, 1991.

Price, Frank James. *Troy H. Middleton: A Biography*. Baton Rouge: Louisiana State University Press, 1974.

Proceedings, Findings and Opinions of the Court of Inquiry Convened by Order of the President of the United States in the Case of Lieutenant Colonel G. K. Warren. 3 vols. U.S. Government Printing Office, Washington, D.C., 1883.

Province, Charles M. *Patton's Third Army: A Daily Combat Diary*. New York: Hippocrene Books, 1992.

Rabinovich, Abraham. *The Yom Kippur War: The Epic Encounter that Transformed the Middle East*. New York: Schocken Books, 2004.

Raines, Rebecca Robbins. *Getting the Message Through: A Branch History of the U.S. Army Signal Corps*. Washington, DC: US Army Center of Military History, 1996.

Raus, Erhard *Panzer Operations: The Eastern Front Memoir of General Raus*, 1941-1945. Steven H. Newton, tr. Cambridge, MA: Da Capo Press, 2003.

Reinhardt, Hellmuth. *Size and Composition of Divisional and Higher Staffs in the German Army.* Foreign Military Studies. MS- P-139. Heidelberg: Historical Division, Headquarters, US Army Europe, 1954.

Robertson, W. Glenn, Jerold Brown, William M. Campsey and Scott R. McMeen, compilers. *Atlas of the Sioux Wars.* Fort Leavenworth: Combat Studies Institute, 1993.

Rommel, Erwin. *Attacks.* Vienna, VA: Athena Press, 1979.

Ross, Charles D. *Civil War Acoustic Shadows.* Shippensburg, PA: White Mane, 2001.

Rush, Robert S. *Hell in the Hürtgen Forest: The Ordeal of an American Infantry Regiment.* Lawrence, KS: University Press of Kansas, 2001.

Scott, Lieutenant-General Winfield. *The Memoirs of Lieut-Gen. Scott, LLD.* New York: Sheldon & Co, Publishers, 1864.

Sharon, Ariel, with David Chanoff. *Warrior: The Autobiography of Ariel Sharon.* New York: Simon and Schuster, 1989.

Shazly, Saad el. *The Crossing of the Suez.* San Francisco: American Mideast Research, 1980.

Shepperd, Alan. *France 1940: Blitzkrieg in the West.* Campaign Series No. 3 London: Osprey, 1990.

Sheridan, Lieutenant-General Philip H. *Annual Report, Military Division of the Missouri*, November 25, 1876, enclosure to the 1876 *Annual Report of the General of the Army.*

Shulimson, Jack, Leonard A. Blasiol, Charles R. Smith and David A. Dawson. *The Defining Year: 1968.* U.S. Marines In Vietnam. Washington, DC: History And Museums Division, Headquarters, U.S. Marine Corps, 1997.

Stolfi, R.H.S. *Hitler's Panzers East: World War II Reinterpreted.* Norman, OK: University of Oklahoma Press, 1993.

Task Force Modularity, US Army Training and Doctrine Command. *Army Comprehensive Guide to Modularity, Version 1.0.* Fort Monroe, VA: US Army Training and Doctrine Command, 8 October 2004.

Taylor, Charles R. *DDB-2680-41-78 Handbook of Soviet Armed Forces Military Symbols.* Washington, DC: Defense Intelligence Agency, 1978.

Terry, Brigadier-General Alfred. *Annual Report Department of Dakota*, 1876.

Thompson, George R., and Dixie R. Harrison, *The Signal Corps: The Outcome (Mid 1943 through 1945)*, The United States Army in World War II: The Technical Services. Washington, DC: Office of the Chief of Military History, 1966.

Tilley, John A. *The British Navy and the American Revolution*. Columbia, SC: University of South Carolina Press, 1987.

Tolson, John J. *Airmobility 1961-1971*. Vietnam Studies. Washington, DC: Department of the Army, 1973.

Toomey, Charles Lane. *XVIII Airborne Corps: From Planning to Victory.* Central Point, OR: Hellgate Press, 2004.

Turnbull, Stephen. *Genghis Khan and the Mongol Conquests 1190-1400*. London: Osprey, 2003.

US Army. *Tactical Symbols (German Army).*" Trans by Hist Sec, US Army War College, 1926.

US Department of the Army. *FM 3-0, Operations*. Washington, DC: Department of the Army, 14 June 2001.

US Department of the Army. *FM 3-90, Tactics.* Washington, DC: Government Printing Office, July 2001.

US Department of the Army. *FM 5-0, Army Planning and Orders Productions*. Final Draft. Washington, DC: Department of the Army, 15 July 2002.

US Department of the Army. *FM 6-0, Mission Command: Command and Control of Army Forces.* Washington, DC: Department of the Army, 11 August 2003.

US Department of the Army, *FM 6-20-10 Tactics, Techniques and procedures for the Targeting Process.* Washington, DC: Department of the Army, 8 May 1996.

US Department of the Army, *FM 17-15 (Test) Tank Platoon Division 86.* Washington, DC: Department of the Army, October 1984.

US Department of the Army. *FM 21-26 Map Reading.* Washington, DC: Department of the Army, January 1969.

US Department of the Army and Department of the Air Force. *FM 21-30 AFM 55-3 Military Symbols.* Washington, DC: Department of the Army, 1951.

US Department of the Army. *FM 21-30 Military Symbols*. Washington, DC: Department of the Army, May 1960.

US Department of the Army. *FM 21-30 Military Symbols*. Washington, DC: Department of the Army, May 1970.

US Department of the Army. *FM 100-5, Operations*. Washington, DC: Government Printing Office, July 1976.

US Department of the Army. *FM 100-5, Operations*. Washington, DC: Government Printing Office, 20 August 1982.

US Department of the Army. *FM 100-5, Operations*. Washington, DC: Government Printing Office, 5 May 1986.

US Department of the Army. *FM 100-5, Operations*. Washington, DC: Government Printing Office, 14 June 1993.

US Department of the Army. *FM 101-51, Department Of The Army Planning System*. Washington, DC: Department of the Army, 1949.

US Department of the Army. *FM 101-5, Staff Organization and Operations. Washington,* DC: Department of the Army,25 May 1984.

US Department of the Army. *FM 101-5, Staff Officers' Field Manual, Staff Organization and Proce•dure*. Washington, DC: Department of the Army,13 July1950.

US Department of the Army. *FM 101-5, Staff Officers' Field Manual, Staff Organization and Proce•dure*. Washington, DC: Department of the Army, July1960.

US Department of the Army. *FM 101-5, Staff Officers' Field Manual, Staff Organization and Proce•dure*. Washington, DC: Department of the Army, 13 June 1968.

US Department of the Army. *FM 101-5-1 Operational Terms and Symbols*, Washington, DC: Department of the Army, 30 September 1997.

US Department of the Army. *FM 101-5-1 Operational Terms and Symbols*, Washington, DC: Department of the Army, October 1985.

US Department of the Army. *FM 101-5-1 Operational Terms and Graphics* Washington, DC: Department of the Army, 31 March 1980.

US Department of the Army. *TM 30-548 Soviet Topographic Map Symbols.* Washington, DC: Department of the Army, June 1958.

US Department of the Army. "Worth Fighting For," PowerPoint presentation given to all Army person•nel as part of a briefing on the *Army Campaign Plan* in April 2004.

US Department of Defense. *Department of Defense Interface Standard MIL-STD-2525B: Common Warfighting Symbology*. Washington, DC: Department of Defense, 30 January 1999.

US War Department. *Field Service Regulations, United States Army, 1923*. Washington, D.C.: War Department, 1923.

US War Department. *FM 17, The Armored Force: Employment of Armored Units (The Armored Division)*. Washington, DC: War Department, undated [probably 1941].

US War Department. *FM 17-5, Armored Force Field Manual: Armored Force Drill*. Washington, DC: War Department, June 18, 1943.

US War Department. *FM 17-10, Armored Force Field Manual: Tactics and Techniques*. Washington, DC: War Department, March 7, 1942.

US War Department. *FM 21-30, Basic Field Manual: Conventional Signs, Military Symbols and Abbreviations*. Washington, DC: War Department, 1939.

US War Department. *FM 21-30, Basic Field Manual: Conventional Signs, Military Symbols and Abbreviations*. Washington, DC: War Department, November 26, 1941.

US War Department. FM 21-30, *Basic Field Manual: Conventional Signs, Military Symbols and Abbreviations*. Washington, DC: War Department, October, 1943.

US War Department. *FM 100-5, Field Service Regulations-Operations*. Washington, DC: War Department, May 22, 1941.

US War Department. *FM 100-10 Field Service Regulations-Administration*. Washington, DC: War Department, 1940.

US War Department. *FM 101-5, Staff Officers' Field Manual, The Staff and Combat Orders*. Washington, DC: War Department, August 19, 1940.

US War Department. *FM 101-10, Staff Officers' Field Manual, Organization, Technical and Logistical Data*. Washington, DC: War Department, 1941.

US War Department, *The War of the Rebellion: A Compilation of the Official Records of the Union and Confederate Armies*. Washington, DC: Government Printing Office 1880-1901.

US War Department, Adjutant General Office, German Military Documents Section. *The German General Staff Corps: A Study of the Organization of the German General Staff*, April 1946.

US War Department. Military Intelligence Division. *German Military Symbols*. Washington, DC: War Department, 1 April 1944.

US War Department. Military Intelligence Service. *German Military Symbols.* Washington, DC: War Department, January 1943.

US War Department. Military Intelligence Service. *FM 30-22 Foreign Conventional Signs and Sym•bols.* Washington, DC: War Department, July 1942.

Utley, Robert M. *Frontier Regulars: The United States Army and the Indian 1866-1891.* Lincoln: Uni•versity of Nebraska Press, 1984.

Van Creveld, Martin. *Command in War.* Cambridge, MA: Harvard University Press, 1985.

Van Creveld, Martin. *Fighting Power: German and U.S. Army Performance, 1939-1945.* Contributions in Military History, Number 32. Westport, CT; Geenwoord Press, 1982.

Wade, Norman M. *The Battle Staff SmartBook: Step-by-Step Visual Guide to Military Decision Making and Tactical Operations.* Lakeland, FL: Lightning Press, 1999.

Wade, Norman M. *The Operations and Training SmartBook: Guide to Operations and the Battlefield Operating Systems.* 2d revised Edition. Lakeland, FL: Lightning Press, 1999.

Wainwright, Charles S. *A Diary of Battle: The Personal Journals of Colonel Charles S. Wainwright, 1861-1865.* Allan Nevins, ed. New York : Harcourt, Brace & World, 1962. Reprinted Gettysburg: Stan Clark Military Books, 1987.

Washington, George. *The Diaries of George Washington 1748-1799: Volume II 1771-1785.* John C. Fitzpatrick, ed. Houghton Mifflin, Co., 1925.

Warner, Ezra J. *Generals in Blue: Lives of the Union Commanders.* Baton Rouge: Louisiana State University Press, 1964, reprint 1981.

Wittenberg, Eric J. *Little Phil: A Reassessment of the Civil War Leadership of Gen. Philip H. Sheridan.* Washington, DC: Brassey's, 2002.

Wray, Timothy A. *Standing Fast: German Defensive Doctrine on the Russian Front During World War II Prewar to March 1943.* Fort Leavenworth: US Army Command and Staff College, 1986.

Zaloga, Steven. *Red Thrust: Attack on the Central Front: Soviet Tactics and Capabilities in the 1990s.* Novato, CA: Presidio Press, 1989.

Zucchino, David. *Thunder Run: The Armored Strike to Capture Baghdad.* New York: Atlantic Monthly Press, 2004.

About the Author

Boston native John McGrath has worked for the US Army in one capacity or another since 1978. A retired Army Reserve officer, Mr. McGrath served in infantry, field artillery, and logistics units, both on active duty and as a reservist. Before coming to work at the Combat Studies Institute, he worked for 4 years at the US Army Center of Military History in Washington, DC, as a historian and archivist. Prior to that, Mr. McGrath worked fulltime for the US Army Reserve in Massachusetts for over 15 years, both as an active duty reservist and as a civilian military technician. He also served as a mobilized reservist in 1991 in Saudi Arabia with the 22d Support Command during Operation DESERT STORM as the command historian and in 1992 at the US Army Center of Military History as a researcher/writer. Mr. McGrath is a graduate of Boston College and holds an MA in history from the University of Massachusetts at Boston. He is the author of numerous articles and military history publications to include *Theater Logistics in the Gulf War*, published by the Army Materiel Command in 1994; *The Brigade: A History*, published by the Combat Studies Institute in 2004; and was the General Editor for *An Army at War: Change in the Midst of Conflict*, published by the Combat Studies Institute in 2006. Aside from a general interest in things military and historical, his areas of particular interest include modern military operations, the German army in World War II, August 1914, and the Union Army in the Civil War. He also has a keen interest in ancient history, historical linguistics, the city of Boston, and baseball.